Belleruth Naparstek's guided-imagery programs have been distributed by the Veterans Administration, Oklahoma City disaster services, Columbine High School, and the Red Cross, among many others.

"Belleruth Naparstek is a first-rate therapist and a gifted teacher. Her use of the compelling voices of trauma survivors is the heart of *Invisible Heroes,* while the effective imagery program and elegant scripts provide the framework for healing. She has written a classic that will be utilized by patients, loved ones and therapists for years to come."
—Ruth M. Buczynski, Ph.D., President, The National Institute for the Clinical Application of Behavioral Medicine

"Belleruth Naparstek is both a compassionate therapist and an authority on the role of imagery in health. Her new book on PTSD ingeniously combines her therapeutic work with the latest brain research on how to heal from trauma. The world certainly needs this information now more than ever."
—Christiane Northrup, M.D., author of *The Wisdom of Menopause* and *Women's Bodies, Women's Wisdom*

"Belleruth Naparstek's theories, based on her vast experience, are profound and very sound. *Invisible Heroes* is simple to read and full of practical solutions—it is a real gift to the many in need."
—Candace Pert, Ph.D., author of *Molecules of Emotion*

"Surgery is controlled trauma. Finally I understand why we cannot just 'talk' patients back to full recovery. Here is a blueprint for using the right brain to deliver health."
—Mehmet Oz, M.D., author of *You: The Owner's Manual*

For My Art with the Heart
June 1, 1938—April 24, 2004
His life was a blessing and an inspiration.

"My children need me. They have homework and karate lessons and swimming. I smile at their teachers. No one would guess that I am out of bed and out of the house for only a very short time each day, summoning the energy to appear normal for my children. I leave the house at three, makeup in place. I look perfect. I return exhausted. No one knows the hell I'm living."

—From the journal of a recovered incest survivor

CONTENTS

GUIDED IMAGERY EXERCISES

STAGE ONE: REESTABLISHING SAFETY AND CONTROL

STAGE TWO: HEALING AND INTEGRATION

STAGE THREE: CLEANUP AND RENEWAL

FOREWORD

Widely known for her work in the use of guided imagery in the healing of trauma, Belleruth Naparstek has written a comprehensive but extremely reader-friendly book detailing not only the neurophysiological basis for this technique, but also the nuts-and-bolts of its application. She has provided a comprehensive, well-referenced review of the latest theories in the physiology, epidemiology, and clinical features of PTSD, in a format that is also accessible to the lay public. Numerous case studies graphically illustrate her main points. In her Guided Imagery Program for Traumatic Stress, she provides a series of imagery techniques for the stages of trauma healing that are comprehensive enough that the program stands alone as a therapeutic tool for the reader. She provides a thorough and even-handed review of the other therapeutic techniques that involve imagery, some of which have become quite popular despite their somewhat controversial theoretical base. Finally, she reviews concepts of transformation in trauma, providing hope for its victims.

This is a remarkable book that is likely to find application as a reference manual for trauma psychotherapists as well as an enlightening and educational book for trauma victims and the general lay public.

—Robert C. Scaer, M.D.
author of *The Body Bears the Burden: Trauma, Dissociation and Disease* and *Trauma Tells the Tale: Understanding Your Life*

INTRODUCTION

A NEW WAY OF LOOKING AT TRAUMA

I think heroes are people who do good or necessary things at great personal cost. Heroism must be judged by the courage and grit required to do what needs doing. That's why trauma—that great terrorizer—produces heroes. No one has to override fear the way a trauma survivor does.

Sometimes the heroism looks like nothing at all. When a phobic rape survivor makes herself go to an evening PTA meeting, even though her heart is pounding with terror and her body is drenched in sweat—that's a form of heroism. When someone has been so traumatized by a recent auto collision that he cannot get behind the wheel of a car without freezing with fear, but he forces himself to breathe and take the wheel and drive to work anyway—that's heroism, too. And when a Vietnam veteran with post-traumatic stress forces himself to interview for a job, even though he wants to bolt, and it takes every ounce of will, courage, and determination he's got to override the intense fear and shame he feels—emotions that, by the way, make no sense to him and cause him to question his own sanity—that's heroism as well.

Post-traumatic stress creates such daunting fear and heart-stopping distress that it produces legions of heroes, whose every day is a test of their mettle, commitment, and courage. This book is filled with their gentle but powerful voices. I thank them and salute them.

• • •

A t dusk one day in early spring 1997 I was nervously picking up my messages at an outdoor pay phone, on a dicey block on the edges of the Adams Morgan neighborhood, in Washington, D.C. That week I was in the middle of a book tour, with a little time between interviews, so I was hurrying to make sure there were no emergencies brewing at home. Looking nervously around me, I raced through my messages, skipping and deleting them as fast as I could, until a I heard a voice that stopped me in my tracks. It was a refined woman's voice, so open-hearted, urgent, and sincere, that I forgot about my questionable surroundings and listened to the whole message, and then played it back again so I could copy down her number and call her right back.

It was a psychologist I didn't know, a Dr. Beverly Donovan, from the Veterans Administration (VA) hospital in Brecksville, Ohio, calling to ask if I would please make some guided imagery audio recordings for traumatic stress for the Vietnam vets she was working with. She had just come out of a particularly heart-wrenching group session—this is what had come across so powerfully in her voice. She'd been thinking about calling me for weeks, but that session did it. She said her program used a few imagery tapes of mine to help with basic relaxation and self-soothing, and the men liked them, but she felt something more intense was needed—something that would go deeper and catalyze more active healing. Would I please consider making a trauma tape for these men?

I warned her that I couldn't start for a while, that such a project would take a lot of time and would require a substantial budget just to meet costs. I also told her I'd need to sit in on many of her group sessions, until I felt I had a full sense of what the men were dealing with. She agreed to all of my conditions.

Within a few months I'd joined the next cohort—seven hard-looking, edgy Vietnam veterans, newly clean and sober, who'd qualified for the very intense, rigorous course of treatment, called the Transcend program, created by Dr. Donovan and her colleague, Dr. Edgardo Padin-Rivera. As a therapist of thirty-plus years, I thought I'd heard and seen it all, but what these men had suffered was a world all to itself. By the time the Veterans Administration told Bev and me that there was no budget after all—neither for a new tape nor for anything else—it was too late. I was completely committed to my seven scruffy guys, the Transcend program, and the imagery project. My audio company footed the bill.

The guided imagery we eventually created was tested and refined, first with another Transcend cohort, then with support groups and staff from a rape crisis center, a domestic violence shelter, and assorted people traumatized by disease, fire, auto collision, surgery, crime, and devastating loss. I was struck by how often this simple tool was able to offer immediate and profound help.

Eventually the trauma imagery made its way into national distribution through the central office of the Veterans Administration, and to Oklahoma City, Columbine High School, and Ground Zero in Manhattan. Particularly with the massive numbers of people affected by 9/11, we were able to learn more about what kinds of imagery worked best for whom and when, getting a handle on different stages of healing from trauma. The imagery is currently being tested in randomized clinical trials at several trauma treatment centers and is showing promising results. The seven now-not-so-scruffy guys are pleased and proud of their seminal contribution and keep up with the latest developments through Bev.

The truth is, I had always been drawn to work with traumatized people, throughout the thirty-three years of my clinical practice. There is a natural gravitational pull between certain therapists and certain kinds of clients; my practice was always full of people suffering intensely from any manner of devastating circumstances: the mother who, when backing out of her driveway, accidently ran over and killed her baby; the psychiatrist whose job it had been at age ten to transcribe her non-English-speaking Holocaust survivor parents' horrific stories for court testimony; victims of gang rape and childhood incest; people who'd been stunned by life-threatening diagnoses and near-murderous treatments; and those forever changed by collisions, crime, combat, workplace accidents, and natural disasters. As with Beverly Donovan, this was the work of my heart and always had been.

PTSD is far more common than most of us think. All of us know several trauma survivors who've suffered from it, and very likely someone very close to us has been in its nasty grip. It can come from events as diverse as a car collision, an ICU stay, an assault, a flood, an industrial accident, a difficult delivery, a heart attack, kidnapping, earthquake, or grievous loss. In spite of the wide range of catalytic events, PTSD symptoms look pretty much the same: flashbacks, nightmares, intrusive thoughts, agitation, numbness, insomnia, irritability, depression, concentration problems, anxiety, panic, shame, guilt, temper, estrangement, and sudden startling—that's the short list.

While I was busy crafting, testing, and tweaking guided imagery narratives for various trauma survivors and assessing their impact, rapid and powerful forces were at work in the fields of psychobiology, neurophysiology, developmental psychology, epidemiology, and clinical psychiatry. A revolution was taking place in what has since been called the Decade of the Brain, which permanently altered the way clinicians approach and heal post-traumatic stress. To put it plainly, we didn't used to be able to help people with post-traumatic stress, at least not in any consistent way. Now we can. We learned we've been going about it all wrong—and how to do it right.

This is because with PTSD, language can be a trap. If a deeply traumatized person is prompted *only* to speak and think about the events that created his distress, without enlisting help from the imaginal, emotional, sensory, and somatic capabilities of his right brain, his symptoms can actually get worse instead of better. Encouragement to "talk about it"—a therapist's and, for that matter, a good friend's stock-in-trade—can catalyze a tailspin of flashbacks, nightmares, and overwhelming anxiety.

This is because the language centers in the brain have been impaired by a cascade of biochemical responses, set loose by our built-in, biologically driven, survival reaction during the time of the traumatic event itself. This biochemistry of terror washing through us at mind-boggling speed will often help save our necks, but it can also leave us with hobbled speech and short-circuited memory, at least when it comes to thinking and talking about the specific horror.

So methods are needed that can blessedly sidestep the booby-trapped language centers in the brain by making clever use of imaginal, multisensory, motor, and emotional pathways—pathways that are in a heightened state of receptivity, due to the very same biochemical hit that disabled the capacity for words in the first place.

These right-brain methods that dip into the imaginal realm are now available, thanks to a confluence of a few revolutionary arenas of investigation and an unprecedented amount of interdisciplinary collaboration between them. For this we must thank the genius and dedication of quadruple-threat investigators who can conceptualize, practice, research, and write: Bessel van der Kolk, Judith Herman, Robert Scaer, Edna Foa, Rachel Yehuda, Peter Levine, and Francine Shapiro come to mind, to name just a few.

Interest in post-traumatic stress has been intensifying since the late 1970s, with the return of thousands of severely traumatized veterans from the Vietnam War. This led to systematic investigation of the incidence of trauma in other populations as well—normal cross sections, as well as rape and assault victims, Holocaust survivors, whole communities reeling from natural disasters, police, and firefighters. These surveys and population studies, proliferating in the United States and around the world, compared and contrasted who suffers, as well as how, when, and where, and came up with some compelling cross-cultural consistencies. These epidemiological findings were the first important new source of data.

Second, thanks to the new imaging technologies—MRIs, PET scans, and the like—we suddenly had ways of understanding the innermost workings of the human brain and the physiological and biochemical dynamics of traumatic stress as never before. We now had insights into the differences between the right and left hemispheres, how the brain encodes memory and experience, and which parts are affected by terror and helplessness. This was the second powerful cache of new data.

And third, we were blessed with frustrated clinicians, experimenting with new techniques because the regular methods weren't helping or were making people worse. Several practitioners managed to come up with effective short-term treatment tools that seemed to get the job done, even if they didn't always know why, then proceeded to codify and quantify their results. This opened the way for others to cobble together variations on these techniques, and a creative cycle of practical, effective new therapies was born within a very short two decades.

Francine Shapiro created Eye Movement Desensitization and Reprocessing; Peter Levine, Somatic Experiencing; Edna Foa, Prolonged Exposure Therapy; Gerald French and Frank Gerbode, Trauma Incident Reduction; Roger Callahan, Thought Field Therapy; Gary Craig, Emotional

Freedom Technique; and so on—the list is long, and these and other methods are spelled out elsewhere in this book. Suffice it to say here that the common thread that runs through them all is *imagery,* the key to the right brain, the power cell that propels healing when other systems are too debilitated to pull their weight.

Many people suffering from post-traumatic stress don't understand their symptoms, which can be very severe and easily mistaken for serious and permanent mental illness. The new discoveries have been so rapid and so profound, there is no way the public at large could possibly be current with them. I want survivors to read the information in these pages and feel relief, because by doing so they will understand that they are probably not crazy after all.

I want them to know that they can recover from their daunting symptoms—not just learn to cope with them, but transcend them and thrive. I want them to have practical, solid guidelines—ten of them, to be exact—for what they can do to hasten their full recovery. There is even information in here that will help a substantial number of trauma survivors make sense of their chronic pain conditions and find ways to deal with fibromyalgia or irritable bowel symptoms.

This book makes a clear and compelling case for the pivotal nature of imagery in healing trauma. It offers a three-stage healing program of guided imagery exercises for healing traumatic stress that anyone can use; it describes the most successful, imagery-based, short-term therapies available; and it provides a resource listing of materials—books, audiotapes, and videotapes—as well as websites to assist with locating expert local providers.

This book is for my fellow practitioners too, especially the ones who have been so busy practicing that they haven't had time to keep up with the explosion of new research and clinical applications. I've taken the liberty of synthesizing a lot of disparate information—astonishing, wonderful information!—from many fields and presenting practical, clinical implications and conclusions they can use.

If practitioners want to incorporate imagery into their practice, they will find very thorough guidelines and scripts here, and resource information about what materials to start with, and where to get training.

I could not have written this book without the help of at least sixty trauma survivors and clinicians, who became my e-mail pen pals, coaches, consultants, and muses, responding patiently, thoroughly, and quickly to my endless questions and requests for clarification.

I salute the therapists, doctors, and social service workers—warriors of the heart—who slogged through the devastation of Ground Zero and Kosovo, the vet centers, the domestic violence shelters, and the incest support groups. Thank you for enlightening me with your wisdom and for sharing your mistakes as generously as your triumphs.

I don't know how to thank the many trauma survivors, who shared so much of themselves, even though this sometimes meant opening old wounds and revisiting old pain. Still, they did so with a grace, willingness, and generosity that took my breath away. Their eloquent voices illuminate and enliven these pages and make information that might otherwise be dry and abstract, wonderfully immediate and real.

Many of these articulate storytellers would have been written off as hopeless cases just a few short years ago. But they have fully reclaimed their lives, emerging triumphant from what looked like an irreparably shattered sense of self. Each of them went about their recovery with creative desperation, using and discarding many kinds of tools and approaches. The field was so new, so much in flux, and so self-contradictory that each of them had to make their own way, discover their own wheel. Bless them for doing so.

Here is what one survivor had to say about the importance of sharing the triumphant truth of her recovery for the benefit of others:

> I am so eager for this book to get out, so all the world can know . . . that healing from the worst of atrocities is possible (so never give up!), and not only minimal healing and eking out a life, but thriving with deep happiness and centeredness and contentment and joy and inner peace. Tell 'em, BR!

The first part of this book looks at the nature of traumatic stress and how it assaults mind, body, and spirit. It clarifies the spate of new research findings about PTSD and spells out the syndrome's cognitive, emotional, physical, and behavioral impact. This information, in and of itself, will relieve many readers, who for the first time will be able to identify and make sense of their symptoms, or understand what's been happening to someone they love.

The second part of this book examines what it is about guided imagery that works so beautifully to heal the pernicious effects of trauma, and why PTSD's tenacious, intense symptoms are so amenable to its gentle but powerful ministrations.

It offers a multilevel guided imagery program to help with each of the three stages of trauma: the immediate aftermath, the heart of the healing work, and the long-term aftermath. These programs work well alone or in tandem with other kinds of therapies. Their flexibility and complementarity are part of their power and appeal.

There are also descriptions of the best of the other new imagery-based solutions that have shown up in the last decade—an array of relatively quick, effective techniques with dizzying alphabet names like EMDR (Eye Movement Desensitization and Reprocessing), IRT (Imagery Rehearsal Therapy), TIR (Trauma Incident Reduction), SE (Somatic Experiencing), PET (Prolonged Exposure Therapy), TFT (Thought Field Therapy), EFT (Emotional Freedom Technique), TAT (Tapas Acupressure Technique), TPR (Trauma Pattern Release), and the exuberantly titled WHEE (Wholistic Hybrid EFT/EMDR), to name a few.

All these therapies are suggested against the backdrop of a reliably effective, broad-based, ten-pronged approach for healing traumatic stress— all the things that can be done in concert to support and maintain healing, including information on when professional help and medication should be recruited, and how to go about finding the right kind of help.

The final chapter describes the special gifts, strengths, and blessings that recovered trauma survivors possess. There is a Resources section as well.

PART I
UNDERSTANDING TRAUMA

1 THE MANY FACES OF TRAUMA AND RECOVERY

A wide range of situations can catalyze post-traumatic stress, and there are many avenues—seemingly different, but very much related—to recovery. Here are some personal stories from trauma survivors that provide a sampling of traumatic situations, individual reactions, and roads to recovery.

A CHILD WHO NEARLY DROWNS

A four-year-old boy, playing in his backyard, accidentally falls into the deep end of the pool, where he struggles briefly to reach the concrete lip but quickly sinks under the water. He winds up floating at the bottom of the pool. Thanks to some quick action from his seven-year-old sister and his frantic mother dialing 911, a nearby emergency rescue team is able to get to him in time to resuscitate him.

The little boy suffers no permanent physical damage, but he is showing signs of emotional distress in the days and weeks after the accident. Two weeks later he's afraid to fall asleep, and he suffers from persistent nightmares. He's back to wetting his bed and sucking his thumb by the third week. He's fearful most of the time, clinging to his mother and becoming distraught when she's out of sight. Getting him to stay in his preschool class is out of the question. Oddly, his symptoms seem to be getting worse instead of better.

A child psychologist comes to visit him and his mom at home and, with an impromptu arrangement of pillows and cushions on the floor, helps him reenact the accident. To the mother's surprise, her son is eager to play this game and enters into it enthusiastically. First the boy is running and jumping in the make-believe backyard, whooping and laughing. He is play-acting exactly what happened that afternoon. With a prompt from the therapist, he slips and falls into the "pool," landing headfirst into the soft cushions as the therapist holds him around his waist.

The therapist is now carefully watching the boy's movements and sees that his little feet are kicking ever so slightly, and his arms are flailing about. He asks the four-year-old how scared he is, and the boy says very, very scared. He struggles for a while longer and then becomes very still, lying facedown on the pillows. They do this several times, and as they do, with each succeeding reenactment, the event is getting less scary and more playful.

Next, the therapist encourages the boy to play-act the story with a different ending. The boy immediately goes back to the running and jumping and then falling into the pillows. This time the therapist comments on how he is kicking his feet and stroking his arms. Still holding him around the waist, he encourages him to kick harder and to swim more coherently, back toward the edge of the imaginary pool. The boy kicks and strokes more vigorously, and together they make it safely to the lip of the "pool," and to the waiting arms of Mom, who swoops him out with a cheer. The therapist, who has all along been functioning as the play-by-play announcer of this event, also cheers.

The boy loves the game, and they play it over and over, from start to finish. Each time the boy manages to kick and "swim" more effectively, displaying more and more mastery and confidence as he makes his way over to his mother. The cheers get louder.

That night he goes to bed without a whimper and sleeps a deep, untroubled sleep. Indeed, he shows no further evidence of emotional upset in the days and weeks that follow. His symptoms have been routed by the simple strategy of engaging his body and imagination to reenact the drowning, then replay it with a new ending—his own, forceful, effective kicks and strokes taking him to safety.

A POSTCOLLISION TRAUMA

Charlotte takes her turn pulling forward at a four-way stop sign, when, out of the corner of her right eye, she sees a shiny, dark metal mass speeding toward her. Instantly hyperalert and buzzing with adrenaline, she turns her head and watches with the attenuated perception of the terror-stricken, frozen in her seat, as a black minivan does its slow-motion roll toward her. She knows there's nothing she can do, and she is dead certain she will not survive the impact.

After what feels like a very long time of helpless waiting—actually only a few seconds in clock time—the van hits its mark with a loud, sickening crunch. The entire passenger side caves in, and the car is totaled, but Charlotte nonetheless shakily opens her door and wobbles out, unharmed. She is both spacey and wired, and she doesn't stop trembling for several hours.

That night she cannot sleep. She keeps seeing the rogue van, rolling inexorably toward her, as she sits frozen in her seat. And each time that image intrudes, her heart starts pounding, and she's again flushed with sweat and terror. For the next several weeks she's distracted and disconnected during the day, and sleepless and upset at night. Interrupting her, day and night, is this one flash of memory of the moment when she is helplessly watching the van rolling toward her.

At the suggestion of a friend, Charlotte goes to a counselor who is a specialist in this sort of thing. The counselor sits her down, hears the story of the accident, sees the flush of fear, the frozen posture, and notes all the symptoms. She asks good questions.

As a result of the conversation, the traumatized driver realizes that this van, coming out of the blue in the way that it did, took away her sense of everyday safety and predictability. She now understands that stop signs don't necessarily mean that people stop for them.

The counselor has Charlotte sit facing a horizontal bar of flashing lights and asks her to follow the lights with her eyes as they move back and forth, from right to left to right. She is able to do this easily enough. Then she asks her to recall the incident again, while following the lights, back and forth, with her eyes. She is able to do this. They repeat the exercise, this time with her voicing her feeling that nothing feels safe, that life is unpredictable and dangerous.

The therapist then asks her to remember the moment when she opened the car door and stepped out of the wreckage. She recalls that at that instant she was thinking with almost giddy wonder, *Holy shit, I'm alive!* It's a brief but miraculous feeling, carrying with it, she realizes, the optimistic implication that Somebody Up There must be looking out for her. Perhaps it's her dead father, or maybe it's a guardian angel, she says. She is asked to recall this moment of realization while following the moving lights, which she does. They repeat the exercise, this time with her voicing the assertion that she is protected by unseen forces.

Charlotte leaves that session feeling much better and is asymptomatic the subsequent week, but she returns a week later just to be sure. They repeat the entire sequence of the previous week, but instead of the light bar, this time the therapist gives her two odd little palm-sized implements that look like computer mouses to hold in her hands as she recalls the van rolling toward her and the moment of realizing she's still alive. They vibrate in her right hand, then her left, then her right, alternately buzzing her palms as she reimagines these two moments.

She leaves that second session with the memory of the collision perfectly intact, but it has no punch, no emotional charge. It doesn't jar her or upset her. Nor does it intrude on her, unbidden, later on. She just remembers the accident as something that happened to her. And she no longer assumes—and rightly so—that everyone stops for stop signs.

I have no idea how that happened—how watching some moving lights and having buzzers going off in my hands could result in extracting the terror from the memory of that experience. But that's what happened. Even after the first session with the lights, I was back to sleeping normally and concentrating and remembering decently. And a good thing, too, because I was getting pretty stupid at work—jumpy and irritable and making lots of mistakes—probably just from no sleep! I'm not sure how long that could have gone on. I suppose it would have dissipated on its own sooner or later, but it seemed to be getting worse, not better, and my work situation might have deteriorated pretty badly, I'm not sure. This was the second miracle. The first was my not getting killed; the second was not staying an emotional wreck!

A LIFE-THREATENING ILLNESS

A pediatrician is diagnosed with multiple myeloma, a virulent form of bone marrow cancer. He and his wife are disoriented and shaken but cope well with the shock of the diagnosis and the ensuing hardships of chemotherapy. They are a team and support each other during months of strenuous treatment, culminating in bone marrow transplantation. He comes very close to dying during the course of his treatment, but he slowly comes around and recovers. Nonetheless, he is in a weakened state for far longer than he ever expected. He hurts all over, and he still can't do many of the things he used to take for granted. He misses his patients, the challenge of his work, and the feeling of being useful and appreciated. He wonders if his life will ever get back to normal again.

All during his ordeal he remains patient, even-tempered, and considerate. With the help of his wife, he asks sensible, proactive questions, keeps up on the latest medical research, and studies his options carefully, every step of the way. His friends, colleagues, doctors, and nurses marvel at his attitude and forbearance.

His wife notices he is a little emotionally flat and out of it, but she assumes this is caused by fatigue from his physical condition, which is still compromised from the rigors of treatment. He is not sleeping well, and he has nightmares that take him to a very black and frightening place, from which he awakens short of breath, in sweat-soaked sheets. Every now and then he confesses to her that the slow recovery is discouraging. Something inside of him seems to have permanently changed, and he's not sure he even knows who he is anymore.

In this fatigued state, waiting for his strength to return, he finds himself slipping into reverie a lot. The days float by in this dreamy state. One day he finds himself imagining there are invisible, kindly, protective helpers around him who seem to just show up of their own accord. This leaves him feeling very moved—very emotional and weepy, but feeling better somehow.

He starts invoking this reverie on a daily basis. Some of his visitors are faceless, but he recognizes some of them, too—on different days it's his father, a best friend from high school, Jesus, two of his favorite nurses from the BMT unit at the hospital, a baseball coach, his wife and kids, the golden retriever he had as a boy, his grandmother. Sometimes an unfamiliar but angelic-looking visitor shows up, mysterious and power-ful. All of these companions communicate wordlessly that they love and care for him and are looking out for him. They also seem to be acknowl-edging his courage, affirming how difficult it's been for him, and offering him strength and support. He actually begins to feel a physical warmth in his body from their imagined presence around him. These "visits" always move him to tears.

He starts looking forward to these reveries and protects his alone time so he can be sure to experience them. He takes to evoking his pro-tectors before bedtime each night, too, to fend off the nightmares. His pediatrician self chuckles at the ritual, because this is the magical think-ing of a two-year-old, and here he is, enthusiastically deploying it himself.

The effect was profound and always touched me deeply. It brought me a peace and comfort I desperately needed. And it put me back in touch with my own feelings, which up till then had been curiously removed and disconnected from me. How strange to think that until those "helpers" came calling, I hadn't realized how traumatized I'd been by my illness. In fact, my illness had completely undone me. And that undoing claimed a central role in my mental status, recovery, and healing.

It was during those dreamy times that I actually got the enormity of what I'd been through and the toll it had taken. I suppose it was the first time I took pity on myself for having suffered through all that. I had been too busy, just surviving before then, getting through each day. The truth was, I was still reeling from the shock and horror of my diagnosis, and I was too disconnected from myself to even know it. It wasn't till I started crying that I could integrate the fear of that experience and move past it.

I still return to that imagery in my own mind when I need to recapture that feeling of being safe and peaceful. It always helps.

A VIETNAM VETERAN

A Vietnam veteran, addicted to alcohol and marijuana, returns to the United States suffering from nightmares, flashbacks, a terrible temper, and the fear he'll wind up killing someone. During his two years of duty, he'd dodged random rockets countless times as they landed all around him, and he'd watched his best friend get half his head blown off. Most of the men he'd been close to were either injured or killed. For most of his time in Vietnam, he'd stayed stoned on alcohol and marijuana laced with opium. He's come home with every kind of post-traumatic stress symptom, complicated by addiction.

Considering himself dangerous, untrustworthy, and full of poison, he decides he's unfit to stay with his family. So he leaves home to hole up in a rat-infested, condemned building in New York City—no lights, no bed, and no heat. He bootlegs electricity from the place next door and settles in with throwaway furniture he picks up from the street. For protection, he keeps by his side a butcher knife, taped to a broom handle, and a chain studded with razors. These two handcrafted weapons establish his reputation as someone not to be messed with and help him fend off intruders who don't know any better.

He feels he has demons inside of him that have to be exorcised—these impulses to hurt people need to be cleansed out of him somehow. His healing regimen is this: every day, for sixteen hours a day, he plays John Coltrane on a record player he's found in the trash. Having once played tenor sax himself, he finds something in this music that reaches him. John Coltrane is his mentor, idol, and savior.

> The music could touch the tender side of me . . . and the rage, too. It was like being cleansed. The music was so pure and lovely, but so edgy and real, it went right through my body. I started to see beauty again. As long as it was playing, all the garbage that had been dumped on me was no longer part of me. It was like a spiritual enlightenment. For a long time, the only thing I could stand to do was listen to that music, over and over again. Sixteen hours a day, seven days a week. That was my healing. Other things came later—a very special woman and a job at a methadone clinic. But it was the music

that purged me, delivered me back to my true self. It drove the
demons out and restored my humanity. Dr. Coltrane found
me and brought me back.

A SURVIVOR OF RAPE

A thirty-six-year-old mathematics professor goes into therapy for flashbacks, nightmares, hypervigilance, and insomnia—symptoms that have
only surfaced in recent months. She also suffers from a deep distrust of
men, stemming from the time she was raped at the age of twelve by her
nineteen-year-old brother. From that day on the world stopped being a
safe place for her. Everything changed. She became isolated and emotionally withdrawn, never telling anyone what happened. She put it all
away, or so she thought, until decades later, when flashbacks and nightmares erupted through the surface of her supposedly quiescent mind.

Even though she has always been a very verbal, intellectual kind of
person, she has a hard time finding words and getting them out in her
therapy sessions. She cannot speak coherently about the rape. When she
tries to, she becomes overwhelmed and confused, and the nightmares get
worse.

After several months of very slow-going work, her therapist gives her
a CD of some guided imagery to listen to at home. The imagery is specifically geared to post-traumatic stress; it doesn't explore the incident but
instead guides her into her own broken heart, where she surveys a damaged landscape that symbolically mirrors her symptoms (*crumpled piles of
shattered dreams; smoking slag heaps, crackling and steaming with helpless
anger; startling geysers of terror, suddenly breaking through the surface* . . .).
She then is taken to a tunnel, where she is led deeper into her heart,
emerging into a place that is still beautiful, undamaged, and whole. Pieces
of her shattered life are returned to her by helpers and guides. She takes
back into her heart whatever she is ready for, and travels back, up and out
of her heart, which still is damaged but less so. She listens to this imagery
over and over again for several weeks.

I generally never showed emotion, but the first time I listened
to the imagery, I cried at length. It was so intense and so on the

mark for me, it was stunning. I credit listening to the imagery over the next several months with my being able to open up in therapy. I used it perhaps twice a week. It was so powerful and intense that I couldn't do it every day. Over the two months or so that I used it, I tapered off to once a week. That was plenty.

I'm not sure how, but it made it easier for me to get to the important things with my therapist. It allowed me to circumvent all my little avoidance mechanisms—I have a lot of them. And I'm not quite sure how to explain this, as it is pretty unquantifiable and foggy, but before listening to the imagery, I felt pretty hopeless about ever being rid of some of my more unpleasant symptoms. After months of listening, I felt confidence and hope—a feeling I was in charge of my own well-being and able to effect change in my life.

Since that time my symptoms have lessened dramatically. While I used to have flashbacks several times a week, I have had only one in the last four months or so. Nightmares are also a rarity. I now have a few close friendships with some wonderful men. I'm still working on the hypervigilance and insomnia.

A CHRONICLER OF HORROR

An oral historian, working for a local university, collects stories from people who were directly and indirectly involved with the attack on the World Trade Center. She interviews rescuers, firefighters, terrorized eyewitnesses, people evacuated from their homes and work, people trapped in poisonous clouds of dust and debris, and family members who suffered terrible losses. This is not the first time she has undertaken such work. She also interviewed 150 Holocaust survivors for another project and collected memories from World War II combat veterans for yet another.

She finds the work fascinating and important but also painful and sometimes overwhelming. An active, empathic listener, she absorbs a great deal of the pain, terror, grief, and anguish that she hears in the course of her work.

She understands that this is "vicarious trauma" and that it comes with the job. Her colleagues meet in informal support groups to help one another debrief and let go of the horrors of the day. "Compassion fatigue," they call it. But still she wakes up in the middle of the night with grotesque images from her interviews crowding her mind. She cannot get back to sleep, and she is uneasy, restless, and jumpy during the day.

She develops her own method of putting away the images that disrupt her sleep. She takes her mind to when, as a little girl, she would hike with her father in the mountains of upstate New York. It was their special time together, when she had him all to herself. She remembers, in precise sensory detail, the sharp smell of the air and the pine needles, the rustle of wind through the trees, the feel of the sun dappling her face, the solid weight of her backpack, and the satisfying sense of strength in her legs. This detailed, tactile recall seems to increase the power and depth of the memory, making it quite real to her body.

Most of all she remembers the absolute joy of laughing and talking with her father and listening to his deep voice telling funny stories about the family. Going back to these times with her dad, her body relaxes, her mind grows peaceful, and her heart smiles. This memory has such a delicious power and valence for her that the disturbing images can't compete with it. By going hiking with her dad in her imaginal world, she not only allows herself to fall asleep; she brings herself back into balance so she can continue with her valuable work. She reclaims her natural optimism, patience, and generosity of spirit. She ends her meditation with a prayer for the well-being of all the people whose stories she has heard.

* * *

All of these people—the nearly drowned boy, the collision survivor, the bone marrow transplant patient, the Vietnam vet, the rape victim, and the oral historian—were suffering from varying degrees of posttraumatic stress. And all were helped, in differing ways, by strategic doses of *applied imagination*.

In each instance, what got them through was imagery, sometimes guided by a therapist, sometimes by an audio program, and at other times spontaneously generated from within. For some, the imagery was accompanied by prescribed ways to move, or by flashing lights or buzzers, and sometimes it was just a flat-out rescue by the imaginal world, all by itself.

These imagery-based solutions use the right hemisphere of the brain—perception, sensation, emotion, and movement—rather than the left side's standard cognitive functions of thinking, analyzing, verbalizing, and synthesizing. And that's why they work. Trauma produces changes in the brain that impede a person's ability to think and talk about the event but that actually *accentuate* their capacity for imaging and emotional-sensory experiencing around it. Imagery uses what's most accessible in the traumatized brain to help with the healing.

As we will see in detail in later chapters, the part of the brain that creates cognition and language takes a hit from the biochemistry of the trauma experience. On the other hand, the imagistic, emotional, metaphoric, and sensory avenues of the right brain are sensitized, hyperacute, and overfunctioning. This is why survivors will fall into using it intuitively and naturally, even if they haven't been taught to do so. With a little direction, coaching, and guidance, they are able to deploy it even more effectively and consistently.

But too few survivors know this and, sadly, too few professionals as well. So people are not only baffled and alarmed by their symptoms; they are more often than not seeking—and getting—the wrong kind of help from people accustomed to using discussion, thinking, and language—help that often misfires.

It's not that talk therapy is bad. The emotional support of a sympathetic listener is as critically important as it ever was. It's just that it's not enough by itself. If a person has been deeply impacted by trauma, it's more than likely that he first needs to find an oblique route through the imaginal realm, using metaphor and symbolic language, to help him manage his symptoms, find a sense of safety, recontact his wholest self, and make language a viable avenue again.

Once the imagery has established a beachhead of safety within the survivor, then the tools of language and cognition can be enlisted to help with healing. But without the imagery first, the thinking and talking can run aground and catalyze even more severe symptoms, such as flashbacks and nightmares.

It is a sweet irony that something as gentle and undervalued as imagery can carry so much clout for healing such a miserable, tenacious, and painful condition as post-traumatic stress. The truth is, it can restore a terrified little boy to equanimity; bring back a sense of calm and safety to a shocked collision survivor; redeem a murderous, disenfranchised combat vet; reclaim a deeply wounded survivor of incest and rape; bring peace to a desperately sick man, still reeling from his dire diagnosis; and heal a woman whose open heart has been shattered by hearing too many terrible stories.

2 FRANNIE'S STORY: A HUMBLED THERAPIST'S EDUCATION

One of my earliest and most enduring lessons on the power of imagery for healing trauma was delivered by Frannie, a client of mine from my psychotherapy practice nearly twenty years ago. Frannie's and my struggle with her PTSD left me a lot humbler and smarter, opening me up to learning everything I've been able to gather since about post-traumatic stress. Were I to evaluate her for treatment today, my approach with her would be faster, more efficient, much more effective, and far less stressful for her. At the time I was offering the best practice my colleagues and I knew to provide—practice that is woefully inadequate and regretfully still in use by the majority of my professional colleagues.

Here is what happened, to the best of Frannie's and my mutual recollection. The slow, winding trajectory of my learning curve is a nice teaching story for showing where the entire field has been, and where it is now heading.

FRANNIE'S UNDOING

Frannie was in her late thirties, the successful CEO of a large service organization. She didn't come to see me because she had PTSD. She came because she'd become suicidally depressed when her fiancé, someone who also happened to be her best friend and professional mentor, ended their five-year relationship.

Frannie was devastated and heartsick—so depressed that for a while she had trouble getting out of bed, eating, or sleeping. Inside she felt empty and worthless and couldn't imagine getting beyond the loss of this man. Because she'd given up so many of her own friendships and interests to fuse with his, losing him meant losing everything, or so it seemed to her. Baffled, grief-stricken, shocked, and enraged, she couldn't imagine letting him go.

She suspected he'd taken up with someone else—a mutual friend— which proved to be true. She'd done some mild forms of stalking— driving by his house, calling him and hanging up the phone when she heard his voice, and looking for ways to manipulate him into talking with her just one more time. Finally, her depression became so intense that her friends got worried enough to make an appointment for her to see me, and they brought her to my office.

FROZEN BUT STILL WRITING

In those early days she sat across from me like a stone, barely able to speak. Her eyes had a certain dead look at their center, a look I'd seen before. It worried me because, to my mind, it broadcast the very real possibility of suicide. In the weeks and months that followed, her face remained wooden and impassive, her voice was devoid of inflection, and her speech had long pauses that trailed off to nowhere.

Fortunately, she wrote copious notes at home about what she was feeling and thinking and would hand me sheaves of neatly written yellow legal paper at the beginning of each session. The writing revealed the extent of her pain, her self-hatred, her discomfort at sitting in front of me, and her hopes for redemption in spite of all that. More than anything it was her journaling that told me who she was. Her writing was a revelation. It was a stretch to reconcile the anguished, complex, self-aware, highly reactive person who had written those words with the block of stone sitting across from me.

Over the weeks and months that followed, she remained depressed but slowly started to pull out of the deepest depths. Her eyes had glimmers of life back in them, which meant this was the time to pay careful attention to the option of suicide. She now had enough energy to pull it off.

I wrested promises out of her that she wouldn't do herself in, and she kept her word.

Eventually, she began to acknowledge that her life with this man was over, and that helped her begin to let go of her tortured, doomed goal of winning him back. This meant facing the full force of her grief, anger, disappointment, and sorrow, but she was able to withstand all of that, as daunting and painful as it was. Slowly her concentration and functioning at work began to improve, and she began to reclaim other parts of her life— old friends and favorite activities. So far, so good. I was still in territory I understood, and we were moving right along at a decent, productive clip.

After several months the suicidal emergency was over. We now had the luxury of exploring her history and going deeper into her healing. Frannie wanted to think better of herself, and she wanted to understand how it was she'd so easily squandered her identity on this debilitating relationship, so she could prevent it from happening again. She described her family of origin: a harsh, abusive father; a kindly but vague, distant, insubstantial mother; and two troubled, angry brothers.

She also told me about Kyle, a fiancé she'd been engaged to many years earlier, a good man who was loving and kind to her, her best friend, in fact. He'd died prematurely of a brain tumor.

THE EMERGENCE OF BOOBY TRAPS

It was about here that I entered uncharted territory and stopped knowing what I was doing. At about the same time Frannie started talking about Kyle, she began having panic attacks at seemingly random times during the day. She also began experiencing verbal paralysis and terrifying flashbacks in my office when she'd start talking about him.

It was always the same peculiar sequence: she would get a strange look on her face; her eyes would open wide and roll with fear; her breath would stop in her throat, and her forehead would get shiny with sweat. Then she'd hitch and twist her body—especially her head and neck—to the right, away from me, then come back, front and center again, closing the sequence by demurely crossing her ankles and looking straight ahead. It looked very strange, like a hallucination, really. I didn't know what to make of it. From our work together, I knew that she wasn't even close to being psychotic. But this looked really bizarre—like a lot of the repetitive, stylized posturing I'd seen in people with severe mental illness—and I spent a lot of time trying to make sense of it. Whatever this was, I knew something was going on that felt very real to her and was causing her enormous distress.

When I would ask her what was going on, she'd become mute. I persisted. Eventually, over the weeks and months that followed, she was able to tell me in disjointed, choppy fragments, about a horrific traumatic event associated with Kyle.

THE RAPE

It turned out that one night, after visiting Kyle at the hospital and coming back to her locked car in the parking lot, she was viciously assaulted by a rapist who came up from behind her with a knife, grabbing her by her very long ponytail. He raped, beat, and stabbed her many times. She was absolutely certain at the time that she would be killed. Eventually he ran away, leaving her for dead in a pool of blood on the asphalt. She was found by staff arriving for work and brought into the same hospital she'd been visiting just hours earlier.

My pressing Frannie to tell me the story of the attack at this point in our work together is something I would never do now. Asking her for words taxed her needlessly and precipitated a cascade of flashbacks and other distressing symptoms, at a time when she had no tools or skills to cope with them. And because her ability to describe the incident in words was impaired by the trauma itself, this process took weeks and even months, and dragged out her suffering enormously. In many psychotherapy practices, this is still going on, out of sheer, well-meaning ignorance, just like mine.

So Frannie never got very far into the story without precipitating a flashback, where she was suddenly reliving the experience in all its heart-stopping horror. Once I finally had the outline of the story, it was plain to me that those strange facial contortions and the torquing of her neck and upper body meant she was back in that parking lot, trying to twist away from her attacker. But by the time we'd gotten most of the story out of her, months later, she was having multiple flashbacks and severe distress, night and day.

WORSENING SYMPTOMS AND STALLED THERAPY

Not only did the intensity of these episodes fail to dissipate with their retelling; if anything, they seemed to be getting worse. This was baffling to me. My experience and training, and certainly the prevailing clinical wisdom of the day, had always led me to believe that as people shared the horror of their experience with a trusted, empathic, but neutral listener, its intensity would evaporate. Often there would be a kind of catharsis involved, where feelings would come to the surface, and people might cry and rage for a while, but afterward, they would feel better, because something painful and isolated had been released or, at the very least, shared.

This didn't happen with Frannie. There was no catharsis and no evaporating of anything. Each time she began sharing the particulars of the attack, she would topple headlong into the abyss of that experience. It was as if she had a deep rut in her brain, where the wheels of her narrative just got stuck, crazily whirring around over and over again but getting nowhere, causing everything to shake and wobble and then come to a shuddering halt. There was no getting past the rut. So there Frannie would be, cowering and shaking in terror, back on the asphalt, getting raped and stabbed all over again. Rather than helping her heal, I was retraumatizing her.

It was finally becoming clear to me that Frannie and I couldn't talk our way through this. My standard therapeutic plan was not working. Frannie was supposed to fully download and share the horror of the attack by telling the story; get her feelings out about it and cathartically release her anguish; examine her subsequent behavior and her altered view of herself; shed whatever irrational guilt, self-blame, and shame she was carrying around about the attack; experience her delayed grief over the loss of her fiancé; and integrate the experience into her life, with a renewed, if altered, sense of meaning and purpose. But the plan wasn't happening.

I was all the more puzzled because we had all the necessary ingredients for success: a strong therapeutic bond, great mutual trust and respect,

Frannie's extraordinary courage and strong motivation to stay with it, the placebo effect of her faith and hope in my skill (however unwarranted) and in the therapeutic process, and a good track record of making psychological headway together on other knotty issues.

I couldn't understand why we weren't getting anywhere. (Indeed, all of those elements undoubtedly did help in the long run; they kept Frannie from running away from all the distress our work was causing and kept her involved in treatment long enough for her to finally get the help she needed.)

TAKING A NEW TACK

Baffled, frustrated, and hating what our work was doing to her, I took my dilemma to the clinical colleagues in my practice, who met weekly in peer supervision to discuss just such difficulties, and we came up with a default game plan. Instead of trying to work with her story of what had happened to her in the parking lot, they suggested that I teach Frannie some relaxation, breathwork, meditation, and guided imagery—some garden-variety "self-regulation" tools to help her master and calm the waves of panic and terror she was now experiencing each day. In other words, my peers were giving me very uncharacteristic advice for a group of traditional, analytically oriented therapists: address her symptoms, and to hell with their deeper meaning or where they originally came from. Her symptoms were now her biggest problem.

This sounded like it was worth a try to me. I didn't know at the time that these very techniques were exactly what would constitute the best way to help Frannie heal, period. I was simply looking for some symptom relief and damage repair.

In our next session, I asked Frannie if she'd mind backing away from our discussions of the rape and instead work on some self-soothing skills. She rolled her eyes and said, "I thought you'd never ask."

So we switched midcourse. Frannie learned various meditative, imaginal, and relaxation skills to increase her ability to calm herself at will. I was delighted and a bit surprised to discover how very adept she was at propelling herself into the relaxed focus of a reverie state. As I was to later discover, most trauma survivors are old hands at accessing the daydreamy mind-state of a light trance, and Frannie was no exception. Indeed, she was a champ at meditating and imaging.

One of her favorite guided meditations had her imagining herself in a safe place, surrounded by loving, protective beings. For a while this was the only viable sanctuary she had to retreat to, and it allowed her to calm herself after a flashback or nightmare.

In a different meditation, she breathed in and out of her limbs, her hands and feet, and her organs. This allowed her to get more in touch with her body, something she badly needed to do. Her body had become such an uncomfortable place to inhabit since the rape that she'd spent many of the ensuing years disconnected and disaffected from it.

In yet another guided exercise, she would place her awareness inside her body, in sequence, from head to toe, where she could sense how it felt on the inside of her. Being able to locate sensation inside her body and sense what was going on within was a revelation to her. This newly redis-covered ability to inhabit her own body was the prerequisite for some profound changes that could now occur—just by placing her awareness back inside her own flesh. She acknowledged she hadn't been in there for decades, from even well before the rape. Her father's abusive outbursts had sent her consciousness scurrying out into the ozone from as early as her grade school days.

It turns out that most trauma survivors can use help with reinhabit-ing their bodies. One of the most natural, biologically driven responses to acute pain and suffering is to "dissociate," to disconnect from the body, move into an altered state, and get some emotional distance from what's happening. This is a highly utilitarian kindness to the self when terrible things are happening, but it can become a problem later on, when the person stays disconnected, often without even knowing it.

Awareness needs to get back in the body—otherwise, people don't know what they're feeling, aren't in tune with their needs, and are prone to being pushed around by others. They're like a leaf blown about by the wind. Their very spaceyness broadcasts their attractiveness as prey to po-tential attackers, because it's clear that nobody's home to mind the store. It's not a healthy way to function on a day-to-day basis. Accidents as well as victimization occur in this state. It was clear that Frannie needed to get back in touch with her body, and this guided exercise helped her do so without taxing her incapacitated or vulnerable spots.

As one might expect, the more she got connected to her body, the more she became aware of her feelings. It wasn't always clear to her what they were exactly, but she could sense that they were in there: powerful, scary, and roiling about, just below the surface. This is another feature that's typical of post-traumatic stress—first a disconnectedness with feelings, gradually evolving, as things improve, into an undifferentiated blur of emotion that needs some defining.

THE STONE METAPHOR

What opened the door to the next stage of Frannie's healing was a metaphor—a simple but seminal symbolic image—that came to her during a session with an energy worker I had referred her to for ancillary work. Laura Chapman, a local Gestalt-trained psychologist, body worker, and energy healer, had been helping Frannie perceive what was happening on the inside of her body with simple awareness meditations during her energy sessions.

During one session, after some simple relaxation and breathwork, Laura asked her if she could identify what she was feeling in her chest, which was chronically wheezy and asthmatic, and if she could assign an image or symbol to it that described it best. Frannie told me years later that she would think to herself, as she thought in many of her sessions with me, *What complete bullshit,* but she went along with it anyway, having no better plan in mind. Feeling as if she were play-acting, she answered that it felt like there was a stone on her chest. The more she investigated this, the more she felt the stone was *in* her chest—that her heart had turned to stone.

The "game" became more and more real to her over time. My notes record that she told me:

> There's this heavy feeling in my chest . . . it's big, cold and
> heavy, like a big rock sitting in my chest . . . it's so heavy, it's
> like a cannonball, made out of lead . . . and it's so old, it's
> rusty, like a cannonball from the Revolutionary War that's
> landed right in the middle of my chest.

Frannie later told me that she was weirdly of two minds: even while she could feel the weight of the stone-cannonball, she also didn't believe it was there. Both positions coexisted in her mind for several weeks. Then at one point Laura began to run energy to her heart, and the light touch to the center of Frannie's chest caused waves of tremendous grief to come washing through her. She'd contacted a bottomless sorrow. This began a period of many weeks when she would cry in my office, then go home and sob through much of the night. The next day she would go to work, where she would function astonishingly well, then come home and sob some more.

The cathartic work had begun, not through talking and thinking, but through touch, the metaphor of the stone, and the feel of its weight in her chest. During this releasing phase, Frannie became very attached to two guided meditations by Stephen Levine from his book *Healing into Life and Death*. One was his Meditation on Grief, and one was Meditation on the Heart of the Womb. I recorded them for her, and every night she would cry herself to sleep to the sound of my now-familiar voice guiding her through these two gentle guided imagery meditations.

She was still somewhat frozen-looking and still couldn't say much to me directly, but she continued to write up a storm of notes for me to read. Pages and pages of long yellow legal paper, covered with fragmented, out-of-sequence thoughts, feelings, memories, hopes, fears, observations, and impressions would appear in the mail or be mutely handed over to me at the beginning of a session. (I was not allowed to read them until after she left.) These pages continued to offer precious insight into how alive, aware, and feelingful she was beneath the burdensome weight of that stone.

With both Laura and me, Frannie found she was able to talk about the stone in a way that she could not talk about her feelings. She could examine the stone, describe it, connect to it, move her awareness into it, and talk to it. Sometimes the stone represented her pain, and all she could do was practice breathing in and out of it. Sometimes it would be hot, burning, and ugly with shame, repulsion, and disgust. At other times it was softer, less threatening, more malleable—more like sorrow—and she could befriend it. Sometimes she felt sorry for the stone and offered it solace.

It was becoming clear to me that Frannie's talking about the stone allowed her to talk about herself in a safe, cushioned way that got around tripping off that dreaded flashback switch and allowed her to have insight about herself. It was a way of circumventing the booby traps and getting to the same place that words would have brought us to, had her language capacity not been so hobbled. I was starting to feel excited and hopeful. Perhaps we would see our way past the rape and its terrible effects after all, in spite of the missteps I'd taken.

After many weeks of relating to the stone, Frannie reported with considerable excitement that she was developing an ability to distinguish between her feelings, experiencing for the first time the difference between love, grief, pain, sorrow, shame, and anger. The indirectness of the metaphor was also enabling her to name and describe her feelings— something she had trouble doing otherwise. This, like her newfound connection with her body, had revelatory impact. It was a wondrously exciting discovery that held out immeasurable redemptive possibilities. She was discovering herself and realizing that she wasn't just an undifferentiated, incomprehensible, inchoate ball of emotion. She was getting a grip on her internal experience, and as she did so, more and more of her own energy was becoming freed up and available to her.

HEALING AND THE RETURN OF JOY

Eventually, over the course of about two years, the stone melted, bit by bit. It got softer, smaller, and more malleable. And one day, when she went into her meditation to check on how it was doing, it just wasn't there anymore. She told me:

> The stone had turned into my heart. Now it's just my heart. I can breathe in and out of it now, connect to it, feel everything through it. My heart is back, and I'm connected to myself now . . . I have mercy on myself now.

Today, many years later, Frannie is essentially free from debilitating flashbacks and intrusive images. She can talk about the parking lot and the rape without reexperiencing it. At the time we stopped our work together, I wasn't sure if this would ever happen, but it did. The way back to having language for her experience was through the nonverbal gifts of imagery and metaphor, focused awareness, feeling, and body sensation.

With her newfound self-awareness and attunement to her body, she can now notice when she's beginning to get tired or strung out and will deploy her breathing, imagery, and meditation skills to get back into balance and keep from going emotionally off kilter. She doesn't want to unwittingly court any of those hideous symptoms again, and she knows how to keep herself resilient and strong.

Only once, at a vacation resort, when somebody came up suddenly from behind her and jokingly grabbed her around the neck, did she start flashing again. It lasted a matter of seconds. She quickly took herself outside, leaned up against a tree, and started breathing and imaging. The friend came up to her while she was still flashing to ask her if she was okay, and she couldn't answer. Language had fled for as long as the flashing took over. She signaled for him to leave her be and calmed herself with her imagery skills. Later she was able to explain to him what had happened.

Her only remaining symptom at present is a spring-loaded startle response that activates when certain aspects of the attack are replicated. (This is usually the last element of PTSD to disengage and disappear.) When she startles, she may experience very briefly a fragment of a flashback—just for a second or two—but it lacks its old intensity and disappears immediately.

> There came a point when I realized it [the rape] just wasn't inside of me anymore. It's part of my experience, but it's not IN me anymore. It's not part of my being. It's funny, because before, I'm not sure I could have said what my being was . . . my sense of myself was incoherent—just a lot of electrical shortages, mixed-up connections, and constant interference. But now I do have this sense of myself. The rape was something that happened to me, but it's not me.
>
> I think about how I used to be afraid of the world and human beings . . . just about every adult scared me. Fear governed my life. I never traveled. Now I scuba dive, bird-watch, hike through rain forests, snorkel with sharks and barracudas,

explore volcanoes, canoe in the tropics with snakes hanging
down from trees, camp with strangers, hang upside down to
photograph flocks of toucans—pretty amazing.

Getting in touch with my body and discovering that stone
on my chest—that was the turning point of my healing.

By the way, Frannie has been in a committed, loving relationship now
for several years. She continues to love her work and to excel at it, but she
also has an interest in various artistic pursuits—her writing and photog-
raphy, among other things—and talks about maybe working as a volunteer with traumatized vets at her local VA hospital when she retires.
Curiously enough (or perhaps not curiously at all), she no longer experiences her asthma symptoms. Those disappeared with the stone.

TRAUMA GONE UNDERGROUND

In hindsight, it is clear that Frannie had a classic, textbook case of PTSD.
Like many trauma survivors, she'd been emotionally constricted since
the rape but functioned well enough at work and coped decently well in
most of the areas of her life—at least at a certain, emotionally superficial
level. But when she was abandoned by the most important person in her
life, everything unraveled, and her trauma symptoms started popping up
to the surface with a vengeance, past the cushion of emotional dead space
that had grown up around them, as if waiting for just this opportunity to
make themselves known. We see this often: *The reaction to a traumatic situation can go underground—for weeks, months, years, or even decades—until
some magical combination of external events plus internal readiness turns the
PTSD symptoms loose.*

LAYERS UPON LAYERS

Like many trauma survivors, Frannie wasn't just suffering from the effects of the rape. As a child, she'd grown up with a raging alcoholic father,
so she knew the helplessness of terror long before she ever entered that
dangerous parking lot. The rape was layered over earlier instances of vio-

lence and abuse, experienced through the sensibility of a powerless child. *It's not unusual for a traumatic event to recapitulate earlier events in some way or another, giving them added punch and destructive power.*

In addition, the rape and the loss of her innocence were compounded weeks later by another grievous loss—the death of her fiancé. But because she was badly injured and contending with the daily rigors of intense medical treatment to cobble her physical self back together, Frannie never got to process the enormous grief that was lurking just beneath the horror of the assault. As cruel as these two terrible events were, coming one on top of the other, this scenario is not all that unusual. *We often see a sequence of horrible things piling up on a person after a traumatic event—either directly related to the original incident; or else brought on by the PTSD symptoms themselves, which are prone to spawn their own set of difficulties; or, as in the case of Kyle's death, occurring independently, in the way that bad things often happen—in bunches.*

MEMORY STORAGE

Frannie's flashbacks, precipitated again and again by her trying to describe the actual assault in words, thrust her into a full-blown reexperiencing of the rape, right there in my office, with all its original terror, struggle, and certainty of annihilation. Each time, words left her, and for five or six seconds she would become an inchoate mass of emotion, sensation, sweat, and struggle. Then the experience would pass, and she would return to normal, with no memory of what had just occurred. Again, this is typical of PTSD. *Trauma memories are not absorbed by the thinking brain, the way ordinary memories are. Rather they are shelved in disconnected sensory fragments, somatic sensations, and muscular impulses, in the more primitive areas of the brain. As such, they are walled off, disconnected from awareness, and inaccessible to cognition. Nor do they fade over time; instead, they either maintain their original strength or grow even more intense, fueled by repetition.*

BETWEEN NUMBNESS AND ALARM

Similarly, Frannie's emotional flatness, numbed expressivity, and wooden appearance were not unusual fallout from her PTSD legacy. Enjoyment, celebration, and the ability to savor the pleasurable parts of her life were simply not options for her. The only times she experienced any feelings at all were when she was fearful, anxious, or angry. *Many trauma survivors shuttle back and forth on a limited track between the poles of emotional numbness and agitated discomfort. They are either deadened or in a state of anxious alarm or fury. In other words, they get the worst of both worlds and rarely experience the rich, nourishing feelings and pleasurable sensations of a life worth living.*

CONTAMINATION AND SHAME

Shame plays a huge part in PTSD. I'd always been aware that Frannie came to my office smelling pleasantly of fresh soap and shampoo, well dressed and carefully made up. At the time I ascribed it to extraordinarily fastidious grooming habits. It wasn't until much later that she confessed to me how, during those dark months and years, she'd felt so dirty and ashamed, so unworthy of sitting with me (presumably a regular, normal person), that she took great care to come to her appointments scrubbed and clean, dressed to look as pleasant and "acceptable" as possible—even if it meant leaving her office early so she could go home and bathe first. *This too is classic PTSD fallout—the obsession with cleanliness is the result of feeling sullied, contaminated by ugliness, and unfit to mix with the rest of the human race.*

HIDING OUT

Avoidance is another key element. For a long time Frannie avoided most people, places, and activities. She went to work, she saw Laura and me, and she went home. That was her life. A few persistent friends stuck by her in spite of this, fruitlessly leaving encouraging messages on her answering machine. For over a year she rarely called back. *This too is typical*

PTSD behavior: avoiding the huge stress that simple daily activities and connections impose. Life is pared down to the bare essentials, which are work enough.

PROWESS AT MEDITATION AND IMAGERY

Like most trauma survivors, Frannie was a natural at using imagery and the altered state to help herself heal. The trance state was her powerful ally, and she was adept at achieving it, rapidly and deeply, thanks to a trauma-induced intensification in her brain's visual, sensorimotor, and emotional centers. So although Frannie was disabled by her traumatic experiences, she was also, in certain ways, empowered by them. *As debilitated as most PTSD sufferers are with using words to process their trauma, they can readily respond to nonverbal engagement—to images, symbols, metaphors, sensations, and feelings; to drawing, writing, conscious breathing, and movement.*

•   •   •

It's time now to take a deeper look at the nature of traumatic stress, to see in a clear, organized way what was so muddled to me at the time I was working with Frannie.

FIERCE UNDOING:
3 THE NATURE OF TRAUMA AND THE DILEMMA OF RUPTURED IDENTITY

For Frannie and for everyone else who suffers from it, post-traumatic stress is the result of a heart-stopping mix of terror, helplessness, and horror that floods the mind and freezes the body during an overwhelmingly threatening event. Later on, the disturbing and acutely uncomfortable symptoms of post-traumatic stress will show up in varying combinations, intensities, and durations. But at the time of the actual event, its defining nature is an instantaneous and automatic takeover of intense feelings of helplessness, terror, and loss of control, and the perception of impending annihilation by overwhelming force.

SYMPTOMS

Sometime later, whether it's immediately afterward or following an interval of days, weeks, or even years, some people will start to experience a classic array of aftereffects. This generally consists of terrifyingly vivid flashbacks, nightmares, and night terrors; intrusive thoughts about the event or events; sleep and concentration problems; anxiety, panic, and maybe phobias; depression, chronic joylessness, and emotional numbness; mental confusion, memory impairment, and possibly amnesia; waves of shame, guilt, grief, and anguish; irritability, hypervigilance, suspiciousness, and eruptions of temper; detachment, estrangement, deep loneliness, and—usually last to disappear—sudden startling from reminder stimuli.

CATALYTIC EVENTS

The kinds of events that have the potential to catalyze this traumatic stress reaction vary widely, but it's important to make clear that most people exposed to them *don't* get persistent PTSD from them. Most people are affected for a few weeks or months, and then the symptoms go away and stay away.

These catalytic events are as diverse as traffic collisions and near-miss accidents, combat, grievous losses, life-threatening diagnoses, ICU stays, traumatic deliveries, childhood illnesses, disfiguring accidents, heart attacks, spinal cord and brain injuries, rape, muggings, fires, near-drownings, childhood abuse, domestic violence, living in a war zone, hurricanes, floods, landslides, earthquakes, tornadoes, prolonged exposure to the elements, torture, terrorist attacks, violent assaults, imprisonment, and kidnappings. In spite of this wide variety of catalysts, the effects of trauma look surprisingly alike. The symptoms resemble Frannie's.

Trauma reactions can come as the result of one single terrifying event or, more often, an incremental compounding of events over time. Most cases of incest, domestic violence, kidnapping, and capture involve repeated abuse over time, which necessitates adapting to a life of perpetual fear. This repeated undoing of someone's personhood over time will usually have deeper and more devastating effects than one event, however horrific.

A recent trauma experience can be an eerie echo of an earlier one and can kick loose dormant but all-too-familiar symptoms. Or a single event can create ripples of problems for future behavior, compounding into greater and wider problems, compromising a simple recovery from the original event.

VICARIOUS TRAUMA

One needn't be directly involved in a situation to be traumatized. An acute reaction can come from just *watching helplessly*, at close range, as something terrible happens to someone else; or it can come from being a *responder to* or *chronicler of* horrible events. Police, firefighters, reporters, therapists, oral historians, and emergency health workers are vulnerable to these reactions when they witness too much repeated ugliness for too long.

Some children empathically absorb trauma from their parents, even though they are one generation removed from direct exposure to the horror that their mothers or fathers experienced. Children of Holocaust survivors are classic examples of a group that's been widely affected by this kind of vicarious traumatic stress.[1]

ACUTE STRESS REACTION

In most cases, the acutely uncomfortable symptoms will subside of their own accord after a few weeks or months. Most women, and even more men, will be only temporarily affected and will recover on their own, without help, when exposed to the majority of traumatic stressors. For these people, just knowing something about their temporary symptoms and how and why they occur is valuable and reassuring.

Jillian's story is typical of what happens after a traumatic event, for most people, most of the time:

> I was a naïve, exuberant college junior from a small New
> England town who got mugged in a Chicago park by a gang of
> six preteen boys, while taking a midday walk with a
> companion to celebrate the onset of spring. The boys, who
> had ditched school, surrounded the two of us, shouting and
> cursing at us to get our white asses out of their park, hitting us
> with tree branches and sticks. They ran away when my friend
> started bleeding copiously from what turned out to be a minor
> scalp wound.
>
> The two of us were taken by police cruiser to a nearby
> emergency room, where our cuts and bruises were tended to.
> After talking to the police, I was discharged, and I retreated to
> the safety of my apartment. I felt shaken and weird. But as the
> afternoon wore on, I became more and more agitated and
> fearful. I was very upset and disturbed by vivid images of
> the hatred on those boys' faces. It made me feel ugly and

ashamed—devalued in some unexpected way—even though I wondered how they could hate me so—they didn't even know me!

When I wasn't faulting myself for stupidly choosing to walk in that park—other students, it turned out, knew it wasn't safe—I was experiencing replays of the attack. Again and again I would be creeped out at seeing the contemptuous faces, hurling curses at me, pounding the two of us with their ad hoc weaponry. My heart would race, and I'd break into a sweat and get very scared.

All that afternoon I tried to distract myself with schoolwork or TV, but I just couldn't focus. I called friends on the phone, but I couldn't really talk to them. They were very sympathetic, but I felt disconnected, cranky, jumpy, and upset, and I just wanted to hang up. Once off the phone, I'd feel lonely and scared and want to call someone all over again. Neither condition was satisfactory. No matter what I did, I couldn't get away from my distress.

That evening I had plans to go to a cast party for a college production I was appearing in. I was scared but also looking forward to getting out of the apartment and being with friends who cared about me. I asked my friend from the ill-fated walk in the park to accompany me. Even though he had taken the much harder beating, he was not nearly as troubled as I was and seemed to feel pretty normal.

When I arrived at the party, my friends, who knew about the incident, gathered around me to express their concern. My reaction to being in the center of a circle of people for the second time that day was to totally freak out. I felt an uncontrollable rush of panic. I couldn't catch my breath. I broke an incredible sweat, started to shake, and had to get out of there.

My friend immediately steered me out of the party and into the hallway, where, after many minutes, I was able to calm down. But I couldn't go back to the party. He took me home, and I felt like a baby but I asked him to stay with me and sleep in the same room with me that night. I needed an asexual, protective, brotherly presence, and he was it. He was very kind and never made me feel like an idiot.

I stayed jumpy, frightened, and agitated for several days. The images in my waking hours were mirrored by nightmares during sleep. My concentration was bad, and I stayed grouchy and out of sorts, pretty disconnected from my friends, and kind of numb. Except for rehearsals—I think I was okay with them, for some reason. Maybe because they took my focus off the event completely, and I already knew my lines, so I didn't really have to concentrate so hard.

Finally, after about two or three weeks, I noticed I was beginning to feel more like my old self again. My friends told me my sense of humor was coming back. I started feeling a little playful again. I wasn't as jumpy or frightened. The nightmares and the waking replays were slowing down.

The only time I reexperienced a reprise of acute symptoms was when it came time to testify against the boys in court. The night before the court date, I couldn't sleep. I had the intense distress again, the cold sweats, pounding heart, and hyperventilating all over again. And weirdly, I felt afraid of seeing my attackers again, facing the people who'd hated me enough to hit me and call me names.

When the boys filed into the courtroom, dressed in their best white shirts, with their hair slicked down, looking so young and scared—hauled in by stern mothers or grandmothers, who demanded that they apologize to us in person—I was shocked. In the park they'd seemed so big, overpowering, and threatening. In the courtroom, they were only frightened kids—scared to be in court, and I think even more scared of their mothers. I found myself feeling sorry for them. Seeing those vulnerable faces definitely shifted something. There were no more nightmares after that.

Jillian had what therapists call an *acute stress reaction,* and the symptoms subsided after a few weeks. With the help of some social support and structured activity, people generally reorient and bounce back, incorporating the traumatic event into the fabric of their lives. Jillian is still the same person to herself. She was able to give the incident a minor place in her personal narrative, which she summarized in this way:

> I was a college junior who was unexpectedly attacked in the park one beautiful spring day. It badly frightened me, and for weeks after, I was a wreck. But I got through it, and I'm fine now. I have to say that since then I'm more careful about where I go, even in broad daylight, and I no longer take my personal safety so much for granted. Those naïve days are over—a good thing!

It's when symptoms stubbornly persist beyond six months—the arbitrary divide declared by the diagnosticians—that we add the D in PTSD and call it post-traumatic stress *disorder*. This is when the flashbacks, nightmares, overwhelming feelings, avoidant behavior, and intrusive thoughts don't disappear but instead tenaciously persist, either becoming chronic, getting steadily worse, or else waxing and waning, submerging and resurfacing, but generally relentless and persistent over the months and years.

SYMPTOMS RESURFACING

There are numerous reports from septuagenarian World War II combat veterans who hadn't experienced their PTSD for four or five decades, until an open heart surgery or domestic terror attack catalyzed the reemergence of hellishly fresh images and emotions from a previously forgotten combat episode. A typical recounting:

> I have been under treatment for deep depression that overcame me in the fall of 2001. We had just returned from a long and tiring driving trip at the end of August. I was excited to be home and to invite some of our friends to my seventy-fifth birthday party on September 9. It was a grand evening but must have taken much more energy than I knew.
> I could not stand to watch the TV scenes of the destruction of the Twin Towers over and over again. It

brought back too many memories of the devastation I had seen in 1945 in Manila and Tokyo and Sendai, Japan. We did not know, of course, if that was the beginning of the total destruction of New York and another war. At the end of that week, when it seemed that there would not be a war, we were struck by a strong tropical storm.

We live on a tropical island, and the rain and wind beating on the house encouraged us to pack a few important things in our van and leave for the mainland. All the traffic lights were out, and even the hospitals were on emergency power, the wind blew very hard, but we felt safe in the heavy van. Fortunately, the center of the storm came ashore a few miles south of us. We could not return home over the same bridge, as several large trees had fallen across the road after we passed.

Every day for the next week and a half, I felt very tired and became increasingly nervous, agitated, and depressed, with less and less appetite. Fortunately, I did seek and find professional help. Listening to guided imagery has been a great help. We still hear it almost every night. My wife usually falls asleep during the visualization, but I look forward to the affirmations, which help me greatly.

PTSD reactions, as we will see later on, are physiologically as well as psychologically based, and they can be so disruptive, frightening, and bizarre that some people fear they're losing their minds. After all, a flashback involves "seeing things," "hearing things," and even "smelling and tasting things" that seem real but aren't actually there. These multisensory images appear and disappear as if they had a life of their own. In that sense, they look and feel very much like a psychotic hallucination, even though the beholder is quite sane and entirely oriented to what constitutes reality and what doesn't.

So intensely distressing, disturbing, and disorienting are these symptoms when they persist that people wind up developing avoidant routines just to keep from experiencing them, a consequence that often catalyzes a whole other set of problems at work and at home. This is sometimes the most destructive aspect of PTSD altogether, this secondary set of aversive responses that short-circuit the normal ebb and flow of life.

Nonetheless, even with some variant of persistent, post-traumatic stress, most people learn to live and work around their symptoms; they manage the emotional fallout with somewhat impaired but good, useful lives—even without knowing about the new, effective tools that are now available to help them move beyond their symptoms.

A minority of PTSD sufferers are seriously incapacitated by disabling symptoms and suffer from a daunting array of destructive social, marital, and vocational aftereffects. But even people this seriously affected can be greatly helped by these new approaches, although they clearly take more time and require other kinds of interventions as well.

We will be exploring in the chapters ahead why some people, like Jillian, get better on their own after a few weeks of unpleasantness; why others, like her companion, have no aftereffects whatsoever; and why others are still far more deeply and tenaciously affected.

But first we need to look a little more carefully at the nature of the impact of a traumatic episode, and the rupture in identity and meaning that it can produce.

SPLINTERED BELIEF AND LOSS OF PREDICTABILITY

Most of us are blandly oblivious to how much comfort we take from our belief that the world is a predictable place, until it demonstrates its random cruelty in some dramatic way. We structure our lives upon a platform of interlocking assumptions: my office building will be there tomorrow; my home is safe; Daddy knows best and protects me from harm; the ground will stay firm and steady beneath my feet; oncoming drivers will stay in their lanes; and in a pinch, people—including myself—will behave decently and honorably.

These assumptions enable us to get on with the business of living, because our attention doesn't have to be diverted by thousands of miniconcerns about what's coming next. By knowing what to expect, and by taking certain basics for granted, we can efficiently focus our efforts on making a living, maintaining relationships, learning new skills, rearing our children, creating art, having fun, and living our lives.

When the platform of assumptions collapses under the deadly weight of a horrific event, everything else goes down with it, and suddenly there's no place to stand. It's as if the world has broken its promise, revealing itself to be capable of devastating chaos and cruelty. Traumatized people, in the eloquent words of Judith Herman, feel "utterly abandoned, utterly alone, cast out of the human and divine systems of care and protection that sustain life."[2] Because of this profound loss of trust in the world, the resulting sense of alienation and doubt pervades every relationship and every activity. The traumatic event, by its very nature, has revealed, with its cruel disregard for the survivor, that his point of view *counts for nothing*. Events have rolled over him, proving he doesn't matter. Once this sense of place, of trust, is lost, things are no longer what they seemed to be, and doubt and fear start to color the entire landscape.

The trauma carves a painful dividing line in the survivor's personal narrative, a line that splices his life in two: there's the person he was before, and the person he's become since. Profoundly undermined, he is lonely, fearful, disoriented, and unnerved by the certainty that he is not who he thought he was, and indeed the world is no longer amenable to past interpretation.

This loss of a sense of safety can be more frightening and devastating than the original event. Because of it, attention must be directed to every slight signal in our perceptual field, because we now are operating from the position that nothing is certain and we can be ambushed at any turn. This vigilance takes up enormous cognitive space, capturing most of our attention, employing vast numbers of our brain cells, and sapping our energy reserves. Frannie put it this way:

> Nothing made sense anymore. Everything had to be reevaluated in the light of the fact that I no longer knew anything. I actually felt stupid or like a Martian or something. Remember that science fiction title, *Stranger in a Strange Land*? That was me. Nothing was safe. Nothing made sense. I was confused and scared all the time. Every morning I woke up (or stayed up most of the night) with a sense of gnawing dread in the pit of my stomach. I was afraid to get out of bed. It took every ounce of strength I had just to get up and face an unrecognizable universe. It was simply exhausting. I get tired just thinking about it.

THE RETREAT OF FAIRNESS AND
THE LOSS OF CONTROL

Along with the collapse of bedrock assumptions about the predictable nature of the universe comes a different kind of loss: that of our sense of
control and self-efficacy—the idea that by dint of our individual actions
and efforts, we can make good things happen for ourselves and keep the
bad things away. Consciously or unconsciously, we cling to ideas like *If
I'm nice to him and do what he tells me, he won't hit me; if I eat right, exercise,
and take my herbs, I won't get sick; if I'm a good person, my children will be safe;
if I stay out of bad neighborhoods, I won't get mugged.* These poignantly optimistic causal connections have two attractive implications: for one thing,
they mean the world is a fair, moral, and reasonable place; and for another, they mean we can choose correctly and keep harm at bay.

Equally important, our self-esteem is bound up in this belief in our
ability to impact our world. We see this in eighteen-month-olds. A fat-
legged toddler whoops with joy when she discovers she can knock over
her tower of blocks. She is compelled to do it again and again, and each
time the delight is undiminished, because she's learning a critical lesson:
She is a prime mover; she can make things happen.

We see it on the face of a four-year-old child who has just realized
that the sound of his own voice is producing an echo and making a really
big noise in a church with good acoustics. He repeats it over and over,
never tiring of the idea that he is the originator of this magnificent sound.

The joyous self-love from such accomplishments is a good part of
what drives all of us—children and adults—to master more, to grow and
develop and learn, even in the face of frustration, fear, and the anxiety of
leaving the familiar comfort of already-mastered terrain.

And because it is built into our human hard-wiring to love ourselves
for being able to make things happen, the converse is also true: we lose
self-regard when bad things happen that are beyond our control. The essential insult of trauma is the helplessness it generates, and the inade-
quacy and powerlessness that we feel in its grip.

Rational or not, we can't help but feel it's a reflection on our worthiness that, when confronted with a terrifying and terrible event, we didn't
prevent it, escape it, or fix it. So we somehow lose value to ourselves and,

at a level we may not even be aware of, we feel guilty and ashamed. Valerie, an adult survivor of years of childhood sexual abuse, struggling with bulimia, writes:

> People like me have lived in darkness so long that the light seems wrong; we've known misery for so long that goodness and happiness produce overwhelming feelings of shame and unworthiness . . . I continue to grapple with my issues, but [with help] I now have a vision of where I can be . . . what I might deserve to hope for.

We all operate from this sort of thinking, whether we know it or not, and if we've been lucky enough to have sidestepped notable misfortune over the years, we are probably unknowingly taking credit for it in an unconscious subtext of smugness. Even if we know better, we slip into the erroneous belief that our good fortune is a reflection of our worthiness, our goodness, our wisdom. The idea of virtue rewarded and control achieved is just too attractive a proposition to pass up.

Trauma, of course, by its very nature, is a situation of feeling an outsize helplessness and a paralysis in our ability to affect a situation. Those who wind up finding something useful to do in the midst of a traumatic event, who can take charge and effect some measure of improved outcome, usually wind up without symptoms, or with fewer or lighter symptoms, than those who are frozen in helplessness. (This is unfortunate, as we shall see later on, because freezing is a natural, built-in, biologically driven response to overwhelming threat; there are certain predeterminants that hardwire some of us to fall into immobility when presented with the proposition of imminent annihilation that we are helpless to stop.[3])

The notion that we are in charge of our fate is so reassuring that we'll stick to it even if it puts us at fault. Nine times out of ten, victims will hold themselves accountable rather than blame a traumatic event on the cruel vagaries of fate. At least if it's their fault, they can adjust their behavior and see to it that it doesn't happen again. The world is still making sense, and they are still at the helm. So the prevailing logic, deep down, is *If this bad thing happened to me, I must have done something to deserve it.* The more atrocious the bad thing, the greater the inferred blame. This is preferable to accepting the truth of random horror.

This is the logic seen most clearly in children. I remember one morning in the summer of 1965, when I was running a Chicago day camp, an eight-year-old girl on our bus told me with big, solemn eyes, in response to the shocking news of Richard Speck's random, sadistic murder of eight student nurses, who had been sleeping innocently in their nearby apartment, "Well, they must have done something very mean to him," nodding her head with great certainty in order to underline the truth of this sure fact.

We adults are only a tad more sophisticated. We frequently blame ourselves directly. At the very least we feel the guilt of not having done something to prevent the trauma from happening. Sometimes we feel the shame of having been scared, frozen in horror, or just plain ineffective at doing anything about it. And as long as we can focus our attention on our own behavior, we don't have to stare into the abyss of a world capable of shocking and unexpected cruelty that renders us flat-out helpless.

And so it was with Michael Risenhoover, an Oklahoma police captain who'd been on the force for over sixteen years, in the town of El Reno, on the outskirts of Oklahoma City. He was burdened by this kind of thinking after the 1995 bombing:

> Before the events of April 19, 1995, in the course of duty, I'd witnessed many horrible events and had even held dead children in my arms. I guess I felt like I was superman. I tried to take care of the whole world. I would comfort victims and families, and somehow I was able to keep my tears locked away with my feelings.
>
> Then on April 19, 1995, I lost my best friend and many other friends in the Oklahoma City bombing. This tragic event seemed to open up my emotions and tears that would not stop.
>
> I went between feeling there was something I should have done, some way I should have saved more people, or even somehow prevented what happened, and another feeling that the whole world was insane. My wife said I changed after the bombing. I kept going to work every day like a robot, trying

not to feel the pain and trying not to pull the trigger when I put the pistol in my mouth.

So, not only does the external world become unrecognizable and senseless, but the survivor's sense of *worth* in that world evaporates as well. Whatever sense of esteem and value was enjoyed previously, based on a sense of efficacy, competence, and ability to make the right things happen, all of this is gone with the wind. Instead, shame, guilt, and self-blame take up residence, either by stealthy invasion or with a howling, anguished takeover.

SHATTERED IDENTITY

I'm not sure I could have said what my being was . . . my sense of myself was incoherent—just a lot of electrical shortages, mixed-up connections, and constant interference. But now I do have this sense of myself. The rape was something that happened to me, but it's not me.

This was Frannie's description of her disrupted sense of self. Most of us have a fairly coherent idea of who we are, even if we're not particularly aware of it. There are central notions and descriptions of ourselves that we feel generally hold true, regardless of what's happening in the moment.

We might even describe ourselves in the course of conversation, saying things like "Oh, that's not me; I would never do that," implying an understanding of our core traits or values. A woman might think, *I would have been happy with that sort of relationship in my twenties, but I've grown up a lot since then,* implying an awareness of her own personal narrative, a familiarity with the trajectory of her growth in the course of her own life's story. A man might get butterflies before entering a crowded cocktail party, but he might quickly identify the sensation as a familiar one before any sort of social gathering and remind himself, "This doesn't necessarily mean you'll have a bad time; this is just the way you get before parties." Again, this is the small daily evidence of a sort of basic, intact personal sense of self—an understanding of the way body and psyche characteristically respond to things, learned over the years. Sometimes in an interaction between two friends, there will be a sudden realization—"She and I are so different when it comes to things like this!"—and again, it presupposes a sense of a self, an intact identity.

Such self-awareness grounds us and supports us. We take deep comfort in knowing who we are, in being able to describe ourselves *to* ourselves and to others, too. Our capacity to see ourselves evolve over the years, like the protagonist in a story, is critical to our sense of wholeness, growth, and self-worth. We depend on our ability to differentiate ourselves from others—even when the comparison isn't always favorable. We have a need to know where we stand and how we stand. It's a sense of having a stable core, a center of gravity that allows us to feel we can claim our spot on the planet, and claim our membership in the human race.

Most of the time this view of ourselves as a consistent, coherent entity is something we take for granted, the unseen operating system that drives our behavior and provides context for our daily doings. It's critical to our conscious functioning, our choice making, and our self-evaluation. And when it's missing, we find ourselves swimming in chaos. Trauma disrupts internal continuity, interferes with coherence, and at least temporarily shatters identity. And when that's gone, nothing is right.

Lynne, the survivor of brutal childhood abuse from a mentally ill mother, describes the early truncating of her sense of self and the splicing of her life's story, because of her needing to lock away from her own awareness the terrible things that were being done to her:

> As many survivors do, I learned to leave my body [during the abuse], to go out to the rainbow, to not feel pain. I locked each incident away in its own little compartment—none could touch the other. I learned to hide the pain, and no one ever knew. For many years I didn't even remember, as each incident was locked away inside me. I never even remembered what happened the day before.

It wasn't until Lynne turned forty that the stories started erupting into her awareness, through nightmares and physical symptoms. This is commonplace with survivors of childhood abuse. There usually comes a point in the adult survivor's life when a deep, wordless intelligence, working underground, determines that it is time to begin to acknowledge and integrate the lost stories, that the person is now strong enough to reclaim the shattered pieces of her self.

> At age forty, I began to have horrific nightmares and waking memories. As if I were watching a video, scenes would come forth, and then stop, and come forth and stop. Little by little I remembered my life and felt the pain of the abuse as if it were actually happening. I started therapy and found some comfort and healing in sharing my story with my therapist. After a number of years in therapy, and much healing, I realized I was still having horrific body memories and found that the slightest sound, or a scent, or another person's anger, would trigger these memories and feelings. One night I even woke up in terrible pelvic/vaginal pain, after dreaming the memory of being abused.

Painful and difficult as these emerging experiences are, they mark an important beginning; they are announcing that it is time for healing and reclaiming the self.

LOSS OF MEANING

Without a belief in a fair and moral universe, a sense of control of one's fate, a coherent sense of self, and a continuous personal narrative, life makes no sense. Living becomes a pointless exercise in getting through the day. People reeling from trauma are thrown into a crisis of meaning that goes far beyond disillusionment; they are plunged into an abyss of despair.

Many sound like Michael Risenhoover, the Oklahoma police captain, who said that the whole world suddenly seemed insane to him. Where before his life held great meaning and moral certainty for him, the heartless cruelty of the bombing and his helplessness to fix anything undid all of that. For a while he considered suicide as a sensible response. Eventually he quit the force, left the state, and after many months built a new life for himself.

John, a World Trade Center survivor, said:

Everything I held to be true got turned upside down. Nothing
made sense anymore. All those smashed bodies, flying body
parts, incinerated people . . . I don't know what was worse, the
screaming or the silence . . . so many destroyed . . . for what?
all their lives, their cares, their hard work, their loves . . . it all
went for nothing in a matter of minutes. How can you care
when everything is instantly destroyed like that? I just stopped
caring. I stopped wanting to get up in the morning and try
anymore. For what?

Indeed, it is those who can eventually bring meaning to bear on their
suffering who are more likely to recover and thrive. Viktor Frankl, a psychiatrist who survived Auschwitz and the death of his wife, parents, and
brother, was able to use his experience of dehumanized suffering to develop a brilliant new form of psychotherapy that explores the essence of
what makes life worth living as its core investigation. He decided:

that human life, under any circumstances, never ceases to have
meaning, and that this infinite meaning of life includes suffering
and dying, privation and death . . . The hopelessness of our
struggle did not detract from its dignity and its meaning.[4]

He described the epiphany he experienced while trudging for miles
on blistered feet in freezing darkness, in an icy wind, kicked and prodded
by rifle butts and shrieking commands. First he discovered that he could
manage the pain and discomfort if he could evoke the image of his wife's
beloved presence:

my mind clung to my wife's image, imagining it with uncanny
acuteness. I heard her answering me; saw her smile, her frank
and encouraging look. Real or not, her look was then more
luminous than the sun, which was beginning to rise.[5]

It was in the company of these magical, sustaining images that he arrived at the premise that kept him from psychological destruction and restored his sense of meaning:

A thought transfixed me: for the first time in my life I saw the truth . . . that love is the ultimate and the highest goal to which man can aspire . . . The salvation of man is through love and in love . . . In a position of utter desolation, when man cannot express himself in positive action, when his only achievement may consist in enduring his suffering in the right way—an honorable way—in such a position man can, through loving contemplation of the image he carries of his beloved, achieve fulfillment.[6]

Frankl found meaning in his suffering, and that alone may have been what saved him from the abyss. And while doing so, he also spontaneously discovered the power of imagery to provide healing, strength, resilience, and transcendence in the midst of horror.

4 WHO SUFFERS: HOW, WHEN, WHERE, AND WHY?

Now would be a good time to step back from the compelling stories of individual survivors and the drama of the therapist's office, to take a broader, more detached look at what population studies tell us. These surveys show us planet-wide trends that remain consistent, regardless of country or culture; and they show us our differences by virtue of gender, class, age, or race. The findings allow us to better understand bedrock truths about our human condition, our assorted vulnerabilities and hardinesses, our survival wiring, and our built-in responses to terrifying events. Epidemiological studies expand and refine our hard-won, hit-or-miss, clinical insights about post-traumatic stress.

This new research is coming at a time when it is sorely needed. Not only is the worldwide incidence of violence, starvation, torture, and war increasing in both developed and undeveloped nations, but climate changes are becoming more extreme, resulting in more hurricanes, droughts, landslides, floods, and earthquakes around the planet. One obvious effect of all this devastation is more trauma-related debilitation.

The new studies and surveys highlight the complex nature of post-traumatic stress. How we get through a terrible event, and the toll that event ultimately exacts, is a convergence of a great many interacting forces: the nature of the traumatic stressor itself; our degree of exposure to it; our age, gender, and ethnicity; our inborn neurological wiring and biochemical predispositions; our psychological history; our social support networks; and our coping behavior before, during, and after the event.

Just looking at the simple prevalence of PTSD in various populations around the globe delivers substantial insight into its nature and ours. For instance, the most obvious findings show that across cultures, countries, and generations, *women* are far more vulnerable to traumatic stress than men, and *children* far more so than adults. This is an important finding we will be revisiting, because both women and children tend to have broader and quicker access to the right side of their brains, where the processing of images, emotions, body awarenesses, intuitions, and sensory perceptions occur. These capabilities are profoundly affected by trauma; they also provide the wherewithal for a speedier recovery.

THE NATURE OF THE TRAUMATIC EVENT

People's reaction to a traumatic event depends in part on the nature of the event itself and some of its main features. This is a piece of what shapes the internal aftermath. A lot of work has been done on this, and we now know many of the key variables.

PROXIMITY

Many of the survey findings reflect simple common sense. For instance, PTSD is more likely for those at the epicenter of a traumatic event than for those in its surrounding or adjacent areas, although a lesser percentage of people on the periphery will still be deeply affected. Similarly, some risk exists even for those who are not directly impacted but have friends or acquaintances who were. Even repeated watching of a traumatic event on TV creates a higher percentage of vulnerability to posttraumatic stress.[1]

For example, roughly six to eight weeks after the attack on the World Trade Center, about 7.5 percent of the population of Lower Manhattan, defined as south of 14th Street, had full-blown symptoms. But closer to Ground Zero, in the area south of Canal Street, the incidence was up to 20 percent.[2] This ratio of impact to proximity also holds up for people nearest an affected area during a flood in southern France; an earthquake in China; a landslide in Sarno, Italy; a hurricane in Nicaragua; an avalanche in Iceland; and a bombardment zone in Gaza.[3]

In all cases, however, regardless of the nature of the traumatic event, whether it be a flood or an earthquake or a motor vehicle accident, it is important to keep in mind that it is not the external danger per se but the *internal perception* of danger that generates the potential for symptoms. If a person is in danger but doesn't know it, she remains immune. On the other hand, a near-miss collision can activate a traumatic stress response as powerfully as an actual accident. It is the fact of the brain predicting impending annihilation that puts the biochemistry of trauma into play.

DURATION

Another factor commonly associated with soaring rates of PTSD is a longer duration of exposure to the trauma, or a greater number of exposures within a certain period of time—in other words, the "dose" experienced. Again, this clear-cut association is a phenomenon that holds up worldwide. We find outsized percentages of people with full-blown PTSD symptoms—usually well over half a population—in shelters for battered women, where traumatic abuse has a duration that is often measured in decades. We see these kinds of percentages in domestic violence survivors in Germany, South Africa, and the United States.[4] Another example of long-standing, cumulative trauma is the experience of children exposed to war. Again, vulnerability is extraordinarily high in children all over the globe, from the Middle East to Kosovo and Sarajevo.[5] We see it in people subjected to torture in Zimbabwe and in those exposed to starvation in North Korea; in those detained in refugee camps in Cuba; in the general population of juvenile delinquents in the former Soviet Union; in Tasmanian adolescents in juvenile detention; among prostitutes in Washington, D.C.; and in women attending HIV clinics in the United States.[6] All of these groups have in common an extended duration and frequency of cumulative, traumatic life events.

Duration has an impact on the helpers as well. UN human rights workers in Kosovo experienced an increase in PTSD symptoms after they had worked on the site for longer than six months.[7] Duration and frequency of the "dose" are equally critical to emergency responders, hospital staff, police, fire, and rescue workers, and international volunteers.[8]

EXTENT OF BRUTALITY

Another critical factor is the degree of *brutality* of the traumatic event itself. Atrocities and interpersonal violence have a more devastating effect on the human spirit and psyche than, say, a natural disaster, even though both can be equally terrifying, life threatening, and consequential in terms of actual injury or material damage suffered. When people are subjected to malevolence and brutality at the hands of their fellow human beings, the ravaging symptoms of PTSD go wider and deeper.

This is why 46 percent of women who are raped develop post-traumatic stress, as opposed to only 9 percent of women involved in an accident,[9] even though the physical injuries may be far greater from the accident, and why 75 percent of concentration camp survivors, a population that suffered an unusual level of demeaning brutality, compounded by both frequency and duration, are so likely to be fully symptomatic.

BETRAYAL

Similarly, betrayal looms large as a factor that generates more severe symptoms, given its intimate connection with beliefs about safety, self-worth, and the trustworthiness of others.[10] Sexual abuse by a trusted family member, friend, or community authority yields the astronomical rate of 87 percent PTSD in its victims. Add loss to horror, terror, and betrayal, and you have the 100 percent PTSD rate in children who have watched the murder of a parent (usually by another family member).

THREAT OF DYING

Of course, life-threatening situations are more likely to increase the likelihood of subsequent post-traumatic stress.[11] But even more than the actual threat is the *perceived* threat. A recent study of heart attack survivors with PTSD showed that it was not the actual severity of the heart attack that predicted a greater likelihood of the patient going on to develop post-traumatic stress, but rather the *perceived* severity of the heart attack, from the patient's point of view.[12]

PERPETRATING VIOLENCE

Odd as it may sound, perpetrators of violence suffer from PTSD as well as their victims. Studies that differentiated between those who perpe-trated violence and those who were victims of violence show differences in symptoms and degree of impairment. Secondary analysis of the 1,638 responses to the National Vietnam Veterans Readjustment Study revealed that perpetrators reported more violent outbursts and greater severity of intrusive symptoms, as well as a greater sense of alarm, alienation, sur-vivor guilt, and sense of disintegration. On the other hand the victims surveyed experienced greater memory and concentration problems.[13]

Other assessments concluded that perpetrators of atrocities in war-time are far more likely to suffer from PTSD than fellow combatants in the same cohort who have otherwise experienced the same events.[14] It ap-pears that participating in brutal behavior results in profoundly destruc-tive effects on the human spirit; one can be on either side of the violence equation to be shattered.

This is an area that cries out for more study. For years, clinicians have posited that perpetrators of violence are in their own sort of dissociated, disconnected "trauma trance" as they wreak havoc on others, in spite of the fact that they are neither helpless nor passive. This complex, paradox-ical circumstance is only now beginning to be explored.

SOCIETAL CONTEXT

The meaning and significance assigned to a traumatic event by the larger culture makes a difference in its impact. For instance, in-depth interviews of Finnish World War II veterans in a rehabilitation hospital revealed an extremely low rate of PTSD, alongside a relatively high sense of sub-jective well-being, in spite of a significant rate of disability and health problems found in this cohort of septuagenarians.[15] Because the larger Finnish society viewed this war as honorable and good, participation in it figured prominently in the men's sense of integrity, courage, and honor. They still spoke passionately of their fighting spirit, their strong bonds of loyalty to one another, and their contribution to making the world a safer place.

This stands in sharp contrast to veterans of the "forgotten" Korean War, who reported significantly more severe symptoms than their World War II counterparts.[16] Most dramatically different, of course, were the devalued veterans of the Vietnam War, who returned to communities that shunned and reviled them. They experienced the highest rates of PTSD—a whopping 30 percent.[17] Indeed, it was this epidemic of PTSD that catalyzed the creation of the diagnostic category and the subsequent explosion of studies and findings under discussion here. These and many other studies show how the significance that the larger community attaches to the traumatic catalyst has the power to cushion or exacerbate PTSD symptoms.

UNPREDICTABILITY

Another feature of a traumatic stressor that makes symptoms worse is its degree of unpredictability. Behavioral psychology has long demonstrated that a distressing event that can be counted on to come and go with regularity is far less psychologically destructive than one that follows no rules. Our sense of safety, control, and empowerment are still intact when we can anticipate an event, adjust our behavior, and know when there will be a return to normalcy. The child who knows that Dad is a dangerous monster when he drinks on Saturday night but is safe to be around the rest of the week has some predictability to protect and stabilize him, unlike the child whose parent launches into full-blown rages at random, unexpected times.

This dynamic is even found when an abused child behaves in such a way as to provoke or solicit abuse from a routine predator. It appears maladaptive and is often misinterpreted, but in fact this is the victim's way of reducing distress by controlling when an attack will occur.[18]

INJURY

Not surprisingly, should a traumatic event produce significant injury or mutilation, the survivors' vulnerability to PTSD is higher. This effect seems fairly universal, whether the survivors are recovering from a car collision in England or an earthquake in China.[19]

LOSS

When a traumatic event results in the loss of a family member or close friend, symptoms are exacerbated and risk of PTSD is higher. Loss of one's home or even important possessions will also increase vulnerability. When, on top of these losses, one's country or culture is also taken away, as is the case with displaced persons or refugees from war-torn or famine-ravaged countries, the toll is higher still.[20]

BEING TRAPPED

Post-traumatic stress by definition involves feelings of helplessness and powerlessness. When someone is literally physically trapped in a danger-ous or terrifying situation, the survivor's likelihood for experiencing PTSD escalates. After a major earthquake in Turkey, a thousand survivors from the epicenter region were interviewed to see which factors led to significant PTSD. Those who were trapped under rubble were far more likely to have severe symptoms than those who were not, even when they were less seriously injured than people who were not trapped.[21]

An extreme example of being trapped is what happens when a surgery patient is unsuccessfully anesthetized during an operation. Esti-mates of how many surgery patients remain aware under unsuccessful anesthesia in the United States each year vary widely, ranging from a low of 30,000 to a high of 140,000. When this occurs, the risk for post-traumatic stress is high.[22] Being sensate but unable to communicate cre-ates intense feelings of helplessness, terror, and if not perceived pain, the fear of pain. A recent batch of studies demonstrates that temporary functional paralysis due to failed anesthetic yields a period of intense post-surgical acute stress and a likelihood of eventual vulnerability to longer-term PTSD.[23]

Other circumstances of being trapped include various forms of captivity—in prisons, slave labor camps, brothels, cults, kidnappings, and of course, families where children or economically dependent wives are stuck. In addition to entrapment, these circumstances heap on additional factors of psychological domination, repeated exploitation, betrayal, and brutality, all of which compound and exacerbate symptoms of PTSD.

SURVIVOR TRAITS

In addition to the way the specific nature of the trauma affects the prevalence and severity of symptoms, so do different traits in the survivor—variations in gender, age, ethnicity, psychology, personal history, neurobiological wiring, coping behavior, and unique social circumstances. These individual attributes and factors also configure to make for either increased risk or an extra cushion of protection.

The same Turkish study that found entrapment to be such a powerful factor also revealed that earthquake survivors with full-blown PTSD symptoms were more likely to be female; to have experienced the death of a family member; to have a history of psychiatric illness; and to be less well educated than the average.[24] Similar findings have surfaced around the globe.

GENDER

As mentioned earlier, women are consistently more vulnerable to PTSD than men. In any general population, a greater percentage of women will develop post-traumatic stress over their lifetime—roughly 10 to 12 percent of them, as compared with 5 percent of men. This is in spite of the fact that men will be exposed to significantly more traumatic events than women over a lifetime.[25]

This is the case around the globe, from country to country and culture to culture. The evidence is overwhelming. Studies looking at a gen-

eral population of British students, French terror-bombing attack survivors, Dutch adults trapped in a ballroom fire, Spanish drivers after a serious motor accident, psychiatric inpatients in the United States and in
Israel, Danish eighth graders, Chinese adolescents after an earthquake,
Nicaraguan survivors of Hurricane Mitch, South Africans suffering war-
time and domestic violence, survivors of the Vaucluse flood in France, and
a Canadian survey of trauma exposure in Winnipeg all show women to
be as much as six times as likely as men to develop PTSD, once they are
exposed to comparable trauma.[26]

The fact that, planet-wide, women are more vulnerable to PTSD
than men speaks to the likelihood that something survival-related, built
into the neurobiology of being female, accounts for this reaction. Neurologist Robert Scaer, who for twenty years was the medical director of
rehabilitation services at Boulder (Colorado) Memorial Hospital, studied
the effects of trauma on the central and autonomic nervous systems of
whiplash victims and other accident survivors, reporting on his conclusions in his cogent, cutting-edge book, The Body Bears the Burden.[27] In it, he
reminds us of the anthropological theories of Richard Leakey, as adapted
by childhood trauma expert Bruce Perry. Perry's discussion offers the
clearest and most reasonable Darwinian explanation for this dramatic
cross-cultural difference.[28]

Perry suggests that when primitive, hominid tribes battled one another, the victorious tribe slaughtered the defeated adult males but captured the women and children, either as slaves or as full-fledged members.
This allowed a victorious tribe to acquire some fresh DNA to ensure the
tribe's future robustness.

It would make sense, then, that male warriors needed a sustained
fight response in order to be able to battle to the death. But women facing capture, rape, humiliation, and other downwardly spiraling events
could freeze, dissociate, get through, and survive. This would allow them
to look after their captured children, too—another population that is
much more likely to freeze and dissociate.

Perhaps this is why adult men, for the most part, ended up struc-
turally with greater separation of function between the analytic, logical
left side of the brain and the intuitive, emotional right side of the brain,
whereas women are endowed with greater connectivity between the
hemispheres.[29] Where the left side is associated with the functions of

cognition, logic, analysis, verbalizing, judging, strategizing, and deciding, the right is more about sensing, imagining, apprehending, feeling, perceiving, and intuiting. Women, with their greater ease of access between the hemispheres, get to have more instantaneous communication between the thinking and feeling parts of the brain; between their verbal and emotive centers; and between judgment and sensation. Men, on the other hand, seem better built for strategic thinking and decision making that is separated from emotional data.

Perhaps when the flooding biochemicals of terror wash through the body during a traumatic event, the female brain gets more of a bilateral bath, contributing to the freeze response, whereas men might be more protected by the built-in roadblocks in the less interactive structure of their hemispheres, allowing them to better fight to the death. We will explore this concept more fully in later chapters. But for now the main thing to note is this powerful and universal gender finding.

The fact that older women, beyond childbearing years, are much less likely to get PTSD than their younger counterparts when faced with a traumatic stressor, also supports Scaer's hypothesis. It also suggests that the hormonal activity of a woman's childbearing years, interacting with the biochemistry of extreme stress, may play a significant part in the freeze response, dissociation, and the greater likelihood of acquiring PTSD.

In a large study of over three thousand American women who had been sexually assaulted, women over age 55 were compared to women between the ages of 18 and 34 and were found to have far lower odds of developing PTSD.[30] This is not just the case for older women, however. An Australian survey revealed that older women *and* men are more protected from PTSD than their juniors.[31] Clearly there are complex variables operating, and we are only beginning to understand their interaction.

Another obvious reason older people are less vulnerable has to do with the stronger sense of identity, worth, and integrity that most older adults possess, accumulated over the years, and that is harder to undo by trauma, garden-variety stress, what other people think, or anything else, for that matter.

One last point regarding gender: sex differences were found to be less dramatic in some countries. For instance, in both Australia and in Israel[32] women were still found to be at greater risk for PTSD than men, but the differences were smaller, suggesting that culture may play a part in modifying the gender differences of trauma.

CHILDREN

Another universal finding is that children are more vulnerable to PTSD than adults. The younger the child, the greater the likelihood of post-traumatic stress occurring, and the more severe the symptoms. Again, this was found to be as true for the children who survived the great Hanshin-Awaji earthquake in Kobe, Japan, as it was for U.S. children from Alabama who had either lost a parent or experienced a tornado, or for child survivors of an industrial accident in the Briey region of France.[33] This finding can be explained, at least in part, by the less complete differentiation in the formative brains of children, as compared to those of adults, compounded by their less sophisticated thinking and language capacity, and of course by their very vulnerable identities, still so much in flux. Children, too, are more likely to freeze and dissociate when experiencing helpless terror, in the same way that women of childbearing years do, supporting the Leaky hypothesis about a Darwinian survival mechanism.

The younger a Vietnam soldier was at the time of his encounter with combat stress, the more vulnerable he was to post-traumatic symptoms.[34] This finding shows that youthfulness continues to be a risk factor even into young adulthood. It was generally assumed that the age factor had to do with the tentative sense of psychological and psychosocial identity that is a normal part of adolescence; but it may also be related to some of these biophysical factors and the greater fluidity in the still-developing eighteen-year-old brain, leaving teens more affected by these events than their elders.

Even with young children, the male-to-female differences hold up, compounding vulnerability for young girls and leaving two strikes against them: once for being a child and once again for being female.[35]

PSYCHOLOGICAL HISTORY

Not surprisingly, previous psychological problems or a family history of mental illness increases a person's vulnerability to post-traumatic stress. Particularly the presence of major depression, anxiety or panic attacks, phobias, and a whole range of mood disorders, either in the survivor's history or the family history, will up the ante on vulnerability, regardless of country or culture.[36] Some studies point to the likelihood that major depression or panic attacks help *predispose* a trauma survivor to post-traumatic stress; still others suggest that once post-traumatic stress comes calling, the sufferer has a subsequent tendency toward depression, panic attacks, and phobias. Cause and effect are easily confounded.

People who have suffered previous traumas are more vulnerable to PTSD, as are people who experience traumas immediately after the original event. This has proved to be as true for a general population of Danish eighth graders as for Cuban refugees and adult survivors of the war in Kosovo who settled in the United States. Additional life stress, either just before or just after suffering a traumatic experience, is another strong predictor of PTSD. So is previously reported childhood abuse.[37]

EDUCATION

For reasons that are not entirely clear, those with less education are consistently more vulnerable to PTSD than the well educated. This was found to be the case in a variety of settings: with those affected by the attacks on the World Trade Center; with survivors of an earthquake in Turkey; with Afghan refugees settled in the Netherlands; and, most compellingly, in veterans of the war in Vietnam who were identical twins.[38]

Childhood trauma expert Bruce Perry suggests that education leads to more highly developed cortices in the brain, creating greater ease with abstract thinking, which, in turn strengthens the ability to modulate impulses and hyperactivity in the more primitive brain structures that are so intensely affected by trauma.[39]

ETHNICITY

Several studies show a relationship between ethnicity and vulnerability. In a study of the effects of Hurricane Andrew on more than four hundred residents of southern Florida, comparisons among Caucasians, Hispanics, and African Americans revealed that whites had the lowest rate of PTSD (15 percent), and Spanish-preferring Latinos the highest (38 percent), while African Americans fell between these two extremes (23 percent).[40] Even when additional analysis corrected for variations in location, income, degree of exposure, and individual vulnerability, these ethnic differences still held up.

Similar findings from post–9/11 surveys in New York have shown that Hispanics were affected in greater numbers than the general citizenry.[41] Some investigators postulate that this could be related to the presence of greater poverty and fewer options among these recent immigrants, resulting in a greater sense of feeling helplessly trapped in a city newly perceived as dangerous. Others suggest that Latino expressivity, a normal feature of the culture, might cause an unsophisticated interviewer to give more weight to dramatic description than is actually warranted.

SOCIAL SUPPORT

People who are single—either never married or divorced—are more at risk than those who are married. And people who have social support among their peers, either at the time of the trauma itself or in the weeks and months immediately following, fared better than those who did not. When social support networks are disrupted as a result of the trauma, as was the case for teenagers affected by the attacks on the World Trade Center and displaced from school, and for adults undergoing the isolation of bone marrow transplantation, people were far more subject to symptoms. One important meta-analysis involving seventy-seven different studies showed that disturbances in social support after a trauma are even stronger predictors for PTSD than a person's pretrauma situation.[42]

The point is made conversely by our previously introduced fellowship of elderly Finnish World War II veterans, who were in poor health, disabled, and institutionalized but high in esprit de corps and low in PTSD, thanks partly to the esteem accorded them by Finnish society for their meaningful contribution, and in part to their own cohesive community spirit, built up during the war and continuing in various Finnish veterans' associations after the war, still intact in the less-than-prime context of the nursing home.[43]

REACTIONS AROUND THE TRAUMA

Certain critical responses that occur right at the time of exposure to the traumatic event are high predictors of PTSD. These findings are important to our understanding of post-traumatic stress and have led to some key discoveries.

PANIC AND ACUTE STRESS

In a study of the population below Manhattan's Canal Street after the 9/11 attack on the nearby World Trade Center, researchers found that those who experienced a panic attack either right before or right after the destruction of the towers had a greater likelihood of developing post-traumatic stress. A study of 350 residents of Guam who experienced five different typhoons within a three-month period showed that the presence of an acute stress reaction right after a traumatic event is a partial predictor of the later development of full-blown post-traumatic stress in the weeks or months to come.[44]

DISSOCIATION

As alluded to earlier, possibly the most pivotal finding—certainly the most intriguing one—involves the presence of dissociation during the time of a traumatic episode. Dissociation is very strongly associated with vulnerability to post-traumatic stress.

With dissociation, people disconnect from their awareness of their sensations and emotions. They have a sense of being detached from reality, floating above or outside of what is occurring, watching neutrally as if it were happening to someone else. Memory is usually impaired during this time, and sometimes the sense of time and place is distorted as well. (A mild, everyday version of this phenomenon is "highway hypnosis," when we drive past our exit on the highway in an oblivious trance, not remembering how we got there.)

People dissociate when they are terrified or in pain and have no escape but to leave via mind and spirit. It is a form of built-in, automatic cushioning from reality, activated by stress hormones. It seems to coincide with the biologically driven freeze response to threat that is an adaptive mechanism present in every species. Women dissociate significantly more than men.[45]

This phenomenon of dissociating is critically important to the study of post-traumatic stress, essential to understanding and healing it. We will be revisiting this powerful natural defense again and again. For now, suffice it to note that people who dissociate are highly amenable to imagery. They respond quickly, easily, and profoundly to healing techniques that involve shifts in consciousness—guided imagery and various forms of meditation.[46]

So it is fair to say that dissociation is both a blessing and a curse. It bestows a blessing when it allows people to tolerate the intolerable during times when there is no other way out; it becomes a curse when it heightens risk for the symptoms of post-traumatic stress once the situation has passed; but it again becomes a blessing when it is turned on its head and deployed as a healing tool, through the beneficent grace of imagery and meditation.

BIOCHEMICAL ANOMALIES

One flamboyantly observable biological marker that is directly connected with dissociation is the release of cortisol,[47] one of the more easily measured hormones that surge through a body triggered by stress. As will become evident in our upcoming discussion of the physiological effects of trauma (see Chapter 5), chronically elevated cortisol can suppress immune functioning and wear down the cardiovascular system. On the other hand, cortisol that is chronically underproduced presents a whole other set of potentially debilitating health and mental health problems.

Under normal circumstances the body automatically returns to homeo-static balance with regard to the production of cortisol and other stress hormones.

But scores of studies measuring people suffering from post-traumatic stress show a uniquely out-of-whack profile of the body's ability to regu-late this stress-induced, fight-or-flight hormone, which is released by the adrenal glands. The working hypothesis is that there are inborn differ-ences in how people respond neurobiologically and hormonally to over-whelming stress. Some are more prone to dysregulated cortisol levels; this constitutional risk factor explains why some people suffer severe post-traumatic reactions, while others can be relatively untouched by horrific experiences.[48]

Investigations of recently traumatized adults suffering from acute stress reactions reveal the presence of heightened cortisol levels, which coincide with agitation, hypervigilance, edginess, and a spring-loaded temper. Usually these elevated responses settle back down over the next weeks or, more likely, months, once the stressor is out of the picture.[49]

For instance, in a study of 115 people involved in an overwhelmingly severe ice storm in Ottawa, Ontario, salivary cortisol levels were found to be elevated one month later but had diminished by the one-year anniver-sary. A similar cortisol elevation was found in UN soldiers after a mine ac-cident in Lebanon, then five days later, and again two months later, followed by a return to normal levels at nine months. Clearly the cortisol activity of someone acutely stressed by a one-time event is likely to follow this pattern of spiking for a while and then, after several months, drop-ping back down and stabilizing.[50]

On the other hand, a long-term adult trauma survivor with chronic PTSD will generally display abnormally *low* cortisol levels. This is con-nected to a dominant post-traumatic stress symptom of numbing and avoidance—a kind of dulled existence that can extend for years. Should someone with this profile get upset or agitated, however, we would see a temporary, extreme spiking in the release of cortisol, then a dip back down to the lower, flattened levels.

One particularly revealing longitudinal study tracked the blood work of Vietnam veterans with chronic and severe post-traumatic stress over a time period of ninety days of Exposure Therapy treatment—a form of therapy that, at the outset, produces stress in the survivor. Scrutiny revealed a static condition neither of cortisol underproduction nor its over-production. Instead these vets had a dynamic tendency to overreact in both directions, a kind of regulatory dysfunction in the entire hypothalamic-pituitary-adrenal axis. Their general coping mechanism of being dis-engaged, avoidant, and numb, associated with low cortisol, would be overridden whenever the vets were subjected to the more stressful as-pects of their therapy, when they were encouraged to remember, reimag-ine, or narrate the details of their traumatic history, at which time their cortisol levels would shoot through the roof into overproduction.[51]

This pattern shows up in several other studies as well—those involv-ing Holocaust survivors and their children, for instance, and other long-term survivors of chronic abuse and trauma. Again, the levels of cortisol are consistently low, but when triggered by stress, they spike and then drop, skittering back and forth between abnormally high and abnormally low levels. What would be a relatively small stressor to most people will trigger a dramatic biochemical cascade in someone with PTSD, which co-incides with their general hyperreactivity, followed by a drop to below-normal levels along with a return to avoidant numbing. In someone with chronic PTSD, low cortisol levels can persist for decades.[52]

Children show a different response, equally intense and dramatic. A study of fifty-one children with a history of trauma revealed heightened adrenal activity and cortisol production. Consistent with other studies, the cortisol levels for the girls were significantly more elevated than those for the boys in the study.[53]

No other emotional condition, including depression, panic attacks, or anxiety disorders, will produce this quirky profile. It is unique to post-traumatic stress and is its signature biochemical and neurophysiological footprint on the survivor. Possibly no other so-called "mental" condition demonstrates the merging of mind and body as much as this one does. It is important to keep this melding of psyche and soma in mind when, in Part II, we discuss the benefits of relaxation and imagery for survivors with PTSD, as these techniques are known to have a balancing effect not just on mood and energy but on zigzagging levels of cortisol as well.

DRINKING AND INTOXICATION

A fascinating finding from a few studies of various survivors of nightclub fires is that imbibing alcohol or actual intoxication during the time of a traumatic event has very real protective value and significantly decreases the odds of acquiring PTSD.[54] Alcohol decreases physiological arousal, inoculating against severe anxiety states and lowering physiological reactivity.

Alcohol can also perform this agitation-lowering function in the weeks and months following a traumatic event, and initially it can sedate a spiking cortisol reaction resulting from sudden alarm states, anxiety, flashbacks, and nightmares. It is therefore no surprise that there is a high prevalence of alcoholism in long-term post-traumatic stress survivors.[55]

At some point, however, the benefit becomes a liability. Should addictive dependence set in, withdrawal produces its own stress reaction, exacerbating the PTSD symptoms and creating its own vicious cycle.[56] Alcohol consumption becomes a coping strategy with a limited shelf life.

SENSE OF CONTROL DURING THE EVENT

People who, at the time of the event or events, felt that they had some control over the situation and managed to find things they could do to improve it fared significantly better than those who felt relatively helpless.[57] People who found ways to rescue their co-workers, manipulate their attackers, evacuate an endangered site, outmaneuver a sadistic captor or enhance their odds in some other way were less at risk than those who found themselves helpless and incapacitated.

It is not clear, however, whether this is a matter of cause or effect. People who are congenitally predisposed toward a dissociated freeze response (and thus are more likely to suffer from post-traumatic stress) are less able to assess their situation and respond to it in a grounded, practical way, because they are not entirely present. On the other hand, those who manage to maintain their sense of control and proactive responses in an emergency may be containing their tendency toward dissociation in the very act of taking charge of what they can.

SELF-BLAME AND NEGATIVE BELIEFS

Those with a tendency to blame themselves for the bad things that befall them are at higher risk for post-traumatic stress. When crime victims at an Amsterdam police station were assessed to determine who was most likely to develop PTSD a few months after the crime, those who blamed themselves were the ones most likely to have persistent symptoms.[58]

Another study, carefully designed to assess beliefs about self-worth, general safety, and the trustworthiness of others, compared people who had never been assaulted with those who had been assaulted, sorting out who had persistent PTSD and who did not, both before and after the attack. Results clearly showed that assault victims who did not develop PTSD were significantly more positive in all three belief areas, and that the persistent PTSD group felt much more negatively on all three measures than either the no-assault group and the assault group who did not go on to develop PTSD.[59] The investigators felt that positive preassault beliefs may have played a buffering role, minimizing the impact of the assault.

But again, cause and effect can easily become confounded here. It is quite possible that the presence of persistent post-traumatic stress symptoms color existing beliefs more negatively after the fact, souring attitude and puncturing positive beliefs with the persistence of relentless, disheartening symptoms.

SUBSEQUENT HEALTH PROBLEMS

Some dramatic overlaps have been found between post-traumatic stress and certain physical health problems. For instance, one comprehensive Israeli study showed that an extraordinary 57 percent of people diagnosed with fibromyalgia also suffered from significant, persistent post-traumatic stress symptoms, a percentage far greater than the 8 percent we would normally expect to find in the general population. Similarly, an American study of fibromyalgia patients found a 56 percent rate of PTSD, while another showed that 57 percent of fibromyalgia patients reported a history of sexual or physical abuse. It should be noted that the vast majority of fibromyalgia patients are women.[60]

Similar results were found in those suffering from chronic fatigue syndrome, multiple chemical sensitivity, irritable bowel syndrome, and other baffling chronic pain conditions that have in the past been misguidedly attributed to hypochondria and depression. Interestingly, long-standing autoimmune diseases with more respectable and "legitimate" reputations, such as rheumatoid arthritis and multiple sclerosis, have more mixed profiles that sometimes but not always reflect a connection with post-traumatic stress.[61]

Given the intimate connection between fibromyalgia and post-traumatic stress, it is not surprising to learn that Gulf War veterans have higher-than-normal rates of fibromyalgia, as do traumatized Lao and Mien refugees who have resettled in the United States.[62]

One intriguing finding, discovered by a group of researchers from the University of Trier in Germany, is that the very same low cortisol levels found in people with chronic post-traumatic stress also exist in those with chronic fatigue syndrome, fibromyalgia, and similar disorders.[63] Their research suggests that persistently low levels of cortisol in traumatized or chronically stressed people promote an increased vulnerability to stress-related disorders. They posit that this trauma-induced dysregulation of cortisol, along with better-known factors such as genetic vulnerability, previous stress experience, and individual coping styles, configure to determine who develops these functional disorders. It certainly could go a long way toward explaining why relaxation, breathwork, and imagery are so helpful to people with fibromyalgia, irritable bowel syndrome, and chronic fatigue syndrome.

A scientist at Washington State University breaks down the biochemical impairment mechanism even further. Martin Pall suggests that a likely suspect is the elevated level of nitric oxide and its potent oxidant product, peroxynitrite, in the tissues of people with fibromyalgia and multiple chemical sensitivity. Peroxynitrite creates its own circular feedback that results in a tendency to stay at elevated levels once it has spiked. High levels of peroxynitrite can be found both in people with post-traumatic stress and in fibromyalgia sufferers. It also manages to proliferate to a lesser extent in people with chronic fatigue syndrome and those with multiple chemical sensitivity.[64] We will discuss the mechanics of this in detail in the next chapter.

Meanwhile, suffice it to say that people with post-traumatic stress experience more physical health problems and seek medical help more readily than the average person, whether they are combat veterans or patients at an Israeli clinic. They are more likely to suffer from major depression, panic attacks, phobias, and eating disorders such as bulimia and anorexia, and they are more frequently addicted to drugs or alcohol.[65] Clearly persistent post-traumatic stress can tax the body's homeostasis and lead to greater somatic vulnerability.

To sum up, research has pointed to a host of significant findings with profound implications. We now know that women and children are more at risk of developing post-traumatic stress across any and all countries and cultures; that proximity to the traumatic event and its duration play a critical role; that the degree of brutality and the level of threat increase vulnerability, as do elements of betrayal, unpredictability, injury, loss, and physical entrapment. We know that being the perpetrator of a horror increases the likelihood of PTSD, and that the meaning and significance that a person assigns to his or her experience can have either a buffering or a debilitating effect.

We now understand that an individual's history of psychiatric problems increases the odds of PTSD, as do lower education, subsequent stress, and lack of social support. Panic at the time of the trauma, or acute stress right after it, also increases vulnerability. Dissociation at the time of the trauma adds tremendous risk, and drinking or intoxication at the time of the trauma reduces it.

Epidemiology gives us our first handles on understanding the biochemically driven nature of post-traumatic stress's persistence, and on the way this syndrome is intimately connected to dysregulated cortisol levels.

We know that the way people cope with trauma makes a difference: that a sense of control during and after the event is a buffer; and that negative beliefs about self and others, and a tendency toward self-blame, coincide with more persistent and profound symptoms.

Finally, we see an increase in health problems, somatizing, and medical visits in people suffering from PTSD. Among people with some of the more baffling chronic pain conditions, such as fibromyalgia, chronic fatigue syndrome, irritable bowel syndrome, and multiple chemical sensitivity, the number who have PTSD is extraordinarily high.

5 THE PHYSICAL EFFECTS OF TRAUMA

Trauma sets in motion a biochemical chain of events that can result in chronic pain and an unusual number of medical problems. This diary description, written by a woman who was molested at the age of seven, is a commonplace story:

> When I was in my twenties, after the birth of my first son, I began to experience bouts of depression and irritable bowel syndrome. I had feelings of worthlessness, even though I loved being a stay-at-home mom with a wonderful, loving husband.
>
> Five years later, after the birth of my second son, I began to have a lot of headaches and physical pains—pains so severe that it was difficult for me to get out of bed or out of a chair. I became unable to do my housework, care for my sons, or have any fun with my husband.
>
> I sought help everywhere, but no one had an answer. Most doctors thought I was having mental problems and only imagining the pain. They said it was because I was a homemaker and feeling unfulfilled, and I needed to get "busier." So busier I got—and sicker I got!
>
> Finally, mercifully, after seven years, in 1987, I went to a neurologist because the migraines and tension headaches were becoming a new and unmanageable symptom in this whole mess. He immediately diagnosed me with fibromyalgia and assured me I was not "mental" and I was not creating my own

symptoms. I had a condition that they were just beginning to recognize and that unfortunately, at the time, there was little help for. But just hearing him acknowledge me as a person with pain and suffering was immensely comforting.

WHOLE-BODY SUFFERING

The most common physical or somatic complaints that immediately follow a traumatic experience are restlessness, hypervigilance, problems with falling asleep or staying asleep, generalized anxiety, inability to relax, shallow breathing, fatigue, and an exaggerated startle response at sudden noises, the sight of reminiscent cues, or unexpected touch. A goodly number of people also experience headaches, backaches, TMJ, various skin complaints such as itching and rashes, and unintentional weight loss.

In the immediate days and weeks following a traumatic experience, when external conditions have returned to normal, the body continues to remain on alert, reacting to relatively neutral cues in the environment as if they were warnings of a continuing threat of annihilation.

If chronic post-traumatic stress sets in during the weeks, months, or years that follow, survivors frequently manifest an unusual number of health-related complaints, resulting in more office visits to the doctor and more physician-diagnosed conditions, including cardiac and arterial problems, difficulties in the lower gastrointestinal tract, and various dermatological and musculoskeletal complaints.

In addition, baffling chronic conditions can start showing up in disproportionate numbers. Often categorized as *functional* diseases, because there is no obvious physical cause that explains them on standard medical tests, these conditions include chronic fatigue syndrome, fibromyalgia, irritable bowel syndrome, alopecia, multiple chemical sensitivity, reflex sympathetic dystrophy, interstitial cystitis, and myofascial, low back, and pelvic pain.[1] Many of these conditions have a distinctly autoimmune dynamic, which given the sequence of biochemical reactions to trauma makes perfect sense. But first things first. Let's take a look at what happens in the body during a traumatic event.

BLASTED BY BIOCHEMICALS

These notes from the journal of the survivor of a major collision offer a strong example of the changes in the body and in perceptual capacity during an overwhelming, terrifying event where annihilation appears imminent.

Thirty years ago on the north side of Chicago, I was in a car accident while driving in the funeral procession of a good friend and fellow grad student. He had taken his life by walking into Lake Michigan on a cold February morning—the final, manic expression of an undiagnosed bipolar disorder. I was grief-stricken and stunned.

I drove toward the cemetery, foggy and disconnected. Out of habit, and because I wasn't paying attention, I stopped for a red light at a busy intersection. Belatedly I realized that funeral processions weren't supposed to stop for red lights, so I hurried on into the intersection, where I saw, barreling toward me from my right, a heavy, dark blue, shiny Pontiac, going what must have been 35 miles an hour. It appeared huge to me, much bigger than a normal car. It was like a Stephen King monster car on steroids.

Everything turned into slow motion, just like those clichéd action scenes in the movies do. My thinking became hyperacute as I calculated that I didn't have time to get out of the way. I also had time to regretfully acknowledge the clinical observation that my husband of less than a year would be especially distraught, because a car had killed his mother, too, just like this one would be killing me. I've no doubt that had I known what I know now about the destined collector's value of my soon-to-be totaled car—a 1965 Mustang ragtop—I'm sure I'd have had time to regret its demise, too.

The Mustang and I took an incredible wallop that completely bent the frame and caved in the entire passenger side. I can still hear the sound of the impact—a sickeningly loud thunk of metal crunching. But I somehow got out of the car without a scratch. When I went on wobbly legs to call my husband at the pay phone in the gas station across the street, I noted in a detached, mildly interested way that I couldn't get my shaking finger into the holes of the rotary dial. I had to use both hands to steer it into the right numbers.

Long after this happened, as mild and insignificant as this event was in the larger scheme of my life, that huge, shiny, dark blue Pontiac continued to roll toward me again and again, in night dreams and waking flashbacks, raising the little hairs on my neck and filling me with sweaty, heart-racing terror. For several years after the accident I refused to be the driver in a funeral procession. And to this day, if I'm driving along and notice out of the corner of my right eye a car entering my roadway from a street on my right—and only on my right—even though it's perfectly safe, my body will involuntarily wince, and in an instant my heart is racing and I'm buzzing with adrenaline.

Three things from this incident impressed me: the detached clarity of my mind as I watched the car come toward me; the queer stretching of clock-time that gave me room for so much analysis in so few seconds; and the way those moments of terror stayed stuck in my mind and body, long after any emotional connection or intellectual preoccupation with them had dissipated.

This driver's response to her accident is a direct result of the neurophysiology of her survival wiring and the biochemical blast it produced throughout her system. The body has a built-in, instantaneous, and awesome reaction to threat.

The more primitive areas of the brain contain a web of ancient circuitry that we share with our mammalian brethren, a matrix that is exquisitely attuned to signs of potential danger and that triggers an immediate, body-wide response to threat. At the heart of this ingenious cable network, in the lower middle of the brain and tied to other regions through a maze of nerve fibers, sits a small, almond-shaped structure called the amygdala. This part of the brain is the storehouse of emotional memory, and it is instantly activated when we sense danger. (Laboratory rats with surgically removed amygdalas are fearless rats. They are also vulnerable rats and, sadly, stupid rats with very short life spans.) For obvious reasons—speed and survival—the amygdala does not wait around for instructions from the conscious, thinking sectors of the brain, to act. It functions independently and instantaneously, instinctively triggered by the merest possibility of danger, the broadest hint of perceived threat. In its extraordinary capacity to commandeer our brains and drive our actions, it overrides the more refined neocortex, which is built to analyze more detailed information and decide on a more finely tailored response. The amygdala, with its direct sensory input, allows us to act before we know why.

Triggering a potent emergency response within nanoseconds, it launches a biochemical cascade. First it jolts the neighboring hypothalamus into producing a hormone known as corticotropin-releasing factor (CRF), which in turn signals the pituitary and adrenal glands to flood the bloodstream with stress hormones: adrenaline (epinephrine), norepinephrine, and cortisol. This results in the familiar sensation of being instantly infused with hyperalert, buzzing energy, a feeling familiar to anyone who's ever experienced a near-miss in traffic or some other perceived threat to life and limb. This is all preparation for the intense neuromuscular activity needed to ensure survival—fight or flight.

The norepinephrine zap to the central nervous system increases a person's immediate alertness and focus, short-term memory, pupil dilation, ocular divergence (to increase the range of peripheral vision), and increased muscle tone in the limbs, now at the ready for a massive expenditure of energy.

At this point we could be experiencing this dramatic jolt and still only be in the realm of a thrilling amusement park ride, sexual arousal, stage fright, anticipatory excitement, or pregame jitters. It's the determination of the *meaning* of the situation as dangerous and life-threatening that mobilizes a full-blown fight-or-flight response. This crucial piece of analysis is happening simultaneously in the hippocampus, the part of the brain that compares new information with past associations, and in the orbitofrontal cortex, the brain's problem-solving and planning department.[2]

If a bona-fide threat is determined, these same stress hormones orchestrate an immediate shutdown of any function that is superfluous to immediate survival. Digestion, immunity, hunger, sleepiness, sexual appetite—all take a backseat to the life-or-death struggle at hand. Readying for fight or flight, blood pressure rises and the heart beats faster, the better to pump oxygen and nutrients to the limbs. The vessels in the stomach cooperate by constricting, in order to force blood to the now supertoned extremities. The lungs go into overdrive, and breathing quickens to take in and disperse greater amounts of oxygen. Perspiration increases, to regulate an otherwise escalating body temperature. And the liver blasts the muscle tissue with energizing doses of glucose, so the limbs can be spring-loaded for action.

Along with the infusion of norepinephrine, endorphins are released as well: the brain's pain-killing neurotransmitters. These endogenous opioids with their magical analgesic effect account for the famously increased pain thresholds found in those in extreme alarm states. The survival value is obvious: self-protective responses to pain won't get in the way of whatever life-saving maneuvers need to be done, unhampered.

When either fight or flight actually occurs, the huge amount of energy and tension stored in the body is discharged. Then, when the threat has passed and the energy-spending phase is over, the parasympathetic nervous system takes over, settling down the overfunctioning systems and bringing the body back into balance. It does this by releasing a neurotransmitter known as acetylcholine to slow the heart rate, lower blood pressure, and shunt blood away from the muscles and back to the organs in the center of the body. Digestion is reactivated, sexual interest resumes, and nutrients can again be stored away for future needs. This postemergency time is when people will suddenly notice that they are famished, exhausted, or both.

The body is always cycling in and out of varying states of excitation and relaxation, shuttling between energy expenditure and energy storage in what is usually an ingeniously fluid, dynamic balancing act of healthy, homeostatic equilibrium.

THE FREEZE RESPONSE

There is a third biologically driven response to danger, however, that can send this balanced cycling between sympathetic and parasympathetic nervous systems haywire. That is the reaction of *freezing*—the immobility response.

The pure freeze response is best demonstrated by animals overtaken by predators in the wild. Immobility is activated when fight or flight is pointless, and nothing proactive can be done to save the day. This totally instinctual and unconscious immobility reflex happens when an animal is about to be caught by a pursuing predator—it collapses and becomes limp, even before it's seized. In this state of suspended animation, the body releases additional doses of pain-killing endorphins, to inhibit wound-licking and other behaviors that could compete with last-ditch, life-saving activity.

Other dramatic changes occur in the freeze state as well, with responses rebounding from the extreme tension of alarm to their opposite of near-paralysis. Tense muscles collapse and become still, blood pressure takes a steep dive, and the racing heart slows down to a barely perceptible crawl.

Freezing has obvious value for possibly aborting an attack when death is imminent and other options have been rendered useless. Some animal predators cannot see what isn't moving. Perhaps more critically, "playing possum" can trick a predator into thinking she has time to leave the scene of her presumed kill to gather up her offspring for dinner, thus giving the dinner time to escape. In addition, the opioid release of the freeze state provides the value-added bonus of preventing a painful death, if death in fact must occur.

With freezing, the immobilized body of the prey animal undergoes huge biochemical extremes in a very short space of time, cycling lickety-split from an intensely aroused alarm state to a biologically enforced vegetative state, all the while collecting and holding unhealthy amounts of undischarged biochemical residuals from each phase.

In the wild, this biochemical overload doesn't usually pose a problem. The animal almost always gets eaten while still loaded up on high doses of epinephrine, endorphins, and acetylcholine and dies a virtual pharmacopoeia of a meal.

Should the immobilized prey somehow survive, however, it will perform some very interesting energy-discharge maneuvers after the predator leaves and the environment is again determined to be safe. Almost all animals immediately begin trembling or shuddering. Sometimes their movements resemble the last act of running, or whatever their final motor attempts at survival were, just before the freeze imperative took over. It is as if the last protective motor or muscular activity is locked in memory and needs to be completed, released with all the retained energy from the aroused state.[3]

After the trembling or shuddering stops, the animal will usually perspire for several minutes, followed by a series of deep, sighing breaths. Then it regains its feet, staggers around a bit, shakes itself, and runs off—unlike humans, apparently none the worse for wear. In fact, a rabbit in the wild will undergo this ritual several times a day with no ill effects.

The same sequence actually occurs among animals in subtler ways all day long, even without a direct threat to survival. A gazelle may hear a sound, become alert, tense its muscles, and scan the environment with cocked head, ears, and eyes. When the landscape is perceived to be safe, it will shudder and return to its calm state of grazing. Energy is activated and released, and then, as the system settles, it gets stored for the next time it is needed.

Humans also freeze when an overwhelming, life-threatening situation overrides any viable possibility of fighting or fleeing. And helplessness, you will remember, is the sine qua non characteristic of a potentially PTSD-generating event. But when humans freeze and survive a dangerous episode, for reasons that aren't entirely clear, they don't automatically discharge all the overload of autonomic energy upon recovery, the way animals do. Most of us don't do enough shaking, shuddering, perspiring, or deep breathing to discharge the physiological tension after the danger has passed, and this creates some unique dilemmas for the species.

One man describes a mugging where, to his chagrin, he experienced this involuntary, automatic immobility response:

> I was walking to the subway. It was late, the street was dark, and I was in a rough neighborhood, but I didn't give it much thought. I was young and athletic and had a natural confidence in my ability to take care of myself.
>
> When I crossed the street, two men came out from an alley, very quickly. Two more came up from behind. One pressed a gun into the side of my head. Another twisted my arm behind me. I was ordered with a lot of cursing to fork over my wallet.
>
> I would have been glad to, but I couldn't move. I'm a talker, but I couldn't talk. I just stood there, frozen.

They relieved me of my wallet, delivered a few punches and kicks, and then ran. I still just stood there. Finally I was able to get out of there and call the police.

Later I was ashamed of my reaction, I didn't talk about it to anyone for a long time. It was a far cry from my view of myself, and a betrayal of my standards.

DISSOCIATION AND MORE ENDORPHINS

When people freeze, they also dissociate. In fact, dissociation, which you may recall is the single strongest major predictor of the eventual development of PTSD, can be seen as the human correlate of the immobility response in animals. People flee the scene *psychically*, by becoming distant, detached, and emotionally disconnected from the realities on the ground. The focused and superalert mind becomes numb, possibly because of a fresh blast of pain-obliterating endorphins. Memory access and storage are impaired, and amnesia is likely for at least some of the events that happen during this period.

Not only do humans generally lack the adaptive discharge response of shuddering, perspiring, and deep breathing their way back into full functioning when the crisis is over, but they tend to assign negative meaning to their natural, biologically driven immobility response. Freezing is usually judged as as cowardly, ineffectual, and somehow weak-willed—as if will had anything to do with this automatic survival mechanism.

Perhaps that highly evolved frontal neocortex of ours, with all its societally structured thinking and planning capacity, leaves us experiencing our helplessness and immobility as devastating evidence of a character deficit. Perhaps our complex brain wiring throws a few neurological monkey wrenches into the works. Whatever the reasons, this aborted energy discharge quite possibly lays the groundwork for imprinting the trauma more deeply into the circuitry of the brain, encoding it into unconscious memory and in the arousal patterns of the central nervous system. In other words, it's very possible that this truncated freeze response is a major factor in creating the dysfunctional conditions that can lead to post-traumatic stress syndrome.

THE VICIOUS CYCLE OF KINDLING

The problem for those who go on to develop PTSD is that the cycling back and forth, from parasympathetic to sympathetic activation, doesn't stop but instead becomes a self-sustaining neurological feedback circuit. The pattern becomes imprinted in the irritated, sensitized neuronal networks involved. It may initially remain underground, but eventually it emerges as a self-perpetuating system. What's worse, if left to its own oscillating pattern, the symptoms become increasingly entrenched, and often they worsen. For its similarity to spontaneous combustion, this self-sustaining, underground pattern has been named *kindling*.

Here is how it very likely works. The undischarged freeze response results in a sustained, high-level alarm state that produces excitability and supersensitivity in the neuronal networks in the affected part of the brain—mainly in the hypersensitive amygdala, the major center for emotion and sensation processing.

Remember that our hard-won survival imperative has geared our brains to unquestioningly and automatically remember and deeply imprint any danger-related information. All it takes is one terrifying, life-threatening event to make a profoundly memorable dent.

After such an event, when we experience spontaneous memories, flashbacks, or nightmares, the amygdala again becomes activated. It also might become activated from even vaguely related external cues of threat—a loud noise, a reminiscent smell, a movement from the corner of the eye, a familiar landscape, the shadow of a person approaching from behind. However it occurs, the aroused amygdala then triggers an alarm state all over again—releasing even more norepinephrine and cortisol, activating the same muscle and nerve fibers, followed by the same parasympathetic rebounding attempts to modulate the reaction with dissociation, endorphin release, and general suppression of sympathetic nervous system function. All of this occurs because of the well-meaning but abortive attempt on the part of the primitive brain centers to keep us alive by relentlessly imprinting past threats on our memory traces and behavior patterns—automatically and persistently.

Because the amygdala's hyperactivation results in impaired narrative memory and reduced synthesizing ability in the hippocampus, trauma-related memories become exaggerated and increasingly intrusive, at the expense of conscious memory, language, and analytic thinking around the event. The cycle takes on a life of its own. People suffering from PTSD oscillate between adrenalized arousal and analgesic flatness, with a tendency toward more and more numbed-out disconnection over time.

Initially people are hypervigilant a great deal of the time, easily propelled into a full-blown alarm state. This state of affairs can last for months or even years, accompanied by inordinately high levels of cortisol and other stress biochemicals in the body. Eventually, however, the system's dysregulation tips in the opposite direction, and people with late-stage, chronic PTSD spend more and more time in a shut-down state of dissociated numbness, occasionally punctuated by hyperaroused alarm.

To make matters worse, it's not just external cues that activate an alarm response; muscular activity can trigger it as well. Memories, flashbacks, and nightmares can kick loose involuntary neuromuscular responses. Certain muscle groups tense and brace all over again, in the patterned ways they did during the traumatic event. And even when these muscle groups are later used for simple, normal, repetitive, daily activities, the muscle stimulation alone can trigger arousal in the patterned neuronal response, jogging memories, flashbacks, nightmares, and panic attacks and resulting in a new blast of norepinephrine, followed by a subsequent dose of opioids. In this way, the kindled feedback loop can be activated through the muscles and skeletal system, too. A response can be triggered from any point in the closed system. (This is no doubt why massage therapy and pressure-point work can activate memories and flashbacks, sometimes from traumatic events that have occurred decades ago.)

CHRONIC PAIN CONDITIONS

This constant activation of the alarm state leads to an accumulation of metabolic waste products in the muscle fibers, and the release of kinins and other chemical pain-generators in the tissue, resulting in myofascial pain and the appearance of those seemingly intractable chronic conditions such as fibromyalgia, chronic fatigue, irritable bowel syndrome, chronic headache, TMJ, and more.[4]

And because these conditions are generated in the brain stem and the motor reflex centers in the spinal column, and routed through a perturbed automatic arousal circuitry, peripheral forms of treatment provide only temporary relief. Constantly activated by everyday sensory cues, normal muscle movements, and spontaneous memories, symptoms grow and become more and more entrenched over time. In other words, this nasty gift from the kindled feedback loop, if not interrupted, will just keep on giving.

Our epidemiology research has already shown us an astounding percentage of people with baffling chronic pain conditions and "functional" diseases that have no obvious causes, who have been found to have prior histories of severe trauma. Probably if we could tease out the subset of traumatized people who experienced substantial dissociation during their trauma, and a truncated freeze response in the midst of it, we might find closer to one hundred percent suffering from post-traumatic stress. Unfortunately for them, they are often assumed to be malingering or engaged in attention-seeking behavior for neurotic reasons, instead of suffering from a very serious, self-perpetuating condition with a potentially worsening trajectory.

Included in this group of maligned and misunderstood patients would be scores of people suffering from pelvic and low back pain; orofacial and myofascial pain; genitourinary and abdominal pain; interstitial cystitis; fibromyalgia, chronic fatigue syndrome, and reflex sympathetic dystrophy; irritable bowel syndrome, inflammatory bowel disorder, multiple chemical sensitivity, and migraine. Interestingly, these are all conditions that have become dramatically prevalent over the past decade or two. We may hypothesize that the reason is that traumatic stressors have become ubiquitous in our world.

Of course, the better-understood somatic complications of post-traumatic stress, and any sort of chronic stress for that matter, have to do with the wearing down of the cardiovascular system by constantly up-regulated stress hormones. Hypertension and coronary artery disease are the most common manifestations of chronic stress.

On the other hand, chronic late-stage post-traumatic stress leads to chronically lowered cortisol levels, which in turn result in a variety of autoimmune disorders. The connections between post-traumatic stress and rheumatoid arthritis, lupus, multiple sclerosis, and similar conditions are just beginning to be examined.

THE UNITY OF PSYCHE AND SOMA

What becomes increasingly clear, the more we scrutinize and study these connections, is the ludicrousness of trying to distinguish between the "psychological" and the "physical" aspects of post-traumatic stress or indeed any other condition. More dramatically than any other condition, PTSD demonstrates the larger point that all physical disease and all emotional illness represent some sort of conflated disturbance in the regulation of our neurobiological, endocrinological, and immunological systems. So-called physiological disease and so-called mental illness are both manifestations of disturbed self-regulation. Trauma changes the brain and therefore simultaneously changes the body. Trauma changes the body and therefore simultaneously changes the brain. Differentiating between the physiological and the psychosomatic for anything other than teaching purposes is meaningless and misleading. Psyche and soma are simultaneously affected and utterly indistinguishable, one from the other.

6 THE COGNITIVE EFFECTS OF TRAUMA

Typical cognitive difficulties following trauma involve recurring intrusive thoughts, flashbacks, memory lapses, and trouble with focus, concentration, and sustained attention. It's often hard for trauma survivors with active symptoms to learn and retain new information, especially complex verbal material. There's a sense of being scattered, distracted, and unable to focus on work or daily activities. Making simple decisions can feel overwhelming. Sometimes there is impairment in psychomotor ability as well.

For most people, these initial symptoms disappear with the passing of time. But people with chronic, long-term PTSD can face some daunting cognitive challenges. Typically they notice some decline in their normal ability to sort out relevant matters from the general bombardment of information. It becomes hard to ignore what is unimportant, and over time all sorts of things might be noticed and reacted to with equal emphasis.

Over time the triggers for intrusive memories and flashbacks can become more and more subtle and ancillary, and even irrelevant stimuli can provoke reminders, making the world an increasingly more threatening place. In this way, perception becomes increasingly biased toward noticing what is worrisome or frightening, at the expense of registering what is pleasurable, beautiful, and nourishing. Even neutral sensations eventually bow to the unpleasant ones. In other words, the world becomes flatter and uglier.

TRAUMATIC MEMORIES AND NIGHTMARES

Memories of the traumatic event are immediate and intense, experienced as if they were happening all over again in the present. Unlike normal, narrative memories that shift, distort, and fade over time, traumatic memories remain fixed, timeless, and contemporary, delivering the same intense sensory material and emotional punch each time. These terrifying sights, sounds, smells, body sensations, and tastes, reexperienced with extreme vividness, resist integration or absorption. They are unaltered by the passage of time and don't change with subsequent experiences.

Nightmares repeat too, replaying the same traumatic scenes over and over again. Early research by the noted traumatic stress pioneer psychiatrist Bessel van der Kolk observed that the content of the nightmares of veterans with PTSD had stayed the same for fifteen years.[1]

This odd permutation of memory comes from the amygdala and the biochemical blast it sends through the brain during the original event. This hormonal flooding provides the wherewithal to fend off threats to life and limb, but it also ensures that a traumatic memory will be imprinted deeply as a one-time-and-forever learning experience. The survival value is obvious: should a reminiscent cue ever come across our perceptual field again, signaling even the hint of a similar scenario, we are now wired to instantly react. Once was enough for our neurobiology to get it. Now we're hardwired for an immediate response that bypasses cognition altogether.

This can happen because the brain has made some critical changes as a result of its initial rendezvous with terror. The locus ceruleus, a structure that signals threat to the amygdala and that regulates the brain's secretion of adrenaline and noradrenaline (catecholamines), is now hyperreactive at even a very mild or neutral cue containing a reminder of the original trauma—a loud noise, a shadow, the smell of sulfur, a sudden touch on the back. So the intrusive images and sensory fragments invade consciousness, provoked by a harmless trigger, creating more distress.

From their nature, it is clear that traumatic memories are processed and stored differently from our memories of ordinary events. Normal memories are encoded verbally and are easily translated into communicable language. But traumatic memories are experienced as emotions, sensations, and physical states. They are like an undigested lump of per-

sonal history, stored separately in a primitive compartment and uninte-
grated into the survivor's verbal and cognitive understanding of himself.

At the same time, in some situations, especially with cases of childhood sexual abuse, there can be partial amnesia, and sometimes an entire
childhood is obliterated to conscious recall. The younger the person was
at the time of her traumatization and the more prolonged the experiences, the greater is the likelihood of substantial amnesia in adulthood.[2]

One woman who suffered severe abuse from her family, from the
time of her birth to the age of seventeen, could literally remember nothing of those years, except for a few names and places, until meditation in
a personal growth workshop broke loose some fragmentary images that
she then realized she had been seeing all along in her nightmares.

When this kind of memory fragment pops loose and surfaces, it has
an immediate, vividly sensory, emotionally intense quality. Often there is
a specificity and uniqueness to the memory that makes it clear that it is a
genuine piece of the person's history and not something that's been
manufactured.[3]

Julie, a woman I was seeing in therapy, suddenly, in one session, remembered the feel of a cold floor on her cheek as an emerging sensory
fragment; then she saw the old-fashioned pattern of small hexagonal
black-and-white floor tiles that were once commonplace in houses of a
certain vintage; then the old-fashioned claw feet of a bathtub. Simultaneously she was flooded with intense feelings of fear, dread, shame, nausea,
and sadness. For a while she was speechless and began shaking and sweat-
ing, huddled on the love seat across from me. She reported that her body
felt very cold and curled up in a ball. In spite of her reluctance to remember these things and her sense of dread about what was surfacing, something inside of her had decided it was time.

Later on Julie began to piece together the sadistic enemas she had en-
dured when visiting her grandmother and aunt. Still, the memories felt so
distant and strange to her, so disconnected, that she would wonder aloud
if she wasn't perhaps making it all up. It didn't feel like a regular memory
to her. But as she retrieved more and more detail, things began to make
sense to her, and other aspects of her childhood that she'd wondered or
heard about began to fall into place. This is how it usually goes. More and
more fragments pop loose, eventually revealing more and more of the
story, like pieces of a puzzle.

Like Julie, the trauma survivor faces an odd contradiction. At the same time that the vivid memory fragments are coming into consciousness, the person has difficulty relating precisely what happened in words and thoughts. He or she experiences the sensory and emotional elements of the event but can't make cognitive sense out of them. The phrase "speechless terror" is not hyperbole; people literally *cannot talk* when affected in this way. Indeed, PET scans establish the physiological basis of this phenomenon, by showing a diminishment of oxygen and reduced perfusion in the verbal centers of the brain during flashbacks.[4] Often this difficulty in verbalizing is generalized to a reduced capacity to articulate any feelings at all—a state of affairs that is pervasive enough to have its own name: *alexithymia*.

TIME DISTORTION

Trauma invariably produces a distorted sense of time as well. This bending of clock-time—either stretching time or losing it—is usually temporary, associated with the biochemistry of hyperactivation or numbing, but in chronic, long-term PTSD it can become chronic and habituated. It is in the nature of dissociating or slipping into a trance state to lose time or distort time.

In extreme instances, severely affected people can miss meals, confuse night and day, neglect personal hygiene, and engage in random, disjointed behavior. Survivors often describe a sense of the days disappearing and time being lost.

DISTRACTEDNESS

Another usually temporary problem is constricted attention, which affects the survivor's ability to take in new information and access stored information. On top of this, a general distractedness makes it hard to remember details. This will often come across as "flakiness," forgetfulness, or even mental deficit. With chronic late-stage PTSD, neuropsychological tests might reveal pervasive problems with short-term memory and attentional focus.[5] For some, adult attention deficit disorder gets diagnosed alongside the chronic PTSD. One woman, since recovered, described walking into a store like this:

> Going into stores and seeing all the things on the shelf would induce another kind of panic—too much stimulation for my nervous system, which was already in its eggbeater-gone-crazy mode.

Some studies have found a degree of impairment of higher-level information-processing and decision-making in some people, who can overlook critical details in making a choice or solving a problem. They might reach conclusions based on narrow, impulsive, or stereotyped initial impressions.[6] As a result, common sense, logic, and judgment can suffer.

Bruce D. Perry M.D., Ph.D., an expert on the brain development of terrorized, neglected, and abused children, explains that a traumatized brain is compelled to train its focus away from language and verbal content, toward non-verbal danger cues—body movements, facial expressions, tone of voice and the like, searching for threat-related information. Cognition and behavior are mediated by the more primitive parts of the brain—the brain stem and midbrain—at the expense of abstract thinking and absorption of language and ideas. People suffering from this are often diagnosed as having attention deficit disorder with hyperactivity (ADD-H), but for some this label can be misleading. It is not that these survivors cannot stay with a given task, but rather that they are *hypervigilant*. Only when sufficiently calmed, can they attend to the meaning of words.[7]

Perry goes on to explain that this is why interventions that are based on a cognitive, problem-solving approach alone cannot impact terror-driven behavior. It's like mixing apples and oranges—the primitive brain and midbrain cannot process cognitive solutions aimed at the higher cortical structures. This is why imagery, with its subverbal, calming voice tone, soothing music and nonverbal reassurances of safety, aimed straight at the aroused lower brain, is far more effective with traumatized people, taking them to a level of safety where they can again process the meaning of words.

OBSESSIVE THINKING

In addition, some people adopt a way of coping with the generalized fears and anxieties of PTSD by rigidly planning, organizing, and scheduling every minute of the day—and then replanning, reorganizing, and rescheduling it all over again. The immediate gain is that the survivor binds up some of the intense anxiety that is always being churned up, by focusing attention elsewhere, on this or that minutia. But when done in excess, this coping mechanism piles up even more challenges onto the already-taxed cognitive faculties, as a great deal of thinking "space" is taken up with managing obsessive detail, leaving that much less room for functional, workaday thinking, analysis, and synthesis. It can also become an annoyance to friends and family.

One survivor described what she used to do in this way:

I used to spell words continuously, often on my fingers, in a pattern I worked out just for that purpose. Sometimes I would count in that way instead of spell. I see it now as an attempt to introduce an orderly pattern in my system, in order to counter the overwhelming anxiety and panic.

This woman, since recovered, is still extremely detail-oriented and meticulous in her thinking and planning, but in a way that is useful to her life.

Sometimes, as a result of these difficulties, people go to great lengths to avoid making decisions. It is important to note that none of these cognitive shifts have anything to do with coincidental brain injury or inherent intellectual difficulties. Research shows that many people with this kind of PTSD-related, cognitive impairment have college- and graduate-level degrees and plenty of proven intellectual capacity.

Again, it is important to remember that for most people this state of affairs is temporary. The vast majority of trauma survivors leave these symptoms behind after a few weeks or months. And now, with the new treatments available, many can reduce these effects even after years.

There is good neurological reason for these symptoms. Let's start by taking a look at the observable, physical changes that occur in the circuitry of the traumatized brain.

THE HIPPOCAMPUS

In long-term trauma survivors with post-traumatic stress disorder, brain MRI studies show a significant reduction in the volume of the hippocampus, the cognitive area of the brain that analyzes, associates, compares, and contrasts current events with past experiences. Some shrinkage has been shown in Vietnam combat veterans suffering from chronic late-stage PTSD[8] and in female survivors of childhood sexual abuse.[9]

In both human and animal studies, high and prolonged levels of cortisol appear to be the culprit.[10] Although glucocorticoids have great adaptive value because they're critical for modulating that initial acute blast of norepinephrine at the first sign of threat, prolonged exposure to them wears down the neurons in the hippocampus. And post-traumatic stress is by definition a matter of extended activation of the stress response, with the repeated release of adrenaline.

Other changes in regional brain structure from PTSD have been found with positron emission tomography (PET) scans, taken while a traumatized subject is read a detailed narrative of his or her trauma—a condition designed to deliberately elicit flashbacks and activate the whole biochemical, neurological, and emotional cascade.[11]

OTHER CHANGES IN THE BRAIN

PET scans show that this provoked arousal generates an increase in metabolic activity in the right hemisphere—specifically in the amygdala and the parts of the limbic system connected with it—where threat-related memories and emotion-laden events are processed. In addition, increased activity in the right visual cortex occurs with the appearance of the flashbacks provoked by the narratives. Perhaps most tellingly, Broca's area—the speech center of the brain—shows reduced activity and loss of oxygen, consistent with an inability to verbalize emotion and emotion-laden events.

Comparable scans of people without PTSD failed to reveal this intriguing pattern. Even a study that compared the scans of *identical twin* Vietnam War veterans, one with PTSD and one without, showed a difference. These matched pairs, who presumably started out with identical brains, had scans that diverged considerably, offering the most powerful evidence of a PTSD-generated change in regional brain functioning.

Further, when researchers scrutinized the anterior cingulate—the section of the brain tasked with quieting down the hyperactivated amygdala after a threat has passed—they discovered that it failed to go into gear. In other words, the normal braking of the arousal response was simply not in place the way it normally is, and instead the self-perpetuating, kindled circuit of chronic arousal had taken over.

As noted earlier, urinary cortisol levels in people with post-traumatic stress are atypical. It's long been established that people suffering from acute stress have elevated levels of cortisol and norepinephrine in their urine and saliva. But people with chronic or long-standing PTSD show relatively low, stable levels of cortisol—one could even say *suppressed* levels of cortisol—while carrying unusually high levels of norepinephrine. One explanation for this odd profile might be some sort of adaptation by the brain and body to continuously kindled arousal—too many "cries of wolf" to the nervous system, so to speak. It responds by stopping its heightened cranking out of cortisol at the sounding of every alarm. (Tests show that the capacity to release cortisol is still there, so we know that the body has not simply run out of these supplies.)

DISSOCIATION

Another explanation, however, might have to do with the pervasive, cumulative effects of dissociation, the altered mental state that disrupts conscious awareness and that has been found to be both a key predictor and a key feature of chronic PTSD.

Here is a powerful description of this mechanism, from a woman who experienced severe abuse as a child. She would, in her own words, "go out into the rainbow":

> I think I began leaving my body even before I was two years old.
> As I've recovered, I have had such images of abuse happening,
> and not feeling any pain as a child. People always remarked
> about what a "high pain tolerance" I had. As I remembered

and dealt with the abuse, I actually had severe body memories as the trauma was revealed to me and as I worked to release it.

The first actual memory I have in which the rainbow came to me was around age six. My mother was in a psychotic state and was screaming in my face as she bent my back over the footboard/post of my bed. She hit me over and over again with a belt buckle, and her body was right on top of me. Her face was red, and spit kept coming out of her mouth onto my face. I turned my head to avoid this and, through the bedroom window, saw colors flooding into the room. I felt the colors and actually saw them on my hands as I raised them to protect myself from my mother's rage. The rainbow light filled the window, and I saw many colors on the walls of my room. Suddenly I felt as though I were bathed in the colors—and it was as though I was watching my mother hurt me from up inside the colors.

When my mother's rage finally stopped, I saw from up in the rainbow that I had cuts on my left wrist and bruises on my skin. I didn't feel anything at all. I don't remember ever feeling physical pain again after I was able to "go out in the rainbow" for safety. I had no idea how much time passed, but I know it was dark when I finally was "present" again.

She adds, with the gallows humor found in many survivors,

There were many other times where I found myself up on the ceiling, and even on top of the refrigerator in the Bronx where we lived, but they were not as pretty as the rainbow. Too much dust up on the fridge!

Dissociation, a uniquely human element in the universal, biologically driven freeze response, involves a sense of unreality, a feeling of distance from what is happening, a numbing of physical pain and other somatic sensations, emotional detachment, and distortions of time and place, including post-traumatic amnesia.

As I mentioned earlier, numerous studies have shown that people who dissociate at the time of a trauma are at greatest risk for developing

PTSD, and if they do develop it, they continue to dissociate more and more as their condition evolves.

When people dissociate, by definition, a lot of their capacity becomes impaired, at least temporarily. Their ability to focus, pay attention, think clearly, solve problems, see escape routes, stay grounded to the details of external reality, and remain emotionally connected to events on the ground—all are substantially diminished. This is because of the constriction, withdrawal, and detachment that are the essence of this altered mind state—the price we pay for the reduction of pain, fear, and emotional distress during the trauma.

The numbing and constriction involved in dissociation suggest the release of natural opioids that can suppress cortisol and prevent the modulating effect of glucocorticoids on the acute effects of epinephrine. Indeed, the presence of chronically high levels of norepinephrine suggest the presence of endogenous painkillers, as these two kinds of biochemicals tend to show up together.

The presence of the body's built-in analgesics could also account for some of the dulled or reduced intellectual capacity noted earlier. In a sense, dissociated people appear "stoned" because they are—riding on a kindled loop of endogenous opioids, continuously served up drugs with cyclical regularity. This also accounts for their generalized fogginess and loss of emotional tone.

The distorted perception involved in dissociation can show up in several ways. Most commonplace is the sense of having an out-of-body experience, both during the traumatic event itself and then later on, at times of heightened anxiety or when a flashback intrudes. Often described as floating up to the ceiling and being able to watch and hear events unfold from there, it is most commonly reported by adults who experienced sexual abuse or repeated violence as children.

The small percentage of terrified surgery patients who have failed to be rendered unconscious by anesthesia and find themselves trapped in a fully sensate nightmare of helpless immobility also report observing their surgery and eavesdropping on the OR staff from their perch on the ceiling—usually in a corner of the room. As odd as this might seem, some of these patients later recount with great accuracy the OR items that were placed on top of an eight-foot-high cabinet at the time of their procedure.

These items were sitting on a surface that could not possibly have been viewed from normal ground level.

Derealization is another aspect of dissociation: the sense that what is happening is unreal or otherworldly. It is also part of the emotional detachment that is fed by biochemical changes affecting the brain. The magical arrival of the beneficent rainbow to the abused, trapped child, described earlier, is one example. Derealization can involve some fairly dramatic memory alterations—a profound slowing down of time, for instance. Often sights, sounds, smells, and sensations are greatly amplified in this state as well. These are called *psychosensory symptoms*.

Amnesia is usually the result of experiencing a traumatic event in a dissociated state. And flashback memories are, in and of themselves, dissociated events that are reprises of the original dissociated event. Just as sensory perception and acuity are affected during the original traumatic episode, so are these distortions manifest during the flashback. Whatever derealized, vivid, or bizarre perceptions accompanied the state of enhanced arousal during the trauma are what gets replayed. Things can be bigger or faster or slower, oddly shaped or colored, and even reveal intense smells or tastes. Body sensation is altered during the flashback as well, most often by a vague sense of numbness, vibratory sensation, and sometimes a sudden weakness in muscle strength.

Flashbacks usually last a matter of seconds or minutes, but they can go on for hours or even days, during which time the person is essentially disabled. During a flashback episode, immediate reality recedes, and people become temporarily disoriented as to their current place and time, because their senses are telling them they are back in the traumatic experience. Except for our dreams, which are by definition psychotic in a normal kind of way, this may be the closest that a perfectly sane, healthy, undrugged person gets to having a hallucination. In truth, they really *are* drugged, but from the inside, by their own biochemicals.

PSYCHIC OPENING AND PRECOGNITION

One surprise benefit that comes from a traumatic experience is the emergence of intuitive abilities that were previously only dormant or occasional. Indeed, the enhanced perception and heightened receptivity that come from the flood of biochemicals washing through body and brain at times of danger are more ingeniously geared to promote survival than most of us think.

Stories abound—from reliable, grounded sorts—of people getting impulses to turn the car illogically right instead of left, just in the nick of time; of someone hearing a voice that warns or advises not to go straight home the night the house burns down; of a child seeing a vision that points to a very unlikely escape route amid the falling rubble of an earthquake. For many survivors, once these intuitive capacities have been popped open by trauma, they stick around for the long haul, to assist with everyday choices, larger life decisions, and creative projects.

One combat veteran from Vietnam actually loved the "high" of walking point, precisely because of the adrenergized charge that allowed him to mystically merge with his environment. In a very real sense, this was a spiritual experience for him, one that had a special, addictive kick. Andy's story illustrates perfectly the survival benefits of activating psychic ability in times of extreme danger:

> Andy was the guy who walked point. His job was to go several yards ahead of the main group and sense danger. It was up to him to declare when it was safe, and when it wasn't. And when it wasn't, Andy was out there, the designated, visible, vulnerable enemy target. The lives of his cohorts were in his very capable eighteen-year-old hands.
>
> Andy got a high from walking point. He described it as a kind of hyperattunement, where he became so alert, he would feel himself merging with the environment and becoming part of the landscape. He could smell even faraway danger in that state. His senses were so sharp, his whole being so fully present and exquisitely alive, that he felt a kind of pure animal joy walking point, like nothing he had ever experienced.
>
> Andy would unnerve the other men with his surefooted clarity and absolute certainty about safety and danger. He always knew. In fact, he developed a reputation for a kind of magical, psychotic invulnerability. Unlike anyone else who walked point, he wouldn't carry a machine gun, which would

have given him a sliver of a chance had he been discovered
by the enemy. On the contrary, Andy's weapon of choice was
an SRL [single rocket launcher]—one shot was all he had.
The men kept their distance and thought of him as a crazy
badass, but they always felt better when it was Andy's turn to
walk point.[12]

Another instance of psychic opening, under a very different set of life-
threatening circumstances, was described in this way by a colleague:

After inadvertently eating a disguised shrimp sauce—a food she
was violently allergic to—at a local restaurant, a young client of
mine went into anaphylactic shock upon returning home to her
empty apartment. She had left her hypodermic kit at her
boyfriend's, and her airways were closing up with alarming
speed. She had the wherewithal to call 911 but wasn't able to
speak into the phone. She knew she had only seconds before
blacking out altogether. Probably it was the adrenaline pumping
into her system that had kept her alive up to this point.
    Just as she was losing consciousness, she heard a voice,
very firmly addressing her by her given name, and telling her,
"Sylvie Anne, get out of this apartment. Find a neighbor. Bang
on a door. GET OUT OF HERE." This she did, passing out
just as the neighbor, who very luckily happened to be home
sick from work that day, opened his door. This is what saved
her life. Had she stayed in her apartment, she would have died.

A musician who miraculously survived a horrendous head-on motor
vehicle accident described his extrasensory experience in this way:

I see the oncoming car lose control, cross the median strip,
and veer straight toward us. It's all happening in slow motion.
Next thing I know, I'm, like, plucked out of my seat by these
huge golden arms, lifting me above the wreck. I mean, I'm in the
arms of an angel, calm as I can be, watching the whole thing.
The whole sky is bright with light, and I'm filled with peace. I
know everything is gonna be all right. It was a state of bliss

and knowing I'd be fine. And I was not on any substances,
man, so don't even go there.

For many people, the intuitive experiences continue and are developed even further. One survivor of severe childhood abuse became very psychic, a commonly reported experience among those who emerge from this sort of history. She was so attuned to her therapist, in fact, that she considered her exquisitely calibrated reactivity to her therapist's moods a liability. She writes:

> The downside was that . . . any minor vicissitudes in her life that I picked up in her presence affected me extremely. It was frustrating, both to her and to me, that I would react so strongly to such minor things and sometimes to nothing external at all. But I was accurately picking up any shift in her nervous system, and my damaged system could little tolerate any further imbalances.

Once this woman's nervous system stabilized and settled down, she was able to take advantage of her intuitive gifts in a positive and welcoming way, using them in her service work, to help others. First she had to heal, naturally. But generally, once a survivor learns how to get past her pain and becomes able to join in the adventure of her life, she has the energy and freedom to enjoy and deploy these capabilities.

For many who open up in this way, this is the beginning of an exciting new adventure in exploring their own consciousness. They frequently have a new interest in matters of spirit that feeds the larger perspective and enables them to move beyond their terrible experiences without denying them. Study groups, meditation circles, new friends, and new ideas feed this renaissance and promote a new romance with being alive.

These are often the people who not only survive their PTSD but ultimately thrive after it. Getting in touch with these powerful human capabilities and spiritual connections that have popped open from the adrenergized terror state leads to more joy, more aliveness, and more productivity in the months and years to come. In fact, one woman extracted from me a promise to mention the heightened creativity and artistic expression that so often comes out of these experiences. These are some of the gifts that lie beneath the rubble of the traumatic experience.

7 THE EMOTIONAL EFFECTS OF TRAUMA

The emotional toll that post-traumatic stress exacts is a powerful and painful thing to witness, let alone bear. As one Vietnam veteran typically reported:

> The memories and flashbacks were so horrible and immediate, I would freeze with fright every time they came. It was exactly like it was happening all over again, only this time it was evidently coming from inside my own head—although you couldn't convince me while it was happening. It felt like it was *really* happening. I thought I was losing my mind.
>
> I also had a lot of guilt and shame for some of the bad things that I did and for the things that I should have done and didn't do. I just wished for it to never have happened, so I could go back to being the innocent, decent person I was before. This was a sad, yearning, painful thing I felt most of the time.
>
> Looking back now, I honestly don't know how I stood it for as long as I did. There were times when, if I could have twisted my head off with my own hands, gouged my eyes out, torn my skin off, to make it all go away, I'd have done it. There was just no way to get away from myself, short of killing myself, because it was all coming from inside of me. I was poison to myself.

The emotional pain of post-traumatic stress is the archetypal, beyond-reason suffering of Greek tragedy. It's the anguish of Oedipus tearing out his own eyes, the howling fury of Medea murdering her children, the outraged betrayal of Antigone digging up the body of her dead brother with her bare hands. It is outsize, abnormal, crazy suffering.

Boston psychiatrist and groundbreaking trauma expert Judith Herman, author of *Trauma and Recovery,* writes, "The survivor is continually buffeted by terror and rage. These emotions are qualitatively different from ordinary fear and anger. They are outside the range of ordinary emotional experience, and they overwhelm the ordinary capacity to bear feelings."[1]

Most psychological description (Herman excepted) is too pale and flat to communicate the roiling emotions of a survivor with post-traumatic stress. The intensity and severity of the feelings involved are better described by poetry, drama, and fiction, or with first-person accounts, such as the ones that follow. Those who haven't experienced these things may suspect these stories are tainted with melodrama or overstated in some way. They are not. This is how it is. People who have suffered similar experiences immediately recognize the truth of them.

IMMEASURABLE SORROW AND DEEP GRIEF

Post-traumatic stress always has great sorrow at the bottom of it. Permeating every reaction and beneath every other emotion, people carry a well of deep sadness over their lost innocence, their shattered dreams, and the disappearance of their reasonable world. They long for the benignly optimistic self that existed before everything changed so cruelly, and they ache for the old sense of safety that was natural enough to be taken for granted. In fact, they long for the ability to take *anything* for granted again, to feel carelessly entitled to any small, thoughtless pleasure of daily life. Many things, large and small, are sorely missed.

Often less abstract losses are involved too, of course—lives, limbs, careers, abilities, homes, relationships. But no matter what the nature of the losses, the sorrow is always there. Even when the noisier, more grandstanding emotions of terror and rage take center stage and push aside the sadness, it can always be found underneath, quiet and deep. The rage and terror come and go in great waves, but grief quietly rules all of it, providing the subtext for everything else. Kissing cousins to it are despair and loneliness.

Michael Risenhoover, the police captain from a nearby town at the time of the Oklahoma City bombing whom we met in Chapter 3, describes the days immediately following the attack:

> Most of the days following the Oklahoma City bombing are somewhat of a blur. Mostly I remember crying. I had never cried so much in my life, and the tears that started during those days continued to fall almost daily. I was a police captain at that time, and tears were considered unprofessional and a sign of weakness, but I couldn't help it. I didn't care who saw my tears. I couldn't and didn't try to hide them anymore—it hurt too much. My tears were the only way I was able to let out the pain that I kept inside, and I found out that I had more pain than I had ever imagined. The Oklahoma City bombing for me was the straw that broke the camel's back. It unleashed all the fear and anger I held for so many years—homicides and suicides, senseless deaths of children and loved ones. All of my pain surfaced, and my sense of identity, of who I once was, would never be the same again.
>
> Eventually, I not only lost my identity but my wife of twenty years as well. My family was shattered. I locked my pistol in my desk drawer and did not carry it on duty anymore. I was afraid that I might hurt myself. In group therapy, I found myself drawn to and feeling close to rape victims. Our fears and memories and sense of loss were so closely related.

A devoted mother who herself survived childhood abuse describes the grief and sadness she experienced over her own lost childhood, as she capably mothered her own well-loved grade-school children. Caring for her own children in the way she wished she could have been loved and protected herself was deeply satisfying and critically important to her, but it also evoked a long-standing, poignant grief:

> The closest emotion would be overwhelming grief and loss of EVERYTHING, primarily my body. With PTSD the body sensations can completely overwhelm any sort of logic—the mind and self disappear, seemingly never to return. Nothing

belongs to me, not even my body. All is lost—there is no anchor, no protector, no mother, no safe place to contain the feelings, so they will fade faster. I ask myself when will this unwanted assault (yes, it's an assault, a taking over of the body) go away, and why can't I control it? Why does this tape replay over and over again? So relentlessly I have to experience the annihilation of my soul. The pain is overwhelming and there is nothing I or anyone else can do to escape it.

I would end my life if I didn't have children—but somehow I know that to live is to win this battle—and I do want to win it. I will not give up. I will fight for myself.

Holocaust survivor Elie Wiesel howls his grief in his powerful writing—the loss of his connection to life, to others, to joy, to his future, and to God. Clearly, this is not just the expression of pain; it is also a declaration of still being alive:

Never shall I forget those flames which consumed my faith forever. Never shall I forget that nocturnal silence which deprived me, for all eternity, of the desire to live. Never shall I forget those moments which murdered my God and my soul and turned my dreams to dust. Never shall I forget these things, even if I am condemned to live as long as God Himself. Never.[2]

In a recent conversation, an ex-client of mine recalled the time in my office when she'd experienced her first full-blown flashback. To my surprise, she mentioned feeling a deep sadness at that moment, a sadness that preceded any other emotion that subsequently came tumbling back. I knew how powerful and overwhelming her feelings of terror, shame, and anger had been, and I'd assumed I'd hear about those first. But sadness was the emotion that preceded all the others. This was Julie, the woman who had the intrusive memory of her cheek on the bathroom floor.

In the session we were discussing, a fragment of a sensory memory had surfaced—the memory of her cheek being cold. This evolved into her recalling her face being pressed against the cold white-and-black hexagonal tiles of her aunt's bathroom floor. More and more pieces of the puzzle emerged, until her whole body was trembling with the memory of the ministrations of a sadistic grandmother and aunt, torturing her with obligatory enemas on the bathroom floor. Here are her own words about that very first memory fragment appearing:

> I can see you sitting in the office. I can see myself sitting there too, huddled in the corner, on the love seat. My legs were crossed, and my arms were crossing my chest. You asked me something. I don't remember what.
>
> I could feel myself drifting away, but I also felt sick to my stomach, and it was like my whole body was electrified—like my finger was in an outlet. I was in disbelief and incredibly sad. I felt so wounded and vulnerable. I just wanted to go cry. I was at the same time totally taken aback. I didn't like what was coming. I mean, I didn't exactly know what was coming, but I knew that whatever it was, I didn't like it.
>
> I had huge goose bumps, I remember. I was shuddering, freezing cold. It was all from this one remembrance of my cheek being cold. Cold from the bathroom tiles. That's what I could see—this pattern of black-and-white tiles on the floor, which was where my cheek was. Then I started to see the whole thing. Lying curled up in a fetal position on the floor, with my gramma and aunt hovering over me. Then I remembered the enemas. And feeling like I was not clean, feeling dirty and ashamed. I couldn't think what I had done to deserve this. It was such a sad feeling.

TERROR, ANXIETY, AND PANIC

Whether the trauma survivor is awake or asleep, the terror of a PTSD nightmare or flashback carries the most intense kind of fear and horror, containing as it does all the helplessness, loss of control, and threat of annihilation of the original event—and sometimes more. The terror is undeniably *physical* as well as emotional, a total body event. Many people describe it as a massive charge of electricity coursing through their bodies.

Here is how one survivor of childhood abuse describes her night terrors, which lasted for several years:

There is no respite. Even at night my unconscious mind purges me of dreams that make me sweat and shake and vomit. I wake up, and the bed is soaked. I gasp for air and try to calm the nightmares, which rattle my soul and activate my entire nervous system. Sometimes it takes a day or two to feel like the fog has cleared from my head after a night like this.

A colleague and friend, a noted writer and successful producer who years earlier survived a violent motor vehicle accident, followed by months of recovery, describes the "classic" panic attacks that overtook her a decade later in this way:

During one of these panic attacks, the thought comes into my head: "What if you can't get out?" (of this elevator, airplane, concert hall, office building—it doesn't matter). Adrenaline shoots into my stomach. Immediately I feel cold and hot— freezing cold hands and feet, but superhot in the torso. I feel like my body temperature rises extremely fast, and I start to sweat. But it's a cold sweat.

My mind keeps shouting this question at me: What if you can't get out? What if you can't get out? (I know this sounds psycho.) My limbs get supertense, especially my hands and thighs. I feel wave after wave of practically convulsive anxiety gripping me, moving through my limbs. My throat gets completely dry. My heart beats so hard, it feels like it's burning in my chest.

Even though all this physical stuff is happening, I don't feel that I'm in my body at all. All I'm aware of is my thought— I have to get out. What if I can't get out? I must get out!

I feel like I don't even blink, that my eyes are stuck open. My breathing gets rapid and shallow. If I try to "breathe into" the tension in my left leg, the tension in my right leg increases. When I put my attention there to breathe into it, the tension goes back to the left leg.

My back gets very tense, my shoulders rise up, and my head tries to almost push down into the body cavity. Impossible, but that's where it wants to go.

Another thing I feel is incredible irritation and anger at almost everything. I feel superhuman strength, like "I could shear the elevator door off if it were to get stuck, or pull a locked emergency exit door off its hinges." Actually, when the anger starts to rise, things slightly rebalance, albeit in an unpleasant way. I actually feel a little better, and I'm not so scared.

After the episode has passed, it takes a really, really long time for my hands and feet to get warm and the adrenaline to subside. And I can make the adrenaline come back just from thinking the thought, "What if I can't get out?" even if I'm standing in a clear, open field.

This even happened to me when I was getting an eyelash tint the other day. You have to keep your eyes closed for fifteen minutes or else the dye gets in your eyes. As soon as she put the tint on my lashes, I had the thought, "What if I have to get out of here but I can't open my eyes? I must open my eyes." I insisted that she wipe the dye off. The whole thing from start to finish, from the thought to the panic attack, was literally about two seconds.

This woman, who is obviously very attuned to her body and extremely skilled at observing herself, even in the midst of terror, provides a near-perfect description of dysregulated hyperarousal, down to the internal biochemical blast, racing heartbeat, shallow, rapid breathing, drench of perspiration, the supertoned muscle in her extremities, pupil dilation, and the feeling of enormous strength and readiness to fight. Overriding it all is the feeling of panic and desperation at being helplessly trapped. She adds:

It's as if your own mind attacks you. This sense of being viciously threatened by your own thoughts is terrifying—there is absolutely nowhere to hide. You're trapped with and by your own mind. At least for me, this is the scariest part of all . . . really intensifies the claustrophobia.

Another survivor describes a very similar set of symptoms:

There was an overwhelming anxiety and panic attacks that would sometimes last all day, till my chest ached from my constantly pounding heart. Often these started with no known cause, though a memory could also set them off. With a nervous system that was always sparking with random electrical charges, anything and almost everything could trigger this response.

Even when she wasn't having panic attacks, she was still subjected to a chronic anxious agitation that existed as the baseline of her "optimal" functioning for many years. Here is how she describes this constant, electrical hum of anxiety:

I used to try to occupy my mind with a lot of concrete detail as a way of trying to calm down the agitation. I can best describe it as a picture of a random, crazy-looking scribble going through my torso, or as an eggbeater that moves randomly 360 degrees, but not in a symmetrical pattern . . . the nerve messages would go in every direction, till it was like a mass of tangled wires, all of them carrying an electric charge. This was the sense of extreme agitation and wanting to jump out of my skin. I was so distressed, I truly did not know what to do with myself.

Another woman writes:

For several years I couldn't go a day without a panic attack. I had a huge fear of driving the freeway, which started when I had to drive to my uncle's [the man who had molested her as a child] to help take care of him. My hands would be like a vise on the wheel. My knees would lock, and I would sweat and hyperventilate. My biggest fear was that I would hurt someone else, pass out at the wheel, and cross the median or something. I found it much easier to be on side roads, where it felt like I had more control. I could at least pull up and catch my breath. It was the biggest relief to finally pull into my own driveway. I'd just sit there and regroup in the car for a while, before going into the house.

Sometimes I'd say to myself a little mantra from my favorite book as a kid, *The Little Engine That Could*. I'd tell myself, "Like the little choo choo, I know I can, I know I can . . ." Or sometimes I'd just do what I used to call a "total kamikaze"— jump in car, carom over, pick up the milk or do the errand, and come home as fast as I could, shaking like a leaf the whole time.

Oh, I'd just as soon have blown my brains out during a panic attack. I'd get in line at the grocery store, and I'd have to leave the cart and get out of there. I'd lie and say I'd forgotten an item, and then I'd just book out of there, as fast as I could. Then I'd get in my car and cry and cry, because I just couldn't do it. And I'd be so exhausted afterward, I'd have to take a nap. And all the time I'd be thinking, "What's wrong with me? Why am I doing this?"

I remember once, I wanted to deposit my check in the bank. I got up to the window, so panicky and sweaty, wringing my hands and looking so scared, the teller thought I was there to rob the bank. She looked at me very suspiciously, like I was a criminal, and made me talk to the bank officer. It was torture. I never went inside that bank again. After that I mailed my deposits in.

I'm okay now, but to this day, if I have to drive on the freeway, I deliberately preoccupy my mind with happy things first.

RAGE

A survivor with post-traumatic stress is stuck negotiating unusual amounts of anger, resentment, annoyance, and irritation on any given day, but when full-fledged fury strikes, the sheer ferocity of it is like a force of nature. Add to that the standard judgments most of us have about how wrong and ugly it is to feel even a fraction of this sort of rage, and the result is an experience that is difficult to assimilate, accept, or withstand.

A Vietnam vet—a tall, gentle African American man of fifty-eight with an easy, good-natured charm and a ready laugh—explained to his support group why he had to move out of his wife's and his bedroom and start sleeping alone in their guest room:

> I have no memory of this, but my wife would tell me that a few times I'd wake up yelling in the middle of the night, trying to choke her. She told me my eyes would be wide open and that would I look at her with complete hatred, like I wanted to kill her. There was no doubt in her mind that I was going to strangle her one of those times. It scared us both to death. I love the woman dearly, and the fact that I had no memory of doing it scared me. She would have to scream and call my name, over and over, scratch my face, and pinch me before I stopped.
>
> I decided I couldn't risk sleeping in the same bed or room with her anymore. I was scared I would kill her before I could stop myself. It made us both very sad. Sometimes I'll just hold her for a while before going to my room.

A police officer who had seen too much ugliness, describes it this way:

> I felt I was dangerous. I had to fight murderous urges. I felt these impulses so strongly, I was afraid they would take over. People always liked me, but I knew I had demons inside that had to be exorcised. I had to get away from the people I loved, to work out the bad in me. It killed me, but that's what I did. I ran away so I wouldn't hurt anyone.

An incest survivor reports that years later, relieved of most of her symptoms, she still has to sleep with the bed in the middle of the room, away from the walls.

> I kept kicking my right foot into the wall during my sleep. I broke my toe twice, kicking the shit out of somebody in my

dreams. I'd wake up in pain—a broken toe hurts!—not knowing who I'd been going after.

One motor vehicle accident survivor describes a waking, conscious fury that only began to surface years after her trauma:

> I now get irritated and angry over nothing, absolutely nothing. It comes welling up in me like a huge wave of heat. I think I actually break a sweat. Sometimes I allow myself to fantasize a full freak-out, just to make the feelings move through me and get out of me, and it sort of works. I imagine that I'm destroying the things around me—beating on windows, pulling overhead compartment doors off their hinges, pushing people, smashing into them, spilling things, breaking things, throwing things . . . stuff like that.

Sometimes the fury is directed at the self. One rape survivor remembers during the worst months of her PTSD symptoms, sitting at her desk, trying to work, and having to fight the impulse to poke pencils into her eyes. Survivors sometimes cut themselves with razors and other sharp objects, in a numbed, dissociated state.

My ex-client Frannie, whose story we heard in Chapter 2, reported a relatively recent experience with an episode of outsize rage that broke through the surface—something that used to overtake her regularly at seemingly random times. She wrote:

> There was a storm, a big one brewing, and the sky darkened, and a chill wind died down to a chill calm. That was going on outside while I was inside; and with absolutely no provocation, my body was taken and filled with a rage so ferocious that I could not breathe or see. Now I know what a "blind rage" is. My entire body was full of a searing fire that ripped through my chest and left me struggling for air.
>
> I got out of the house and sat with my back to the house, desperately trying to breathe and be grounded to something, thinking that my heart and chest would surely explode and I would die right there. Dark, freezing, overwhelming, and a raging

fire all at once. This lasted for about ten to fifteen minutes, so I am told, and once the first wave passed, I was able to open my eyes. I gasped for air and tried to slow down my breathing, wanting to ground myself, feeling like I was going to die if I didn't.

I caught sight of the top of a very tall tree in the back of the property, and fixed my eyes on it, following the tree from the topmost leaf, through the smaller, then larger branches, down through the sturdier branches and into the trunk, where there is the rhythm of the heart and the breath of the tree. Once my energy was focused on this journey, it just kept moving down the trunk, slowly, until it reached the ground.

I began to breathe again and began to feel the fires and the waves of extreme rage subside. I was grounded. The thing about this, though, is that I did not know to go to the tree for the grounding. I think my body did it for me. Maybe it's all the mindfulness and breathwork I've been doing, I don't know.

NUMBNESS: WALKING THE FOG WALK

Survivors oscillate between very intense feelings and their opposite: numbness and internal deadness. This is the emotional counterpart to the wildly oscillating hormonal shifts happening at the bioneurological level. People feel as if they are sleepwalking, barely alive in these periods, and as time goes on, it's the numbness that tends to predominate, taking over more and more days and weeks.

Summoning up great courage and energy they don't feel, people with chronic PTSD haul themselves from task to task, somehow getting through the day without a shred of interest in it. These are days obscured by a foggy anesthesia, times of feeling numbed off, unpleasantly stoned. And indeed these people *are* stoned—on the endogenous opioids flooding their systems from a dysregulated endocrine system.

As one combat veteran described it:

The days just disappear. I don't know where they go, because
I'm not really there. It's not terrible. It's more like nothing.
I'm like a shadow, like the undead, walking around. Like that
movie *The Night of the Living Dead,* that's me.

A similar quote from a World War II veteran appears in Judith Herman's
book:

Like most of the 4th, I was numb, in a state of virtual
dissociation. There is a condition . . . which we called the two-
thousand-year-stare. This was the anesthetized look, the wide,
hollow eyes of a man who no longer cares.

One student who viewed firsthand the massacre at Columbine High
School and narrowly escaped injury himself said he didn't remember
whole sections of many weeks, but that his girlfriend later told him that
being with him was like being with no one at all. It frightened her, how
hollow, apathetic, empty, and lifeless he had become—when he wasn't agitated, irritable, and short-tempered, that is. "I was not a pretty picture,"
he said after regaining his customary sense of humor several months
later. "Being with me was a drag."

As one young mother, a survivor of childhood incest, says:

Sometimes it takes a day or two to feel like the fog has cleared
from my head after a night filled with nightmares. It is like
walking in a fog. I walk the fog walk.

SHAME AND HUMILIATION

Perhaps most corrosive of all are the feelings of shame—the red-hot
waves of self-disgust and embarrassment that rise up and fill so many survivors of trauma, making them want to hide and not show themselves
again. This sense of being contaminated, dirty, defiled, and spoiled in
some integral way becomes a core wound that informs and distorts other
perceptions. There is the sense that they have failed themselves, violated

their own standards. Even though they've been dealt a set of impossible, no-win choices, the stinging self-assessment is that they are at fault.

Psychiatrist Judith Herman calls it "the debased self-image of chronic trauma."[3] In describing the altered identity of survivors of prolonged captivity—and this description could apply to survivors of any traumatic situation—she writes:

> Whatever new identity she develops in freedom must include the memory of her enslaved self. Her image of her body must include a body that can be controlled and violated. Her image of herself in relation to others must include a person who can lose and be lost to others. And her moral ideals must coexist with knowledge of the capacity for evil, both within others and within herself. If, under duress, she has betrayed her own principles or has sacrificed other people, she now has to live with the image of herself as an accomplice of the perpetrator, a "broken" person. The result, for most victims, is a contaminated identity. Victims may be preoccupied with shame, self-loathing, and a sense of failure.

The perennially superscrubbed, soap-scented Frannie, my ex-client who used to go home to shower and change into fresh clothing before coming to my office for her session, felt she was too unclean to show up straight from work. She was not alone in this distorted self-perception. Many people with PTSD become obsessed with cleanliness because they feel so sullied on the inside. She recalled some of the dark revulsion she would feel as she sat across from me, perfusing the room, ironically, with the fresh, pleasing aroma of shampoo and soap:

> In a state of unliving, I'm sitting and staring at you, desperate to verbalize my thoughts, but afraid of the words coming out, even if I could utter them . . . fear of rejection, because what is inside of me is so vile and repulsive . . .
>   It's like living below the earth, where it's stagnant and still, with no air moving. The rank smell of it, the heavy weight of the shame in this filthy, dead place, a greasy film of rancid oil covering me, smothering the life and breath out of me.

At the very least, most survivors are chronically riddled with embarrassment and easily humiliated when confronted by neutral daily events. A mild misunderstanding, an innocent error, or simple ignorance of a customary practice can send a trauma survivor into a tailspin of shame.

One woman, who was victimized herself and was forced to watch the victimization of others during the sadistic ritual activities hosted throughout her childhood by her family, describes the feeling this way:

> One of my long-term symptoms of lingering PTSD is the feeling of humiliation that is just there from being violated; the shame of something/someone outside of me having control over me; and the sense of being less than others, damaged in some way that others aren't. It's a deep-seated embarrassment in front of others, and always wondering, why? And perhaps fearing that I'm really bad to have drawn such negativity into my life. (And unfortunately, simplistic ideas of karma play right into that.)

Some survivors are fully cognizant of the exact moment when everything changed for them, and they were flooded with the first of what would be many attacks of shame. Here is a typical story:

> The trauma that disrupted and immobilized my maturing happened at the age of around seven . . . a much older, teenage cousin attempted to molest me. Being the stubborn and precocious child that I was, I refused to let him do anything to me, but he forced me to perform a sexual act on him, which was horrifying to my "little girl" mind and soul.
>
> All this occurred after he had masterminded a plan to befriend me through sharing his huge baseball card collection with me . . . I *loved* baseball cards. Our parents would often get together in the evenings, and while they were visiting downstairs, he took me upstairs to his bedroom and began to lure me into friendship through the cards. Finally, when he felt he had me exactly where he wanted me, mentally and emotionally, he locked me in the bedroom and this horrendous event happened.

I did not cry out for my parents . . . I felt so helpless and so
very bad . . . he told me he would kill my much-loved dog,
Suzie, if I told . . . I can still visualize my little self coming
back downstairs when it was over. To this day I can still feel
the disgust and fear and shame and confusion and pain that
was swirling through my little body and mind as I joined my
parents . . . *silent* and *changed forever*. This wonderful little child
that was me was never the same again.

The shame needn't, however, be connected to suffering deliberate
humiliation at the hands of an abusive predator. It can be activated simply
by the inherent helplessness and vulnerability in a scenario informed by
benign intentions. For instance, a man who suffered a painful and pro-
tracted recovery from a disabling bone marrow transplant procedure included feeling ashamed as one of the stronger emotions that burdened
him afterward:

I was greatly embarrassed by my bag-of-bones thinness. Who
would have thought I'd be ashamed of being too thin? Me, the
guy who always wanted to lose ten pounds! However, that's
what I felt. I think maybe because it was a symbol of my
abject vulnerability, my total helplessness. I had always been a
resourceful person. I prided myself for being someone who
took care of others. When I couldn't take care of myself, it
shamed me deeply. I became so fragile! Sometimes something
will happen now that reminds me of those months in the
hospital, and a feeling of . . . almost revulsion for myself . . .
floods through me all over again.

LONELINESS AND ALIENATION

Anyone who suffers the extreme anguish of PTSD is further pained by
feeling separate from "normal" people who don't. The sheer intensity of
the suffering, in and of itself, creates a chasm between the survivor and
his fellow humans. Others, after all, are still managing to find comfort,
order, and meaning in their days. There is resentment, too, that where he

must bear the burden of knowing what he knows, others can blithely and obliviously waltz through their lives, apparently unscathed.

Survivors doubt others and themselves. Events have shattered their understanding of life, and therefore their connection with others is tenuous and compromised. Gone is their trust in civility and their belief in fairness. Typically, they feel they must resort to "faking it," playacting their way through their interactions with others, maintaining a fragile surface normalcy that belies their surreal sense of alienation in a counterfeit world. Of course, playacting their "normalcy" serves only to exacerbate their loneliness.

I remember one of the Vietnam veterans warily challenging a brand-new, fresh-faced psychology intern who was sitting in on his PTSD support group for the first time. He was speaking for all eight men in the group, all inpatients struggling to recover from the twin demons of chemical dependency and post-traumatic stress. He asked:

> What makes you think *you're* gonna understand *me*? What makes you think you're even the same *species* as me? There's no way you could get who I am. No way. We're not even from the same planet, sweetheart. I'm from Planet Hell. So if you're here to judge me, I don't want you here. You don't have the right. These guys can judge me if they want to, but not you. If you get that, you can stay.

Perhaps it was the innocence and trust in her pretty, hopeful young face that set him off. Or maybe it was the edginess and irritation that comes from the very raw state of being newly clean and sober. Normally these men took scrupulous care to be gracious, appreciative, and courtly to the female staff on the floor. But at this particular moment he was telling the flat-out truth of how he and the entire group felt. You could hear a pin drop in that room when he spoke those alienated words, because he was speaking for every man in the room.

A survivor of incest describes a typical day in this alienated, disconnected state:

> My children need me, they have homework and karate lessons and swimming. I smile at their teachers. No one would guess

that I am out of bed and out of the house for only a very short time each day, summoning the energy to appear normal for my children . . . I leave the house at three, makeup in place. I look perfect. I return exhausted. No one knows the hell I'm living.

Trauma counselor and abuse survivor Lynne Newman wrote this poem, expressing her isolation. Her poetry-writing was part of the healing regimen that helped her recover from her own terrible experiences:

Like a piece of polished glass
   They all look through me,
And no one ever sees,
   The pain behind my phony smile.

I feel invisible and fragile.
   CRASH! The glass breaks
And the world can finally see
   The jagged splinters of my shattered spirit!

DESPAIR

Hopelessness mounts as abnormally painful symptoms pile on and persist, exacerbated by the isolation and estrangement from others. Despair, always a powerful ingredient in even garden-variety depression, is all the more present with PTSD. Being without hope is considered to be one of the typical attitude distortions that accompany these conditions, a denial of the possibilities and changes that are an inherent part of being alive. When despair takes up residence, it's all the more important for the person to have a stand-in to hold the light until the despair moves on. At these times the person simply cannot do it for himself. Here are two moving examples of this dynamic:

One survivor writes:

I believe part of the depth of my (and perhaps other PTSD people's) depression was due to the fact that I sensed at a very basic level that the damage was total and irreversible. It is impossible to describe the depth of that kind of hopelessness. The damage went beyond the broken bones and burned flesh and atrocities I witnessed. The raw material of my being, below the cellular level, was damaged beyond repair. Or so it seemed to me. Fortunately, Frances Baker, my therapist, held strongly to the belief that I would heal and told me so often. I did not share that belief, but I did trust her cognitively. She was right.

It would be years before I would realize how right she was. At this point in my life, I can see that I have not only healed in the minimal sense of no longer carrying a diagnosed disturbance; I am thriving in a way that I would never have dreamed possible.

Another describes her despair in this way:

That fall I began to lose my battle against despair again. The headaches were excruciating, the depression and anxiety were getting worse. I had no energy, no hope that this would ever go away. On top of it all, I was now also becoming addicted to pain pills.

I had sought help from various doctors over the years, all of whom grew tired of me and my maladies . . . I knew they just hated to see me waiting in their offices, which further added to my hopelessness. I used to ask myself rhetorically, "What is wrong with me?" but now I wasn't even asking that anymore. Instead, my mantra was "What's the point?" and "Who cares, anyway?"

This woman also had a "coach"—a friend she'd met on the Internet who picked up the banner of hope for her and waved it frequently in her face while she traversed this dark time. They shared an extraordinary connection, quite mystical in nature:

She told me she knew she was supposed to be the person who would "stand in the gap" and pray for direction and healing

for me when I was too weak to do it . . . she told me, "You are
in this valley for a reason. There is a bottom to this."

She too was right.

HELPLESSNESS

Many clinicians and theorists say that the essential insult of trauma is the
helplessness it imposes on its victims. We grow as children and thrive as
adults on our sense of efficacy and power; and we shrivel and die when
our sense of control is snatched from us.

One traumatized government worker, who was away from her New
York neighborhood during the 9/11 attacks on the World Trade Center,
described her helplessness and sense of failure upon her return to her dec-
imated neighborhood:

> I could not get back to New York for two days. For weeks I did
> not know who was dead and alive. We had no way to find each
> other. It was chaos. I knew two people on my block were
> missing as well as all the firefighters in my neighborhood. Signs
> were everywhere. We all kept going to Union Square, to cry, to
> pray, to comfort, and to try to understand how so many could
> be missing.
>
> We went from the fact that people we knew were missing,
> to the recognition they were dead, to the final recognition that
> they had been murdered. That was the hardest processing of
> all, at least for me.
>
> All I wanted to do was save lives, but there were none to
> save. I did get involved with animal rescue when I came back,
> because there were animals who had been abandoned by those
> who couldn't get back to their apartments or who had died.
> These were lives I could help save. But it wasn't enough.
>
> Actually, I later initiated a project to get pollution
> reduction equipment on machinery at the World Trade Center
> site, because I finally realized there was nothing I could do for
> those who had died. I needed to do what I could for the living.

I am reminded and surrounded daily by WTC cleanup, events, trauma. But so many have had so much happen, and I truly am one of the lucky ones. I am alive, I am trying to be as healthy as I can be, and I am working on a sweet project to clean up diesel school buses for kids, which will help their respiratory issues.

However, the truths I have had to confront have been very hard. I'm the tough woman who thought she knew all about war, but who knew so little. Facing my own limitations, in spite of my own deep needs to make a meaningful contribution—that has been rough.

My own goal was to leave the world at least a little better than I found it. I've been trying for twenty-five years, in my environmental work all around the globe. I can't judge what impacts my actions will effect, but it's pretty hard not to feel like a total, utter failure.

Innumerable tales from combat reflect similar devastation from not being able to prevent closely witnessed destruction and loss. This dropping of life's illusion that we are in control is a painful awareness that must be borne for the rest of a person's life. For some, it creates profound wisdom, compassion, and spiritual understanding. For others, it just hurts.

Combat vets tell tale after tale of watching helplessly while a buddy's head gets blown off, or a comrade steps on a mine. Medics forget those they saved and fixate on those people they couldn't reach. Their nightmares and flashbacks are reruns of the incidents fraught with helplessness and failure, as if by replaying them, they could maybe make them right.

GUILT, BLAME, AND REGRET

Guilt accompanies helplessness and is almost universal among people with PTSD, whether they were perpetrators of heinous acts themselves—admittedly worse—or simply victims of nature's random violence. They may feel guilt merely for being unable to do anything to ward off disaster, or for surviving when others didn't. People have guilt for not foreseeing a traumatic circumstance, or for failing to sidestep it. Guilt can show up simply because the person was scared or unheroic or paralyzed by terror. Indeed, no matter how brave or resourceful a survivor may have been, when she later reviews her own conduct, she almost always finds it inadequate.

Rape and domestic violence produces the same effect: it is the victims, not the perpetrators, who often suffer guilt. Indeed, most perpetrators and abusers generally agree with the one-sided assessment that the victim is the one to blame.

Dianne Schwartz, author of *Whose Face Is in the Mirror?*, says of her own traumatizing, abusive marriage:

> For a long time I didn't know I was being abused. I just thought I was too uptight, too inadequate, too lacking. I didn't recognize I was a victim. In my eyes I was a woman who couldn't make her husband happy.
>
> I didn't come to the marriage with good self-esteem, because of growing up with a lot of verbal and emotional abuse. So when he would look down his nose at me and tell me I just couldn't get myself together, I basically agreed.
>
> He loved to torture me. I had a little wirehaired terrier I adored named Oreo. He would try to kick her for no reason at all, except that it upset me. I wouldn't allow him to abuse my dog, but I let him abuse me. Ironic, isn't it? I was outraged when he tried to hurt her, but couldn't seem to get angry when he did the same thing to me! One time when I stood up to him over her, he got even by letting her out and telling me, "Look, Dianne. Your dog is out on the road and now she's gonna get run over and die, and it's gonna be all your fault."

As with all abusers, it was her husband's strategy to chip away incrementally at her autonomy and pride, and to brainwash her over time to think that everything was her fault. She was the guilty one, and he was the injured party. She was responsible for his every outburst. Typical of a traumatized victim, she complied, even when cognitively she knew better. Feeling guilty and responsible for her own pain became as familiar as the air she breathed.

In a very different set of circumstances, Andy, the point-walking Vietnam veteran we met in Chapter 6, carried around his own load of guilt for having made a hideous, no-win choice between two evils; he was haunted by guilt for years, until he finally got the right kind of help. A therapist told his story this way:

Andy almost didn't share his most traumatic experience with the others in the group. He waited until the very last day, leaving the room, agitated and upset, to pace in the corridor many times. Up until he began speaking, he wasn't sure if he could do it.

The story he told was this: They had caught an enemy girl—no more than ten years old—in an area where their advance team was doing extremely sensitive reconnaissance work, and it was understood that if they left her alive, she would most certainly disclose their location, exposing scores of American soldiers to deadly peril. They sat her down and tied her to a tree, and then the men shuffled and equivocated, everyone understanding that there were no acceptable choices.

As usual Andy, a mere eighteen-year-old at the time, stepped forward. He crouched opposite the girl, face to face, not more than a foot and a half away from her. The rest of the men backed off, glad to be off the hook, and waited a distance away. For a long time Andy just looked into this girl's eyes, trying to connect with her and know what was in her heart. She looked back, unflinching, defiant—her eyes reflecting an extraordinary, steely courage and the unspoken words: Go to hell.

Andy said it was like looking at himself. She was a perfect mirror, and this was intimate communion of the highest order, between two perfectly matched, huge warrior souls.

After a time—maybe ten minutes, maybe a half hour—he silently slit her throat with his knife. He came back to his cohort with her blood still on his hands. The men wouldn't look at him. They walked on through the jungle, completing their mission, never speaking of it again.

Thirty years later this was Andy's recurring nightmare, whether sleeping or awake . . . seeing the girl's eyes following him wherever he went. Reproaching him, accusing him, hating him. But this was no greater than his own self-reproach, his accusations, or his hatred of himself.

Once back in the States, Andy wrote poems to this girl. He saluted her fighting spirit. He talked to her. He listened to her when she talked back. He asked her for forgiveness. In honor of her memory, he swore never to carry a weapon again, and he never did—even during the times he was dangerously employed as a heroin dealer.

The anguish became less intense. The flashbacks and nightmares eventually stopped. But the sadness and the guilt never left him. He didn't want it to. He felt the sadness and guilt were the correct thing to feel, after all.

As was the case with Andy, a traumatic circumstance usually deals no honorable alternatives. That is why they generate such profound helplessness. Regardless of what the protagonist does or how he acts, circumstances dictate that she will fail utterly, in a terrible, heart-shattering way. Perpetual guilt and self-reproach follow.

Sometimes the survivor will get involved in blaming others—a quixotic maneuver to try and transfer the crushing sense of responsibility elsewhere, and release a burden of a guilt too heavy to claim. This strategy can succeed as a temporary distraction, but sooner or later it collapses in on itself. The heart knows better.

A HEART RIPPED OPEN

In spite of the terror and sorrow, guilt and shame, numbness and rage, a substantial number of survivors emerge from their PTSD experience with a greater ability to feel deeply, experience joy, savor the preciousness of life, and appreciate beauty in a way they never did before. Many are able to empathize with a depth of compassion that wasn't accessible to them previously. In hindsight, they often report that intuitive and creative abilities seemed to open up for them at around this time. They begin writing or sculpting or expressing themselves differently. Many change careers and choose work more congruent with their heart's desire or their newly revealed softness. And many feel a connection with a spiritual side, a sense of meaning, purpose, and grace that they didn't know existed.

The "tough" environmental scientist from Ground Zero in Lower Manhattan writes:

> All of my life I have been shutting down because it is a defense mechanism. I have always known I had good intuitive wiring, but have felt rather foolish discussing or acknowledging it.
>
> When you said trauma can rip your heart open, what a perfect description. Even though my life has been a terrifying one since 9/11, the ability to open up to so much that I have denied is a wonderful gift.

Former police captain Michael Risenhoover says:

> Before the Oklahoma City bombing, I was married, successful, and had a family. I had a nice home and cars and a wonderful job. Now I am alone in a one-bedroom apartment on the West Coast, with very little furniture and not much money. But I am filled with happiness when I see a hummingbird at my feeder. I feel joy in my heart when I see flowers and beautiful sunsets and children laughing and playing. I love my sons, and I enjoy talking to my ex-wife and parents on the telephone. I am happy and full of love. The trauma I endured took my sense of identity, shattered who I was at the time, but in reality, it helped me find my true self—the child inside me, who loves and laughs and likes to play.

I remember the first time I realized Frannie would be all right. She had gone off on her first vacation ever, somewhere on the West Coast to watch birds and explore new terrain, fully festooned with camera, binoculars, and writing journal. For her, vacationing was a radical act, and I wondered how it would go. After a week I got a wonderfully manic postcard from her that read:

You would not believe these sunsets! I had no idea the colors of the sun, dropping into the ocean, could be so incredible! If I could, I'd drive right into them!

Childhood abuse survivor and counselor Lynne Newman writes:

My healing has been deep and profound, and my life is full and rich. I am able to feel deeply, joy and love and compassion, and my heart is open. I feel blessed beyond belief.

One of her poems reflects her journey and how far she has come:

JOURNEY HOME

I've journeyed far upon this earth,
What places I have been.
I've traveled down this earthly road,
Time and time again.

Crossed deserts, barren, without hope,
Through quicksand, hot with shame,
Traveled into caves of fear,
Through hatred's burning flame.

Climbed up karmic mountains,
Felt rage's lava flow,
Crawled into caves of solitude,
With nowhere else to go.

Swam in silver pools,
Where ripples touched my soul,
And voices of my spirit, cried,
"I long to make you whole."

Put down age-old burdens,
Stood on mountain high,

Heart open, vulnerable,
My spirit dared to fly.

Journey's now on different course,
Divinely led, by Grace,
Spirit dancing joyfully,
Warm sunlight on my face.

Ah, journey, how I thank you,
For my soul has always known,
That the traveling would one day bring,
The joy of coming Home.

Lynne Newman

8 THE BEHAVIORAL EFFECTS OF TRAUMA

Linda was a client of mine—a tall, big-boned, appealing, good-natured woman, now fifty-one years old, with a ready, booming laugh and easy, gentle ways, who suffered for years with severe PTSD symptoms. For decades she displayed a classic behavior pattern that is common to post-traumatic stress: elaborate avoidance of many activities, substance abuse, compulsive eating, phobias, isolation, repetitive involvement in exploitative relationships, a tendency to court disaster and sell herself short, self-mutilating impulses, a willingness to let others push her around, impulsivity, and constant eruptions of interpersonal conflict in an ever-narrowing social sphere. These patterns erupted in earnest when she left home for college, presumably to begin her life as an independent young adult.

Linda had been a beautiful child who, for most of her childhood, from the time she was a preschooler up through her adolescence, was routinely molested by a wealthy bachelor uncle and some of his cronies.

Her family had provided tacit permission for the abuse by ignoring the obvious and repeatedly putting her in harm's way. Linda, in her heart of hearts, had apprehended an ugly subliminal truth: that her family hoped for a substantial inheritance from this uncle, and Linda, the golden child with whom he was obsessed, was their ticket to a better future. So, in addition to the indignity, terror, pain, and creepiness of the abuse itself, betrayal by her beloved parents, along with her weirdly elevated status as the family redeemer, figured prominently in her psyche.

For years the adult Linda was buffeted mightily by her symptoms, but she ultimately emerged triumphant, conquering her phobias, rediscovering her self-esteem, and reclaiming her life. She is now a much-loved and respected floor supervisor at a nursing home and is slowly but surely getting her nursing degree, a lifelong dream. It is a testament to her huge heart that she feels genuine forgiveness for her hapless, remorseful parents and compassion for this now-deceased uncle. But it was a long, hard road getting to this point.

THE SYMPTOMS SURFACE

Things started to fall apart for Linda when she left home for college, where she quickly fell into a pattern of drinking every night and sleeping for large portions of the day. She engaged in a lot of casual sex, at the same time feeling very guilty and growing more and more fearful of getting pregnant or catching a sexually transmitted disease. After a few months she stopped going to classes entirely, and after a year and a half she finally flunked out.

She moved back home and got a sales job but described herself as "an emotional wreck" without knowing why. She was terrified of even very small things, afraid to walk across the hall to a co-worker's desk or go to the cafeteria for lunch.

She was also getting urges to cut herself with her letter opener, or to scratch her arms with her nails during sales meetings. This whole new set of urges and symptoms made her fear for her sanity.

In the evenings she anesthetized her rampant anxiety with a lot of beer-drinking, random sex, and unwholesome company. In her own words, she was hanging out with "nasty men, abusers and lowlifes" who used her and disrespected her. After years of this pattern, one of her "boyfriends" hurt her physically. She ended that relationship and decided to avoid sexual relationships with men altogether.

Meanwhile, the years of drinking and overindulging in food had caused her to put on an enormous amount of unhealthy weight. In her high school golden girl days she had been five foot ten and 135 pounds and had dazzled the boys with her long red hair, big blue eyes, huge fringey lashes, and all-round drop-dead-gorgeous looks. Since then she had blown up to a dangerous 325 pounds. She was having trouble walking, everything ached, and she had acquired functional diabetes.

She decided to have gastric bypass surgery, which to date has resulted in a loss of a hundred pounds and the rout of her diabetes. But even at her heaviest, when she would dress in her sloppiest clothes and make herself as unattractive as possible, there were always men who were interested in her. She just had something about her that drew them to her.

Now, with the weight loss, she is a little frightened of attracting serious romantic attention again, but she experiments with makeup and clothes nonetheless.

Her career history followed a similar trajectory. At one point, when she was in her late twenties, she had tried to go back to school. She had always wanted to be a nurse. Even her odd jobs were as a nurses' aide, a hospital transportation orderly, a private duty companion to the elderly and the like. She was a naturally good-hearted, gentle caretaker of the frail and the vulnerable, and people felt safe with her.

She registered for an anatomy class at a Catholic women's college, because she felt safe with the nuns and they always seemed to like and appreciate her, too. But her panic attacks in class caused her to miss a lot of school. Eventually, in spite of all the support from the sisters, she felt she had to drop out.

She went to see the family doctor, a general practitioner, who over-medicated her. (This is not uncommon. The alarming symptoms of PTSD make for some wildly wrong-headed diagnoses and prescriptions from nonpsychiatric providers who simply don't know any better.) He put her on a host of inappropriate drugs, some of them addictive, which may have muffled her anxiety somewhat but that also had her stumbling around, zombielike, foggy-brained, and barely functional.

It was when she was in this stuporous state that she came to see me for therapy. I couldn't tell what was the medication and what was Linda, so I asked her to bring in every pill bottle she was using. I was stunned by the cache of pharmaceuticals she showed me, and after the first order of business—telling her I didn't think she was crazy—the second was getting her to a competent psychiatrist who could wean her off those meds, especially the addictive tranquilizers.

Her withdrawal was brutal, but Linda, who had taken heart from the idea that she wasn't crazy, showed her considerable mettle and toughed it out. As the effects of the drugs wore away, her brains, humor, resilience, and big-heartedness came more and more to the fore. With a little coaching, she began questioning her poor self-assessments, her passive compliance with bad ideas, and started making better decisions for herself.

Later on she was given Paxil for her panic attacks, and that, she feels, changed her life. She has not had a full-blown panic attack since. Over the years that followed, she was able to process and integrate all the compartmentalized traumatic memories, as ugly as they were, and understand and master her symptoms. She's justifiably proud of herself and pleased with her life these days.

Linda experienced most of the behavioral complications of PTSD—she was a textbook case, if ever there was one. She was so overwhelmed by panic that she spent a great deal of time and energy avoiding things, to the point that the parameters of her life became extremely limited. She anesthetized herself with addictive substances and overeating and engaged in destructive relationships that repeated the patterns of abuse she'd experienced in her family. She passively went along with what others told her to do, automatically trading in her own needs for theirs.

If we were to identify the most typical behavioral responses to post-traumatic stress, they would be the ones that follow.

AVOIDANCE AND ISOLATION

One of the most commonplace and problematic behaviors connected with having post-traumatic stress is the need to avoid apparently "normal" activities, because they carry the potential for provoking anxiety, panic, or other overwhelming feelings. Survivors go to elaborate lengths to side-step all sorts of apparently neutral but anxiety-producing situations, often at enormous inconvenience and resulting in many lost opportunities.

Along with their avoidance, people with PTSD usually feel intense shame about being afraid to do everyday, "normal" things and take great care to conceal the avoidant behavior from others—even from close family members and co-workers. Jane isn't phobic about highway driving; she simply prefers the beauty of the more scenic route. Timmy isn't school-phobic; his tummy hurts. An author on a book tour won't fly to the cities his publicist has booked, because he has philosophical issues about the nature of air travel. The need for elaborate ruses and defensive duplicity adds to the survivor's strain, burden, and isolation. After all, inauthenticity is, as we all know, a fatiguing and lonely business.

Sometimes the avoidance is very narrow and specific, and the person is dodging only one specific reminder of the original traumatic situation. For instance, the woman we met in Chapter 1 who suffered a severe motor vehicle accident while driving in a funeral procession, refused to be the driver at subsequent funerals for several years—not a serious interference with daily living. But it would not have been uncommon for her fear to blossom into a more far-reaching phobia about driving anywhere.

A substantial number of survivors, such as Linda, fear going just about anywhere—a condition known as agoraphobia. A certain proportion of rape, assault, incest, and combat survivors will become partial prisoners in their own homes for a period of time, then will tether themselves to an unnaturally rigid schedule for weeks, months, and even years afterward, never making the connection to the traumatic event.

Michael Risenhoover, the El Reno police captain who was involved in responding to the Oklahoma City bombing, writes:

> At some point I started isolating myself, hiding in my home
> and not wanting to be around people, especially people I knew
> either as victims or suspects, and in the small town where I
> lived, almost everyone I knew was either a victim or a suspect
> or both. As far as avoiding places, I have been to the Oklahoma
> City Bombing Memorial twice, once with my therapist and
> once by myself. That was very hard for me to do, and now, by
> living in California, I am probably avoiding the whole state of
> Oklahoma . . . Even nowadays, here in California, when I
> am around people I am very quiet, and I don't make friends
> easily.

For weeks I sat in on a Transcend Vietnam group, a highly effective PTSD recovery program at the Louis B. Stokes VA Medical Center in Brecksville, Ohio. I was working on developing some effective imagery for post-traumatic stress. One of the inpatient vets decided he wanted to visit an uncle who had been hospitalized with terminal cancer at the

Cleveland Clinic, several miles away. He wanted to leave immediately following the group meeting so he could be back in time for evening group.

This man was a jaunty, popular member of the Transcend group, a capable fellow with fine social and comedic skills. He was also smart and competent, and unlike some of the men in the group, he was holding down a job that would be waiting for him when he completed the program. But his nonverbal behavior made it obvious that this business of a hospital visit was a scary and daunting challenge for him. At the time I wasn't sure why—it didn't add up, given this man's outgoing personality. But I could see it was so.

The staff signed his permission slip and gave him directions. He was told he would need to take two different buses to get into town. He became sufficiently agitated that he had trouble following the instructions. The staff person repeated them and then wrote them down for him on a card, but his composure was going from bad to worse, and he wasn't getting the rather simple instructions. Because I was going that way anyway, I ran down the hall, got permission from the floor nurse, and asked him if he wanted a lift. The relief on his face was heartbreaking.

We joked and laughed all the way up to Cleveland. He told stories and happily extolled the seat-heater that was warming his bottom. He gleefully announced that he couldn't wait to tell his best friend and rival in the group that he'd had a date with me. But as we approached the hospital, he got very quiet and appeared to shrink in his seat. I remembered that he'd been a medic in Vietnam, and many of his traumatic experiences had to do with the wounded men he couldn't crawl over to in time, or those he managed to reach but couldn't save.

As a neutral way of getting him to start talking, I asked if he was worried he wouldn't be able to find the right floor. He said yes, then confessed that he was also worried about whether his uncle would be glad to see him. He was scared he wouldn't know what to say to him. Mostly, though, he seemed to be overwhelmed with a generalized panic and the feeling that he didn't have the *right* to be there, like the "normal" people, in that hospital. Nonetheless, he was valiantly determined to visit this uncle, pay his last respects, and say good-bye.

We wound up going up to the room together (more relief), and I stayed only long enough to see the joy on his uncle's face and on his, at the sight of each other. I drove home puzzling over how *hard* everything was for this man—even this act of kindness. At the time I didn't know that this simply came with the territory of PTSD. Avoidance is at the heart of many problematic behaviors.

Another survivor of sadistic childhood abuse writes:

> For several years I was terrified of going to the dentist, the car wash, or anywhere that was confining. I would procrastinate until it was absolutely necessary. The only way I could get through the car wash was to blast the air conditioner on my face, or else dissociate to somewhere better. In the movies and in airplanes, I had to sit on the outside, aisle seat. I actually still try to do that.
>
> I was afraid of "authority figures" of any kind and avoided dealing with them whenever possible. I was even terrified to go to parent-teacher conferences for my children but made myself do it anyway, of course. God forbid anyone should see the fear! It took great effort, and I would be completely exhausted afterward. Nobody ever knew how much work it was to just *not* stay home and hide!

Frannie was ingenious at camouflaging all the situations she avoided while running a large organization and supervising a substantial staff:

> At work, I would intentionally schedule things that would keep me in the background and bring others forward. For instance, I would get around being the speaker at a public meeting, even when I was the logical choice. Or at the last minute I would cancel a speaking engagement that I hadn't been able to hand off to someone else.
>
> Even though I was philosophically opposed to it, I would work with my door closed, because I was afraid someone might walk by or drop in while I was having a flashback. I was very paranoid about that, and I *never* wanted anyone to find out about them. So I avoided spontaneous conversations and hanging out with my staff.

This extended to other aspects of her life as well. She avoided taking vacations, engaging in hobbies, or going out for fun—anything that was not strictly necessary.

> Really, the extreme isolation . . . not going anywhere, not taking vacations, holing up in the house for several years . . . all of that was the way I dealt with experiencing massive amounts of terrifying visual, auditory, and kinesthetic flashbacks.

Even in her interactions with friends, she avoided sharing too much of herself. Intimacy was not an option. During the worst years of her symptoms, she stayed in touch with her oldest and most trusted friends by voice mail only.

> Relationships were and are [even now], for the most part, a matter of me listening to friends and loved ones, but not sharing with them. In recent years a few people I'm close to are now aware that I had PTSD . . . The fear of people stayed with me for a long, long time. The habit of listening and not speaking is a residual, I suppose. I'm still warier than most people when meeting people in new situations.

DISRUPTED RELATIONSHIPS— OVERCONTROL, AVOIDANCE OF INTIMACY

Often survivors of trauma experience a painful pattern of impaired or disrupted relationships with those they care about most. While their symptoms are active, people with PTSD will tend either to overreact and scare people with their intensity, or else to shut down and numb out. For periods of time they have trouble sharing their feelings, expressing their needs, controlling their tempers, and modulating their moods. They are torn between needing closeness and fearing contact.

People with PTSD can become quite secretive and opaque, going to great lengths to avoid any feelingful connection, because feelings of any sort are so overwhelming and painful. For this reason, they sometimes avoid sex, too, for fear of the intensity of feelings it can provoke. Or paradoxically, they may use sex as a compulsive activity, to keep feelings or random anxiety at bay.

The behavior can be quite baffling, even to the survivors themselves, and inadvertently hurtful to those who love them. Generous amounts of patience and understanding are required, usually for an extended amount of time. Some relationships don't withstand the taxing demands of these difficult periods.

Michael Risenhoover again:

> When I first started experiencing the effects of trauma and PTSD, I had no idea what the problem was. I was married, but I became very distant from my wife. For her, it was probably like living with a shadow. I have a hard time remembering exactly what I was doing at that time, but I remember crying a lot by myself and not sharing any of my feelings.
>
> I remember one time going to an awards ceremony for a man who lived in the same town as me, an Oklahoma City police officer who was injured in the bombing. For some reason I told my wife that I had to work that night. I didn't tell her about the ceremony. I didn't want her to come, and I don't know why—I don't know what I was thinking. The man committed suicide not long after that ceremony. My wife got mad at me for not telling her the truth. I still don't know why I did that.

Michael looked up his psychological tests from when he first entered the force, to get a neutral assessment of what he was like before the bombing. He wasn't sure he could trust his own memories, but he thought he'd been a fairly affable, sociable person:

> I know I did socialize with friends on the job, and with my wife, and with my family as a whole. We went camping, and it was a weekly event for me and my youngest son to go fishing. So I think my social life was pretty normal before. I remember having a lot of good times with my wife. I really have a hard time remembering things about my friends or family after the bombing. It makes me sad to think about it . . .

Anyway, I was reading the results of the psychological exam that I took when I was first hired as an officer. It says, "People who score similar to Mr. Risenhoover are healthy, happy, and psychologically well adjusted. They appear friendly and get along well with family, peers, and supervisors. They are socially adjusted and lead active, normal social lives." So I would say I was pretty normal before the bombing and everything else. Seems like a long time ago.

Another uniformed officer, a firefighter from Ground Zero, described his behavior this way:

I needed to be treated gently, but I treated my family roughly. I was grief-stricken, but I stormed around and yelled a lot. I was terrified, but I complained, blamed, and attacked. Instead of crying to my wife, I drank by myself. Finally, she had enough and told me I could see a therapist or she was leaving with the kids. That's when I got some help for myself—when she threatened to walk out the door.

Vietnam combat veteran Michael Norman tells a similar tale:

Unsettled and irritable, I behaved badly. I sought solitude, then slandered friends for keeping away . . . I barked at a son who revered me and bickered with my best ally, my wife.[1]

Difficulties with colleagues in the work setting are commonplace, too. Survivors will ruefully describe themselves as being difficult on their jobs, their irritability, sensitivity, and reactivity creating problems for themselves and for those around them.

A young woman named Dawn, who suffered from post-traumatic stress from an abusive relationship in her past, ruefully describes her behavior this way:

At one point in my recovery process, before I got help, the main behavioral manifestations were intense anger, verbally attacking others without real cause, and then beating myself up. I found

myself almost constantly angry with my co-worker. Little
things that normally would not bother me would set me off. I
would yell at her, then turn on myself. I would beat myself up
and feel terrible about who I was and how I had treated her. I
felt like I was unfit to be part of the human race.

I have since taken personal responsibility for any emotional
injury that I caused this co-worker. I have apologized to her a
few times. Fortunately, she had worked with victims of abuse
before. She recognized what was going on and suggested that I
find some help, which I did.

In their extreme vulnerability, survivors can project their skinlessness
onto others, becoming overprotective and controlling of those they love
most. Many Holocaust parents were found to be notoriously confining of
their children. Parents who were abused as children can become extremely anxious for their own children as they approach the age at which
their own victimization occurred. They might oppress the child with extreme hovering; lay down inappropriately rigid house rules; display a
harsh, punitive kind of strictness; or forbid them from normal activities
such as sleepovers, car pools, play dates, and the like.

Far less likely is the commonly overstated risk of survivors becoming
abusers themselves, as a result of unconscious identification with the perpetrator or because of the very real attachment they developed in childhood for the person who molested them. This outcome is by no means a
foregone conclusion, let alone commonplace. The idea of a "generational
cycle of abuse," much touted in the popular media, is not substantiated
either in the research literature or in clinical experience.[2]

It is true that most people who are perpetrators of abuse were themselves abused as children. But the converse is not true. *The great majority of
people who were abused as children do not become perpetrators.* The vast majority carry their scars in different ways, feeling depressed and empty, perhaps, or finding themselves in relationships that are not nourishing to
them.[3] But they do not become violent.[4] For the most part, these survivors
of childhood abuse go to great lengths to deliver a kind of loving and protective care to their children that they never got from their own parents.[5]

Even the child abuse research literature, consisting primarily of data
collected from the more visibly dysfunctional families that come to the

attention of protective services and the courts, reports that two-thirds of abused children do not become abusive themselves.[6] Further, this percentage doesn't take into account the myriad parents whose abuse never comes to the attention of the authorities, and whose children go on to heroically parent their own children with great care, even while they are silently grieving for their own ravaged childhood. My practice was filled with these mothers and fathers, as were most of my colleagues'.

REENACTMENTS AND FLIRTING WITH DISASTER

It is not at all unusual for a survivor of childhood incest to be raped and assaulted multiple times as an adult. A traumatized combat vet, back in the States, might well find himself in one homicidal barroom brawl after another. A person with an acute stress reaction from a motor vehicle accident might go on to have five or six more minor collisions in the space of a year. Someone who was repeatedly beaten by his father might be drawn to physically abusive sexual partners who assault him in much the same way. Throughout the clinical histories of a goodly number of trauma survivors is a puzzling tendency to replay the essence of the trauma in subsequent life scenarios. They seem to have an unconscious attraction to danger or punishment, an unwitting willingness to court disaster and put body and soul at further risk.

These reenactments have about them a feeling of involuntariness, a compulsive, driven quality. Survivors rarely seek them out consciously, nor do they welcome them into their lives; they just seem to wind up there.

Emily, a survivor of sadistic childhood abuse from a psychotic mother, reflects on the period of years when she seemed to find nothing but abuse, no matter where she turned:

> Oh, yes! I had one "abusive" boss after another. I was triggered constantly and felt like the consummate "victim" with a sign on her back that said "Abuse me!" I'd returned to work after having been a stay-at-home mother for ten years, and was working as a secretary/typist—the low woman on the totem pole in each situation. I couldn't believe that each time I changed jobs, I got

another "mother"! I lived in terror, perpetuating the adrenaline rush of flashbacks, fear, etc.

I also had friends who were very angry people—what a mirror to look in! One woman who was quite disturbed would randomly start screaming at me, even when we were out to dinner. One day, after having done a lot of work on myself, I finally said, "You're being abusive, Rebecca," and I walked out of the restaurant. Hooray! I don't have this kind of friend anymore, and I know I can make choices at any time to leave what doesn't feel healthy. Celebration!

Last July I knew I could quit my probation counselor job. Part of my decision was that I knew I'd finally come full circle—my boss was a wonderful woman, and we had a great working relationship! That cycle, that karma of being "abused" by people in power, was finally finished. What a healing!

Former police captain Michael Risenhoover talks about the dramatic emergence of some uncharacteristic risk-taking behavior of his after his traumatization from the Oklahoma City bombing:

After my wife left, I starting drinking quite a bit and coupled that with some very self destructive behavior . . . I did dangerous things at work, like entering a house that was supposed to be booby-trapped or chasing a violent armed robber without a radio, or single-handedly taking a knife away from a person saying he was going to commit suicide.

If those were the only incidents, someone might say I was just being brave. But I also remember being off-duty and riding my motorcycle 100 mph and then letting go of the handlebars, or playing cowboy poker[7] at a rodeo and winning.

Even out here in California I have been in a fistfight at a bar, which seemed so out of character for me, but it felt good, and that kind of scares me.

It is a mistake to adopt a judgmental attitude toward this puzzling reenactment behavior, as the forces that drive it are neither deliberate nor conscious. Nor is a strictly psychological interpretation accurate: this may look like suicidal behavior, or an attempt to master a distressing memory by dramatizing it with a new, improved ending, but generally this is not the best explanation.

Instead, biophysical evidence suggests that this self-destructive, danger-courting, reenactment behavior is first and foremost a matter of unconscious neurophysiological conditioning, rooted in the biochemistry of the traumatized brain. People are unknowingly addicted to their own biochemicals and are thus *provoking doses of their own stress neurohormones*.

Remember that the central nervous system of a person suffering from PTSD is patterned to shuttle back and forth between massive jolts of adrenaline and equally intense infusions of endorphins. Both endogenous drugs are addictive, but the opioids make for an especially compelling pot of gold at the end of the hyperarousal rainbow. This is the built-in, self-perpetuating reward system for getting worked up into survival mode. Beneath conscious awareness, the person's behavior is being subtly, incrementally propelled by addictive drugs. In effect, the repeated courting, provoking, reenacting, or tripping over danger is driven by the same dynamic that supports chemical dependency, only instead of a synthetic morphine derivative, the brain's natural endorphins are the addictive substances.

We see this when children who are abused by their caregivers experience increased levels of endorphins as part of the traumatization-and-freeze response and thus stay biochemically bonded to their tormentor and attached to their abuse cycle.

It is also dramatically apparent in adults caught in domestic violence situations, with the repetitive pattern of subjugation and abuse followed by passionate reconciliation, a sequence that is also infused, first with adrenaline, and then with endorphins.

We also see it in the "Stockholm syndrome"—the intense bonding that hostages, kidnap victims, and cult members experience with their captors.[8]

Elsie writes:

> I went from a dysfunctional relationship with my alcoholic, emotionally abusive, controlling, irresponsible mother to my marriage to an emotionally abusive, controlling, irresponsible husband. And I wound up with controlling, abusive friends, too.

> That is, until I [became conscious of what I was doing to myself and] decided I didn't want that anymore.

For people caught up in this cycle, the act of consciously deciding to break it is a powerful act of will, requiring motivation, commitment, and strength, because it is, in fact, the same challenge as turning away from an addiction. Elsie intuitively knew to substitute one endorphin high for the other, and she used meditation, imagery, and exercise to ease the "withdrawal" from abuse.

Emily suffered repeated abuse in her childhood from a psychotic mother, incestuous father, and other sadistic adults in her family system, then suffered assaults outside the home as well. It is important to note that, aside from the biochemical patterning that might unconsciously support the assaults on Emily outside the home, another powerful factor is at play here: a typical survivor of chronic sadistic abuse is conditioned to her own victimhood and unknowingly broadcasts herself as "prey" with her body language. A dissociated survivor is more likely to look vulnerable and "attackable" by virtue of her walk, her gestures, the way she holds her head, moves her limbs, and even speaks and expresses herself. A certain degree of disembodied passivity and spacey compliance immediately signals to a predator—well attuned to such cues—that she is an easy mark. This is by no means "blaming the victim." It is simply a piece of the pattern, a compounding of misfortune that the survivor faces. Incest survivors like Emily have a dramatically increased likelihood for future victimization. A high percentage of incest survivors are subject to subsequent rapes, assaults, and domestic violence.

One common variation on reenactment behavior is something called the *anniversary reprise,* when, without any conscious awareness, a survivor marks a traumatic anniversary date with dangerous risk-taking behavior or some other form of self-destructive replay. Psychiatrist Bessel van der Kolk describes a patient traumatized in Vietnam during a night patrol in 1968, when he struck a match to light his cigarette, instantly resulting in his best friend's getting killed by enemy sniper fire.[9] After his return to the United States, this man unwittingly engaged in the same annual ritual each year, from 1969 up until 1986. At the exact day, hour, and minute that his friend was shot, he would attempt to rob a store, using his finger in his coat pocket as his "gun." Presumably the police officer or the person behind the counter was supposed to kill him and even the score, but some-how that never happened. Amazingly, he had no conscious awareness of the annual nature of this event, nor of the anniversary date, nor of the connection with his friend's death, until he finally got some help in therapy in 1986.

SUBSTANCE ABUSE AND ADDICTIVE BEHAVIOR

It is no surprise that traumatized people, who involuntarily trance out through dissociation during flashbacks and intrusive memories, run a high risk of developing dependence on alcohol, drugs, food, and other substances in their attempts to regulate or obliterate overwhelming feelings.

Initially, attempts at self-medication through alcohol, drugs, or food can bring relief and alleviate noxious symptoms. But sooner or later they compound the difficulties, exacerbating discomfort, increasing alienation, and promoting greater dysfunction. On top of that, the need for eventual sobriety and withdrawal ensure that the original hellish symptoms will get even worse.

Research shows that at least 75 percent of returning Vietnam veterans with PTSD went on to develop problems with drugs or alcohol.[10] Similarly, people with histories of sexual abuse are known to be highly prone to the overuse of drugs to modulate their feelings. People have a tendency to abuse both prescription drugs and illegal substances, depending on lifestyle and access.

Various illicit drugs are favored for their differential effects. For instance, heroin is turned to for its potent ability to mute feelings of rage and aggression. Cocaine is generally preferred for its jolting, antidepressant impact. And alcohol functions, at least initially, as a short-term antidote for sleep disturbances, nightmares, and other intrusive symptoms.

Continued using, however, tends to make things worse, producing an ugly rebound effect. People find their symptoms reemerge with fresh vengeance. Nonetheless, the initial impulse is to self-medicate, and in the beginning it often seems to help. This seductive promise of anesthesia that successfully obviates pain keeps the downward cycle going.

Frannie wrote to me:

I used lots of alcohol to try to escape the flashbacks when I had no other means to deal with them. This was before I learned to take advantage of imagery, breathing, and meditation. I figured if I could drink myself into a cloudy stupor, they would subside . . .

What I remember is drinking to kill the pain. This was during the time I was just beginning to realize what was real, and starting to face what had been done to me, and it was more than I could bear. It was coming out in fragmented flashbacks, over time. But I couldn't put it into words. I wanted so much to put it into words. But it was like having it always be there with no way to get it out.

I remember sitting in your office, with active flashbacks, and you asking me to tell you what I was experiencing. I could not formulate a word or a sentence to describe it. I used writing to try to get successive approximations of it, and the stuff kept coming into my awareness.

The frustration and pain are what led me to the drinking.

Sometimes the addictions of trauma survivors are interchangeable. They can take the form of compulsive eating, anorexia, or bulimia, accompanied by dramatic gains and losses in weight. They can also show up as compulsive sexual activity, which has nothing to do with liking or needing sex per se. Instead, these driven behaviors are about trying to get some sense of control over wildly dysregulated feelings, and a biochemistry that has run amok.

Linda says:

In college I drank every night. The habit stuck, and after I left college I continued to drink . . . mostly beer . . . I think so I could become oblivious or at least oblivious enough to be promiscuous and self-destructive.

I also ate compulsively, whenever I was anxious or panicky, which was a lot of the time. I carried food with me at all times, the way some people carry Valium—I had food in my car, in my desk drawers, in my pockets. Then later on, of course, I became addicted to Valium, too.

Elsie writes about her compulsive eating, followed by equally compulsive self-recrimination:

> When the pain was intense I would eat, usually bread, sweets, or chocolate. This calmed me down for a while, but then I would feel so guilty for having done this that I would eat more and more. Then I would blame myself for being such a horrible person who couldn't stick to a diet. This started the whole self-loathing, condemnation cycle. Then I would just eat so much that I would fall asleep.
>
> Food became the way I tried to control my pain. I was focused on all the rituals of food and diets. I thought if I could just solve the eating problem, everything would be fine. This "control" diverted me from the real problem—being unable to process my thoughts, feelings, and bodily sensations. I played countless mind games with food: eating this, not eating that, eating at certain times, exercising too much, exercising not enough, eating only certain kinds of foods with other kinds. It was insanity, because it was always focusing on something outside of myself.
>
> I would do well for a little while and be proud of myself. I would be calm for a while, and I thought I was doing well. Then an emotional trigger happened. I would get agitated very quickly and start all over again, with the trigger, food, binge, control, self-loathing, fear cycle.

Indeed, eating disorders—anorexia and bulimia—are found in high percentages among trauma survivors. Clinicians have always noted this, but now reliable studies are available.[11] The compulsive aspects of the condition, the dysregulated ups and downs, and the shame and self-disgust involved, all fit right into the pattern of PTSD behavior.

SELF-MUTILATION AND REPETITIVE SELF-INJURY

Compulsive self-injury is described by psychiatrist Judith Herman as one of the more spectacularly dysfunctional self-soothing mechanisms in trauma survivors with PTSD. Like compulsive risk-taking, and self-medicating with alcohol, drugs, food, and sex, it is the psyche's attempt to regulate emotional states.

Often mistaken for an attempt at suicide, self-mutilation in fact has little to do with wanting to end one's own life. Like reenactment behavior, repetitive self-injury is not motivated by a desire to kill oneself. A small proportion of people with PTSD do have periods of feeling suicidal or attempting suicide, but that may have more to do with the depression that often accompanies PTSD than with the PTSD itself.

Nor is self-mutilation a cry for help or an attempt to manipulate others, as many people suppose. On the contrary, compulsive cutting, scratching, burning with matches or lit cigarettes, hair-pulling, and other forms of self-injury constitute an attempt at relief. It is more accurately seen as a paradoxical form of self-preservation.[12]

Typically the self-mutilation is preceded by a profoundly dissociated, anesthetized state, along with unbearable agitation and a compulsion to attack the body. Usually the initial injuries produce little or no pain, and the behavior continues until there is a powerful feeling of calm and relief. Many people say they do it to demonstrate to themselves that they exist, or to feel alive and aware of themselves again. Like so many other trauma behaviors, this one is accompanied by massive doses of shame. People wear long sleeves and don elaborately constructed outfits to cover their scars, which they find disgusting and disgraceful.

Heloise writes:

> I was diagnosed with PTSD and borderline personality disorder about ten years ago. I have been in therapy with a psychiatric nurse and psychiatrist since then. I feel that I have reached a point where I am virtually recovered (except in times of extreme stress). I had several hospitalizations over the first five years, due to an inability to cope with the reality of both my present life and the effects of flashbacks, plus the reactions to my original traumas.
>
> I spent many years in a self-destructive mode where I was very self-abusive, including severe cutting and burning with cigarettes. My body is covered with scars, and the last several episodes were so severe that they should have had stitches

except that I was afraid to go to the doctor until it was too late . . . I have not self-abused with blades or pills for almost four years now, and although I do have an urge to cut on occasion, I have learned to find other ways to comfort myself and divert my destructive desires. I use meditation, relaxation, and distraction methods, and they definitely work for me.

According to Judith Herman, survivors resort to self-mutilation when they become so deeply dissociated that they feel utterly disconnected from themselves and others. Ordinary methods of self-soothing don't work to interrupt the feeling of having been dissolved into nothingness, and nothing short of a major jolt to the system is required. It is most often seen in survivors of early childhood abuse.

IMPAIRED VOLITION AND LEARNED HELPLESSNESS

People with post-traumatic stress in general and traumatized survivors of childhood abuse in particular tend to behave in ways that reflect their feeling that their lives are run by forces beyond their control. After all, the central insult of trauma is the sense of powerlessness that overwhelms those it visits. By definition, action is pointless and resistance futile. This is when the freeze imperative takes over, and people dissolve into a state of dissociated surrender. As one patient put it, "I feel like a leaf, blown about by the wind."

This *learned helplessness* informs subsequent behavior. As survivors dissociate more and more with their kindled cycle of symptoms, they become more and more recognizable as "victims" and are all too easy to push around, direct, and commandeer. In this way they can easily be re-victimized by bosses, teachers, pastors, spouses, physicians, therapists, friends, co-workers—indeed, any authority or bully that crosses their path.

Dawn describes such a scenario with her boss, where she became more and more passive and nonreactive:

Part of my job was to report to a supervisor who resembled one of the people who had abused me. The problems arose when he would ask me to do things I didn't think would work with some

of the people we were trying to help. I expressed my
reservations to him, but he wouldn't listen. He kept pushing and
pushing, until I said I would do things his way. I just went along.
I wasn't assertive enough at the time to say no . . . well, okay, I
didn't even really *know* I could say no. I didn't recognize that
he didn't have to be right. I just decided that I was wrong . . .
As a result of the pressure that he exerted, I began to feel like
a little girl again, pushed into a corner and not allowed to refuse.

In another commonly seen scenario with PTSD, an educated, sophisticated professional—a high-powered attorney and human rights activist—who was suffering from PTSD after the 9/11 attack on the World Trade Center, became uncharacteristically passive and allowed an inept physician to overmedicate her to a shocking extent:

I was overmedicated after 9/11. I was in a fog, was a mess, and
trusted in the medical system to decide what was best for me.
I kept telling the doctor how very sick I was from the
antidepressant medication I was taking. I was dizzy and passed
out seven times on the streets and sidewalks of Manhattan.
   He told me I was just upset, and if I took higher doses, I
would feel better. He also said to just sit down when I felt I was
going to pass out, which was not practical advice since it would
come out of the blue and I had no idea when it would happen.
I would just be walking on the sidewalk, and I would lose
consciousness. As soon as I hit the pavement, I would come to.
What was happening was my blood pressure was going crazy—
it would drop rapidly and suddenly there was no oxygen to the
brain. When I hit the pavement, I would instantly come to
because oxygen was again getting to the brain.
   Because I was so afraid and so confused and in the hands of
an arrogant psychiatrist, the situation continued. I finally landed
in the emergency room of NYU Hospital with a team of kind
docs who wanted to understand why I kept passing out. Bottom
line was I was overmedicated. I knew this myself. I was saying
this to him and to others. But not effectively. Not with any kind

of power. I just couldn't speak for myself. It was bizarre, given my track record as a proactive, warrior-woman-type lawyer.

In another all-too-common situation, a survivor of childhood incest describes the abuse she received as a devout teenager at the hands of a priest who was her spiritual director. It was typical of her unquestioning, absolute obedience to this predator that years after their relationship ended, she was still taking the birth control pills he had commanded her to get, in spite of the fact that she had been away from him and leading a celibate life for years. In this case, her trauma-based passivity was compounded by her belief that this man represented the word of God. Here is her painful account of his incremental predations and her responses to them:

He became my spiritual director and I did all I could to follow this path he talked about, reading Reginald Garrigou-LaGrange's treatise on ascetical and mystical theology, reading and rereading Saint John of the Cross and Saint Teresa of Àvila, and continuing to spend all my free time in contemplative prayer.

Then things changed. He started to introduce psychology into the mix, explaining that we have to be psychologically whole to have a deep spiritual life. He talked about, and we then read, Karen Horney and Sigmund Freud. Spiritual direction began to be psychological counseling.

Then he moved to sexual contact. One day he said, "I think we need to spend a whole night together." My mind flew to the saints who would talk and pray together all night. This was an opportunity to make great psychological and spiritual progress with this holy person. I so wanted to love God with all my being and to get rid of anything that stood in the way.

He set a time and picked me up to take me somewhere where we would be undisturbed. We got to a vacant convent and went in. He took me to a room and said to take off my clothes and he would be right back. His words were cold and direct. I was stunned. What was going on? Frightened, I did as

I was told. When he came back into the room, he had no clothes on. I couldn't believe what was going on. Was this a dream? He tried to enter me. Apparently, in my terror, I had vaginismus, though I did not know the term then. We left shortly afterward, and still I could not understand what was happening.

No words were spoken on the ride back. At our next office session, he explained that if I wanted to take vows as a nun, which was my goal, I had to experience sex; otherwise giving it up would be meaningless. I was still in shock and becoming more dissociated (although that was not a term I knew then).

He was clear about his logic, and he was my spiritual director. The books about the lives of saints abounded in stories about the importance of obedience to one's spiritual director and spiritual superior, even extending to logical absurdities. The spiritual director was the voice of God to the soul.

We had another encounter, and a number of them after that. They were awful, and I could feel myself getting more and more disturbed. I lost about a third of my body weight, going down to about a hundred pounds on my five-foot-ten-inch frame. I was profoundly depressed and felt suicidal but knew that suicide was wrong. There was no way out.

Finally, I had an obvious catatonic episode. Living in this craziness had become too much. Trying to live with his twisted logic and make sense of it was crazy-making. I could no longer go to church, and I could not pray; my mind was gone. I was enormously disturbed . . . [A psychiatrist] agreed to take me as a patient . . . He himself was an atheist, but he kept me alive. I terminated therapy after about seven years. Later, I resumed therapy with a psychologist who wisely advised me that I needed to reconnect with my spirituality; that the inner work I had to do would be too difficult without the support of a spiritual path . . .

The losses I suffered were enormous: the loss of my mind, the profound depression, the lost time and potential, the many years of deep inner pain and struggles, the confusion about what was true and whom I could trust (the priest had so distorted reality that I lost confidence in myself and my own ability to know what was true and who I could trust, if anyone), the personal and financial hardships from the huge cost of therapy, the effect that these experiences had on relationships with family and friends, the distrust of religion or anything that was even remotely related to religion, and most of all, the loss of my relationship with God.

It was to be many, many years before my therapist and I unraveled it and I could separate out what was true and what was disturbance. You might think this should have been clear to any right-minded person. I can only tell you it is a different matter when you go into something believing with your whole heart and mind and soul in the goodness of something or someone . . .

I suspect that troubled priests, like other sex offenders, have a way of picking up unconsciously on who is a likely target—perhaps people who have been abused or threatened or violated physically, psychologically, and/or sexually, the way I was.

COMPULSIVE BUSYNESS

One of the less dramatic but frequently observed behavioral side effects of traumatic stress is a compulsive, relentless busyness, a need to occupy the mind so as to keep terrifying images, feelings, and sensations at bay. Many post-traumatic stress survivors describe keeping twelve-hour workday schedules, toiling through the weekend, avoiding vacations, and filling any moments of free time with obsessive thinking, planning, problem-solving and errand-running—all of it compulsively driven, and much of it essentially needless.

Dawn writes:

It seemed that the flashbacks were the worst in the moments when I was resting or trying to take time to just sit. In order to avoid them, I learned to become ultra busy. I scheduled my life so fully that I didn't have time to sit. I was running all the time. Sometimes I would stay up at night until I was completely exhausted in order to avoid the hell that I experienced in my dreams. I would push myself until my body said stop and I would get sick. It was another cycle that repeated itself over and over during that time.

I have since learned that becoming too busy is not an effective coping mechanism. In the process of time, I've learned to change the need to be busy in order to avoid things. (It helps that the flashbacks are not always so evident in my life right now.) Taking time for myself and slowing down are things I had to learn. Paying attention to the signals my body sends when I'm pushing too hard is another thing I've had to learn. Imagery and other relaxation techniques have played an important role in teaching me these lessons.

One of the things that I started doing to deal with flashbacks was imagery. After my therapist taught me how to rewrite the abuse through visualization and walked me through it a few times, I was better able to do it on my own when I had memories that needed to be dealt with. Gaining this tool helped lessen my need to stay busy as a form of avoidance. (Deciding to be brave and choosing to use the tools was also very important!)

It's not unusual for the compulsive time-filling and driven overwork to produce exhaustion that exacerbates symptoms. Elsie reports:

I also worked very, very hard at my job, working many weekends. I did not get proper rest. I rarely took vacations and burned myself out.

These, then, are the main manifestations of PTSD-driven behavior, aspects of which perplex survivors, their families, friends, colleagues, and even their therapists.

Now we can look at what heals post-traumatic stress: how we can deploy the gifts of the imagination and the bounty of the right hemisphere of the brain.

PART II
HEALING
TRAUMA

9 HOW AND WHY IMAGERY HEALS TRAUMA

Guided imagery is a form of deliberate, directed daydreaming—a purposeful use of the imagination, using words and phrases designed to evoke rich, multisensory fantasy and memory, in order to create a deeply immersive, receptive mind-state that is ideal for catalyzing desired changes in mind, body, psyche, and spirit. For most people, imagery is an easy, user-friendly form of meditation that yields immediately felt results. Its gentle nature belies its potency and its research-proven, cumulative efficacy.

GENTLE BUT POWERFUL

Imagery has been found to reduce anxiety and depression; lower blood pressure; reduce cholesterol and lipid peroxides; speed up healing from cuts, fractures, and burns; cut blood loss and length of hospital stay in surgery patients; beef up short-term immune function; reduce pain from arthritis and fibromyalgia; increase comfort during all manner of medical procedures; lower hemoglobin A1c in diabetics; improve motor deficits in stroke patients; reduce fear in young children undergoing MRIs and needle sticks; cut down bingeing and purging in people with bulimia; improve success rates in infertile couples; accelerate weight loss; and improve concentration in developmentally disabled adults, to name just a sampling of outcomes.[1] Indeed, given the last twenty years of research findings from various clinical trials, it is surprising that imagery isn't prescribed as a universal, low-cost, preventive health tool, in much the way that aspirin is used to reduce the likelihood of future heart attack and stroke.

Imagery is effective, in part, because of the way it is able to sidestep linear thinking and logical assumptions and send its healing messages straight into the center of the whole person, where it can affect unconscious assumptions and jostle defeating self-concepts, while floating soft, appealing reminders of health, strength, meaning, and hope. In my own mind's eye, I see the healing imagery washing over every surface of the body and being absorbed, spongelike, by the skin, allowing it to soak into the muscle tissue and bone, all the way down into the cells, where it tweaks the DNA into remembering its original, miraculous blueprint.

In fact, the imagery is taken in primarily through the right hemisphere, by way of primitive, sensory, and emotion-based channels in the brain and nervous system, using our capacity for sensing, perceiving, feeling, and apprehending rather than our left-brain thinking, judging, analyzing, and deciding. Because of this, it is an ideal intervention for post-traumatic stress.

Since guided imagery sidesteps the logical and analytic centers of the brain, it's a useful way to slip around psychological resistance, fear, hopelessness, worry, and doubt and grab a foothold on attitude and self-esteem before the more literal, logical thinking mind, with all its worrying monologue, can even get wind of its presence and start arguing with it.

Indeed, imagery is the gift that keeps on giving. An appealing, quick route to relaxation, it creates a highly malleable reverie state that allows healing images to slip in, where they drop like a depth charge, deep beneath the surface of the bodymind, where they can reverberate again and again, delivering multiple layers of complex, encoded, healing messages by way of simple symbols and metaphors. Key phrases and images, culled by the unconscious mind in a mysterious but ingenious sorting process all its own, pop into the mind during the day and during sleep, on an as-needed basis.

Imagery is fast, powerful, costs little or nothing, and gets more and more effective with continued use. Its end user needn't be smart, rich, well educated, young, strong, or mentally healthy to reap its considerable benefits. Listeners can be bone-tired, disgusted, depressed, disbelieving, listless, resistant, distracted, mentally disabled, physically unfit, or at death's door, and imagery will still be something they can use, because it requires so little of them.

The reasons imagery is such an ideal practice for traumatic stress are plentiful and compelling. We will explore them all, but let us start at the beginning, with the most basic and earliest reasons imagery works, anchored in the development of the human psyche.

MOM, BLANKIES, PEEKABOO, AND THE COMFORTS OF THE IMAGINAL REALM

Imagery has been helping us get through the day—especially the rough days—since our earliest, pretoddling babyhood. When we are anxious, threatened, blue, unsure, or needing comfort in any way, internal images—either unconscious ones or those we overtly conjure—soothe our adult selves, communicate reassurance, confer hope, and remind us of our capabilities and worth. Whether we are consciously aware of it or not, imagery is at the core of our ability to manage anxiety and distress—and helps us to literally and figuratively take the next step.

As infants, we first required Mommy herself, or whoever our primary caregiver was, to deliver food, comfort, touch, or soothing as needed. Mommy resolved our cravings, and as infants, we didn't quite know where she ended and we began. We were one, or so we thought, living the high life in the baby equivalent of the Garden of Eden, where everything was pretty much provided for and life was stress-free.

Sadly, we were soon disabused of this notion of perfect unity and got our first inklings that Mom wasn't all she was cracked up to be, when we found ourselves in need and she wasn't there to promptly fix it. The bad news was hitting home: Mommy was in fact a separate being, and not ours to commandeer. Thrown out of paradise, we were forced to instinctively find ways to comfort ourselves. (The distress of an utterly helpless infant rapidly escalates into a full-bodied response of fury and terror—human infants don't survive without adults, after all. It is, of course, this very kind of primitive distress that adults reexperience during an overwhelming, traumatic event.)

Given our baby-selves' disillusionment with Mom, we quickly learned to take up with the more reliable charms of the thumb, the blankie, and the teddy—*transitional objects,* as they are called in psychodynamic language—to substitute for our fickle caretaker. We got better and better at filling the comfort breach when she was not around, and we gained for ourselves a little badly needed self-sufficiency. Just like Adam and Eve on the wrong side of the gates of paradise, we were forced to learn how to work for a living and take care of ourselves with the implements (literally) at hand.

Our designated comfort item became our first symbol, imbued with magical meaning and power—a marvelous feat of abstraction for such a young being, really, and one that set the stage for later creative and spiritual development. The blankie, teddy, or thumb was the forerunner of many other magical, powerful, comforting abstractions in our adult lives—art, theater, literature, and even, according to many psychoanalytic theorists, religious experience.[2]

And in several ways, truth be told, Teddy was an *improvement* over Mommy, because he was at our complete disposal, ours to command in ways Mommy never could be. Ted was solid and steady as a rock. He was portable and could be tossed around, dragged in the mud, chewed on, smooshed, stomped, or ignored. And unlike Mommy, Ted never changed unless *we* changed him—indeed, we objected strenuously to the outrage of his being altered in any way by anyone other than ourselves. He was not to be washed, misplaced, or loaned out, and no substitutions were accepted. Very simply, he was ours and ours alone to possess, abuse, cherish, or neglect, however our whims dictated.

This marvelous omnipotent control over Ted was a kindly delusion that served us well, helping us learn, grow, and individuate in ways that would otherwise be overly fraught with anxiety. In this way, we found ourselves masters of our tiny universe, bravely toddling through our developmental tasks with our trusted blankie, teddy, or thumb functioning as obedient sidekick, lending us courage and agreeable feedback all along the way.

Sometimes the comfort came not so much from a specific item as from an activity or sensation. Some of us used thumb-sucking, rubbing a cloth against our cheek, crumpling a sheet in our hands, or playing with our hair, fingers, cheeks, or ears as our self-soother, sometimes combining an item with an activity.

Soon enough we took another prodigious developmental leap, with our ability to create another kind of symbolic substitution—this time, by forming a *word* for Mommy, a dazzling feat of verbal derring-do—that allowed us to "possess" her when she wasn't around, simply by repeating the word. Sometimes we assigned the associated Mommy-word—often *ma-ma* or *ba-aa* to the teddy or blankie, so we could claim our mom-substitute both verbally and tactilely, while still accommodating ourselves to the sad truth that we were separate from her (or to be more accurate, that *she* was separate from *us* and out of our control).

The most impressive intellectual coup of all, however, occurred—still in pretoddlerhood—when we found ourselves moving into the realm of complete abstraction, evoking the *image* of Mommy or Teddy when we needed comfort. The image started to install itself on the inside of us, as part memory, part dream, and part fantasy, on its way to becoming an integral part of us, a basic building block of the self. Mommy started to inhabit our imaginal world and, in doing so, became fantastically ours to conjure as needed.

The ubiquitously popular game of peekaboo, everlastingly in demand by the pretoddler set across the globe, addresses this critical next step. Even the dimmest and least sensitive of caretakers instinctively comprehends the importance of this universal game of disappearance and reappearance and knows to initiate it. Peekaboo taught our baby selves to incorporate precious images of comfort into our inner world and transferred the powerful secret of self-soothing.

We all know the drill. It usually starts with the adult caretaker covering her eyes and feigning distress because, apparently, the baby has disappeared; then expressing relief when she can see him again. The baby is fascinated and amused. *He* knows he's still there, regardless of her perception.

Sooner or later it gets to be his turn to cover his eyes, making Mommy disappear. Mommy is now gone, creating a certain degree of tension. When he can stand it no longer, he uncovers his eyes, and—presto!—Mommy is back. Her reappearance is greeted with whoops of laughter and joyous relief. Now the riveting sequence must be repeated, again and again. Each time the baby attenuates the tension a little longer, laughs even harder. Long after his adult caretaker has wearied of this mind-numbing game, the baby is still cracking himself up, entranced by the delicious enormity of the riveting truth he is teaching himself.

After all, he is causing this precious person to disappear and come back to him. He is creating tension and dispelling it, all under his own masterful direction.

And as he extends the period of time she must "disappear," he is more and more able to perceive the tracings of Mommy's image on the inside of his eyes. He is not just retrieving her each time; he is slowly learning to take her in and *possess* her image from the inside out, so he can have her with him all the time.

At some point later on, when he takes his first steps or gets dropped off at the sitter's or is made to play with a new neighborhood friend or is invited to eat unfamiliar food with his play group, he will do so with the help of this familiar, comforting Inner Mommy—a combination of dream, fantasy, and memory, of her voice, her looks, her smell, her touch, and, above all, her love for him—offering reassurance and encouragement from the inside. These inner images are what reassure all of us that the world is safe enough to manage, and we are capable enough to try all sorts of scary, difficult new things.

And later on still, when circumstances conspire to diminish, disable, or defeat our adult selves, it is precisely these powerful, comforting, internalized images, as immutable and reliable as our stalwart Teddy of yore, that sustain and support us. They have settled into our inner landscape to form the bedrock of our self-esteem, resilience, and effectiveness. They are fragments, loaded with meaning: a loving phrase from our mother; our father's approving nod; the reassuring touch and smell of our favorite grandmother; the words of a beloved teacher; the sensual, pleasure-giving embrace of a lover; the adoring trust in the eyes of a child . . . all of these nourishing, multisensory images become the subtext that accompanies us on even the most average of days; and they are what we deliberately conjure at times of overwhelming fear and suffering.

Viktor Frankl describes how he intuitively and automatically evoked the sustaining image of his wife to keep him going during the misery of long, freezing, forced marches to and from a Nazi labor camp. Her image was the mechanism whereby he transcended his suffering.

Whoever did not march smartly got a kick. And worse off was the man who, because of the cold, had pulled his cap . . . over his ears before permission was given.

We stumbled on in the darkness, over big stones and through large puddles, along the one road leading from the camp. The accompanying guards kept shouting at us and driving us with the butts of their rifles. Anyone with very sore feet supported himself on his neighbor's arm. Hardly a word was spoken; the icy wind did not encourage talk. Hiding his mouth behind his upturned collar, the man marching next to me whispered suddenly: "If our wives could see us now! I do hope they are better off in their camps and don't know what is happening to us."

That brought thoughts of my own wife to mind. And as we stumbled, slipping on icy spots, supporting each other time and again, dragging one another up and onward, nothing was said, but we both knew: each of us was thinking of his wife. Occasionally I looked at the sky, where the stars were fading and the pink light of the morning was beginning to spread behind a dark bank of clouds. But my mind clung to my wife's image, imagining it with an uncanny acuteness. I heard her answering me, saw her smile, her frank and encouraging look. Real or not, her look was then more luminous than the sun, which was beginning to rise . . .

In a position of utter desolation, when man cannot express himself in positive action, when his only achievement may consist in enduring his sufferings in the right way—an honorable way—in such a position man can, through loving contemplation of the image he carries of his beloved, achieve fulfillment.[3]

Frankl describes the immutability of his wife's image and its absolute and indestructible nature to him—in other words, how the *image* itself became primary, transcending the actuality of her questionable existence:

In front of me a man stumbled, and another man fell on top of him. The guard rushed over and used his whip on them all.

Thus my thoughts were interrupted for a few minutes. But soon my soul found its way back from the prisoner's existence to another world, and I resumed talk with my loved one: I asked her questions, and she answered; she questioned me in return, and I answered . . .

A thought crossed my mind: I didn't even know if she was still alive. I knew only one thing—which I have learned well by now: Love goes very far beyond the physical person of the beloved. It finds its deepest meaning in his spiritual being, his inner self. Whether or not he is actually present, whether or not he is still alive at all, ceases somehow to be of importance.

I did not know whether my wife was alive, and I had no means of finding out . . . but at that moment it ceased to matter. There was no need for me to know; nothing could touch the strength of my love, my thoughts, and the image of my beloved. Had I known then that my wife was dead, I think that I would still have given myself, undisturbed by that knowledge, to the contemplation of her image, and that my mental conversation with her would have been just as vivid and just as satisfying. "Set me like a seal upon thy heart, love is as strong as death."[4]

By internalizing these steadfast images of loving comfort, we establish the primacy of imagery as our automatic, built-in, self-soothing tool. Indeed, devastating grief is ultimately resolved this way. By experiencing the presence of the lost loved one inside of us, and sensing the way they are carried within our hearts, keeping us company, continuing to advise, inspire, and find unique value in us, we manage. We still "have" them. We see their faces, hear their words, smile at their foibles, hold conversations with them, laugh with them, scold them, and embrace them still. In an absolute and immutable way, they still exist. Eventually the comfort of the image takes over for the flesh-and-blood reality. We slowly trade anguish for sweet sorrow, draw nourishment from the inner companion, and transcend the loss, thanks to the gentle resourcefulness of the imaginal realm.

This is the historical reason why imagery is a powerful tool that all of us know well. We've leaned on it from our baby days. It gets us through and allows us to tolerate separation and loss. Imagery is the blankie all of us adults get to carry around—on the inside.

There are also other reasons imagery works so well to heal the effects of trauma.

THE RIGHT-BRAIN CONNECTION

Brain development expert Bruce Perry has studied how a traumatized brain is compelled to train its focus away from language and verbal content, and to fix instead on nonverbal danger cues—body movements, facial expressions, tone of voice, and the like, searching for threat-related information. Cognition and behavior are mediated by the more primitive parts of the brain—the brain stem and midbrain—at the expense of abstract thinking and the absorption of language and ideas. Only when sufficiently calmed can attention be focused on ideas and the meaning of words.[5]

This is why interventions that are based on a strictly cognitive, problem-solving approach cannot impact terror-driven behavior. The primitive brain and midbrain cannot process cognitive solutions aimed at the higher cortical functions. But imagery, with its calming voice tones, soothing music and symbolic representations of safety, can settle down hypervigilant brain functioning and allow the higher brain to get back to doing its job.

PET scans and recent research have shown how traumatic events leave distinctive footprints on the brain, making survivors far more amenable to imagery than they were before the trauma. Sufferers of acute and post-traumatic stress experience exaggerated sensitivity and heightened reactivity in the parts of the brain that process emotions, sensations, and images—the amygdala and its surrounding neuronal network.[6] As a result, trauma survivors are exquisitely responsive to sensations, emotions, and perceptual cues. Of course, this is what makes up the very essence of imagery, both its content and its style. Guided imagery is thus an intervention of choice, a best practice that is perfectly geared to take advantage of that which is most accessible in the wiring of a survivor.

On the other hand, Broca's area—the part of the thinking brain that translates personal experience into language—loses capacity as a result of a trauma, at least temporarily. This is why people under acute traumatic stress experience their emotions as physical states rather than as verbally encoded happenings.[7] The person sees, hears, and feels fragmented sensory elements of the traumatic event but is hard pressed to translate them into communicable language. When asked to describe an actual traumatic episode, a survivor is often rendered speechless (literally) because of these physiological impediments.

Because the survivor is hindered in her ability talk about the event, organize it into a conceptual framework, or integrate it into her life experience, the usual methods of digesting what has happened through discussion are often inadequate. Words and the "talking cure" are not the promising vehicle for healing that they would normally be under different circumstances.

A certain number of long-term trauma survivors find themselves with yet another hindrance to using the analytical side of their brain. Chronic, severe elevation of stress hormones can result in some shrinkage of the hippocampus—the part of the brain that compares new information with past associations and quickly decides whether something is good or bad, safe or dangerous. As a result, the ability to see things in context and make critical distinctions can suffer, at least in the more extreme cases, while impulsivity and disinhibition can be exaggerated.

The survivor needs to use the best assets at hand to help with healing, and under these circumstances, the thinking part of even an extraordinarily fine mind is not necessarily a shoo-in for first choice. What a survivor does have in abundant supply, however, precisely because of his traumatic experience, is his supersensitive, hyperacute, pumped-up, spring-loaded, and downright *athletic* right hemisphere. These overfunctioning visual, sensory, and emotional channels of the brain make for a powerful natural healing alliance. As Cleveland-area psychotherapist Linda Gould, L.P.C.C., says:

> Oftentimes in trauma, healing cannot be completed because traumatic experience becomes locked in various areas of the brain. We don't work trauma through by just talking about it. Talking is primarily a left hemisphere activity. In order to complete the healing process, a traumatized person must access the limbic system and the right hemisphere of the brain, where images, body sensations and feelings are stored. By activating

this area of the brain and accessing the stored images, body sensations and feelings, a person is able to attach meaning to them and move this traumatic material to more adaptive resolution.

The changes in the neuronal network of a traumatized person make for extreme responsiveness to direct contact with the experiential self, through avenues of sensation, perception, and emotion. In this way the gentle but potent ministrations of guided imagery become a powerful treatment of choice.

REBALANCING BIOCHEMISTRY

Trauma survivors experience extreme swings in their biochemistry, from the jolts of cortisol, epinephrine, and norepinephrine that accompany flashbacks, nightmares, and intrusive memories, to the body's built-in pharmacy of relaxants and endogenous opioids. Most of the time the body rebalances on its own after a traumatic event, returning to normal homeostatic business as usual within a few weeks or months.

Most people, however, experience at least several weeks immediately following a traumatic event when their systems are stressed and out of balance, and when cortisol levels are significantly, abnormally elevated. This is the biochemical counterpart to feeling anxious, hypervigilant, angry, tearful, panicky, upset, irritable, fearful, rageful, or terrified.

Should these symptoms become chronic over several years, the survivor runs the paradoxical risk of then chronically *under*producing cortisol, with depressed levels that are punctuated now and then by occasional alarm states that shoot it through the roof. Suppressed cortisol is usually associated with depression, numbness, joylessness, emotional flatness, inaccessibility, fatigue, listlessness, dissociation, and disconnection.

When chronically dysregulated stress hormones infuse the bloodstream for an extended period of time, they can wear away heart muscle, block arteries, create muscle pain, initiate immune and autoimmune problems, and shrink specific areas of the brain. As luck would have it, however, imagery and allied forms of meditation are proven strategies for gently and nonintrusively steering the body's biochemistry back into balance.

A host of studies with trauma survivors, pre- and postoperative patients, and generally healthy adults show that guided imagery can help regulate cortisol and rebalance the body's biochemistry, most often in the short term and in many cases continuing for several weeks after. Other forms of meditation and relaxation, including mindfulness, yoga, qigong, and massage, are also established aids for restoring biochemical balance in the body, as evidenced by blood, urine and/or saliva testing.[8] As gentle and low key as these practices are, they consistently deliver reliable clinical changes, demonstrated by hard-nosed lab values. For this reason alone, guided imagery, which requires no skill or practice and is low- or no-cost, makes for a choice intervention for post-traumatic stress.

THE RETURN TO MASTERY: REGAINING LOCUS OF CONTROL

The essential insult of trauma is the sense of absolute helplessness it imposes on its victims. First there is the overwhelming loss of control one feels during the traumatic situation itself; then there are the countless reprises of helplessness, when every unbidden flashback, intrusive thought, memory fragment, and nightmare breaks through the surface and explodes into consciousness. These unwelcome bouts of distress from reexperiencing the trauma memory can spread to other situations, allowing the terror, rage, panic, and horror to contaminate more and more neutral situations, until scenarios that used to be experienced as perfectly harmless start to feel threatening.

In the face of all these redundant layers of cumulative helplessness, the survivor needs to restore his own sense of efficacy, power, and self-control. The obvious path to restitution rests in a method that is internally based, easy to deploy anywhere, and delivers immediately felt mastery and relief.

This first-order task for recovery is handily accomplished with guided imagery, a practice that is entirely within the control of the user. Survivors access their own soothing images by tapping into their hyperresponsive imaginal world. There is no dependence on fickle externals. The survivor functions as his own masterful, sole agent, able to engage the technique in private whenever, however, and wherever he wishes. The process is just like having Teddy back again.

Imagery also restores mastery and control by providing an instantaneously effective way to soothe and calm an overwrought psyche. The effect is immediate. People often compare it to finding a different channel with a radio tuner, coming upon a mellow frequency that had not been perceived but apparently had always been there. They are relieved and gratified to discover that they can teach themselves to turn away from their intense agitation and enter a state of peacefulness in a matter of seconds.

One burn survivor, who contends daily with physical pain, strange stares from people, the need to perform hours of onerous exercise each morning, and the despair of feeling weary of it all on a regular basis, was astonished at her reaction to her first experience with guided imagery, proclaiming, "I felt different *right away!* The effect was immediate! It changed my mood! I've got to get this to other burn survivors!"

In fact, the more traumatized people are, the more amenable their nervous systems are to being assisted in this way. The fact that relief can be accessed so quickly and easily, by a simple act of free will, is not just immensely relieving; it also provides a return to a sense of competence and mastery, because most trauma survivors are so *good* at doing this. Imagery delivers power and control back to them and in this way helps them retrieve self-esteem, confidence, and faith in the future.

FIGHTING TRANCE WITH TRANCE: THE POWER OF POSITIVE DISSOCIATION

People who are traumatized are people who, by definition, dissociate easily at random and involuntary moments. Their "spaceyness" renders them vulnerable to very real danger by way of attack, collision, exploitation, accident, and other mishaps that can occur as a result of not being fully present and attentive. People who dissociate usually don't know they're doing it at the time. Unbeknownst to themselves, they slip in and out of conscious awareness, usually when confronted with cues that are reminiscent of the trauma, or at the first sign of any sort of anxiety. The danger lies not in the dissociation per se—we all dissociate to some extent, sometimes at our most creative, transcendent moments. Rather, the problem occurs when the dissociating is neither conscious nor part of a deliberately chosen activity but is an automatic, habituated response that occurs without awareness.

Many people with PTSD were already dissociating heavily before their traumatic event, from previous encounters with terror. We know from innumerable studies that people who routinely dissociated before their trauma are more likely to wind up with full-blown PTSD after it.

In addition, anyone who experiences an immobilized freeze response during their traumatic event was dissociating then and is likely to dissociate subsequently, at least for a period of time. Certainly anyone who has a flashback, an intrusive thought, a nightmare, or any other kind of reexperiencing of the trauma is by definition someone who is dissociating.

Consequently, it is safe to say that people who are traumatized can dissociate at the drop of a hat. The good news is this: guided imagery is a *benign* form of focused, strategic dissociating—consciously deployed dissociation with a purpose—and trauma survivors are *highly skilled* at it. Healing imagery is a way of deploying the trance state in a conscious, positive way—a form of fighting fire with fire, if you will. The healing content of the imagery meets the ugly material of the trauma exactly *where it lives,* in the world of right-brain reverie, sensory fragments, and feeling. Using imagery, we can counter our nightmares with daydreams. The imaginal troops we send out are familiar with the terrain, they recognize the enemy, and they know how to bring us back alive.

Equally important, because guided imagery is a consciously managed process, the very act of using it teaches the person the difference between being "gone" and being "back." In effect, by using it, a survivor is learning how to be grounded and present, and how to come back into fully inhabiting her body when she "spaces" out of it. She is learning to choose when to consciously dissociate in a purposeful, proactive way, for the sake of her own healing.

For this reason, imagery and guided meditation are choice interventions for trauma survivors who struggle with unbidden, unconscious, and unprotected dissociated states. Less experienced therapists sometimes naïvely assume that teaching a dissociative technique to an already dissociating client will exacerbate his symptoms, but research and clinical experience point to the opposite effect.[9] Again, it's a simple, practical matter of using the best tools at hand.

BLESSED DISTANCE AND DETACHMENT

During a traumatic event, dissociation offers the gift of emotional distance when physical escape is impossible. The supremely flexible human mind does its best to make up for the capacity the body has lost. It is a very useful maneuver. Problems occur only when the process cycles out of control and later revisits the survivor in dangerously random ways.

Imagery and meditation offer the same gift of distance, only under structured, benign conditions. In the dual awareness that a light trance state allows, the meditator is encouraged to detach and become the observer of his own internal process at the same time that he is the experiencer of that process. In the altered state, we can be two, three, or more places at the same time. The right side of the brain is not troubled by competing realities: it simply accommodates them all simultaneously.

Both guided imagery and mindfulness meditation are generously endowed with built-in ways to detach, but always with compassion for the self. By practicing a healthy, conscious, deliberate form of detachment from our feelings, our sensations, and our thoughts, we are able to accumulate evenness, strength, resilience, and balance. Under these practiced conditions, emotional and physical pain can become more and more manageable.

Buddhism, a system of thought that is designed to alleviate human suffering, and its principal practice of mindfulness meditation, most clearly makes the case for this sort of detachment. It teaches us to watch our own suffering in the present moment, with detached, neutral curiosity, going from moment to moment with compassion for ourselves. We observe our thoughts, feelings, and sensations as they come into our awareness and as they leave our awareness, always staying in the current moment or, more realistically, *returning* to it. We neither resist what we observe nor cling to it. Instead, we just watch, with the neutral, detached eye of a camera:

I am not my sensations;
I am the observer of my sensations.

I am not my thoughts;
I am the watcher of my thoughts.

I am not my feelings;
I am the observer of my feelings.[10]

By *disidentifying* with our suffering and seeing ourselves as larger than our pain, we give ourselves the distance necessary to transcend it. This becomes a tool for entering deep states of relaxation and well-being, where we can allow ourselves to feel our worry, anxiety, tension, impatience, fear, anger, grief, sadness, loneliness, anguish, and despair without becoming them.[11]

It takes discipline and practice, however, for most of us to achieve these states of clarity and spaciousness through mindfulness, even with the natural advantages a trauma survivor possesses for easily slipping into an altered state. It's not an easy practice—it's an acquired skill. The rewards make it well worth the effort, but it might be asking a lot from trauma survivors to have them start out with it.

Further, because mindfulness meditation is far more open-ended than guided imagery, it doesn't provide the carefully constructed cushion of protective images and built-in emotional safety that imagery does. With meditation, the practitioner's mind can suddenly release intensely distressing images and memory fragments that catch him off guard. This is possible but far less likely with guided imagery, where the cards are stacked against this sort of intrusion by the very way the mind is gently, safely being directed.

Further, because imagery uses evocative, multisensory images that have their own natural pull, it is a far easier and less demanding method for reaching a place of detached clarity and transcendence over suffering. Appealing memories and lush fantasies require less energy and discipline to evoke, as they seduce and distract us away from our pain, carrying us beyond our worries, fears, and obsessive anguish.

In the generous space of the imaginal world, we can gain the necessary distance by any manner of tricks: we can put our pain in a box, float it away on a balloon, project it onto a TV screen and then shut it off with the remote, or draw it with imaginary chalk on a blackboard and then erase it. We can surround our vulnerable, shaken selves with protection and support, by marshaling help from magical allies, remembered friends and champions, favorite animals, powerful ancestors, guardian angels, and other divine helpers.

We can create as many layers of distance between ourselves and the traumatic event as we need. We can go to our favorite place and, once there, discover ourselves surrounded by powerful, loving protectors. We might then come upon a screen, where we see fragments of the trauma projected, but we can shut it off when it becomes too much to bear, or we can change aspects of its nature. So the trauma is cushioned by being placed on a controllable screen, which in turn is located in a benign, fantastical place, where we are provided a protective circle of guardians and allies. Three or more tiers of safety and distance are possible in the imaginal realm.

One therapist describes using this technique when working with survivors from the World Trade Center attacks of 9/11. Her aim, she says, was neither to help these survivors deny the reality of what happened, nor to encourage them to prematurely "get rid" of the hideous images, as that would only be disrespecting what happened and short-circuiting their healing process. Instead, she helped them to incrementally process their experience, through gentle reexposure under conditions of structured distance in the imaginal realm.

> Two of the people I've been working with were working together in a nearby building at the time of the attacks and were traumatized by seeing bodies fall and explode on the ground. This particular sight proved to be the greatest horror for those not threatened directly by loss of their own life or that of a loved one.
>
> My approach was to slowly allow them to process the horror, build some capacity for language for it, and ultimately help them integrate it into their lives, so they could move on.
>
> At first they couldn't talk. One woman just got nauseated when she tried. The other almost immediately got a migraine headache. So I asked them to make believe that they were

watching TV together, and that they were holding the remote control, and they could turn it off when they needed to.

One survivor, Jennifer, who experienced severe family violence of another sort, had terrible flashbacks and memories and ultimately wound up inventing her own unique imagery for giving herself the distance and control she needed over these jolting intrusions. Like the Ground Zero therapist, she felt it was important to *manage* these memories rather than deny them.

> I spent the better part of 2000 dealing with flashbacks, memories, and even spent a couple of weeks in my local psych ward as my mind released all that was tucked away.
>
> Since then I've learned to use imagery as a way to put away thoughts and memories until I am able to work with them—I created a closet with a top shelf. And on the top shelf is a box. My box is rather plain, which belies the strength and depth and fierceness of all that is stored in it.
>
> When a flashback or memory comes that is too disturbing to deal with, or is at an inconvenient time (like when my four-year-old is having breakfast), I go to the closet, open the box, take it down, open it, and put the memory there. When I am ready to work with it, I take it out again. I can then respect the currents of my life today without denying my past or shoving it away.

SIDESTEPPING WORD TRAPS THROUGH METAPHOR AND SYMBOL

For many trauma survivors, directly recounting or reexperiencing the traumatic event is simply too daunting a task, one that threatens to release a flood of emotion that overwhelms and submerges the self. For them, a direct, head-on approach exacerbates symptoms and yields little in the way of positive change, especially when attempted too early in the healing process. And of course, as previously mentioned, many survivors cannot access words for their traumatic experiences anyway. The words simply aren't there.

Fortunately, both the right hemisphere and guided imagery have a natural affinity for symbol and metaphor—a natural predisposition for approaching things *on the bias* and getting around concrete facts with symbolic representations. This is a very good thing indeed for a condition where obliqueness is far more effective than head-on literalness. So when a trauma survivor dips into her imagination and takes a look around, she finds all sorts of ingenious symbols offering themselves to her for scrutiny. What shows up front and center often comes straight from the wisdom of the unconscious, a healing gift from the deepest part of the self.

In fact, imagery pioneer and researcher Jeanne Achterberg evolved in her thinking from believing that accurate cellular imagery is the most potent agent of healing for conditions such as cancer and wound healing, to the idea that imagery of heroic archetypes, mythic symbols, and indirect metaphors, rich with personal and spiritual meaning, far outperforms the more concrete varieties.[12] The imagery she most favored thus shifted from imagining white blood cells attacking cancer cells, or bone cells knitting themselves back together, to images of noble or courageous aspects of the self, perhaps embodied by mythic figures, finding treasures of hidden strength or vanquishing outdated aspects of the self.

Frannie's discovery of the stone in her chest, where her heart was supposed to be, is a perfect example of the power of symbol:

> She found she was able to talk about the stone in a way that she could not talk about her feelings. She could examine the stone, describe it, connect to it, go into it, and talk to it. Sometimes the stone represented her pain, and all she could do was practice breathing in and out of it. Sometimes it would be hot, burning and ugly with shame, repulsion, and disgust. At other times it was softer, less threatening, more malleable—more like sorrow—and she could befriend it. Sometimes she felt sorry for the stone and offered it solace.
>
> It was becoming clear to me that Frannie's talking about the stone allowed her to talk about herself in a safe, cushioned way, that got around tripping off that dreaded flashback

> switch. It was a way of circumventing the booby traps and
> getting to the same place that words would have brought us
> to, had her language capacity not been so hobbled.

So for its ability to skirt around the traps of direct language and literalism, guided imagery lends itself well to healing, providing a kinder, gentler, and more effective route to reaching and tending the deep wounds within.

GROUNDING AND REINHABITING THE BODY

Imagery also has a unique capacity to help a trauma survivor because of its ability to ground a person's awareness back into his or her body. Survivors tend to disconnect from the body in the process of dissociating from emotional and physical pain. In this limbo state of not being quite "home" or "all there," it is virtually impossible to take good care of oneself, identify feelings and emotions, know when external circumstances are unwholesome or dangerous, or just get through the day with any sort of efficient functioning capacity.

Guided imagery that focuses primarily on sensation can very gently guide consciousness back into the body. It accomplishes this by focusing awareness, starting with the head and working its way all the way down to the feet. This is a preferable sequence for survivors of trauma, rather than the other way around, as we want them to get back *in* and *down*, as opposed to floating *up* and *out*.

The sequence usually has the person identify what it feels like in a part of the body—noticing whatever sensations are present in a detached, neutral, interested way, with no praise or blame, just mindful attention—and then consciously breathe into that area and consciously breathe out, before moving on down to the next part of the body.

As simple as this sequence is, it can have a profound effect on a disembodied, disconnected person, offering a physical feeling of stability and a relaxed groundedness they didn't even know was missing. It's as if the psyche's reentering the body provides actual *ballast*. Survivors will even walk and sit differently. They are harder to knock over, in every sense of the phrase.

A wonderful example of helping people reestablish body awareness and ground themselves was used by a traditional psychotherapist with survivors at Ground Zero. She describes this intervention, as simple as it is elegant, in this way:

> During my disaster work on the spot, I just did lots of hugging, holding and taking care of the basics . . . helping people figure out how they were getting home, and who was going to be there to support them. I found myself constantly talking to people about their breathing . . . finding a place inside their center that they could breathe into.
>
> I remember one woman who had lost so many people—I couldn't get her away from the site. I said to her, "You look like you're having trouble breathing." She said, "No, I'm breathing." She had no sense that she was holding her breath—this is what people do when they don't want to take in what has happened—they stop inhaling. Her breathing was so shallow, it was invisible.
>
> So I said to her, "I wonder if you could count your breaths to see if you're breathing as well as you think you are," and this was good, because it got her distracted, and as she started counting, she started breathing better. So then I asked her, "See if you can find a big place inside your center and see if you can breathe into it," and that was enough. That was all she did, but it helped her get calmer. Up until then, her frenetic mood was getting me frenetic, too, and I was starting to feel as desperate as she was. But I calmed myself when I calmed her.

The kinesthetic anchoring of the breathing process works to help people relocate their awareness inside their bodies, and the simple act of counting is just enough of a cognitive distraction to help them do so. Asking people to do much more than breathe and count under the traumatizing conditions at Ground Zero would have been too much for most. But this simple intervention was so effective that this clinician began using it in all her therapy sessions in her office, to ground her traumatized clients.

I would start out each session with breathing. I would call it a
breathing meditation and have the person simply count his
breaths. I would say, "Okay, and every time you breathe in and
out is one . . . and two . . . and three . . . And whenever you
lose count, just go back to one." It was the simplest form of
meditation, and it absolutely worked.

Body awareness is every bit as important later on in the healing process,
because only when people are again perceiving from the inside of their
bodies can they start to feel again and sort out their emotions. As Frannie
noted, early in her healing process her feelings were one giant, amor-
phous jumble, and it took her a while to distinguish one from the other.
Teasing out the differences between anger and sadness was a revelation to
her. But before she could do that, she had to locate the inside of her body
and learn how to place her awareness there.

As this process unfolded, worlds of possibility opened up. For Frannie
and for all trauma survivors, although the difficult emotions get noticed
first, they are not the only ones that get noticed. Survivors take the first
step on the way back to finding the pleasurable ones, too, and to reestab-
lishing love and joy in their lives.

COGNITIVE RETOOLING: LEARNING CONSCIOUS
PLACEMENT OF ATTENTION

It is important to remember that trauma impairs parts of the thinking
brain, at least at the outset. People under acute stress are distracted, scattered, and unfocused. It is hard for them to concentrate and maintain a
sustained train of thought. They are bombarded by unbidden, recurring,
intrusive thoughts, disturbed by memory lapses, and have difficulty learning and retaining new information.

While significant areas of the left hemisphere are under siege, parts of
the right brain are hyperacute and overfunctioning. Rather than strain
the already hard-pressed speech and cognition centers, we can lean on
right-hemisphere tools to help revive these overburdened functions. Imagery and meditation are wonderful ways to teach or retrain our capacity

for *conscious placement of attention* and to sustain that focus of attention where it needs to be.

Indeed, the very essence of mindfulness practice instructs the meditator to witness his thoughts, sensations, and feelings; to watch the way he gets distracted from the witnessing; and then to refocus on the witnessing once more. He learns to gently redirect his mind in much the same way we train a rambunctious puppy to stay on the sidewalk. Mindfulness thus improves concentration and learning in contexts far beyond meditating. Of course, the increased calm, balance, and relaxation it generates also help to improve cognitive performance.

Imagery, too, strengthens attentional focus, although not quite as strenuously or directly as mindfulness meditation. It requires less discipline and shoulders some of the work with its ability to seduce and hold interest, making it a more appealing choice to many people, with or without PTSD. As one research team from the University of Utah School of Medicine put it in a recent research proposal, imagery "provides a highly immersive activity whereby multiple senses are at work . . . as well as recruiting a large amount of cognitive resources."[13] With imagery, the basic instruction to the listener is that she allow herself to absorb the images, letting them wash over and through her, breathing them in with open receptivity but without any proactive striving; and should she notice that her mind is straying from the narrative, she is to gently guide it back. For these reasons, imagery becomes a powerful ally in bringing strength and focus back to the cognitive areas of the brain.

SEROTONIN: THE BODY'S NATURAL "HIGH"

Guided imagery provides a natural reward system for its own continued use, as it increases serotonin levels in the bloodstream and provides a badly needed natural uplift. In particular, heart-opening imagery that is specifically designed to heighten feelings of love, gratitude, and connectivity with the larger world is an especially potent producer of these mood-enhancing neurotransmitters. Training the body to access this natural uplift through imagery helps wean it away from its kindled feedback loop, which shuttles between the alarm state and numbness. Imagery introduces an alternative way of returning to biochemical stability, gently and incrementally interrupting the cycle and providing balance.

The medicines that keep serotonin in the bloodstream by slowing down the speed at which it is absorbed—the SSRIs, or selective serotonin reuptake inhibitors, more commonly known by their brand names: Zoloft (sertraline), Paxil (paroxetine), Prozac (fluoxetine), and Luvox (fluvoxamine)—have the effect of reducing depression, anxiety, mood shifts, obsessive-compulsive symptoms, selective types of insomnia, and some degree of impulsivity and aggression, all symptoms of PTSD. It is no surprise, then, that the SSRIs are currently seen as the first-line pharmacotherapy for post-traumatic stress.[14] Needless to say, any practice that heightens the presence of serotonin in a natural, organic way is a critically important, value-added benefit to an already-powerful intervention.

In addition, increased serotonin in the bloodstream has a demonstrated analgesic effect and lowers the perception of pain. Since trauma survivors are known to suffer from all manner of chronic pain conditions, this is a particularly welcome feature. In PTSD support groups, after an imagery experience, some of the first comments from members usually run along the lines of "Gee, my headache went away" and "This is the first time I can remember my knees not hurting." For many survivors, this alone can be reason enough to maintain the practice until the subtler long-term rewards start to kick in.

REPLACING ADDICTIVE SUBSTANCES

Because of imagery's mood-elevating and pain-reducing benefits, it is a staple in recovery programs and is often deployed to fill the breach when a person is withdrawing from addictive substances. It helps when the physical discomfort of abstinence is new and raw, and it helps when, later on, after a stable period of sobriety, emotional distress threatens to topple someone off the wagon.

As epidemiology research has shown us, a substantial percentage of people suffering from PTSD contend with chemical dependency, usually because of the need to self-medicate their more overwhelming symptoms and get additional relief from chronic anxiety, depression, and physical pain. This gentle, healthy substitute for alcohol and other drugs of all kinds serves them well and helps greatly with withdrawal symptoms, which otherwise would only exacerbate their PTSD symptoms in a vicious cycle.

For these reasons guided imagery is a popular intervention in recovery and twelve-step groups. Recovery literature is filled with guided meditations designed just for these groups.

TO SLEEP, PERCHANCE TO DREAM

Insomnia is a common feature of post-traumatic stress. Pervasive hypervigilance, anxiety, nightmares, flashbacks, intrusive thoughts, and obsessive worry interfere with sleep and the normal replenishment it brings to mind, body, and spirit. Lack of sleep, of course, colors everything else in a trauma survivor's day, worsening fatigue, depression, irritability, anxiety, and pessimism.

In addition, as anyone who has ever fallen into an insomnia cycle knows all too well, lack of sleep has the perverse effect of breeding an even greater lack of sleep. At some point it becomes critical to break the cycle, even if it means using the heavy ammunition of sedatives, because the insomnia, if allowed to persist, will sooner or later upstage every other form of misery. Indeed, research consistently shows that if any one of us goes without sleeping and dreaming for a long enough period of time, we are assured of becoming temporarily psychotic.

Guided imagery has a unique ability to break through a persistent insomnia cycle and gently lullaby a hypervigilant listener into a welcome cradle of sweet, welcome sleep. Its immersive, relaxing context and its menu of multiple sensory images capture the right brain while recruiting enough cognitive resources to divert the left. This is just the right recipe for competing successfully with the obsessive thoughts and worries that render a person sleepless.

Most important, almost all imagery has primitive, calming nonverbal elements—usually a combination of a relaxed, comforting voice tone and soothing, calming music—that is reminiscent of the way a baby is rocked to sleep by a loving parent. By its very nature, imagery's tone and pacing entrain feelings of safety, so an exhausted listener can let down his vigilance just long enough to drop off into sleep.

There are exceptions, of course. If a trauma survivor has had experiences of being soothed and seduced by the voice of an exploitative, predatory parent or other adult, then the sound of any low, soothing, inviting voice, regardless of how trustworthy and nonseductive, may set off alarm bells and produce the opposite effect. This is especially true when the voice is the same gender as the original abuser.

But generally speaking, imagery makes for a wonderful nonpharmacological sedative and is always worth a try. This note from a sleep-deprived imagery user is dramatic but representative:

> At the recommendation of my therapist, Dr. Kathleen B., I purchased a guided imagery tape to help with sleep . . . I had been taking 10 mg of Ambien every night for the past fifteen years (I am surviving chronic depression, chronic pain, and PTSD from sexual abuse). After one night of listening to the imagery, I threw away the Ambien and have had peace-filled sleep every night since then—something I thought I would never have, either with or without medication! I especially like the idea of guardians surrounding me with love and all good things in my life. I also like the idea of "relaxing my heart."

THOSE BIASED AGAINST THERAPY CAN USE IT

Many people are still prejudiced against psychotherapy or counseling, no matter how great their emotional pain. They might find the idea of seeing a therapist a sign of weakness or self-indulgence, or perhaps they don't see the point, as mere talking cannot change the facts on the ground. This is especially true among certain professional groups and work cultures. We see it with combat vets, early responders, uniformed officers (firefighters apparently leading the pack of therapy-resisters), and certain subgroups of mental health and health care providers.

But imagery can be presented as a skill set to learn, a form of training in improved self-control, and as such it is not a violation of a personal code against displays of vulnerability. As many therapists who worked in Oklahoma City or at Ground Zero after 9/11 later attested, guided imagery and other brief, empowering therapies were a great help to the police officers and firefighters who would not accept more traditional forms of counseling. These simple skill sets were taught on the scene.

One psychologist who sees a lot of police officers for grief says:

> They are hard to work with and don't like a lot of intellectual stuff. They would never come to therapy in a million years. But they can be coached to come up with their own "calm scene." And then later on, when they're overwhelmed by a memory or flashback at work, they can close their eyes, right there on the corner, and go back to that calm scene. It's better than reading a book or going to a counselor. They have a tool they can use right away.

SPIRITUAL CONNECTION: CONTACTING THE WIDER PERSPECTIVE

Imagery is highly compatible with religious belief but doesn't insist upon it. It offers the gift of opening up even the most cynical trauma survivor to the spaciousness of the wider perspective, a felt sense of the mystical, and glimpses of long-shut spiritual doorways. After we experience unspeakable heart-shattering events, entering this vaster perspective allows us to apprehend the larger truth that everything really is, at some level of reality, still all right. This is not the same thing as denying the ugliness—we understand that what happened was hideous. But from this other view we can hold both truths at the same time, derive comfort, and maintain hope.

My hard-core physiologist friends would say that this experience of the boundless, the noetic, and the ineffable that imagery catalyzes is the result of our hyperactive temporal lobes, which are known to produce perceptions of religious or spiritual experiences. Psi researcher Michael Persinger reports that when the amygdala and other structures within the limbic system of the brain are electrically stimulated, intense hallucinatory activity is generated, and subjects report seeing apparitions, hearing inner voices, feeling nearby presences, and sensing powerful convictions of deep meaningfulness.[15]

My religious and mystical friends, however, would say that guided imagery is simply the equivalent of an engraved invitation to the divine and to guardian angels, guides, spiritual helpers, departed loved ones, noble ancestors, and benign invisible forces to come calling and lend a hand. They would suggest that these divine allies are available and eager to be called upon for assistance; but, politely adhering to spiritual etiquette, they wait to be asked.

I would put myself in the second camp, although I certainly have no problem with Persinger's physiological facts. Science and mysticism are not mutually exclusive, after all, and I'm certain that hyperactive temporal lobes and God are happy to work hand in hand. But whatever one's bias may be, it makes no difference in practical terms. Scientists, theologians, and mystics would have to agree that people suffering from posttraumatic stress face extraordinary emotional hardship and an unsettling loss of identity, safety, trust, and meaning. They need something *big* enough to hold them as they slog through all that suffering and disorientation, toward their own redemption.

Hope has to come from somewhere, once the normal hope-carrying avenues have melted away. For this reason many people lean harder on their faith or return to it for support. Most will seek out some form of spiritual sustenance, even those who barely believe it exists. A substantial number of those disaffected from the formal religious training of their younger years will look for it. Even survivors who feel betrayed by their religious or spiritual history find themselves envying those who are able to find sustenance. Imagery is a way of accommodating all of these circumstances and helping people get back to a comforting God without setting off their doubts, fears, objections, or emotional resistance. The need is strong.

Christine, a survivor of grotesque ritual cult abuse, eloquently describes the critical nature of maintaining her spiritual connection in order to withstand the rigors of her recovery. Luckily she had a brilliant, seasoned therapist, psychologist Frances Baker, PhD., who understood this need from the very beginning.

I hold a license as a psychotherapist and am a Reiki practitioner, but I am writing from my personal history of surviving satanic ritual abuse of such enormity that I would never have thought full healing was possible. But it was. I had the good fortune to work with wonderful people, like Frances

Baker, Jean Berggren, Jim Kepner, Laura Chapman,[16] to name a few. You see how lucky I am!

Among the things that were most helpful: consciously placing myself in the presence of God (my word) for long periods. No other healing energy or presence was big enough or available enough to counter the huge negative, traumatic energy field that I carried from over seventeen years of the cult experience. Often there were no words in this time with God. Yet glimmerings of understandings began, and most of all the time spent this way felt comforting and healing.

It was not a time of daydreaming, or just making my mind a blank, or problem-solving, or dissociating. I knew what those things felt like, and none of them would have had the healing effect this practice had. Instead, this was a time to just bask in God's love, to take it in. Someone summarized it this way: "I look at Him. He looks at me." Only love here. I cannot tell you what enormous healing, comfort, and true inner wholeness this brought.

Unfortunately, many people do not have access to this, because there is a sense of blaming God for not preventing what happened. I hadn't had that particular difficulty. Having had near-death experiences, I knew that "uncaring" didn't describe the God I had experienced. I didn't understand why things happened, but I knew it wasn't about God's not loving or caring.

However, at the beginning of my therapy, God was unavailable to me, because I had lost my ability to connect, due to my own craziness (normal under the circumstances), resulting from the layers of extreme abuse I went through.

Frances told me in the beginning that I would need to reconnect with my spiritual roots—that without that, the work of healing would be too hard. It was difficult and I felt resistant, but I knew she was right.

I share all this because as I look back, I see this spiritual connection was a crucial component in my healing. The time spent with God began to open ways of viewing things that, when I try to assign words to them, sound superficial or

Pollyanna-ish or like I'm trying to whitewash the experiences
or rationalize them away.

But inner experiential knowing rebuilt my core in a way
that nothing else could. And I am unendingly grateful for
Frances's clarity about where my healing would come from.

The need for spiritual sustenance and support is great, but people
have very different attitudes toward and relationships with the divine,
particularly after their shattering experiences. This is another reason imagery has such extraordinary appeal. When properly constructed, it has a
chameleonlike, open-ended ability to tap into a person's inner gateway to
whatever his or her unique spiritual connection—or lack thereof—is. It
can borrow language that won't compete with the specific religious
teachings a person holds fast to, and in fact, it will support and enhance
their spiritual connection with an immersive experience of lush, sensory
images and heart-opening feelings.

At the same time, the language can be open enough to sidestep confining religious labels and theological constructs that could set off alarm
bells and start red flags waving among the disaffected. Guided imagery
thus becomes an equal opportunity form of prayer for religious and non-
religious alike. Atheists get to have their healing dose of spirit, without
having to overtly sign up for any labels that are anathema to them.

Here is what one traditionally religious Christian woman wrote
about the importance of being able to bring Jesus into her fill-in-the-
blanks healing imagery:

I feel that it is important to note the role that God has played in
my healing. I know that without His help I wouldn't be where I
am today. Jesus Christ and His power to heal are important
parts of the visualizations that I do. He is real to me. His power
to heal is real. I depend on Him for strength every day.

For her, the imagery made the presence of Jesus more real, more viable,
and more accessible. It made her contact with the divine something she
could apprehend, sense, and experience. As a result, her experience of
prayer became more potent, personal, and sustaining.

Another woman, whose childhood sexual abuse was perpetrated by twisted predators disguised as devout people of God, couldn't bear to participate in regular, spiritual practice or prayer. Religious terminology and church ceremony sickened her stomach and made her want to bolt.

In a poignant e-mail message, she describes the tentative stirrings of reconnection that relatively neutral imagery was able to afford her. What she does not say directly, but is heartbreakingly apparent, is how painful the loss of her spiritual connection was, after it came to feel dangerous to her:

> I got your tape for PTSD, and tried to listen to it. I had to turn it off. I could not handle it for a while. I got it back out and listened to the whole thing. I actually could feel a sense of connectedness for a brief few seconds. I entertained the thought that there really might be a loving God.
>
> In reference to the comment about some people wanting the word "God" out of the tapes, I'm glad you said you would not take it out. This is one of the first times that I heard the word "God" and did not get all the dark feelings . . .
>
> [The imagery] helps me imagine that there could be something basically good about me, like a "home" I came from that was pure and light . . .
>
> I want so much to be able to accept that things were not rosy as a child, and realize that that's okay. I want to move forward, and I want to think of the universe as more friendly . . .
>
> I would love to believe that I have guardian angels, or beings looking over me, just hanging around. I do know, however, that they cannot stop bad things from happening.
>
> But to go back in the past, and think that maybe there was something there with me, somehow shifts the memory for me. I hope it's true.[17]

In its neutral, nonthreatening way, imagery makes God possible again, in many shapes, formats, names, and guises. It is a great gift to give back to anyone but a special blessing for a survivor of trauma.

10 GENERAL GUIDED IMAGERY WISDOM AND TACTICS

Many people in need of healing, whether physical or emotional, manage to intuitively come up with their own homegrown imagery to help in their recovery. Some are able to consciously construct these healing images, proactively drawing from a combination of daydreams, memories, and fantasies that they know will strengthen and support them.

For others, the process is more like a magical visitation. Images bubble up to the surface of awareness, seemingly of their own accord. These profound experiences, served up from the lush bounty of the imaginal world, provide assistance in powerful ways—sometimes subtly and incrementally, and sometimes with bold panache.

SPONTANEOUS IMAGERY

Here is a sampling of some of the spontaneous imagery experiences that came to the aid of a wide range of trauma survivors.

One survivor of childhood terror methodically shifted her reaction to a terrible memory through imagery of her own devising. This memory involved a night when she watched some terrible rituals performed on others and was herself raped, assaulted, and threatened with death:

> The most graphic way I can explain my own process is to say
> that one of the memories that I needed to deal with on my
> healing journey was a particularly harrowing night in a barn at

my uncle's farm . . . even after resolving many of the existential dilemmas this experience posed for me, and after the intense flashbacks had subsided . . . I would still notice physical anxiety if I thought about that memory.

With an intention to truly heal that space, a gentle process emerged over a few months . . . I moved through the "close call" aspect for the final time and saw myself rejoin myself rather than leave a part of me behind in that barn.

A week or so later I had the notion that it was time for the barn to burn down in my internal picture of it all, but I also didn't want to create "more harm."

That dilemma resulted in the notion of having a fire chief come and do a controlled burn. For several weeks, when I would go to the place in my imagination, I was aware of the "burned earth" waiting for something else. Then I noticed green starting to pop up, and I seemed to be growing a garden.

In the garden there were primarily wildflowers and paths winding through. Near the "front" of the garden was an old bench where someone could sit if they chose. Near the "back" corner of the garden, if you were to look closely, you would see a small bunny statue with a commemoration of the healing journey that transformed the space. (I had watched a rabbit being sacrificed the original night.)

Now when I find myself thinking about what used to be the "barn memory," my awareness is first of the garden, which always has a light energy and fresh smell to it. If I go further into this place, I am next aware of the final time I visited the memory and the new ending of rejoining myself (as opposed to the fracturing that occurred at the original time).

And if I go further than that, I do have a vague awareness of the original trauma. But my physical and emotional experience is one of the peaceful garden and a whole self. And my heart rate does not get faster, and my breathing does not stop the way it used to when I used to remember this place.

Psychologist Beverly Donovan, Ph.D., coordinates the Transcend program at the Louis B. Stokes VA Medical Center in Brecksville, Ohio.

This impeccably designed and highly successful treatment program for combat-related PTSD and addiction, co-created with Edgardo Padin-Rivera, Ph.D., yields many stories of spontaneous imagery from the veterans.

Dr. Donovan describes one vet's healing journey, filled with transformative grace, which still moves her as she tells it:

> Sometimes these visualizations are like a spontaneous spiritual healing . . . something emerges that is exactly what is needed in order to heal. This is an amazing thing to witness. It's as genuine as anything in "real time."
>
> One man had a recurring nightmare of being chased by a faceless tribe. It always left him terrified, breathless, and sweaty. So this one time, as he was describing the nightmare with closed eyes, he was clearly reexperiencing it. He became panicky and out of breath, so I asked him what he needed to do, right then and there, about the situation.
>
> With his eyes still closed, he replied, "I need to ask them why they're chasing me. I have to turn and face them." So he did. He asked them why they were chasing him.
>
> The chief of the tribe said, "We will stop chasing you, if you will stop destroying your life." They put down their weapons. And he made a solemn resolution right there on the spot, with great emotion, to stop destroying himself.
>
> Then he wanted to know why they were faceless. So he asked them to take off their masks. He said to the chief something like "I need to know who you are. I need for you to take off your mask." And it was his friend Chicago, who was killed on the base during a good-bye party. He had left the party early, and his face was blown off by incoming fire. This man had been the one to stumble upon him and find him, as he was leaving the party.
>
> He understood right away that this was Chicago, trying to reach him, trying to tell him he was okay and to stop punishing himself for still being alive. It was one of those amazing moments, when everything really did shift for him.

Many of the spontaneous imagery experiences of the vets have this theme of forgiveness and permission from fallen comrades to go on and live their lives. Another example occurred when one of the men was listening to a guided imagery narrative. Guided experiences are often most effective when they are designed in an open-ended fashion, so that they can serve as a platform for launching the listener's own unique images:

> This happened while Jim was listening to an imagery tape. His imagination broke away from the text, and he saw the man who had been his friend and mentor come right into the room with him. He'd been talking about this friend earlier, when he'd come to realize that he wasn't just grieving for him; he was actually very angry with him for leaving him and dying on him, when he still needed him.
>
> The friend had been hit by sniper fire, right in front of Jim, and his brains had splattered all over him. The next day, when he went back to look, he couldn't find his body, and this bothered him greatly.
>
> During the imagery, Jim saw him in the room, laughing, teasing, and telling him to move on . . . that it was hard to see him suffering all these years, and that he was okay . . .
>
> After that imagery experience, Jim quit having nightmares about him. Once, on an anniversary date, it came back, but he again invoked this imagery and again got a pep talk from his friend, and that particular nightmare never came back again. Absolution happens.

One twelve-year-old boy in protective custody in New York City had had an unusually harsh life. He'd lost his father when he was still quite small, and shortly afterward his mother became sick. He stayed with her while she was dying and then, after he lost her, went to live with the very decent man who had married her during her illness. He was very attached to this man, who looked after him like a father, but within a year he too had died of cancer.

This child had enormous grief and anger, and his sadness ran so deep that it was hard to get close enough to him to help him. He started to become more emotionally accessible when he began daydreaming about his favorite room in the house he used to live in when he was very little, before all the troubles started. This was the only way he could settle himself down. He described his daydreams to his therapist, who reports:

> He started imagining himself in that room, back in his earliest years, when his father was still alive. He could see all the paraphernalia in one room, the shelves, the tabletops, his toys stashed in a corner. He could feel the nub of the sofa fabric, and he could smell the room quite vividly, too. His favorite item was a picture on the wall of him with his mother and father, all smiling. In his imagination, which is very vivid, he is playing with one of the toys in his hands, on the sofa, and he expresses surprise at how small and pudgy his little boy hands are.

Returning to this time and this room helped him to find safety, and he reinhabited it again and again to calm himself. He outgrew the need for inhabiting this spot until the attacks of 9/11 reactivated his fearfulness, and then the first place he went back to was his room.

Dawn, who as a child had been thoroughly abused and terrorized, liked to conjure this image for herself as she thawed from her chronic numbness, to help herself deal with a host of emerging feelings she was only beginning to sort out and understand. The imagery didn't have to make sense to anyone but Dawn:

> I still do visualizations when faced with emotions I don't understand. One of my favorites is imagining the outline of myself on a carpet. On the carpet, I visualize different colors of paint, each representing a different emotion (to me, emotion is best expressed in color). I then find the super-duper vacuum, and with the help of friends, I vacuum the carpet until it is sparkling clean. The mess that is in the vacuum is then turned into beautiful opalescent glitter that I shoot into the air. I let the sparkles float until they cover me. The glitter represents joy and learning. I think it is important to recognize that any pain we experience can and will change as we are willing to work

with it and allow those who can help to do so. I can't change
the memories; they happened. But in allowing myself to learn,
I can find purpose in the pain and, I believe, eventual joy from
the growth that comes from adversity.

One woman felt her agitation so viscerally that imagining her activated nervous system made the most sense to her:

I visualize the nervous system as you see it in anatomy
drawings, branching out everywhere, and then I look at it as
all lit up, which is not hard, because of its electrical nature. I
think most trauma survivors actually identify with feeling like
the trauma is right in their nervous system, which it is, so this
also has logical appeal. Sometimes I pull the trauma out
through my head, sometimes I let it flow out the fingertips
(where some of the meridians flow out).

A man in his fifties suffered a traumatic shock years earlier as a little
boy when his mother, a recent immigrant from China, had a psychotic
break. The memory that kept flashing back for him was of his mother
standing over him (looking absolutely huge), wielding a large, flashing
kitchen knife, while he remained mute and paralyzed with terror. His imagery, as reported by his psychologist, Anne Chapman Kane, Ph.D.:

I imagine the scene again, just as it occurs in my flashbacks.
Only this time, my adult self goes right over to the little boy
(also me), picks him up, and takes him away, saying soothing,
kind words and holding him gently but firmly close. I am
protecting him (me) from my crazy mother. Crazy as it
sounds, it feels wonderful.

According to Dr. Kane, an expert in hypnosis and imagery, this simple
homemade scenario helped more than any other intervention she had offered her patient. It alleviated his anxiety, sleeplessness, depression, and fear.

Another survivor elicits even more potent protective forces to look
after her:

I choose people I would like to have had as parents, and
then I feel them around me, filling me with their being. Each
time I have done this, I have felt permanently changed. I
always choose saintly figures on the other side, because it was
so clear to me about the magnitude of the energy I would be
needing in order to heal.

Another homegrown, spontaneous imagery experience, designed to
help make the shift from helplessness to empowerment, was reported in
this way:

One practice I have started goes like this: I consciously get in
touch with one trait I have, even if in small measure, like
peace. Then I feel it growing inside, using whatever images
help it to grow, drawing from all the energy in the cosmos,
and increasing it until it is very large inside. Then I
consciously focus on radiating it outward. I might send it to
someone who has asked for help, or for world conditions, or
anywhere that comes to mind. As I send it out, I keep the
inflow coming so I can keep sending more. I sense this will
help me to continue the transition from feeling passive and
helpless to a sense of my own energy and ability to serve.

Therapists themselves can make good use of imagery, to help them
maintain their resilience and keep from absorbing too much pain.
Manhattan-based psychologist Dr. Anne Chapman Kane, in the months
following 9/11, felt the secondary trauma that came from hearing in disturbing detail the terrible things that people saw or experienced. The repeated stories were taking their toll, and so she devised this imagery for
herself:

I find I need to do my own imagery these days, to keep from
absorbing all the horror. So before, during, and after my
sessions, I imagine that I am a lightning rod. The horror goes
right through me and into Mother Earth.

Frannie still remembers the imagery she used to lull herself to sleep as a child, when she needed to retreat into something that offered beauty and safety:

> When I was a young child, in the dark of my room each night, on all four walls, near the ceiling, about eighteen inches high, marched many colorful animals, all following each other as in a parade. They moved and danced and moved their heads from side to side in unison. They let go of each other and turned around in a regular rhythm, to the beat of an exotic and beautiful chant with stringed instruments and reeds and ancient Asian and African pipes. There were beautiful, massive but agile elephants, so strong, yet so delicate, trumpeting the way; and swans in flight, so graceful; and fearless lions and tigers; giraffes so silent and gentle and tall; ibis and heron and hummingbirds and butterflies, dolphins and whales, all in a chorus line for me! All connected to each other by their trunks and tails—an awesome, powerful, and supportive group of sentient beings of the universe.
>
> Their song was for me, to entertain me, and for that time the fear would go away. I would gaze up and follow them with my eyes and ears around the room, and I was transformed as they sent their nods of affirmation toward me. I sang with them while they moved in slow motion and in unison. I looked forward each night to this escape, to be with these loving creatures that knew how to keep me safe from harm, and to bring me the light of their hearts in that dark room.

SCRIPTED GUIDED IMAGERY VS. SELF-GENERATED IMAGERY

Some people are not comfortable devising their own imagery, or don't feel confident in what they come up with on their own, even when they produce excellent material, entirely made to order, and of the utmost compatibility with their personal agenda, taste, and needs. Others like to start out with an "official" expert version, just to be sure they are getting the hang of it, then launch with greater assurance into imagery of their own devising.

When Phaedra Caruso, Ph.D., and Trudy Helge, Ph.D., were doctoral candidates in psychology, they studied chemotherapy patients at the Mt. Zion Infusion Center at the University of California at San Francisco Medical Center.[1] In their study they compared two kinds of guided imagery—the self-generated, unique, fill-in-the-blank type, and a standardized, physiologically based imagery narrative that was completely scripted—along with a third technique: a progressive relaxation tape. All three interventions were recorded by the same person—imagery expert Martin Rossman, M.D.—and offered to three different intervention groups of randomly assigned cancer patients in the context of a four-session course.

When the data were analyzed and broken down, Caruso and Helge found that both kinds of guided imagery performed equally well, and significantly better than the progressive relaxation, in reducing depression and anxiety for the patients—indeed, increasingly so over time. But there was an interesting internal difference between the two kinds of imagery. After one session the personalized imagery group seemed to have less anxiety and feel more excited and hopeful about the intervention. But over the course of the four sessions it was the standardized, scripted imagery group that showed the steadiest improvement, and unlike the self-generated imagery group, these patients stayed with their technique. The self-generated imagery group, on the other hand, had several dropouts.

Dr. Caruso thinks this difference in usage and efficacy has to do with the placebo effect of having greater confidence in the "expert" version. Over time she felt that the self-generated imagery group became less and less confident about whether they were in fact on the right track and coming up with what they needed, which interfered with their wholehearted usage. The group with the scripted imagery suffered no such doubts.[2]

This confidence factor holds true for therapists, too. Many start out working with someone else's scripted, recorded version until they can figure out the basics of structure, content, and style, and sooner or later they feel that they are on firm enough footing to take a crack at creating their own imagery with their clients.

ONE-ON-ONE IMAGERY VS. RECORDED IMAGERY

Some practitioners feel very strongly that the best kind of imagery is personalized, one-on-one imagery, where a guided imagery practitioner works directly with an individual, continually modifying and adjusting the narrative through ongoing give-and-take dialogue and corrective feedback from the client.[3] This certainly is an excellent approach. It has the advantage of making the client a fully empowered co-writer and collaborator, and it unquestionably produces imagery that is uniquely designed for the end user.

But it doesn't work for everyone. Some people don't want a professional appointment with a practitioner, and others can't afford one. Many people—trauma survivors in particular—prefer to do their inner work in private, away from even the kindest sort of scrutiny by a therapist. (I have had clients take a recording and ask to be allowed to listen in a vacated office next to mine, so that they know I'm nearby but not watching them. They feel self-conscious.)

Some are so sensitive to what they think the therapist needs or wants to see from them, by way of a positive reaction, that they get all bollixed up in those expectations and lose sight of who they are doing this for. And of course some people with PTSD are too phobic to leave the house altogether, and that fact alone makes a portable recording the intervention of choice, short of a home visit.

Of course, the recorded guided imagery should do its best to offer fill-in-the-blanks imagery that allows its listeners to customize what they hear; and up front it should instruct its users to be the executive editors of the imagery, inviting them to delete or add content as needed. And people really do this: they hear different portions or images when they are ready for them. I have actually had people ask me if a certain image or phrase was *always* on a recording, because they only just heard it for the first time after weeks of listening. This is the genius of the unconscious, always looking out for its owner. People generally hear what they need to hear, when they need to hear it. So even on a scripted recording, they titrate the dosage of what they take in.

Nonetheless a general, scripted recording needs to be carefully field-tested, because even the most sensitive writer of imagery has inevitable blind spots and is sure to blunder into tender areas that are best avoided.

For instance, after our trauma imagery passed muster with the combat veterans and was presented to groups of rape survivors, they were understandably distressed by the word *penetrating*, which I hadn't even realized was in there, to describe a quality of light. Needless to say, that word was excised. And when the same imagery was then tested with a group of domestic violence survivors, they made it clear that the image of being seated while surrounded by helpers and guides had to go. As one woman said, "Honey, if they're standing, I'm standing. Nobody stands over me anymore. And no one comes up from behind me, either. I want to be able to see who's coming." These concerns do not come up with one-on-one imagery, but with scripted imagery extra care is necessary.

THE LISTENER'S VOICE VS. ANOTHER'S

Another variable that people frequently wonder about is whether it isn't inherently more effective to have people record their imagery in their own voice. The assumption is that surely the timbre and cadence of a person's own voice would be the most congruent, compatible, and *absorbable* sound going into their ears. In fact, this is often a wonderful idea and absolutely right. And if the person can add his most preferred, sympatico music underneath his own voice, better yet.

But again, it's not that simple. Some people hate the sound of their own voices. Others get distracted by evaluating their "performance" instead of immersing themselves into the imagery. Some feel awkward or self-conscious doing the recording, and others just don't have the energy—they much prefer to be given something that's already made. These are case-by-case situations that need to be evaluated on the merits and practicalities at hand.

ADULTS VS. KIDS

Imagery is not just for adults—on the contrary, children love it and are especially skillful at it. Flexing their imaginations is a natural activity for them, and they'll do it with or without our assistance. Younger kids prefer shorter words and shorter sessions, and there are some wonderful children's audios available;[4] but in a pinch they will manage to benefit even from inappropriately adult-sized recordings with polysyllabic words. They naturally get the flavor, intention, tone, and mood. Some parents and grandparents actually hold a preverbal baby in their laps while listening to imagery themselves, and swear that the baby absorbs the imagery from them, almost by direct induction, through their skin.

Contrary to popular assumptions, teenagers make the best guided imagery end users of all. I suspect this is because they are already awash in an age-appropriate, hormone-induced trance state that is just a natural part of adolescence. I've had the secretly amused privilege, many times, of watching surly, slouching, teenage boys and girls—kids whose tough exteriors, scary, indifferent looks, and weird headgear have become semi-permanent accessories—drop like stones into their imaginal world. Once there they would be horrified to know that their faces became disarmingly and angelically sweet.

The trick with teenagers is to not be fooled by the shriveling disdain and contempt they so skillfully direct at adults (therapists and community workers who themselves affected this look when they were teenagers are least likely to be fooled, as they understand all too well the mush that lies beneath), and to offer them imagery with an end goal they can get behind—imagery geared to help with peak performance at sports or music, for instance.

Staff at one residential treatment center for chemically dependent teens—some with severe behavior problems who are court-ordered for a thirty-day stay—report that a favorite activity for these tough kids is Spirituality Group, where they listen to various guided meditations. It has become a tradition for many of them to bring blankets and stuffed animals to the session so they can curl up and listen like the children they are and still need to be.

SOME BASICS OF SCRIPTED GUIDED IMAGERY

The guided imagery narratives that follow can be read quietly and then reimagined; spoken aloud to someone; or recorded for yourself or someone else, then listened to on tape or compact disk.

Ideally, they are spoken over compatible music and recorded in such a way that the words and music provide a relaxing, immersive experience, carrying the listener effortlessly into a calm, receptive state, and making the lush, rich world of his or her imagination even more accessible than usual. This combination of relaxed reverie, heightened receptivity, and healing images allows alchemical changes to occur in mind, body, and spirit.

For those who prefer to speak or record in their own voice, or who wish to make changes to the words or phrases, here are some key pointers.

POINTERS FOR THE NARRATOR

VOICE

If we've learned anything from accumulated feedback over the past decade and a half, it's that, as important as your words are, they will never be as critical as the quality of your voice and the intention behind it. Most people start out a little too fast, high-pitched, and too effortful, but usually after reading a few paragraphs they automatically slip into the relaxed cadence and gentle flow of their own natural rhythm and timbre, which is so essential to effective guided meditation.

If you are creating a recording, the best thing to do is to keep on going and then go back and rerecord the beginning to match your now-slowed-down, more natural pace. If you are reading to someone, chances are they have also started out a little too speedy, and you'll just be starting where they are and slowing them down along with you into a more relaxed, immersive pace.

The most important thing to remember is to speak naturally, the way you would to a friend sitting next to you, during a relaxed, quiet conversation. Your voice is low and soft, the way it always is when you are relaxed. (The more tense we are, the higher our pitch.) This not only entrains a calmer pacing but encourages listeners to match you by getting their awareness back down into their bodies, through the example of your own low, embodied voice. Under these conditions, even if your voice is somewhat strained starting out, your throat will relax and you will probably wind up sounding fairly smooth.

This is *not* a dramatic reading, so you want to be free of artifice and emotional punctuation. In fact, you very much want to keep out of the listener's way by maintaining a fairly even emphasis—they'll know for themselves what content needs their attention and what is irrelevant, and they will supply their own emotional flavoring. Your voice is there to provide a quiet, trustworthy, undistracting platform from which the listener can access his or her unique reactions and responses. So your voice can't be calling attention to itself. Neither should there be even a hint of seductive, manipulative, or controlling flavor. Have some other people listen to it as a check if you are not sure about the tone you are communicating. It goes without saying—but I'll say it anyway—that the last thing on earth you want to be doing is issuing an unconscious sexual invitation to your listener.

Of course, if you are recording in a studio or using a good microphone, you have ideal conditions for communicating a gentle intimacy. Your voice can be as soft and low as you please, and the microphone will take care of the volume.[5]

A personal supply of room-temperature water, tart Granny Smith apples, and throat-soothing tea with honey and ginger revives even the weariest, scratchiest voice. Keep away from the lemons, though. They may appear to be helping your voice initially, but ultimately they will dry out your throat.

MUSIC

Music plays a powerful and underappreciated role in increasing the power of guided imagery, and just as with the voice, effective music does not draw attention to itself or compete with the listener's images by being too interesting in and of itself. Appropriate music stays *under* the words, supporting their relaxed, emotional impact without creating anything additional on its own.[6] Most people have no idea how helpful the music is to the whole experience, precisely because of the way it stays in the background and doesn't ask for attention.

In one study by guided imagery expert Lucille Eller, R.N., Ph.D., with HIV clinic patients at University Hospitals of Cleveland, the recorded interventions tested were guided imagery and progressive relaxation.[7] The music track was removed from the imagery tape, so that both treatment conditions would be "pure" and would match each other. The study found that the guided imagery was less impactful than anticipated. The HIV patients still reported a reduction in anxiety and depression, but the results were far less dramatic than previous reports had led investigators to expect. The best explanation was that without the music, the imagery had lost some of its potency.

In most cases where relaxed listening is the goal, the music does well to offer slow, spacious chords (like breathing) with a rhythm that matches a strong but relaxed heart rate of about sixty beats per minute, give or take.[8] Most people intuitively choose music that does this. The exception is when you are devising imagery to increase energy, motivation, or physical movement—then you want to use rhythm that is faster and stronger, and possibly more emphatic instruments, such as horns and drums, or an ostinato of strings.

There is a danger of overthinking all of this, however. Most people are guided by wise intuitive preferences, if they have the opportunity to choose their music. Therapists who work one on one with individuals like to have a selection of background music CDs from which the person can choose. Or they use music that they know doesn't create objections in most people.

There are a few exceptions to this music-is-better rule, however. Professional musicians can get sidelined by their tendency to analyze the music ("Why on earth is he using an oboe in there? What was he thinking?"), so that the music actually impedes their ability to immerse themselves into a relaxed, receptive state for the imagery. Similarly, people with great sensitivity to music or strong musical tastes may have such a powerful evaluative reaction that they are better off without it. In addition, people used to the quiet of mindfulness meditation may also prefer some quiet space between words.

All that being said, I strongly recommend musical accompaniment for most people. It adds greatly to the experience and enhances the healing power of the images. Indeed, scores of studies show that an intervention of music in and of itself will lower heart rate, blood pressure, respiration, and anxiety as well as improve mood. This includes trials with people undergoing various disturbing medical procedures such as colonoscopy, breast biopsy, radiation therapy, ventilator therapy, and coronary bypass surgery as well as with people suffering from chronic diseases such as COPD (chronic obstructive pulmonary disease).[9] With music we can increase the impact of the imagery with a synergistic and potent intervention that boasts its own fine track record.

REINFORCING THE SENSE OF MASTERY AND CONTROL

In any imagery session it is important to make sure people understand they can stop the session at any time. As with any approach or technique, but especially with survivors of trauma, people must be able to set their own pace and feel free to call time out or stop participating altogether at any point along the way.

If a person is listening to a recording, having her finger on the pause button is powerful insurance. If the imagery experience is with a practitioner, that clinician is of course obliged to show sensitivity and flexibility, deferring to the wishes, needs, and concerns of the client. This is always true but is especially true for trauma survivors, who are striving to reclaim ownership over themselves as the first order of healing.

Some will feel safer if they can leave their eyes half open and just stare down at the floor, rather than close them completely, the way most listeners like to do, during an imagery session. That works fine. In fact, some forms of meditation specifically ask that the eyelids be kept at half mast.

Similarly, it's best to use language that communicates an easygoing acceptance of whatever images care to show up in the listener's inner world. The listener is not there to follow authoritative instructions but rather to explore his own journey with the help of some gentle, external support. Imagery always works best in a permissive, relaxed, unforced atmosphere, processed as it is in the right hemisphere, where dualities of right and wrong, correct and incorrect, are irrelevant.

So, too, it is best to avoid the imperative verb form, so that inadvertently "bossy" language doesn't marshal unnecessary fear or resistance in the listener. This is the difference between the directive "Feel the air on your skin" and the suggestion "And you might notice the feel of the air on your skin" or perhaps "Allow yourself to enjoy the feel of the air on your skin" or even "Feeling the air on your skin." Sentences needn't be complete. Gerunds and hanging adverbial clauses work just fine. The right brain is not concerned with syntax. The idea is simply to communicate that all of this imagery business is a choice.

This is in sharp distinction to traditional hypnotherapy technique, which is authoritarian by choice. Hypnotherapy tells the listener, "Feel the air on your skin," and assumes he can and will do so, building in some automatic "success." Standard hypnotherapy worries that saying "And you might notice the feel of the air on your skin," leaves room for doubt and suggests to the listener that he might not be able to do this.[10]

To complicate matters further, there is another method of hypnotherapy, devised by Milton Erickson, that is entirely antiauthoritarian in style and far more compatible with what I am calling guided imagery.

As a rule of thumb, I am fairly certain, based on years of feedback from many quarters, that people—at least in the United States—have far more trouble with being told what to do than they have with an inferred implication that they maybe won't be able to follow the suggestions put forth. And that goes double for trauma survivors.

Finally, some traumatized or highly anxious people may feel better or safer reading the imagery script first, before the actual experience of listening to it. Leslie Root, Ph.D., and her team at the Gulf Coast Veterans Health Care System in Biloxi, Mississippi, used this approach with their support groups of twenty-two male veterans with PTSD and found that the men were more amenable to using the highly evocative and intense imagery once they'd first had a chance to read it over and discuss it with one another.[11] In addition to reading it over, the men also felt the group support lent a sense of safety as well.

IMAGERY CONTENT

Content is best left open-ended, in order to allow listeners to fill in the blanks with meaningful images of their own. People's imagery needs to be congruent with their personal values, aesthetics, experiences, and comfort zone, so you always want to encourage people—either in a recording or in an individual session—to let their own images come up for them, rather than yours.

Words and phrases that recruit all the senses are most effective, especially those that address the kinesthetic or feeling sense. Evocative sensory images—sight, sound, touch, feel, taste, and smell—activate the power of the right hemisphere, intensify the reverie state, and make the imagery more potent.

It is also a good idea to liberally sprinkle your narrative with symbols, similes, and metaphors. This kind of poetic language has a deep impact on the receptivity of the right brain and at the same time is oblique enough to sidestep terrifying literal images. In content areas where people are skittish, resistant, or fearful about approaching the actual idea of something, they will often be able to work with a symbolic representation of it. Like Frannie and the stone, the effect can be quite magical.

Another simple but very effective tactic that can help with fearfulness, reluctance, or resistance is using the imaginal device of a stage, a movie screen, a TV set with a remote switch, or a telescope upon which the images occur—anything that offers an imaginal layer, one that provides additional distance from the imagined content.

Imagery that elicits emotion is generally more effective than imagery that does not, and when a listener responds with emotion (usually tears), it is a good sign that the imagery is working in a deep way. Some trauma survivors in a numbed phase may pull back from having their feelings evoked, and it is of course up to them to decide if they are ready. But the majority welcome the return of emotion with relief, even when the feelings aren't pleasant. There is a sense of coming back to life again with the return of grief, anger, love, longing, shame, regret, fear, helplessness, and sorrow.

ADDITIONAL IMPACT

Groups potentiate the effects of imagery, and increase its impact on individual members, because of the contagious nature of the reverie state. I mean this literally. I like to seat people close together for this reason. If I'm given a large room to work with a small group, I'll cluster the chairs in a corner. If people are sprinkled around an auditorium, with space between them, I'll ask them to please come forward and clump together. Cancer and cardiac patients commonly report that after experiencing imagery with their hospital support group, they were much better able to use it at home by themselves.

For trauma survivors especially, listening to guided imagery with a supportive group of people who have survived similar horrors lends an extra measure of safety, support, and trust to the experience. For this reason support groups, family groups, therapy groups, and training groups are an ideal platform for offering guided imagery.

Touch is a powerful accompaniment to imagery, both to help with relaxation and grounding and to increase the images' kinesthetic power. When a person is being encouraged to breathe deeply into her belly, for instance, it can be very powerful for her to put her hands over her belly and feel the rise and fall of the abdomen; or to imagine that the warm energy from her hands is gently being absorbed by the skin, softening and calming any agitated places inside. Imagery for opening the heart can be assisted by putting the flat palm of the hand over the breastbone or center of the chest.

Some trauma survivors who are already working with therapeutic massage, energy work, or other touch therapies as part of their treatment regimen may want to play their imagery during these treatments as a valuable added component. Of course, this can only work with trustworthy practitioners who display sensitivity, respect, and good boundaries in their work.

OBSERVABLE RESPONSE

Numerous nonverbal cues let a practitioner know when people are responding to guided imagery. Participants become preternaturally still, and even if they temporarily interrupt their immobility to scratch, shift position, sneeze, or yawn, they return to that unusual stillness. Their faces become very smoothed out, and regardless of their coloring, their skin acquires a pinker undertone as blood moves into the face. Their expression becomes very soft and calm—beatific, actually. Sometimes when I am working from a stage and looking out over a large audience of people immersed in imagery, I feel like I am in a room full of angels.

POINTERS FOR THE LISTENER

For the person who is listening to healing imagery—whether in a live session or from a professional or homemade recording—this basic information can help make the experience as powerful, comfortable, and effective as possible.

Many clinicians who work individually with clients record their imagery sessions, so that their clients can take a tape or CD home to work with, between sessions. The suggestions that follow are not intended to trump their individual instructions but rather to serve as a general guide.

GENERAL DRILL—RULES AND REGS

I like to encourage people to pick the same corner of the house, or the same chair at the office, for their imagery sessions. Closing the door, shutting off the phone, and doing whatever is possible to avoid disruption (or worrying about disruption) is also a good idea.

Try to listen to the same imagery once or twice a day for at least three or four weeks. Developing a routine with it will ensure that it gets scheduled into your day. An inherently impactful time is when waking up or when falling asleep, that dreamy time between wakefulness and sleep, when you already have a powerful reverie state working for you.

But here's an important rule of thumb: any time spent with the imagery is better than no time. Even five minutes can confer a significant benefit. So don't pass on a daily session just because you don't have the full twenty or twenty-five minutes.

If an entire narrative feels like it's too much to take in, do just a small piece of it and try to add a little more each time you're ready. Over time you will adjust to it and it might seem less impactful, but in actual fact it will be affecting you more and more profoundly.

Listening to the same imagery for several weeks may produce what is called a *saturation effect*—you feel tired of it and don't want to listen to it anymore. This is a good time to switch to another narrative and let the new one soak in. Eventually you may have several to choose from, each of which will sound fresh to you again after a break.

On the other hand (as we once learned from a quirky experiment with a guided imagery / weight-loss group, artificially configured for a national TV news program, which met for a year and doggedly listened to the same weight-loss imagery every day of that year), if you choose to continue to listen to imagery you are thoroughly sick of, it will continue to benefit you, even as it annoys you and drives you to distraction.

HOW TO SIT

It is best to sit straight, with your head, neck, and spine aligned. This is better for you physically, as you will be fairly motionless for a while and you don't need to be acquiring kinks and cricks; and it helps you to be more open and receptive to the imagery.

Try positioning your hands in the same way, each time you listen to the imagery. You might fold both hands over your belly, or place one palm flat over your breastbone—any comfortable, accessible position that you can later use anywhere. Over time this hand placement will become a kind of conditioned response, a postural cue that will help you move immediately to a place of relaxed calm, with or without the audio. This can come in very handy when you're out and about and something distressing happens. You can then access relaxation and healing very quickly, simply by placing your hands the way they were when you were relaxing to your imagery.

Some trauma survivors are happier keeping their eyes half open during their imagery rather than shutting them completely. That works fine.

CONSCIOUS ATTENTION

You don't need to pay perfect attention as you listen. As you relax more and more deeply, you are likely to drift in and out of focusing on the imagery. If you notice your mind wandering, you can gently guide it back, but it's not essential. This spacey kind of awareness comes with the territory, so don't feel you must sharply focus on the content in the same way you would study for a test. This process uses a different part of your brain, and it likes to meander.

In fact, it's a good idea to let go of any rigorous expectations about how to do this exactly right. Imagery works best in a permissive, relaxed, unforced atmosphere. There are many ways to listen effectively, so don't get stuck on feeling you have to do this in just one "correct" way. The right hemisphere doesn't understand the idea of "correct" anyway, so never feel that you must follow a suggestion or do exactly what is said.

Even if you fall asleep while listening, the imagery will still have a cumulative, healing impact on you over time. Certain hard-driving Type A sorts of people are incapable of being relaxed and awake at the same time. They nod off immediately and never hear a conscious word. Yet a few people with diabetes, who track their blood glucose measurements each day, have assured us that their levels zigzag down in a steady progression from daily listening, even though they fall asleep before the introduction is half over. One such person was determined to stay awake to hear what was on the imagery, so she listened to it while walking around her kitchen table. She reported that she immediately recognized every image on the tape—even the physiologically detailed cellular imagery of which she had no previous knowledge was entirely familiar to her, just below her conscious awareness. If, like her, you prefer to stay awake just to know what you are listening to, you too might try sitting up with your back away from the chair, standing and leaning against a wall, walking, or listening with eyes half open to help you stay awake.

Because of its ability to produce deep relaxation and inattention in the listener, you shouldn't listen to guided imagery while you are driving or doing anything that requires alertness.

SELECTIVE HEARING

Different parts of the imagery will capture your attention at different times. You'll tend to notice what you are ready to hear. Let your unconscious provide this service for you—it tends to be a wise and compassionate editor.

Of course, give yourself permission to ignore or change whatever is on the narrative that doesn't suit you. Your "inner editor" will tend to do that for you anyway, as well as fill in the blanks with your own personal, appropriate images on an as-needed basis. They may change over time, depending on what you need, and they may not make immediate sense to you. Try to keep an open mind, and avoid immediately judging or analyzing what shows up. Let the images evolve in their own way, rather than forcing meaning on them too soon. Sometimes you can get more mileage out of letting the symbols or images stay ambiguous for a while. Trying to figure them out before their time can lead you down forced, artificial paths.

If your unconscious mind wants to take over and supersede the narrative, let it. Don't get stuck in following the literal recording unless you want to. And always feel free to stop anytime—that's what that pause button is for.

LESS BECOMES MORE

Keep in mind that skill and efficiency increase with practice; people improve dramatically. Over time they find themselves moving more and more quickly and deeply into a healing reverie, on an as-needed basis during a working day. After a few weeks of regular use, most people are able to access a level of deep healing imagery in the time it takes for a traffic light to change. In fact, you could say that guided imagery functions in a way that is the opposite of addictive substances—the more you use it, the less of it you need.

UNIVERSALITY AND ACCESSIBILITY

The good news about imagery is that just about anyone can use it. It's an equal-opportunity intervention. You don't have to be smart, rich, grown up, psychologically sophisticated, mentally balanced, physically strong, supermotivated, or well educated for it to work for you. It likes everybody.

For most people, imagery is a far easier form of meditation than mindfulness, mantra repetition, or following the breath, as it requires less discipline, tends to more easily capture attentional focus, and is inherently more interesting.

Nor do you need to believe the imagery will help you for it to work. Even a skeptical, reluctant willingness to give it a try is quite enough. Imagery has a lot of adherents who started out with negative assumptions about it.

On the other hand, a small minority of people find imagery taxing and annoying. Some people hate to sit still and get agitated when they are invited to relax. There is no sense in torturing them with twenty minutes of guided imagery, twice a day. They have a host of far more compatible interventions to choose from—walking meditation, biofeedback, qigong, yoga, and many brief, behavioral approaches described in detail in Chapter 14.

RECRUITING ALL THE SENSES

It's best to engage all your senses, imagining sights, sounds, smells, tastes, and feel as fully as possible. The rule of thumb here is the more sensory avenues the better. In fact, the term *visualization* is misleading because it implies that we're limiting our imagery to visual imagination. The fact is, only about 55 percent of the population is strongly wired visually, and the other 45 percent could get the wrong idea that they are incapable of using imagery because they don't "see" things in their imagination.

If anything, it's best to focus on the kinesthetic or feeling sense as the premier perceptual avenue for healing. Remembering or imagining how something feels in the body is especially powerful for trauma survivors who need more grounded body awareness, and whose symptoms are located in their bodies.

EMOTIONAL AND PHYSICAL REACTIONS

Don't worry if the imagery brings forth unexpected emotion. It has a way of making people tearful, either because their hearts are touched, or because they are releasing grief, or both. The onset of emotion means that the imagery is reaching you the way it was designed to. Let the tears rinse through you—it's good for you.

You may find you have other physical responses. Some people get a runny nose, cough, yawn, feel heaviness in their limbs, get tingling sensations along the top of the scalp or in their hands and feet, or experience minor, involuntary muscle movements. These are all normal, transitory reactions. Don't worry about them.

Expect to become unusually still when you are listening to imagery, although you probably won't be aware of it at the time. (This is one reason it is a good idea to sit straight—to avoid cramping.) Your face and hands may become a lot warmer or, in some people, cooler. Your voice is likely to be deeper and lower immediately after the imagery, and your speech slower and more relaxed. Irritations and worries that you had when you started are likely to vanish, and you will probably feel more open and receptive. You may notice people responding to you differently. Imagery usually makes people more attractive and more approachable.

CONDITIONS THAT ENHANCE IMPACT

It often surprises people to know that imagery is more impactful on a person in a group than alone. There is something contagious about the reverie state. When people are surrounded by others, in close proximity, in a group where everyone is listening to the same guided imagery, their response goes further and deeper than what happens when they are alone. This is even true of people who are uncomfortable in groups. It's as if they are able to hitch a ride on the powerful coherence of the group brain wave. Once the group achieves a new, deep level, individuals can repeat it alone. So, listening to imagery with a whole support group, study group, therapy group, or family group is an extrapowerful way to experience it and very helpful for people who have trouble meditating on their own. The opportunity for discussion afterward, with people who have had similar experiences, can provide even more support.

Music usually increases the power of the imagery, adding interest and emotional flavor to the experience. It is important to choose music that is compatible, pleasant, and not too obtrusive, because you want it not to compete with the imagery but to support it. A small percentage of people prefer no music at all, especially if they are professional musicians or are extremely sensitive to music—they become distracted by their natural tendency to analyze and evaluate it.

Touch is a powerful accompaniment to imagery, both to help with relaxation and to increase your ability to absorb the images with your whole self. If you are already using methods such as therapeutic massage, energy work, Reiki, Zero Balancing, or other kinesthetic modalities, you might consider doing that work while playing the imagery.

SIDE BENEFITS

Keep in mind that the act of listening to imagery is very likely to yield additional benefits, by its nature and regardless of its content. Because it elevates endorphin levels, imagery will lift your spirits, reduce anxiety, and alleviate pain from headache, arthritis, and other chronic conditions. It can also do a nice job of pulling you out of obsessive rumination or preoccupation with old resentments, slights, and injuries.

PERSONAL ADJUSTMENTS

Some people like to open their imagery session with a personal prayer or request for help and guidance. The heartfelt invoking of divine assistance sets intention, adds to the feeling of relaxation and calm, and invites spiritual assistance to come calling. It can only help.

●　　●　　●

Now we can look at the specific guided imagery narratives designed to heal the three stages of recovery from traumatic stress: after the immediate impact; during the heart of the healing; and for whatever residual aftereffects might remain after the core trauma is healed.

11 GUIDED IMAGERY FOR THE FIRST STAGE OF TRAUMA: REESTABLISHING SAFETY AND CONTROL

This book offers a three-stage program of specific guided imagery exercises, for the most general applicability, and for the widest range of survivors and circumstances. It provides imagery for the immediate aftermath of trauma, designed for simple, basic self-soothing, to help the user quickly settle down and return to calm when disturbing images and memories intrude into consciousness. The second-stage imagery goes deeper, to help the user reestablish a connection with the world of feelings, face down unpleasant symptoms, and move under them to the core of the hurt, in order to cognitively and emotionally integrate what has happened. And the third stage helps with the longer-term fallout from the trauma, after the core difficulties have been healed: the toll trauma takes on confidence, self-esteem, the possible emergence of compulsive or addictive behaviors, or difficulties with relationships.

WHERE TO START

There is no definitive, cookie-cutter timetable for these stages, but generally speaking, early-stage imagery is good for right after the traumatic event, up through several weeks—sometimes even three to six months—later. For some the first stage will be all that is required, and they will have no need to go further with the more elaborate imagery. Second-stage imagery can be used anytime, from a few days or weeks after the traumatic event, to several months or even years later. It is strictly a matter of personal readiness *to tolerate feelings.* The self-regulation imagery remains helpful to people during this phase, to help them settle down when the emotions get too distressing. The third stage of imagery is, again, a matter of individual readiness, when people have the strength and energy to dismantle any dysfunctional patterns they've acquired along the way.

Most people do not need to do half of what is offered here. One or two exercises from each stage is usually plenty. For most survivors, I recommend Peaceful Place Imagery and Imagery for Restful Sleep in the first stage; Imagery to Release Grief and Imagery to Heal Trauma in the second; and Imagery for Confidence and Imagery for Anger and Forgiveness in the final stage. This imagery seems most likely to help the greatest number of people and alleviate the worst of the symptoms—either by itself or as a component of a broader treatment program.

But the wider selection allows you to pick and choose and offers alternates for the sake of variety, depth, and subtlety. The "menu" makes it possible for you to tailor a program for yourself or, if you are a practitioner, for your clients.

These guided exercises have been used with good results by combat veterans; rape, assault, and domestic violence survivors; victims of incest and childhood abuse; natural disaster survivors; people recovering from life-threatening illnesses; and those who experienced the terrors of Columbine High, Oklahoma City, and the attacks of 9/11. They have also been used by early responders, therapists, journalists, EMT workers, uniformed officers, Red Cross volunteers, and other emergency relief personnel.

Survivors whose wounds have seasoned over time may prefer to begin with the more intense imagery of the second stage. Many adult survivors of childhood abuse, who have already done personal work on themselves, are often ready and eager to go straight to the heart of their healing with Imagery to Heal Trauma. This is also true for people who suffer from secondary or vicarious traumatic stress—early responders, uniformed officers, therapists, emergency service personnel, pastors, and reporters often prefer to start out with the more intense and specific healing imagery of stage two.

But most people, between the immediate aftermath of a traumatic event and several weeks later, generally do well starting out with simple, unambitious imagery that helps regulate anxiety and manage overwhelming feelings, flashbacks, and thoughts. This is what they need, what they can manage, and what they find useful at the outset.

The program is highly versatile. It can stand on its own, and for some, it is the only thing they will use to recover from trauma. But it is also an extremely compatible complement to other methods. It makes for great homework for people already in counseling or therapy. It doesn't compete with the other effective behavioral methods, tools, and modalities described in Chapter 14. Rather, it serves as an integrative force for other modes of help, cohering mind, body, and spirit—conscious and unconscious elements—around the central task of healing.

You may read through these narratives, then use the imagery while listening to a favorite piece of music. But they are more effective when you hear them directly and have nothing to do other than listen. You can record them in your own voice and subsequently play them; or you can ask a trusted friend, family member, or professional helper to read them aloud; or you can purchase professionally produced and scored pieces, where technical proficiency and well-scored, well-mixed music partially make up for the absence of a familiar voice and more personal touch.

STAGE ONE

The imagery a trauma survivor needs immediately after a traumatic episode, or in the earliest stages of post-traumatic stress, offers simple, easy-to-follow, self-soothing tools. It is different from the more layered, complex, multifaceted imagery that is helpful later on, in the weeks, months, and even years that follow, when symptoms have seasoned, festered, or become chronic; or have gone underground and then resurfaced after a period of uneasy but apparent quiet.

Immediately after a traumatic episode, people are most often looking for imagery that will gently divert their attention and offer simple, temporary relief from extreme distress. They want an oasis of time where they can feel calm, grounded, and back in control. Even five minutes of getting away from the horror and helplessness flashing in their heads is gratefully received. At this stage the imagery cannot make too many demands on an already overtaxed psyche, because people are already stretched to the limit.

So in the immediate aftermath, we are not trying to "fix" anything (although for some, these exercises might serve that purpose). We aren't looking to help produce catharsis, deep insight, profound change, intellectual understanding, existential meaning, or spiritual transcendence. We're after *relief*. We want to serve up imagery that will gently hold, support, divert, calm, and affirm the survivor. We want something that will enlist his or her self-regulation skills with minimal demands and show that it's possible to master the emotional roller-coaster ride they find themselves on. This is imagery of modest but worthy ambition—imagery that gets a person through the day and helps promote good sleep at night. As modest as these goals are, they are badly needed and greatly appreciated. For calming a ravaged soul, this imagery delivers the goods. In the immediate aftermath of trauma, its value is priceless.

What follows is imagery to gently divert attention, while at the same time grounding, calming, and soothing the listener.

1 PEACEFUL PLACE IMAGERY

This imagery is a standard choice for trauma survivors and their counselors. It has the advantage of being easy to use, and because of its fill-in-the-blank nature, it elicits each person's unique memories and sensations of happier times, places, and situations.

People with a history of abuse and hardship will sometimes say they have no happy time or place to go to—that the people in their lives were disappointing or cruel, and no place on the planet feels safe. But when gently pressed, they can usually find something from which they drew nourishment—either a loving animal, a kind adult who made a brief but memorable appearance, a spiritual connection of some kind, or some imaginal companion that got them through. The lush inventiveness and generosity of the imagination can always serve up the right conditions for these purposes, as it probably did back then, too.

Some people with an obsessive nature can get caught up in trying to figure out the absolute best possible place to choose for the exercise, running the risk of never getting beyond that threshold, because they can't decide. ("Well, I like the mountains . . . but then again, the ocean is really nice, too . . . and I do enjoy walking in the woods.") For them, getting too many choices is a liability, and it's best to encourage them to *just pick one*, for the sake of the exercise. They may take comfort from the notion that they can always go back and choose a different scene the next time.

This meditation and the ones that follow are the "long form." People may prefer their own shortcuts. The operating principle is simply *whatever works*. People should do whatever makes these guided exercises easy, practical, and usable on a frequent basis.

PEACEFUL PLACE IMAGERY

Please take a moment or two to position yourself as comfortably as you can, allowing your body to be well supported . . . and gently letting your eyes close, if they want to . . . and arranging it so your head, neck, and spine are straight . . .

And letting your hands rest comfortably somewhere on your body . . . on your chest or midriff or abdomen . . . so you can feel the rise of your body when you breathe in . . . and the way it settles back down when you breathe out . . . and you're becoming more and more attuned to the feel of your breath moving in and out of your body . . .

And now, taking a nice, deep, full, cleansing breath . . . and breathing out, fully and completely . . . feeling the expansion of your belly with each breath in . . . and the way your body subsides with each out-breath . . .

And again, breathing in . . . and this time, imagining that you're sending the warm energy of your breath to places in your body that might be sore or tense or tight . . . and releasing the tension with the out-breath . . . so you can feel your breath going into those places . . . warming and softening and loosening them . . . and then, gathering it all up . . . and breathing it out . . .

So that more and more you can feel safe and comfortable . . . relaxed and easy . . . watching the cleansing action of your breath . . .

And any unwelcome thoughts . . . those too can be sent out with the exhale . . . so that for just a moment, your mind is empty . . . free and clear space . . . and you are blessed with peaceful stillness . . .

And any emotions you might sense inside . . . those too can be noted and breathed out of your body . . . so you can be still and quiet . . . like a smooth and glassy lake with no ripples . . .

And now, if you would . . . see if you can imagine a place . . . where you feel safe and peaceful . . . relaxed and easy . . . and it might be a place you used to go to . . . or somewhere you go to now . . . or a place you've always wanted to be . . . it could be by the ocean . . . or in the woods . . . or up in the mountains or desert . . . it doesn't matter . . . just so you choose one of the places that feel good and peaceful to you . . .

And allowing the place to become real in all its dimensions . . . looking around you . . . enjoying the colors . . . the play of light and shadow . . . the scenery, in all its detail . . . looking over to your left . . . and over to your right . . .

And feeling whatever you're sitting against or lying upon . . . whether you're leaning against a friendly old oak tree . . . or lying on sweet meadow grass . . . or walking in the woods, on a fragrant carpet of spicy pine needles . . . or you might be walking in the surf, with cool, wet sand oozing between your toes, and gentle waves lapping at your ankles . . . or maybe you're just sitting on a nice, warm rock in the sun . . .

And listening to the sounds of the place . . . birds singing . . . or the rustling sounds of a soft wind through the leaves . . . or the powerful, rhythmic crash of ocean waves . . . or the gentle soothing sound of a bubbling brook . . . just so you're letting your ears become attuned to all the beautiful sounds of this place . . . that is so safe and peaceful to you . . .

And smelling its rich fragrance . . . whether it's the sharp, bracing scent of salt sea air . . . the sweet, heavy fullness of flowers and grass . . . the pungent, dark green smell of peat moss in the forest . . . sometimes the air is so rich and redolent, you can practically taste it on your tongue . . .

And noticing the feel of the air on your skin as it caresses your face and neck . . . and it might be crisp and dry . . . or balmy and wet . . . so you're just letting your skin enjoy the nourishing presence of this place . . . that is so safe and peaceful to you . . . and letting its healing energy soak into your skin . . . letting it fill you . . . feeling it move into muscle and tissue and bone . . . all the way down into each and every cell . . .

So with every breath, you're inhaling the nourishing beauty of this place . . . bringing it into your body . . . breathing it into your heart . . . and with each exhale, you're more and more able to release whatever you wish to let go of . . .

Breathing deeply and easily . . . taking the peaceful beauty of the place into your body with each in-breath . . . and letting it move all through you . . . and breathing out whatever you wish to release . . . strong and steady . . . in and out . . . peaceful and easy . . .

And so, whenever you are ready . . . taking another full, deep breath . . . and gently, with soft eyes, coming back into the room whenever you are ready . . . knowing in a deep place that this place is inside of you . . . that you are better for this . . .

And so you are . . .

2 IMAGERY TO GROUND AWARENESS IN THE BODY

This next narrative is another commonly used exercise that, for all its simplicity, is surprisingly effective in calming and stabilizing people who have been recently rocked by trauma. It also helps them to breathe more normally. Traumatized people tend to inhale and exhale very shallowly. As a rule, people unconsciously slow down their inhalations to a very shallow minimum when they don't want to "take in" what has happened. Just from breathing more deeply and consciously, they will feel better.

This is an imagery alternative to counting the breaths, which is also a good, simple exercise at this stage. Note how in this narrative, awareness is guided from the head down, not from the feet up. This interrupts dissociation by encouraging people to settle awareness down into their bodies and more fully inhabit their skin.

IMAGERY TO GROUND
AWARENESS IN THE BODY

Please make yourself comfortable . . . positioning yourself so that you're allowing your body to be fully supported . . . and arranging your head, neck, and spine to be well aligned . . . as you shift your weight to be as comfortable as possible . . .

And taking a full, cleansing breath . . . breathing out as fully as you can . . . and another . . . deep down into the body . . . and again, breathing out fully and completely . . .

And turning your attention inward . . . focusing inside . . . curious about where your body might feel tight or tense or sore . . . and where it feels loose and open . . . so just letting your awareness move around inside your body . . .

Starting with your head . . . noticing any sensations in your head . . . and breathing into your head . . . and releasing discomfort with the out-breath . . . so that your head can feel clearer . . . more comfortable . . .

And moving your awareness into your neck and shoulders . . . and sensing how they're feeling . . . noticing any tightness or heaviness that might be there . . . and breathing the energy of your breath into them . . . and breathing out . . .

Noticing with detached interest how it feels inside your arms . . . in your elbows . . . your wrists and hands . . . and breathing the healing power of your breath into them . . . loosening trapped energy with the power of your breath . . . and breathing out . . .

Moving your awareness into your chest . . . sensing any tightness or discomfort . . . and inhaling all around and through it . . . releasing with the exhale . . .

And taking an extra moment to focus on your heart . . . becoming aware of how it feels, all around and through your heart . . . and you can breathe the kindness of your breath . . . into your own heart . . . letting the softness of your breath . . . nourish your heart . . . breathing out anything you might wish to release . . .

And now letting the energy of the in-breath move down your back . . . loosening your spine . . . and breathing out . . .

Filling your belly . . . sending the power of your breath deep into your center . . . and breathing out . . . as fully as you can . . .

And moving your awareness into your hips and bottom . . . aware of the soft power of the in-breath, releasing discomfort . . . softening tight muscle . . . as you breathe out . . .

Sending the breath into your legs . . . your knees . . . your calves and ankles . . . your feet . . . all the way down to the tips of your toes . . . breathing in and out . . .

So you're just taking a moment to check in with your body . . . your oldest friend . . . your steadiest companion . . . gently acknowledging with kindness and respect . . . as you would to any loyal friend . . . that you know it hasn't been easy . . . but it will get better . . . as you breathe in and out . . .

Continuing to send the breath into any tightness . . . letting it warm and loosen and soften all around and through it . . . and then releasing with the out-breath, deeply and fully . . .

Letting your awareness settle down into your body . . . allowing your spirit to softly settle into it . . . like a gentle, misty fog . . . softly rolling into every valley . . .

And just letting yourself feel the fullness of it . . . breathing fully and easily into every corner of your being . . . softly acknowledging the sore, weary places . . . and the strong, solid places . . . no praise, no blame . . . just noting what is so . . .

So you are breathing in . . . and breathing out . . . aware of the healing action of the breath . . . tending to your insides . . .

And whenever you are ready . . . taking another full, deep breath . . . and gently, with soft eyes, coming back into the room whenever you are ready . . . knowing in a deep place that you are better for this . . .

And so you are . . .

3 IMAGERY TO FOCUS ON THE HEART

This brief imagery exercise focuses awareness on the heart, directing attention to the beating of the heart—the central oscillator for the whole system. Even the energy of very scattered, distressed people can become more coherent as they focus on this imagery, and they will feel more grounded, present, and strong.

In addition, by the simple placement of attention on the pulsing of the heart, numbed-off feelings will often rise to the surface, bringing life back into emotionally deadened spaces. For this reason, people who are not yet ready to feel their emotions, even in a general way, may not want to work with this imagery right away.

Similarly, people who have had recent heart surgery may not like this imagery either, since focusing on their heart can remind them of their newly encountered vulnerability.

But for just about anyone else, this is a potent, easy exercise.

IMAGERY TO FOCUS ON THE HEART

To begin with, see if you can let yourself get comfortable . . . settling down into your body . . . and shifting your weight until you feel well supported . . . with your head, neck, and spine straight . . .

Getting more and more comfortable with each deep, full, cleansing breath . . . inhaling all the way in . . . letting your belly rise with the in-breath . . . and subside with the out-breath . . . soft and steady . . . *(pause)* . . .

And with the next breath in . . . sending the warm energy of the breath to any part of your body that's tense or tight or sore . . . sensing how it warms and loosens and softens any uncomfortable places . . . releasing them with the out-breath . . . so that more and more, you can feel comfortable and easy . . . with the healing action of your own breath . . .

Aware of any distractions that might surface in your mind . . . and breathing those out, too . . . so that for just a moment, your mind is still and empty . . . for just a split second, it is clear . . . and you are graced with stillness . . . like a lake with no ripples . . .

And noticing how you can focus your attention on your heart . . . as you place your awareness there . . . curious about how it feels all around and through your heart . . . and perhaps even putting the flat palm of your hand over your heart . . . to help you keep your attention there . . .

Connecting to the powerful rhythms of your heart . . . sensing how it pulses life and strength all through your body . . .

And now, imagining that you are breathing through your heart . . . as if the air were actually coming in through your heart . . . *(pause)* . . . and going out through your heart . . . soft and warm and steady . . .

Feeling a warmth and fullness gathering all around and through your heart . . . soft and nourishing . . . as you focus your attention there . . . and breathe your breath, right through the center of your heart . . . *(pause)* . . .

Still aware of the steady rhythm, in and out . . . your whole body beating with the steady rhythm of your heart . . . and even feeling the air around you begin to pulse with the steady power of your heart . . . your whole body radiating this powerful pulse . . . creating a force field of energy all around you . . . an expanding cushion of vibrant, dancing light and color . . . tingling on your skin . . . *(pause)* . . .

Sitting in the seat of the heart . . . in the center of its warmth and power . . . steady and strong . . . peaceful and easy . . . breathing your breath through your heart . . . for however long you wish . . . *(pause)* . . .

And knowing you can come back at any time . . . just by closing your eyes, and placing your hand over your heart . . . and breathing through it . . . and sensing how you pulse with it . . . strong and peaceful and steady . . .

So . . . whenever you are ready . . . you can, very gently and with soft eyes . . . allow yourself to come back into the room . . . knowing in a deep place that you are better for this . . .

And so you are.

4 IMAGERY FOR PROTECTION AND SUPPORT

This imagery is a bit more complex but has some extra healing punch. It offers the same calming effects as the other narratives, but with some additional feelings of safety, protection, and uplift from its deliberately heart-opening imagery. When people are asked to recollect those who have loved them, their own loving feelings tend to kick in, and this affords them not just a dose of emotional sustenance but a nice jolt of uplifting neurotransmitter that reduces pain and raises spirits.

Depending on the circumstances, some people may say that all the loving people are gone now. This thought has the potential to propel people into a state of despair, anger, or grief, where they can get stuck and lose the benefits of the exercise. The best way to counteract this thought is to see if it is possible to just stay in the moment, tapping into the nourishing *image* of the loving person, time, or place. It is the *image* of the loved one, after all, that functions as the "blankie," perpetually offering support, regardless of physical availability, just as the image of Viktor Frankl's dead wife kept his body alive and sustained his spirit during his soul-deadening time in the labor camps. The sensory images on the right side of the brain make no distinctions between past, present, and future. They just *are*. For some, however, the losses will be too fresh and the grief too strong for them to use these images of loved ones. And they don't need to; there are plenty of other exercises to choose from. But for those who can use this imagery, it serves up a strong dose of high-test healing.

Still others, especially those who suffered a harsh, abusive, or neglectful childhood, may say that they simply have no loving people or resources to recall—an even more devastating thought that can create enough distress to end the imagery session right there. Usually, however, when gently pressed, people can and do come up with sustaining memories— of a kindly adult, a teacher or neighbor, or perhaps a special pet who offered steady, loving support, or an imaginary friend, a nourishing relationship to nature, a felt sense of spiritual help, or a deep, wordless connection with the divine. The fact is, *something* gets them through, or they wouldn't be walking or talking.

Indeed, brief but well-timed, positive interactions with nourishing adults or even other children can go an awfully long way, repeating over and over in memory and fantasy and creating sustaining images that get children through. However, if it is just too much work for the listener to wrap his or her mind around this, or if the notion of loving beings just perpetuates too much pain, it's best to skip over this imagery exercise and use some others instead.

And finally, some may say that some of those who loved them were their betrayers and predators, and they do not want them around them. It is important to make clear that they are in control, and that this imaginal conjuring is *by invitation only*. Predators need not apply, and should they somehow show up, they can be just as easily banished. All things are possible in the benificent territory of the imaginal world.

In spite of these caveats, most people derive a great deal of support, strength, and relief from the imagery that follows.

IMAGERY FOR PROTECTION AND SUPPORT

Please begin by making yourself comfortable, shifting your weight so you're feeling well supported . . . *(pause)* . . . and gently allowing your eyes to close . . .

Letting your hands rest comfortably somewhere on your body—on your chest or midriff or abdomen—so you can feel the rise of your body when you breathe in . . . and the way it settles back down when you breathe out . . . and you're becoming more and more attuned to your breath, as it moves in and out of your body . . .

Inhaling deeply and slowly, all the way down into your belly . . . *(pause)* . . . and breathing out, fully and completely . . . feeling the expansion of your abdomen with each in-breath . . . and the way it subsides with each out-breath . . .

And again, breathing in . . . and this time, imagining that you're sending the warm energy of your breath to any part of your body that's sore or tense or tight . . . *(pause)* . . . and releasing the tension with the exhale . . . so you can feel your breath going to all the tight, tense places . . .

warming and loosening and softening them . . . and then, gathering up all the tension . . . and breathing it out . . . so that more and more, you can feel safe and comfortable, relaxed and easy . . . noticing your breath . . . with friendly but detached awareness . . .

And as you continue to breathe in and out . . . deeply and easily . . . and you might begin to notice a tingling in the air all around you . . . the pleasant, subtle feel of energy on your skin . . . tingling and vibrating . . . as if you were surrounded and protected by a magical cushion of air . . . alive with humming energy . . . tiny waves of it, sparkling and dancing with light and color . . . becoming fuller, denser, with every breath . . . a force field of protection and safety . . . softly pulsing around you . . . gently insulating you from anything you don't want or need . . .

And now, sensing this cushion of energy drawing to it all the love and sweetness that has ever been felt for you by anyone at any time . . . pulling in all the caring, all the loving kindness that has ever been sent your way . . . every prayer and good wish . . . permeating and filling the field of energy around you . . . every smile, every nod of respect . . . every thank you and gesture of gratitude . . . pulling it all in like a powerful magnet . . . calling every good wish home . . . and so increasing the powerful, protective field all around you . . .

And perhaps even sensing around you . . . the presence of those who've loved and nurtured you . . . or those who love you now . . . or who will love you in the future . . . just the ones you want with you . . . and sensing them around you now . . . maybe catching a fleeting glimpse of somebody . . . or noticing an old, familiar scent . . . or hearing the timbre of a dearly loved voice . . . possibly feeling a presence by your side . . . or the soft weight of a gentle hand on your shoulder . . .

People from your life . . . alive or long gone . . . there might even be a special animal . . . a powerful ancestor . . . a guardian angel . . . sweet spirits or magical beings . . . special helpers and healers . . . allies, teachers, and guides . . . all come to lend assistance . . . invoked by your intention to heal, fully and completely . . . and some might be familiar and some not . . . it doesn't matter . . . just so you feel their protection and support . . . breathing it into your heart . . . letting it fill you . . .

Breathing in all that love and care, fully and deeply . . . all the way into your heart . . . filling up with it . . . feeling its warmth spread all through your body . . . gently pulsing out from the center of your heart . . . and diffusing through your body . . . spreading widely and evenly, like ripples in a pond . . .

So you can feel a peaceful calm and balance settle over you . . . evening you out . . . filling you with a nourishing softness . . . as your heart becomes more and more peaceful . . . steady and calm . . .

Breathing in the protection all around you . . . knowing it is always there . . . yours to notice, whenever you wish . . .

And so . . . whenever you are ready . . . taking another full, deep breath . . . and gently, with soft eyes, coming back into the room whenever you are ready . . . knowing in a deep place that you are better for this . . .

And so you are . . .

5 AFFIRMATIONS

Affirmations are an alternative to a straight twenty-minute dose of imagery, and some people, traumatized or not, prefer them to guided imagery. They are positive statements designed to combat negative thinking. They are briefer and require less concentration than imagery. In fact, they are a little like imagery bytes. They don't ask fidgety listeners to sit still—you can even be folding laundry, shaving, driving, or doing some other rote task while listening to them.

They are also a bit more cognitive in nature, expressing supportive ideas in the first person, while still appealing to the right side of the brain with voice tone, images, and music. They work incrementally, as a kind of conscious, positive brainwashing. It's not the same as denial—these ideas don't have to be believed in order for them to work. All that is required is an openness, based on hope that over time they can be believed.

People are encouraged to listen to each statement in a state of open, relaxed attention, breathing in deeply with each one and repeating it softly to themselves, either aloud or in their minds. Even those who start out feeling that they are hokey and silly—and I'd have to include myself in that group—often find them astonishingly effective.

AFFIRMATIONS

I declare my intention to heal myself in body, mind, and spirit.

More and more, I understand that I will heal in my own way and my own time.

I invite assistance from friends and loved ones, past, present, and future, to lend me their support and strength.

I see myself surrounded by their love and caring, and I feel it all through me like a warm wave.

More and more, I can acknowledge and accept the times I feel anger, loneliness, sorrow, guilt, terror, despair, or shame.

I know that the more I can acknowledge and accept what I feel, without criticism or blame, the more I allow myself to heal.

More and more, I can accept my feelings, soften around them, and breathe through them.

I am better and better able to be kind and gentle toward myself.

More and more, I can release the thoughts and feelings that disturb my inner sense of balance and peace; I can send them out with the breath, in the interest of my own well-being.

More and more, I can let go of worrying about things I cannot control, and focus on my own inner peacefulness.

More and more, I can sense the peaceful stillness at my center.

I see myself becoming more and more patient, with myself and others.

More and more, I know that when I can let go of harsh expectations, of myself and others, I allow myself to heal.

I know that I am learning to listen to my body and sense what it needs.

More and more, I can appreciate my body, respect it, and take good care of it.

More and more, I can notice when muscles tense and tighten in my body, and I can soften and release them with my awareness and my breathing.

More and more, I can consider the possibility that my body is my ally, my oldest friend, and my steadiest companion.

I know that when I appreciate my body, respect it, and take good care of it, I allow myself to heal.

I can see and feel radiant sunlight warming my body, sending comfort and solace deep into my heart.

I can see and feel a powerful blue-green wave of healing, washing through me from head to toe, clearing away unwanted debris and taking it out with the tide.

I can see and feel a warm, glowing blanket of magical comfort surrounding me, enveloping me with peace and safety, soaking its peaceful energy into me.

I welcome my increasing ability to perceive the invisible assistance around me, guiding me back to my own strength, courage, and resourcefulness.

I salute my ability to survive and my courage to heal.

I understand there are treasures to be found as I heal from my past.

I know there is a core part of me that can never be diminished or destroyed.

I know that beneath the darkness that overtakes me at times, there is a place where I am radiant with the beauty of my own being.

I look forward to the time I will reclaim my full strength and express the range of my gifts.

I know that my heart is large enough to hold my suffering and transform it.

More and more, I can see the beauty all around me and draw nourishment from it.

More and more, I can take the time to touch a leaf, smell the morning air, and receive the caress of a soft breeze on my face.

I welcome my awareness of the peaceful power deep in my heart, the seat of my strength, and the home of my spirit.

The blueprint that I hold in my mind's eye is the picture of myself, vital, strong, calm, and steady; focused, joyful, and fulfilled.

I salute my own courage, commitment, and persistence in my efforts to reclaim my strength.

More and more, I know that my heart can heal with the vast energy of its own loving-kindness.

I can feel around me a protective cushion of energy, containing all the kindness, good wishes, prayers, gentle smiles, and sweet gestures of gratitude that have ever been sent my way.

I know that I have things to do, gifts to give, purposes to accomplish. I require my full strength and courage and peace of mind for this.

More and more, I know that my suffering has meaning, and I will understand this in my own time.

I know that I am held in the hands of God, and I am perfectly, utterly safe.

And so you are . . .

6 IMAGERY FOR RESTFUL SLEEP

For someone with post-traumatic stress, a few consecutive hours of satisfying sleep are a precious and hard-won commodity. Most trauma survivors experience a period of time when falling asleep is difficult, and falling back to sleep after being jolted awake by a nightmare is harder still. Because sleeplessness breeds its own set of pernicious symptoms, it is very important to be able to interrupt a sleep deprivation cycle.

This imagery has enough cognitive content in it to distract the worrying left brain away from its obsessive thinking, and enough evocative, soothing, "blankie" imagery to lull the right brain to sleep.

With this imagery, the notion of being surrounded by protection is important, particularly for adults who were molested at bedtime when they were children.

Especially with this imagery, where the goal is to encourage a dropping off into sleep, it's best to record the imagery on a compact disk. A cassette is likely to make a noise when it clicks off, and that can jar the person awake again.

IMAGERY FOR
RESTFUL SLEEP

To begin with, please allow yourself to get comfortable, allowing your body to feel the support beneath it . . . softening and settling into your position . . . and gently letting your eyelids close . . .

Becoming aware of the rise of your body as you breathe your breath in . . . and the way it settles back down as you breathe your breath out . . . soft and steady . . .

Breathing in . . . and breathing out . . . and with the next in-breath, sensing the warm energy of your breath moving into places that are sore or tight or tense . . . warming and loosening and softening any discomfort . . . and releasing it with the exhale . . .

Breathing into your mind . . . *(pause)* . . . and breathing your thoughts out with out-breath . . . so that for just a moment, your mind is free and clear space, still and quiet . . .

Sending the breath into any emotions . . . and releasing them with the out-breath . . . so you can feel more and more balanced and steady . . . quiet and still . . . like a lake with no ripples . . . smooth and clear as glass . . .

Becoming more and more aware of the gentle, healing power of the breath . . . moving in and out . . . soothing and tending to your interior . . . as you settle, more and more, into safety and comfort . . . relaxed and easy . . .

Your body feeling heavier and heavier . . . allowing the soft weight of your arms and legs . . . head, neck, and torso . . . settle and sink into the support beneath you . . . still aware of your own peaceful breathing . . . soft and steady . . . in and out . . .

Letting the weight of your head settle softly into a welcoming place . . . as your scalp releases any tightness . . . and tension drains away from your forehead . . . and you might even feel the space between your eyebrows melting . . . your eyelids growing heavy and soft . . .

Feeling the loosening all through your face . . . around your mouth . . . as muscles in your jaw and around your ears let go . . . leaving a softness in your face . . . continuing to breathe . . . deeply and easily . . . your body rising and falling with each gentle, nourishing breath . . . soft and steady . . .

Breathing into your neck and shoulders . . . sensing the gentle power of the breath . . . infusing and softening the tight places . . . warming and loosening . . . cleansing and clearing . . . releasing with the out-breath . . . and feeling the shift as your limbs release and soften . . .

Breathing into your heart . . . allowing the gentle power of the breath to move all around and through your heart . . . and breathing out, softly and easily . . . each breath taking you deeper down . . . into your body's healing rhythm . . .

Feeling the heaviness of your arms . . . how they sink softly into the support beneath them . . . muscle tissue releasing . . . tension ebbing away in the wrists and hands . . . your fingers curling gently . . . in their own soft gesture of peace and comfort . . .

Breathing into your abdomen . . . feeling the gentle rise as the breath comes in . . . moving into any uncomfortable places . . . warming, soften-ing, and loosening . . . and releasing any discomfort with the exhale . . .

Feeling the heaviness in your legs . . . as tightness melts away . . . let-ting them sink into the welcoming support beneath them . . . muscle tis-sue releasing . . . tension draining in the ankles and feet . . . your toes soft and comfortable . . .

Feeling all through your body, the infusion of heavy softness . . . as every layer, every cell in your body . . . responds to the sweet permis-sion . . . to safely surrender into rest and renewal . . .

As if gentle guardians were treading on soft feet . . . trustworthy and protective . . . as they gently close the curtains . . . and create a soft and quiet space . . . free of distraction . . . gentle and safe . . . smiling at you with loving eyes . . . and maybe touch your brow with a caring hand . . . a ranging the covers around you . . . just so . . . and you might sense a special animal . . . loyal and loving . . . nuzzling your hand . . . resting its head by you . . . watching over you . . .

And others might place themselves around you . . . to guard and protect you . . . inviting healing dreams into this soft and quiet space . . . and effortless answers . . . conjuring the sweetest of memories to come calling . . . to tiptoe in as you dream . . . in the sacred space of sleep . . .

Sensing how their loving presence has even changed the feel of the air in the room . . . creating a space for you . . . as inviting as a loving lap is to a child . . . as steady and soothing as a rocking chair . . . or a mother's heartbeat . . . as soft as kindness itself . . .

And you can know . . . that these gentle guardians have filled the space around you . . . with all the love and sweetness that have ever been felt for you . . . by anyone at any time . . . that they have pulled in all the loving-kindness, all the caring . . . that has ever been sent your way . . .

Every prayer and good wish . . . every sweet smile and heartfelt thank you . . . every nod of affirmation . . . pulling it all around you like a powerful magnet . . . calling every good wish home . . .

All that goodness, softly settling into the space around you . . . infusing the air . . . so that every in-breath is a blessing . . . and every out-breath is a thank-you . . .

And you know . . . that your body knows how to find rest and renewal here . . . healing and growth . . . vision and knowing . . . as you melt into the welcoming support that holds you . . . and looks out for you . . . as you slip into the steady rhythm of your interior . . . safe and easy . . . comfortably at home, deep in your body . . .

And you know . . . in your heart . . . that this rich and nourishing place is always here . . . yours to visit whenever you wish . . .

By closing the curtains . . . and dimming the lights . . . and tuning in to the breath . . . as you sink into the support beneath you . . . surrounded by powerful guardians and loving allies . . . encircled by safety and blessings . . .

And knowing in a deep place . . . that you are better for this . . .

And so you are . . .

(*Let the music continue for as long as there is space for it, and let it fade gradually, so as not to awaken the listener who is, we hope, sleeping by now.*)

12 GUIDED IMAGERY FOR THE SECOND STAGE OF TRAUMA: HEALING AND INTEGRATION

During the second stage of trauma, which can begin anywhere from a few days or weeks after the traumatic event or events to several months or even years later, the simple, self-soothing, stage-one imagery can still be used on an as-needed basis for promoting relaxation and calm, especially because imagery in this stage can be evocative and disturbing.

This second-stage imagery is for delving deeper, whenever the survivor is ready to go beyond managing symptoms and coping with distress to directly pursue healing. Once the self-soothing skills are in place, this is easier to do. The backup system for managing distress is in place. This is the time for sorting through a complex array of intense feelings, in order to cognitively and emotionally integrate what has happened.

If you haven't enlisted one already, a good therapist, coach, or counselor can offer tremendous assistance. It is always a good idea to choose someone who is empathic, skillful, and grounded. But for traumatic stress, it is also important that this person understand the nature of PTSD, how disturbing and pseudo-psychotic the symptoms can appear, and the need for right-brain practices to promote healing. Better yet, if the practitioner is conversant with appropriate local resources and can make referrals to other practitioners who specialize in some of the PTSD-specific healing techniques (spelled out in Chapter 14), they are invaluable.

Unfortunately, Ann Landers's favorite fallback position—calling the local mental health center or professional association of psychologists or social workers or psychiatrists—won't necessarily get you the right person. It will get you a properly pedigreed name on a list, and that's a place to start, but you don't want to stop there. It is risky to settle for someone who is simply the next name on an automatic intake list (although through blind chance, you just might get lucky).

You need to ask questions and network, starting with whoever took your call, until the same names keep coming up. I like to encourage people to ask, "If I were your wife (or husband or sister or brother or son or daughter), to whom would you send me?" If you can get a personal referral from someone who knows you and has a sense of the kind of person you'd best connect with, and who also knows something about the nature of post-traumatic stress, that is best. But even then it's a good idea to interview two or three practitioners before deciding on one, and you ought to be able to do that on the phone.

Unfortunately, someone in the throes of PTSD might not have the energy or proactive push to do all this preliminary networking and sorting. But it's important—important enough to deputize a trusted family member or friend or colleague to do it for you, if you are not up for it yourself.

People who fare well in their recovery process either function as their own "general contractor," finding various nonverbal right-hemisphere techniques for themselves at various stages of their recovery, or else they have therapists and friends who help them with suggestions and referrals, recommending a whole mix-and-match laundry list of effective practices at different stages along the way.

The imagery for this stage goes deeper and deliberately aims to help the survivor reestablish a relationship with the world of feelings; face down unpleasant symptoms; move under them, to the core of the hurt; and reestablish a connection with a broader, more spiritual perspective, big enough to hold and transform the enormity of the pain and loss. Now that the ability to self-soothe is in place, this is possible and the time is right. The survivor sets the pace and leads the way. The therapist, if there is one, follows.

7 IMAGERY TO SUPPORT AWARENESS OF FEELINGS

Many people with traumatic stress, especially of the long-standing, chronic variety, are somewhat numb to their feelings and find it hard to sort them out. For some, like Frannie, everything feels the same; others feel nothing at all, because of the fog that has overtaken them. So it's important for survivors to understand that identifying undifferentiated sensation in the beginning is an important first step. This exercise may have to be repeated several times before any fine distinctions can occur. People should be patient with themselves and trust the process. The key here is to ask the body and the world of sensations to provide the answers, rather than the thinking mind. The body has its own innate wisdom for choosing the timing for these revelations. And always, if anxiety or distress threatens to become overwhelming, we return to the simple exercises for relaxation and self-regulation from stage one.

IMAGERY TO SUPPORT AWARENESS OF FEELINGS

Please get comfortable, shifting your weight so your body can feel fully supported . . . arranging it so your head, neck, and spine are straight . . .

Each in-breath rich and full *(pause)* . . . exhaling comfortably and fully . . . breathing deep into the belly . . . *(pause)* . . . and breathing out . . . as you turn your attention inward . . . checking to see how it feels inside your body . . . just a gentle, curious inventory . . . of how you are just at this moment . . .

And you might sense your energy level . . . or sense a certain mood . . . or have a feeling about your sense of well-being at the moment . . . as you continue to breathe deeply and easily . . . interested . . . curious . . . but detached and neutral . . .

Noticing the places inside your body where you might be tight or tense or sore . . . and where you might feel relaxed and open . . . so you're just letting your awareness travel inside your body . . .

And you might start with your head . . . noticing how it feels inside your head . . . whether it seems tight and cluttered . . . or comfortable and open . . . or nothing in particular . . . and you're just aware of what is there . . . not trying to make it different . . . or change it in any way . . . just noticing . . . neutral and detached . . . *(pause)* . . .

And moving your awareness into your neck and shoulders . . . curious about how it feels inside your neck . . . *(pause)* . . . and across your shoulders . . .

And down into your chest . . . into your heart . . . continuing to breathe deeply and easily . . . as you sense how it feels all around and through your heart . . . noticing any heaviness or tightness . . . with friendly but detached interest . . . no praise, no blame . . . *(pause)* . . . just doing this simple inventory . . .

And checking to see how your whole chest feels . . . *(pause)* . . . moving your awareness around to your back . . . *(pause)* . . . traveling the entire length of your back . . . *(pause)* . . . and moving around to the belly . . . looking to see what it feels like in your abdomen . . . noting any sensations in the belly . . . *(pause)* . . . continuing to breathe deeply and easily . . .

And moving your awareness down into your bottom . . . seeing how it feels along your whole pelvic floor . . . *(pause)* . . .

And down into your legs . . . noticing how it feels inside your thighs . . . and knees . . . and calves . . . all the way down to the feet . . . and the very tips of your toes . . .

Sending your breath into the very center of your body . . . wherever you sense that to be . . . *(pause)* . . . and breathing out . . . *(pause)* . . . and breathing in again . . . deep into the very center of your body . . . letting the energy of the breath disperse to wherever it's needed . . . *(pause)* . . . exhaling fully and easily . . . *(pause)* . . .

And you know . . . that you can ask your body to show you what it's feeling . . . leaving space for it to answer . . . as you continue to breathe in and out . . . open and steady . . . as you ask your body to show you . . . where your feelings are held . . . so you're just letting the intelligence of the body show you what needs showing . . .

Clearing away a space . . . and letting the wisdom of the body reveal itself . . . because it might show you a place that's denser and heavier than the rest . . . or perhaps a soft sadness around the heart . . . or a place that's sharp with pain . . . or maybe a wary feeling in the belly . . . or perhaps you find the clench of anger in your legs . . . and wherever a feeling is held . . . you can just let it begin to reveal itself . . . however subtle and elusive . . . knowing you can be curious . . . neutral and detached . . . the explorer of your own inner terrain . . .

And with another deep, full breath . . . ready to take a closer look at this feeling or mix of feelings . . . and breathing out fully and easily . . . going to wherever it sits . . . curious about its texture . . . *(pause)* . . . and size . . . *(pause)* . . . its weight and feel . . . *(pause)* . . .

So you're just granting yourself the space to explore . . . interested in its nature . . . its intensity . . . whatever colors it might have . . . *(pause)* . . . or sounds . . . *(pause)* . . . or tastes . . . *(pause)* . . . or smells . . . *(pause)* . . . so that you're moving your awareness all around and through it . . . to whatever degree that feels right . . . in your own way . . . and your own time . . .

And asking the body to continue to show you whatever you need to know about this . . . trusting it to reveal what is needed . . . in its own time . . . as you continue to breathe deeply and easily . . . all around and through this feeling . . . not trying to change or fix it . . . just noticing what is there . . .

Able to trust this process . . . of connecting more deeply with yourself . . . and so giving yourself all the space and time that you need . . . to let the energy of these feelings reveal themselves . . . and begin to shift and move inside you . . . of their own accord . . .

And if the mind wants to assess or judge . . . just turning your attention back to the feeling in your body . . . knowing there will be a time when all of this will make sense . . . and it doesn't have to be now . . . that now is just for experiencing what is there . . .

And so . . . taking whatever time you need . . . continuing to breathe deeply and easily . . . saluting your own courage . . . and your capacity for self-awareness . . .

And whenever you are ready . . . coming back into the room . . . gently and with soft eyes . . . knowing in a deep place that you are better for this . . .

And so you are . . .

8 IMAGERY TO FACE DOWN ANXIETY

Some people want to have proactive ways to deal with anxiety when it comes bubbling up. This imagery goes beyond self-soothing. It's more the "turn and face your enemy" approach, using imagery to meet and greet the anxiety, move in toward it, explore it and get to know it a little better. It borrows liberally from certain components of mindfulness meditation and the mind-set of the spiritual warrior, who faces what is happening in the moment with the courage of the open heart. It won't be for everyone, but those who are ready for it will like where it takes them.

IMAGERY TO FACE DOWN ANXIETY

To begin with, please settle in as comfortably as you can, shifting your weight so your body can feel well supported and arranging it so your head, neck, and spine are straight . . . and it might feel right to place your hands over your abdomen, so you can feel it rise and fall as you breathe in and out . . .

And taking a full, deep cleansing breath . . . *(pause)* . . . exhaling as fully as you comfortably can . . . *(pause)* . . . and again . . . taking another breath . . . deep into the belly . . . *(pause)* . . . and breathing out . . . fully and comfortably . . . *(pause)* . . .

And gently allowing yourself to turn your attention inward . . . focusing inside for just these next moments . . . to see how you're feeling . . . just a gentle, curious look at your insides . . . knowing that the part of you that watches yourself . . . is always neutral and steady . . . detached and calm . . .

Feeling the places in your body where you're tight or tense or sore . . . places that might need comfort and peace . . . and places that feel open and relaxed . . . so you're just scanning the insides of your body . . .

Sensing how it feels around and through your heart . . . noticing any heaviness or tightness there . . . any pain or sadness or grief that might have collected there . . . with friendly but detached interest . . . no praise, no blame . . . *(pause)* . . . as your breath continues to rhythmically and slowly fill your chest . . . releasing with the exhale . . .

So just doing this gentle, curious inventory of your insides . . . no axe to grind . . . no judgments . . . just exploring how you are . . . and what your body is feeling . . .

And now . . . with this same attitude of detached interest . . . taking a moment or two to focus on this discomfort that visits . . . this worry or fear or anxiety . . . looking to explore its nature . . . its special qualities . . . with all the neutral, detached curiosity . . . that you can bring to bear . . .

Noticing where this is held in the body . . . *(pause)* . . . and what it feels like . . . *(pause)* . . . letting it become more and more clearly defined, as you focus the power of your attention on it . . .

Exploring, not with your mind, but with your senses . . . exploring with the courage of your intention . . . to be strong and steady and fully present . . . as you continue to breathe your slow, full breaths deep into your belly . . . releasing any tension with the exhale . . .

Checking to see if perhaps this worry or fear or anxiety has a color . . . or colors to it . . . *(pause)* . . . or if it seems to have a sound or sounds associated with it . . . *(pause)* . . .

Perhaps there is a scent connected to it . . . or a familiar taste . . . so you're just letting the part of you that is detached and neutral and curious explore . . . while you continue to breathe in and breathe out, very rhythmically and fully . . .

Willing to go to wherever it sits in your body . . . curious about its location . . . *(pause)* . . . and how much territory it covers . . . *(pause)* . . . the feel of it . . . *(pause)* . . . the weight and texture of it . . . so just granting yourself the space to investigate its nature . . . its intensity . . . moving your awareness all around and through it . . . curious and detached . . . willing to look at it freshly . . . and see what it has to say to you . . . observe what it wants to show you . . .

And asking the body to show you whatever you need to see about this . . . in its own way . . . and its own time . . . as you continue to breathe deeply and easily . . . all around and through it . . . with full, strong, deep breaths . . . the intrepid explorer of your inner terrain . . . with the courage of the open heart . . .

And making room to let the energy of these feelings begin to shift and move inside of you . . . *(pause)* . . . whenever they are ready . . . and they may or may not be . . . but you know you can feel the shift, once it begins . . . very naturally and of its own accord . . . letting it happen in its own way . . . in its own time . . . as you continue to breathe . . . deeply and fully . . .

And the shift in your body . . . might be subtle and delicate . . . or bold and dramatic . . . it will have its own truth . . . and you can just let yourself feel the change on the inside . . . as something starts to move . . . still feeling detached but curious . . . and breathing full, deep, steady breaths . . . *(pause)* . . .

And now . . . whenever you are ready . . . giving yourself permission to put this away for now . . . knowing you can bring it back and work on it some more whenever you wish to . . . and knowing that this is fine for now . . .

And so, setting this aside for now . . . with respect for all its stubborn power and complexity . . . and with respect for your own courage and resourcefulness . . . knowing that just by facing and exploring it . . . you change it . . .

And so . . . taking a deep, full breath . . . deep into the belly if you can . . . *(pause)* . . . and breathing all the way out . . . fully and completely . . . *(pause)* . . .

Gently and with soft eyes . . . turning your attention back into the room whenever you are ready . . . knowing in a deep place that you are better for this . . .

And so you are . . .

9 IMAGERY FOR SOFTENING PAIN

This imagery exercise is for alleviating sharp pain—either physical or emotional. It deploys resources that are under the complete control of the listener, mitigating the hurt through the energy of the breath and the touch of the hands. And because resistance and muscle tension increase pain, and relaxation reduces it, this simple exercise can be surprisingly effective. The wording and gentle direction also encourage compassion for the self.

IMAGERY FOR SOFTENING PAIN

To begin with, please settle in as comfortably as you can, shifting your weight so your body can feel well supported and arranging it so your head, neck, and spine are straight . . . and it might feel right to place your hands over your abdomen, so you can feel it rise and fall as you breathe in and out . . .

And taking a full, cleansing breath . . . *(pause)* . . . exhaling as completely as you comfortably can . . . breathing into the belly . . . *(pause)* . . . and breathing all the way out . . .

And any unwelcome thoughts that come to mind . . . can be sent out with the breath . . . released with the exhale . . . so that for just a moment, the mind is empty . . . free and clear space, and you are blessed with stillness . . .

And any emotions you might sense within you . . . can be noted, and acknowledged, and sent out with the breath . . . so that your emotional self can be still and quiet . . . like a lake with no ripples . . .

Allowing yourself to become aware of the places that are tight or tense or sore . . . any uncomfortable places in the body . . . and sending the power of the breath into the heart of those places . . . feeling the soft energy of the breath moving all around and through them . . . massaging and opening tight, trapped energy . . . so you can breathe it out . . .

And again, breathing into the core of the tightness . . . with care and concern for that part of your body . . . gentle and easy . . . letting the soft power of the breath release discomfort . . . and breathing it out . . .

And again . . . breathing in . . . and perhaps this time, if it feels right, putting your hands over a place that hurts . . . and letting the warmth of your hands move softly and easily into it . . . encouraging your body to open to the warm energy of your hands . . . and breathing out to release it . . .

Aware of the remarkable intelligence of the body . . . softening and opening and loosening around the places that hurt . . . releasing tight muscle . . . dispersing heaviness . . . dissolving the boundaries that hold densely packed energy . . . and watching the edges disappear . . . floating out on the powerful back of the out-breath . . .

Feeling the warm, healing softness flowing from your hands . . . gently softening and loosening . . . slowly and steadily . . . moving deeper and deeper into the core of any place that needs it . . . gently releasing as it goes . . . and you can sense energy floating free . . .

As you continue to breathe deeply and easily . . . feeling a softness toward yourself . . . a compassion for the places that hurt . . .

Grateful for the power of the breath . . . available to you anytime and anyplace . . . knowing it is always there for you to direct and command . . . at your service . . . as you breathe your breath in and out . . . strong and steady . . .

And so . . . feeling peaceful and easy . . . knowing you can call forth the healing power of the breath . . . and the warm energy of your hands . . . whenever you wish . . .

So gently and with soft eyes . . . coming back into the room whenever you are ready . . . understanding that powerful resources are yours to use whenever you wish . . . and knowing that you are better for this . . .

And so you are . . .

10 IMAGERY TO EASE DEPRESSION

This imagery is a favorite of many of the combat veterans and others dealing with chronic, late-stage traumatic stress. It focuses on alleviating two signature symptoms of depression: the heavy, dulled fog of fatigue, and the loss of self-esteem that accompanies it. It is also designed to help increase energy, instill hope, and encourage the return of some healthy self-love. Depression is a common by-product or accompaniment of post-traumatic stress, making it all the more difficult to heal.

IMAGERY TO EASE DEPRESSION

To begin with, please allow yourself to get comfortable . . . shifting your weight so your body can feel well supported . . . and arranging it so your head, neck, and spine are straight . . . and you might want to place your hands over your abdomen . . . so you can feel the rise and fall . . . as you breathe in and out . . .

And taking a full, cleansing breath . . . inhaling completely and comfortably . . . sending the warm energy of your breath to any place in your body that's tight or sore or tense . . . and releasing discomfort with the exhale . . .

So that more and more, you can feel relaxed and comfortable, safe and easy, sensing the cleansing action of your own breath . . .

And any distracting thoughts or feelings that might be there . . . those too are sent out with the breath . . . so that inside, for a moment, you can be peaceful and quiet . . . clear and still . . . like a lake with no ripples . . .

As you begin to notice a kind of tingling . . . a pleasant, energizing aliveness in the air all around you . . . and it's taking on a kind of a glow . . . a sense that the space around you is alive with vibrant energy . . .

And from somewhere above you, you can feel a cone of powerful white light, softly descending . . . until it forms a tent of vibrant energy all around you . . . surrounding and protecting you with its tingling presence . . . illuminating everything it touches with exquisite brightness . . . highlit definition . . . intensely saturated color . . . giving everything it shines on a fresh, new beauty . . .

You can feel the air around you dancing its sparkling energy on the surface of your skin . . . feeling wonder for such stunning beauty . . . as you feel the tingling energy of the light moving down into your body . . .

softly entering your head and neck . . . warming your shoulders as the
light softly soaks into them . . .

And gently moves into your chest . . . intensifying as it is drawn to the
heaviness around your heart . . . softly massaging and opening . . . soaking into the edges of the heaviness . . . gently but steadily kneading and
softening . . . releasing trapped energy . . .

As it continues down the spine . . . filling the back and the whole
torso . . . soaking into the layers of tissue . . . deeper and deeper . . .
moving into every organ . . . into muscle and bone . . . into each and
every cell . . . cleansing and clearing as it goes . . .

Sending a warm, vibrating softness into the belly . . . gently warming
and opening . . . filling it with the powerful, healing energy of the light . . .

Working its magic deep inside your body . . . moving with deliberate
intelligence to the places where pain and sorrow and weary discourage-
ment are stored . . . and feeling the spaces loosen and lighten as you
breathe into them . . . maybe beginning to sense glimmers of energy
awakening . . . old sparks returning . . .

You gradually become aware of a warm presence . . . more than just
the warmth of the light . . . and you notice that you have companions . . .
gentle, loving beings, immediately recognizable as allies . . . smiling and
nodding in the soft beauty of the light . . . some perhaps familiar . . . or
perhaps not . . . but all of them warming you with their protective presence . . .

One of them softly approaches . . . and with a deep, gentle look, directly into your eyes . . . with great care and utmost respect . . . gently
touches the center of your chest . . . sending a charge of soft, warm energy directly into your heart . . . waves of peaceful, nourishing energy . . .
moving through barriers of dull, deadened spaces . . . melting away
the thick, heavy fog . . . releasing and awakening the powerful core beneath . . . and you can feel energy begin to move through you . . . charg-
ing and renewing each and every cell . . .

Feeling the stirrings of your own energy . . . bubbling up, simmering
and rolling to a boil, from deep inside your center . . . pulsing and vibrating . . . radiating strength and purpose into every corner of your body . . .

You see in the eyes that are looking at you, that they see what you
see . . . that you are healing . . . that your body is now beginning to remember its natural vitality and aliveness . . . and you can feel it deep

inside you . . . breathing in to touch it . . . *(pause)* . . . breathing out to let it move through you . . . *(pause)* . . .

And suddenly you are certain . . . you know with your whole heart . . . your whole being . . . that you are healing . . . that you will continue to heal . . . that the heaviness will lighten . . . that the fog will continue to burn away in the bright, humming light . . . as more and more you are able to release the places where feelings are held . . . breathing out pain and weariness . . . *(pause)* . . . breathing in the aliveness and beauty of the dancing light . . . *(pause)* . . . and releasing sadness and despair with the out-breath . . . *(pause)* . . . taking in joy and hope with the in-breath . . . *(pause)* . . . and breathing out sorrow and pain . . .

Knowing you are healing . . . feeling your heart expand and open to its own vast energy . . . attuned to the brightness of your own being . . . and the generosity of your spirit . . . breathing in to touch it . . . *(pause)* . . . and breathing out to let it move through you . . . *(pause)* . . .

This visitor says, "Remember, we are always here . . . it is you who come and go . . . call for us anytime, and we will come . . . to help you heal . . . to help you remember who you really are . . . ," and gathering up a handful of the glowing, vibrating light . . . gives it to you for safe-keeping . . . your own special supply, to use as needed . . .

And with a special look of deep understanding . . . bows and fades away with the others . . .

And so . . . feeling peaceful and easy . . . you can watch the light slowly withdraw . . . returning to wherever it came from . . . knowing it is yours to call forth whenever you wish . . .

You might feel that something powerful has happened . . . that a major shift has occurred . . . and will continue to occur . . . with or without your conscious striving . . .

And so . . . feeling your hands and feet . . . your breath in your belly . . . as you softly and deeply breathe in and out . . . rhythmically and easily . . . very gently and with soft eyes . . . you can come back into the room whenever you are ready . . . knowing in a deep place that you are better for this . . .

And so you are . . .

11 IMAGERY TO RELEASE GRIEF

People with post-traumatic stress are dealing with a whole range of losses to grieve—lost loved ones, possessions, home, work, community, country, ideals, confidence, hope, innocence, identity, and sense of safety. They have also experienced the loss of who they thought they were and the way things used to be. For most people, sorrow is inevitable, and when the time is right, processing the grief is an important part of the healing.

This imagery starts out similarly to the imagery for depression, but it works with the notion that images held in the heart ultimately take over for what is lost and make those losses bearable. Internal images of what we love are the mechanism that ultimately saves and restores us—the true transitional object, our immutable, reliable "blankie" when all else is lost. Imagery helps us take our first steps beyond a painful time.

IMAGERY TO RELEASE GRIEF

To begin with, please allow yourself to get comfortable . . . shifting your weight so your body can feel well supported . . . and arranging it so your head, neck, and spine are straight . . . and you might want to place your hands over your abdomen . . . so you can feel the rise and fall . . . as you breathe in and out . . .

And taking a full, cleansing breath . . . inhaling completely and comfortably . . . sending the warm energy of your breath to any place in your body that's tight or sore or tense . . . and releasing discomfort with the exhale . . .

So that more and more, you can feel relaxed and comfortable, safe and easy, sensing the cleansing action of your own breath . . .

And any distracting thoughts or feelings that might be there . . . those too are sent out with the breath . . . so that for a moment, your mind can be peaceful and quiet . . . clear and still . . . like a lake with no ripples . . .

Noticing a kind of tingling . . . a pleasant, energizing aliveness in the air all around you . . . a sense that the space around you is alive with vibrant energy . . . taking on a kind of a glow . . .

And from somewhere above you . . . a cone of powerful white light is softly descending . . . until it forms a tent of vibrant energy all around you . . . surrounding and protecting you . . . illuminating everything it touches with exquisite brightness . . . highlit definition . . . vibrating, saturated color . . . giving everything it shines on a fresh, new beauty . . .

You can feel the light dancing its sparkling energy on the surface of your skin . . . and feeling wonder for such stunning beauty . . . you feel the tingling energy of the light softly moving into your body . . . gently entering your head and neck . . . warming your shoulders . . . as the healing energy of the light softly soaks into them . . .

Flowing into your chest . . . intensifying as it is drawn to the heaviness around your heart . . . softly massaging and opening . . . gently kneading and softening . . .

And continuing down the spine . . . filling the back and the whole torso . . . soaking into the layers of tissue . . . deeper and deeper . . . moving into every organ . . . into muscle and bone . . . into each and every cell . . . cleansing and clearing as it goes . . .

Sending its warm, vibrating softness into the belly . . . gently warming and opening . . . filling your torso with the powerful, healing energy of the light . . .

Working its magic deep inside your body . . . moving with deliberate intelligence to the places where pain is stored . . . and feeling the spaces loosen and lighten as you breathe into them . . . all the way down into your legs and feet . . .

You suddenly realize you are not alone . . . that there is a warm presence all around you . . . and looking around . . . you see that you are accompanied by gentle, loving beings . . . immediately recognizable as allies . . . smiling and nodding in the soft, healing light . . . warming you with their protective presence . . .

One of them softly approaches you . . . and with a deep, gentle look, directly into your eyes . . . gently touches the center of your chest . . . sending comfort and solace deep into your heart . . . waves of deep comfort, flowing into the heaviness of your heart . . . soothing the torn, jagged places . . . opening and warming and softening all around the pain . . .

And you can breathe deeply, filling your whole body with this generous, healing energy . . . perhaps letting the tears begin to melt the
armor around the heart . . . as the eyes that gently look at you, nod and
smile . . .

Showing you that it is understood . . . how much hurting you've
done . . . it is understood, the stony-cold aloneness you have felt . . . the
wordless ache of longing . . . the stinging regret . . . the disappointment
of interrupted dreams . . . all the pain is understood . . . breathtakingly
intense at one moment . . . and heavy and dull the next . . . all of it is understood . . .

You feel the warmth of this awareness begin to collect and radiate
through your entire chest . . . sending compassion and forgiveness and
reassurance to every corner of your being . . . as you breathe into the
opening spaces of your heart . . .

And suddenly you are certain . . . you know with your whole
heart . . . with your whole being . . . that there is a place where nothing is
lost . . . where all the love and sweetness, direct or disguised, that you
have ever felt . . . is still alive . . . that all the love you have ever felt for
anyone at any time is alive and well in the vast spaces of your own open
heart . . . placed there forever . . . rich and nourishing and boundless . . .
and it is always available to sustain you . . .

Breathing in to touch it . . . breathing out to let it move through
you . . . feeling the body soften . . . sending a gentle, healing forgiveness
all through you . . . a new compassion for yourself . . . a different way of
looking . . .

Understanding that you are being shown . . . that even this terrible
pain can be a teacher . . . showing you something you need to know . . .
about yourself . . . about who you are . . . and who you are becoming . . .

You know that even this will look different to you in time . . . when
you know more about who you have become . . . when you are connected to your life in a new way . . . and the pain has permanently softened . . . when this sorrow has become part of the depth and richness of
the texture of your life . . .

You see in the deep, gentle warmth of the eyes that look at you,
that it is understood, that you have seen this . . . that you have had a
glimmer of your own healing . . . that nothing has been lost to the vast-
ness of the heart . . . the whole world spins there . . . and so you can

begin to return to the peaceful stillness at your center . . . breathing in to touch it . . . breathing out to let it move through you . . .

Your guide says, "Remember, we are always here. It is you who come and go. Call for us anytime, and we will come."

And gathering up a handful of the glowing, vibrating light, places it in your heart for safekeeping . . . your own special supply . . . to use as needed . . .

And so, feeling peaceful and easy . . . you watch as the light slowly begins to withdraw . . . returning to wherever it came from . . . until it is gone altogether . . . for now . . . knowing it is yours to call forth again, whenever you wish . . .

And taking a deep, full breath . . . you might feel that something powerful has happened . . . that a major shift has occurred . . . and will continue to occur . . . with or without your conscious working on it . . .

And you can see very clearly that you can call forth the healing light . . . the special ones . . . your guide . . . whenever you wish to further the work that you have already done . . .

And so . . . feeling yourself sitting in your chair or lying down . . . breathing in and out, very rhythmically and easily . . . gently and with soft eyes . . . coming back into the room whenever you are ready . . . knowing in a deep place that you have done important healing work . . . that you are better for this . . .

And so you are . . .

12   IMAGERY FOR TRANSFORMING A SYMBOL

When the realities are too painful or too inaccessible to process directly, this imagery offers a triple dose of distance—first by taking the listener away to a favorite place; then by creating a screen in that place, upon which the core images will occur; and finally by using an indirect symbol on this screen to represent the problem or difficulty. As layered and indirect as this imagery is, it's surprisingly effective. Most people do better to select a simple symbol of something they are struggling with before they begin—something to represent one specific dilemma or issue that they wish to shift in a positive direction. The symbol can either change or not, but regardless of outcome, what happens can be illuminating. The wording is designed to encourage patience with the process of change.

Those with an obsessive tendency will need encouragement to pick just one thing and not worry about all the other things they didn't pick. Any symbol will do for a starting place—a rock, a flower, a cookie, a flame, a shoe . . . the imaginal world will be happy to work with it.

IMAGERY FOR TRANSFORMING A SYMBOL[1]

To begin with, see if you can position yourself as comfortably as you can, shifting your weight so that you're allowing your body to be fully supported . . . with your head, neck, and spine straight . . .

And taking a couple of deep, cleansing breaths . . . inhaling as fully as you comfortably can . . . *(pause)* . . . breathing deep into the belly if you can . . . and breathing all the way out . . . *(pause)* . . . fully and completely . . .

And again . . . breathing in . . . seeing if you can send the warm energy of the breath to any part of your body that's tense or sore or tight . . . *(pause)* . . . and releasing the tension with the exhale . . . *(pause)* . . .

So you can feel your breath going to all the tight, tense places, loosening and warming and softening them . . . and then, gathering up all the tension and breathing it out . . . so that more and more, you can feel safe and comfortable . . . relaxed and easy . . . watching the cleansing action of the breath . . . with friendly but detached awareness . . .

And any unwelcome thoughts that come to mind . . . those too can be sent out with the breath . . . released with the exhale . . . so that for just a moment, the mind is empty . . . for just a split second, it is free and clear space, and you are blessed with stillness . . .

And any emotions you might sense . . . those too are noted and acknowledged and sent out with the breath . . . so your emotional self is still and quiet . . . like a lake with no ripples . . .

And now, imagining a place, where you feel safe and peaceful and easy . . . a place either make-believe or real . . . a place from your past . . . or somewhere you've always wanted to go . . . it doesn't matter . . . just so it's a place that feels good and safe and peaceful to you . . .

And allowing the place to become real to you . . . looking around you . . . taking the place in with your eyes . . . enjoying the colors . . . the scenery . . . looking over to your right . . . and over to your left . . .

And listening to the sounds of the place so your ears can enjoy the unique gifts of this place . . . that is so safe and peaceful to you . . .

And feeling whatever you're sitting against or walking upon . . . whether it's sand or pine needles . . . or grass . . . or a quiet, country road . . . or maybe you're just sitting on a nice, warm rock in the sun . . .

And feeling the air on your skin . . . crisp and dry . . . or balmy and wet . . . or maybe there's just the subtlest caress of a fragrant, gentle breeze . . . so you're enjoying the presence of the place on your skin . . .

And smelling its rich fragrance . . . whether it's the soft, full scent of flowers . . . or the sharpness of salt sea air . . . sweet meadow grass . . . or the pungent smell of peat moss in the forest . . .

And as you become more and more attuned to the safety and beauty of this place . . . feeling thankful and happy to be there . . . you might notice a kind of tingling . . . a pleasant, energizing something in the air all around you . . . something that contains expectancy and excitement . . . a sense that something wonderful is just about to happen . . .

And as you look out in front of you . . . just a few feet in front of you . . . you begin to discern a shimmering kind of screen . . . like heat rising from a hot surface in the desert . . . a shimmering screen, but with a certain depth to it . . .

And as you watch the screen, with a kind of detached, peaceful curiosity . . . you gradually become aware that a form is beginning to appear on it . . . becoming more and more defined as you watch . . . until the three-dimensional image of a symbol is quite clear . . . and you can sense that this is the symbol of whatever it is that you want to work with or change in a positive direction . . . becoming more and more defined and crisp and clear . . . and you can watch it with a kind of alert but peaceful detachment . . . calm and curious . . . as it turns, slowly and steadily, so you can see it from every angle . . .

Curious about the colors it has . . . the sounds associated with it . . . there might be a vibration or hum . . . a melody or a rhythm . . .

You might be aware of a scent . . . or a texture . . . there might be a certain kind of hardness or softness . . . to it . . . or it could be heavy or light . . . big or small . . . bitter or sweet or sour . . .

So you're just taking these next few moments to let yourself be curious . . . while the symbol on the screen reveals itself to you . . . and you can watch and listen . . . in a state of friendly, detached interest . . . observing very carefully . . . and with all of your senses . . . *(pause for 30–45 seconds)* . . .

And now, if you would, see if this image on the screen is willing to shift or change in any way . . . noticing if it wants to move in any direction . . . without pushing it or pulling it . . . but just letting it transform in its own way, if it wants to . . . and if it doesn't, that's all right, too . . . in fact, it's good to know, if it doesn't want to . . . but if it does . . . and it might . . . just watching the shift occur . . . in a state of calm and curious detachment . . . observing this transformation, however subtle or bold . . . with all of your senses . . .

Understanding that it need not be complete . . . it need not make any sense . . . but just noticing the shift . . . with all of your senses . . . for however long it takes . . . calm and curious . . . *(pause for 30–45 seconds)* . . .

And understanding that you can come back and work with the screen and this symbol or others, whenever you wish . . . letting it take however long it needs to take . . . and knowing perfectly well that whatever amount of time it takes will be exactly the right amount of time . . . you can begin to let the image fade . . . and again, seeing the screen . . . and letting that fade, too . . .

And once again, seeing yourself in your favorite surroundings . . . feeling safe and comfortable, relaxed and easy . . . although perhaps the colors are brighter . . . perhaps the sounds are more vivid . . .

Breathing deeply into your belly . . . allowing yourself to come back into the room whenever you are ready . . . knowing in a deep place that something powerful has happened . . . that you are better for this . . .

And so you are . . .

13 IMAGERY FOR WORKING WITH AN ISSUE LOCATED IN THE BODY

This is a more potent, embodied version of the preceding imagery and can help in a more visceral and immediate way. Sometimes doing the screen imagery prepares the trauma survivor for this level of in-the-body work. Sometimes there's no problem going straight to this imagery.

Keep in mind that this exercise doesn't require recalling or working with any specific, literal content whatsoever. That is a big part of its value; it trips off no booby traps in the language and cognition centers. Rather, it stays in the realm of body awareness and perception, where the listener can remain comfortable and safe. The person is encouraged to identify a problematic issue (again, those with an obsessive streak are encouraged to pick just *one*) and then, rather than process it intellectually, identify where the issue sits in the body. Then, as with the symbolic imagery on the screen, the issue can either change or not, but either way illuminates. The wording is designed to encourage patience with the process of change and reassure people that they don't have to force the timing.

IMAGERY FOR WORKING WITH AN ISSUE LOCATED IN THE BODY

To begin with, please allow yourself to get comfortable . . . shifting your weight so your body can feel well supported . . . and arranging it so your head, neck, and spine are straight . . . and you might want to place your hands over your abdomen . . . so you can feel the rise and fall . . . as you breathe in and out . . .

And taking a full, cleansing breath . . . inhaling completely and comfortably . . . sending the warm energy of your breath to any place in your body that's tight or sore or tense . . . and releasing discomfort with the exhale . . .

So that more and more, you can feel relaxed and comfortable, safe and easy, observing the cleansing action of your own breath . . .

And very gently allowing yourself to turn your attention inward . . . letting come up into your awareness something you'd like to change or heal in some way . . . so just taking whatever time is needed to let the thing that wants to, show up . . . *(pause)* . . .

Clearing away a space . . . so that something you want to change can show up . . . some issue . . . or way of being . . . perhaps a physical problem . . . or an attitude of yours that you've grown weary of . . . whatever wants to present itself . . . and you might be surprised by what surfaces . . . or, if you might have many possibilities . . . and if that happens, you can give yourself permission to settle on just one of them for now . . . knowing you can come back and work with others later on . . . *(pause)* . . .

And letting yourself be curious to see where this issue sits in your body . . . where it is felt . . . so just taking a moment to let your body show you where this is held . . . *(pause)* . . . and acknowledging its presence . . . just a neutral, honest nod of recognition to it . . . no praise, no blame . . . and just letting yourself feel its presence . . . noticing where perhaps it has always been . . . or where it has settled now . . .

So you're just letting it make itself known to you . . . in any way it wants to . . . allowing it to just sit there, occupying however much space it wants to take . . . as you sense its nature . . . and focus your attention on it . . . and it might seem dense and heavy . . . or light and airy . . . it might stay put . . . or perhaps it slips and slides around . . . and you can tell if it feels hard or soft . . . compact or spongy . . . if there are edges to it . . . knowing you can investigate its nature with detached curiosity . . . neither denying it nor exaggerating it . . . but just noticing what is there . . . not with your mind but with your senses. . . .

Curious to see if it has a color . . . or tone . . . or flavor . . . *(pause)* . . . if there are any strong physical sensations . . . if there is a mood to it . . . or a smell or a taste . . .

So you're letting yourself experience it . . . in your body . . . with all of your senses . . . in a state of friendly but detached awareness . . . sensing it . . . feeling it . . . and observing it . . . with fresh but neutral curiosity . . . *(pause)* . . .

And now . . . noticing if it wants to start to shift or change . . . very naturally and of its own accord . . . if it wants to . . . and maybe it doesn't . . . and if it doesn't, that's all right, too . . . that's a good thing to know, if it doesn't . . . but if it does . . . and it might . . . allowing it to begin to shift in whatever direction it's inclined to go . . . allowing it to happen in its own way . . . in its own time . . .

Just allowing it the room to shift or change . . . breathing in and out, soft and easy . . . and you may sense a change in density . . . or size . . . or temperature . . . you might feel something expanding or shrinking . . . softening or hardening . . . perhaps there's a change in color . . . or tone . . . or flavor . . . sound . . . or smell . . . or perhaps not . . . but you can stay open and curious . . . to whatever wants to happen . . . and to whatever doesn't want to happen . . . it needn't make sense to you . . . and it needn't go to completion . . .

Feeling the shift in the body . . . however delicate and subtle . . . or dramatic and bold . . . as something starts to move . . . *(pause)* . . .

And whenever you are ready . . . giving yourself permission to put this away for now . . . knowing you can bring it back and visit this again whenever you wish to . . . knowing it will keep . . . that this is fine for now . . .

And so . . . setting this aside for now . . . with appreciation for whatever it may be about . . . however clear or vague . . . giving it the respect it deserves . . . for all its stubborn complexity . . . and giving yourself appreciation as well . . . understanding that even lack of clarity and unfinished business can be illuminating . . .

And so . . . taking a deep, full breath . . . deep into the belly, if you can . . . *(pause)* . . . and breathing all the way out . . . fully and completely . . . *(pause)* . . .

And again . . . another soft, full breath . . . all the way down to the bottom of the belly . . . *(pause)* . . . and all the way out . . .

And gently and with soft eyes . . . turning your attention back into the room whenever you are ready . . . knowing in a deep place that you are better for this . . .

And so you are . . .

14 IMAGERY TO HEAL TRAUMA

This most potent and intense imagery is designed to incrementally heal the trauma, layer by layer, by taking listeners on a safely guided journey into their own broken hearts, where they can survey the painful damage that has been done. Symptoms appear symbolically, as part of the landscape, which they are guided around and through. They then move even deeper down, to the part of themselves that is still beautiful and whole. In this exquisite place, their true home, they are given back various shattered pieces of their hearts, in a kind of imaginal soul retrieval. It is important to note that this beautiful, sustaining place is *beneath* the trauma, not *above* it. People have to go deeper into their *bodies* to get there, not up and out into the ethers.

Although this imagery is designed to be used incrementally and repeatedly over time, sometimes the first experience with it has a dramatic healing impact. This seems to be especially true for those whose trauma has been seasoned over the years. Survivors of long-ago incest and rape, and of surgeries, life-threatening diagnoses, wars, accidents, and natural disasters that occurred years ago frequently have immediate and profound results.

People with intense PTSD symptoms that keep them in intense and active pain throughout the day have been known to listen to this imagery as many as one or two dozen times a day, over and over.

Others might have an opposite reaction and prefer to "titrate" the dosage of this imagery, bit by bit, finding it too intense to take in all at once. They might listen to a few minutes each day, adding a little more each time. Some listen to the whole thing, but only two or three times a week.

IMAGERY TO HEAL TRAUMA[2]

To begin with, see if you can position yourself as comfortably as you can, shifting your weight so that your body feels well supported . . . and gently allowing your eyelids to close, if that's comfortable . . . and arranging it so that your head, neck, and spine are straight . . .

And letting your hands rest comfortably on your body . . . on your chest or midriff or abdomen . . . so you can feel the rise of your body when you breathe in . . . and the way it settles back down when you breathe out . . . so you're becoming more and more attuned to the feel of your breath moving in and out of your body . . .

And now, breathing in as fully as you comfortably can . . . and breathing out, completely and easily . . . and with the next in-breath, imagining that you're sending the warm energy of your breath to any part of your body that's sore or tense or tight . . . and releasing the tension with the exhale . . . so you can feel your breath going to all the tight, tense places . . . warming and loosening and softening them . . . and then, gathering up the tension and breathing it out . . . so that more and more, you can feel relaxed and comfortable, watching the cleansing action of your breath . . .

And any unwelcome thoughts that come to mind . . . those too can be noted, and acknowledged, and sent out with the breath . . . so that for just a moment, your mind is empty . . . for just a split second, it is free and clear space . . . and you are blessed with stillness . . .

And any emotions you might be feeling inside . . . those too can be noticed and sent out with the breath . . . so that your emotional self can be still and quiet . . . like a lake with no ripples . . .

And now . . . see if you can turn your attention inward for a moment . . . to see how your body is feeling . . . noticing where it might feel tight or tense, achy or sore . . . and where it feels loose and comfortable and open . . . so you're moving your awareness down into your body . . . taking a moment to pay attention to how it's feeling . . . noticing any sensations in your head . . . your neck . . . your shoulders . . . your arms . . . and hands . . . inside your chest . . . down your back . . . inside your belly . . . down your hips and bottom . . . your legs . . . and in your feet . . . just taking a moment to check in with your body . . . your oldest friend . . . your steadiest companion . . .

Still aware of your breathing, in and out . . . slow and steady . . . and now . . . taking an extra moment to focus on your heart . . . connecting to the powerful rhythms of your heart . . . sensing how it pulses life and strength, all through your body . . . strong and steady . . .

And just becoming aware of how it feels right now, all around and through your heart . . . because it changes from moment to moment . . . and maybe you're aware of some tightness around your heart . . . some fluttery feelings . . . or an ache inside . . . or a heavy sensation . . . perhaps it feels hard around your heart . . . or it might feel exposed and vulnerable . . . you might sense deep pockets of sorrow tucked away inside . . . but whatever you notice, you're continuing to breathe deeply and easily . . . curious but detached . . . noticing what's there with the neutral eye of a camera . . . no praise, no blame . . .

You slowly become aware of a warm and gentle presence beside you . . . very comforting . . . maybe this someone or something is familiar . . . or maybe not . . . but clearly is radiating love and protection and support . . . and you somehow know that this visitor knows you in a deep and true way . . . that this presence accepts you as you are, and carries great comfort and care . . .

And maybe with a soft touch on your shoulder . . . your guide invites you to come along so that together you can explore your own broken heart . . . the gentlest invitation . . . to see if you are willing . . . and somehow, together, you magically enter the weary landscape of your own heart . . . perhaps slipping in through a torn or jagged place . . . to have a look around . . . for the sake of your own healing . . . and so you enter your heart . . .

And it may seem harsh and dark and cold inside at first, as you look around here in this topmost layer . . .

Because you're making your way through crumpled piles of shattered dreams . . . ragged heaps of lost innocence . . . and your guide is at your side, comforting and encouraging you to continue . . . gently pointing out crusty outcroppings of old guilt and self-blame . . . acknowledging with you the chill wind of loneliness that howls through this place . . . helping you move through smoky slag heaps, crackling and steaming with helpless anger . . . gently guiding you around sticky tar pits of shame . . . pointing out the heavy quicksand of self-pity,

And showing you startling geysers of terror, suddenly bursting forth at unexpected times . . . announced by a loud crack as they break through the surface . . . and then gone as inexplicably as they appear . . . and so you walk together . . . gently exploring the territory of your own pain . . .

continuing to breathe deeply and easily . . . always aware of the comforting presence by your side.

And you notice that you can explore this dismal landscape with steady courage . . . like the survivor that you are . . . even though it's not pretty . . . but somehow you know that even in this ravaged, lonely place, there is great power here . . . that treasures are buried deep in the debris . . .

And your guide looks at you with wise and loving eyes and says, "You can't make this place go away, but your courage in exploring it will change it in time . . . and there are gifts for you here, where you'd least expect to find them". . . and leaning down, picks up a luminous object from under the rubble . . . and gives it to you for safekeeping . . . and it might feel warm in your hands . . . a perfect fit as you wrap your fingers around it . . . and continue along your way . . .

Noticing a golden light glowing up from the ground some distance away . . . and walking toward it, you slowly approach what looks to be a glowing cave or hollow . . . with a hazy, golden light filtering out from it . . . and you can see that this is a tunnel, but like no other, because it glows . . . leading down into an older, deeper part of your heart . . . and so the two of you enter . . . continuing to breathe deeply and easily . . . moving along the glowing pathway . . . deeper and deeper . . . sensing a sweet peace in the soft, golden air that gently billows all around you . . . and so you travel together . . . down into the deep center of your heart . . .

Until you emerge into an exquisite landscape . . . a place pulsing with its own peaceful, stunning beauty . . . awash in light and color . . . with air that sings with healing energy . . . dancing gently on your skin . . . and you're captivated by the breathtaking radiance and splendor of this place . . . buoyed and held by the sweet magic all around you . . .

Aware that somehow this place is familiar to you . . . you know this place . . . and slowly you remember that this is your oldest home . . . the part of you that can never be destroyed . . . the exquisite core of who you really are . . .

And you can inhale the beauty of this place with deep, full breaths . . . breathing it in and letting its healing energy permeate every part of you . . . sending soft waves of comfort and peace all through your body . . .

Your companion smiles . . . and with a gesture calls forth a gentle parade of guardians and allies . . . sweet spirits . . . magical beings . . . ani-

mal helpers . . . guardian angels . . . teachers and guides . . . powerful ancestors . . . old and dear friends . . . sweet singers and dancers . . . some
familiar, some not . . . but all smiling and nodding . . . gently approaching, one by one . . .

And you can see that they are holding out to you, with great tenderness and respect, the shattered pieces of your heart . . . delicate, sparkling
shards and slivers . . . lost or left along the way . . . separated from you at
times of great fear and anguish . . . but now, in this place, in the deepest,
oldest, truest part of you . . . they are tenderly offered back . . . still pulsing with life and power . . .

And you know that you can take back whatever you wish . . . whatever you're ready for . . . no more, no less . . . so you can stand at full
strength . . . your full self and much more . . . more wisdom, more
power . . . more compassion, for yourself and others . . . more awareness
of the invisible support, all around you . . . and you might tentatively accept one or two pieces . . . to see how it feels to have them back . . .

And suddenly you are certain . . . you know with your whole
being . . . that you are healing . . . that you will continue to heal . . . that
a time is coming when you will accept your sorrow; dismiss your shame;
release your anger; forgive yourself; reclaim your strength; and express
your gifts . . .

And so, whenever it's time to say good-bye, you thank your visitors . . . and watch them depart . . . and you and your guide make your
way back up through the tunnel lit with golden light . . . step by step, together . . . until, closer to the surface, you reach the darker, cooler landscape of your pain . . . although perhaps it looks a little different now . . .
not quite as dismal or heavy or dark . . .

And as your departing steps crunch through the debris . . . you might
notice other luminous treasures twinkling at you from the rubble . . . and
you may pick one or two up . . . or you may decide to come back for them
later . . . because perhaps you have all you can carry for now . . .

And so . . . together . . . the two of you come back out of your
heart . . . and your guide, with a look of great tenderness, gently touches
the center of your chest . . . and you can feel the soft warmth of it fill
your heart . . . spill over into your chest . . . fill your whole torso . . . your
shoulders, neck, and head . . . move into your arms and legs, hands, and
feet . . . until your whole body is filled with warmth . . .

And with a bow, your visitor withdraws for now . . . and you're peaceful and easy, knowing that you invoke more assistance whenever you wish . . . to further the work you have already done . . .

And so . . . breathing deeply and easily . . . very aware of your hands and your feet . . . the support beneath your body . . . your breath in your belly . . . you can very softly open your eyes . . . becoming aware of how good it feels to stretch and move again, after being still for so long . . .

And knowing in a deep place that you are better for this . . .

And so you are . . .

13 GUIDED IMAGERY FOR THE THIRD STAGE OF TRAUMA: CLEANUP AND RENEWAL

People who suffered PTSD who arrive at the third stage have done a heroic amount of healing, and hopefully they will take time out to celebrate—at least to themselves—the considerable strength, courage, resilience, and stamina that got them to this place. Many survivors certainly come away from their struggle with an even stronger sense of themselves and a deeper appreciation of their own resourcefulness. But many also emerge with a net loss in confidence and self-esteem. Trauma takes its toll, and long after the core of it is healed, there can still be aftereffects.

Some may still be negotiating a certain amount of emotional residue from the traumatic events beyond their control that completely rocked their world; but if they get into the habit of avoiding people, places, or activities during the worst of their symptoms (as most do), they are likely to experience a period of reluctance to get back into the stream of life. Chances are they will get past this, with or without the help of imagery, but imagery can make it easier, offering opportunities for rehearsing success and retrieving nourishing memories of times when they felt stronger and surer.

Imagery is also an excellent way to help dismantle problematic behavior patterns that have come to take on a life of their own—substance abuse and addictive behavior, for instance, which may have gotten started as a way of self-medicating all the mood dysregulation that happens with post-traumatic stress. Compulsive eating and even compulsive working can get entrenched in the same way. The imagery in this chapter offers a healthy alternative way of reducing anxiety and evening out mood, while helping maintain motivation and hope for getting on the wagon and staying there.

Imagery can also help with personal and work relationships that may have suffered from the huge stress placed on the survivor and passed along to those around him. The imagery here can help with intimacy, anger, and even forgiveness.

And finally, imagery can enhance the intuitive and creative abilities that may have surfaced as a result of the increased right-hemisphere activity and heightened arousal from the trauma. Guided imagery can structure ways to better exercise, focus, and deploy these newfound gifts. For all these reasons, it is as valuable for this final phase of restoration and renewal as it was for the first phase of coping and the second phase of healing.

15 IMAGERY FOR CONFIDENCE

Since post-traumatic stress disrupts so much of a person's life, self-confidence can take a major hit. Regular habits, reactions, and ideas about safety are no longer taken for granted, particularly when panic attacks and phobias have been primary symptoms. Defensive avoidance of activities and people can also impair confidence. As a result, even a survivor who has fully recovered from her symptoms might still have some confidence-building to do. This imagery helps and also provides the opportunity for a positive dress rehearsal when someone is planning on trying something that feels scary. (A lot of people use it before exams, tryouts, job interviews, creative challenges, and social occasions, too.)

IMAGERY FOR CONFIDENCE

To begin with, please allow yourself to get comfortable . . . shifting your weight so your body can feel well supported . . . and arranging it so your head, neck, and spine are straight . . .

Letting your hands rest comfortably somewhere on your body . . . on your chest or midriff or abdomen . . . so you can feel the rise of your body when you breathe in . . . and the way it settles back down when you breathe out . . . and you can become more and more attuned to the feel of your breath moving in and out of your body . . .

Breathing in and out . . . feeling the expansion of your belly with each in-breath . . . and the way your body subsides with each out-breath . . .

And with the next in-breath . . . sending the warm energy of your breath to any place in your body that's tight or sore or tense . . . and releasing discomfort with the exhale . . .

So that more and more, you can feel relaxed and comfortable, safe and easy, sensing the cleansing action of your own breath . . .

And any distracting thoughts or feelings . . . those too are sent out with the breath . . . so that for a moment, your mind can be peaceful and quiet . . . clear and still . . . like a lake with no ripples . . .

And allowing yourself to imagine a cushion of peaceful energy . . . gently tingling and vibrating all around you . . . dancing on your skin . . . sparkling with dots of color . . .

A cushion of protective, intelligent energy . . . softly surrounding and protecting you . . . becoming more and more palpable . . . and inside the cushion, you can feel safe and protected . . . able to take in whatever is nourishing to you . . . but insulated from whatever you don't want or need . . .

And now . . . sensing that this cushion of energy is drawing to it all the love and sweetness that have ever been felt for you by anyone at any time . . . feeling it pull in all the caring, all the loving-kindness that has ever been sent your way . . . every prayer and good wish . . . every smile and gesture of gratitude . . . permeating and filling the field of energy around you . . . pulling it all in like a powerful magnet . . . calling every good wish home . . . and so increasing the powerful protective field all around you . . .

And perhaps even sensing the presence of those who've loved or nurtured you . . . those who love you now . . . or who will love you in the future . . . just the ones you want with you . . .

And sensing them around you now . . . and perhaps even seeing a fleeting glimpse of somebody . . . maybe catching an old familiar scent . . . or hearing the unique timbre of a dearly loved, familiar voice . . . possibly feeling a presence at your side or just behind you . . . or the soft weight of a gentle hand on your shoulder . . .

People from your life . . . alive or long gone . . . there might even be a dear old pet . . . a guardian angel . . . a powerful ancestor . . . a teacher or guide . . . sweet spirits and magical beings . . . perhaps familiar, perhaps not . . . it doesn't matter . . . just so you feel their protection and support . . . and breathing in all that love and care . . . deeply and fully . . . all the way into your heart . . .

Feeling the warmth of it gathering in the center of your chest . . . very soft and rich and full . . . all around and through your heart . . . so you can breathe in all that love and care . . . feeling it infuse your whole being with comfort and calm . . .

You might become aware of a warm presence beside you . . . gentle and caring . . . radiating a powerful sense of protection and support . . . and you can sense that this visitor knows you in a deep and true way . . . accepts you exactly as you are . . . but also can see you unencumbered by any limits that may have been imposed on you . . . or that you've imposed on yourself . . . so that for just an instant . . . through these other eyes . . . you have a glimmer of yourself . . . at the height of your potential and power . . . unimpeded, from within or without . . .

And with an encouraging nod, your companion invites you to choose an instance where you want to feel relaxed and confident . . . assured and ready . . .

And you find yourself looking at a large, shimmering screen, just a few feet away . . . and as you watch the screen with a kind of peaceful curiosity . . . you can discern a form beginning to appear on it . . . becoming more and more defined . . . and you realize that this is you . . . feeling very relaxed and easy . . . but also glowing and radiant . . . very at ease . . . comfortable and strong in your own skin . . . and fully engaged in the activity or situation . . . surrounded by all the expected sights . . . and sounds . . . all the sensations of being there . . .

And with the help of your guide, you find yourself somehow entering the magical space of the screen . . . and moving your awareness into this radiant version of yourself . . . relaxed and engaged . . . aware of the feel of your breath in this glowing, energized body . . . the feel of your limbs in easy motion . . . the sound of your breath . . . your voice . . . the feel of your clothing or the air against your skin . . .

Utterly absorbed in what you are doing . . . fully and completely captured by this time and place . . . just doing what you do . . . flowing in perfect sync with yourself . . . free and easy . . . beyond time and place . . .

Merging into the harmony of it . . . feeling the grace of being so crisply focused . . . so awake and alive . . . and yet peaceful and steady . . . trusting mind and body . . . using all your natural grace and ease . . . fueled by the joy of every part of you fully engaged . . .

Suspended in time . . . like an effortless bird, looping and gliding over sparkling water . . . held aloft and carried on the back of the wind . . . kissed by completeness and the joy of being alive . . .

Your companion looks at you with wise and smiling eyes and says, "Remember this feeling. It belongs to you. And whenever you remember it, you reclaim it.". . .

And as if to seal this idea, your guide gently touches the center of your chest . . . and you can feel the warmth and power of this awareness . . . move directly into your heart . . . flow over into your chest . . . fill your whole torso . . . your limbs . . . your whole body . . .

And suddenly you are certain . . . you know with your whole heart, your whole being . . . that you already have what you need . . . you have always had all the courage, patience, fortitude, and trust you've needed . . . yours to claim just by turning inward and remembering . . .

And so . . . together you leave the shimmering screen . . . and just before departing, your guide slips something into your pocket . . . and whispers one more time, "Remember," and with a bow, retreats . . . and you can feel peaceful and easy, the friendly weight of the gift in your pocket . . . and knowing you can call forth this visitor whenever you wish . . . to further the work you have already done . . .

And so . . . feeling peaceful and easy . . . you can once again feel your hands and your feet . . . your breath in your belly . . . stretching and moving . . . and very gently . . . with soft eyes . . . allowing yourself to come back into your normal, waking reality . . . knowing in a deep place . . . that you are better for this . . .

And so you are . . .

16 IMAGERY FOR ANGER AND FORGIVENESS

This imagery addresses anger and forgiveness, one of the most difficult issues facing a trauma survivor, and possibly the last to get resolved, if in fact it does get resolved. The imagery approaches this goal through body sensation and deliberately sidesteps the cognitive content of looking at what produced the situation in the first place.

This gives the listener a chance to work on the issue in a deflected way—on the bias, so to speak—without reactivating the pain and resentment. This indirectness has been found by many to be remarkably effective at giving forgiveness a chance. It does not ask for a quick resolution. The process takes most people a long time and is rarely smooth. Usually it happens in incremental doses, with predictable backsliding into anger and resentment now and again.

One thing to keep in mind: people are sometimes expected to forgive too early in their healing process, either by themselves or others, because it is the "right" or socially convenient thing to do. Premature forgiveness doesn't hold up and can interfere with the trajectory of psychological recovery, because it asks that people lie to themselves. For this reason it is important for people to approach the task of forgiveness only when they are ready to do so from the inside. This means a genuine intention to eventually wind up with forgiveness, no matter how long it takes.

It is neither desirable nor necessary to rush the time it takes to heal authentically from the inside. Indeed, the survivor should feel free to retreat if it feels forced, and try again later at a different point in the process, or perhaps not at all. Generally, it doesn't work to demand forgiveness, from ourselves or others. Staying open to the possibility is a more viable approach.

It also helps to know that forgiveness is usually a gradual, incremental process, not a sudden zap of grace—although that can sometimes happen, too. But usually it occurs by degrees, with stops and starts, progress and backsliding.

The point of forgiveness is not to condone or alleviate guilt for the perpetrator or perpetrators—that is not the survivor's job. Ultimately, guilt and self-forgiveness must be addressed by the guilty, with or without input from the injured party. The point for the survivor is to forgive in order to free up the energy that has been bound up in anger and resentment, and has therefore been inaccessible. The goal of forgiveness is to gain a fuller, more vibrant life. It is a form of kindness to the self.

Some people never get to this stage. Either the hurt is too great, or the work of healing is directed elsewhere. Some do not want to face the raw pain and vulnerability that lie beneath the anger. No survivor should ever feel that forgiveness is something they must do. Some people manage perfectly well without it.

IMAGERY FOR ANGER AND FORGIVENESS

Please begin by making yourself comfortable, shifting your weight so you're feeling well supported . . . *(pause)* . . . and gently allowing your eyes to close . . .

Letting your hands rest comfortably somewhere on your body—on your chest or midriff or abdomen—so you can feel the rise of your body when you breathe in . . . and the way it settles back down when you breathe out . . . and you're becoming more and more attuned to your breath, as it moves in and out of your body . . .

Inhaling deeply and slowly, all the way down into your belly if you can . . . *(pause)* . . . and breathing out, fully and completely . . . feeling the expansion of your abdomen with each in-breath . . . and the way it subsides with each out-breath . . .

And again, breathing in . . . and this time, imagining that you're sending the warm energy of your breath to any part of your body that's sore or tense or tight . . . *(pause)* . . . and releasing the tension with the exhale . . . so you can feel your breath going to all the tight, tense places . . . warming and loosening and softening them . . . and then, gathering up all the tension . . . and breathing it out . . . so that more and more, you can feel safe and comfortable, relaxed and easy . . . noticing the cleansing action of your breath . . . with friendly but detached awareness . . .

And any unwelcome thoughts that come to mind, those too can be sent out with the breath . . . released with the exhale . . . so that for just a moment, the mind is empty . . . for just a split second, it is free and clear space . . . and you are blessed with stillness . . .

And any emotions that you are feeling . . . those too can be noted and acknowledged and sent out with the breath . . . so that your emotional self can be still and quiet . . . like a lake with no ripples . . .

You slowly become aware of a soft presence beside you . . . very warm and comforting . . . and maybe this someone or something is familiar . . . or maybe not . . . but clearly is radiating love and trust and support . . . and you somehow know that this visitor knows you in a deep and true way . . . accepts you as you are . . . understands where you've been . . . sees where you need to go . . . and carries great comfort and care . . .

And with a look of great tenderness, your guide encourages you to focus your attention on your heart . . . and so you notice how it feels, all around and through your heart . . . and maybe you're aware of some tightness around your heart . . . or a heavy, dull aching sensation . . . it might feel hard around your heart . . . or maybe you sense deep pockets of sorrow tucked away inside . . . but whatever you notice, you're continuing to breathe deeply and easily . . . seeing what's there with the neutral eye of a camera . . . no praise, no blame . . .

And with a nod, your guide gently touches the center of your chest . . . and you can feel the warmth of it . . . pulsing into your chest . . . soft waves of comfort moving into the layers of protection that wind around your heart . . . warming and loosening and softening the ropy chords of anger and resentment . . . wound so tightly . . . that they cramp and constrict the lush power of the heart . . . and wall it off from the nourishment and solace it needs . . .

Layers and layers of wrapping, placed around the core wound . . . a kernel of hurt embedded so deeply . . . and walled off so skillfully . . . that inside it remains fresh and new . . . as sharp and as cruel . . . as the moment it first tore into your heart . . .

And so more and more you can breathe in the warmth of this gentle, healing energy . . . pulsing its rhythm to match the beat of your heart . . .

and you can take in more and more with each breath . . . letting it softly soak, layer by layer, into your chest . . . permeating all around and through the tangled knots and tightened chords . . . loosening . . . softening . . . opening . . . wending its way toward that seed of still-fresh grief . . .

And you might feel some space opening up . . . as you find yourself able to breathe more deeply . . . as more and more, the warm energy of the breath infuses you . . . and you might even notice some of the loosened chords falling discarded, in lazy loops at your feet . . . released from the task of holding your heart so tightly . . .

Understanding that you can allow this to take as long as you need . . . because you know . . . that this process must be done with the greatest respect for your own readiness . . . and only when the time is right . . . so you can expose the grief that lies beneath . . . the pain of lost connections and broken ties . . .

And maybe those times will come and go . . . when you can allow yourself to feel the pain . . . breathing into it . . . and letting it reclaim the opened spaces of your heart . . . giving it the room it needs . . . and knowing that this is the price of freedom . . . this is the way back to the richness of connection . . .

And you know . . . that the person you are now can do this . . . that you can breathe into your vulnerable, broken heart . . . giving your grief its due . . . because you are strong enough to just let the pain be, an uncontested presence . . . until it is ready to release . . . when the time is right . . . no sooner, no later . . .

And so it visits you . . . as many times as necessary . . . each time leaving your heart more open and strong, more filled with the power of its own vast energy . . .

And so, more and more, you feel the newly opened spaces . . . as you continue to breathe, deeply and fully . . . feeling the expansion in your chest . . . as warmth and power energize and nourish your heart . . . as you welcome your wounded self back into your own heart . . .

Getting a glimpse of the liberation . . . that comes with kicking off the covers of resentment . . . and dismissing the diversion of blame . . . able to love yourself, vulnerable and new . . . cleansed by grief . . . rinsed by sorrow . . . seeing how you are able to hold steady . . . because you know . . . that this is the price of admission back into the hugeness of your own heart . . . into the fullness of your own life . . .

Your companion smiles . . . and with a gesture calls forth a gentle procession of guardians and allies . . . sweet spirits . . . magical beings . . . animal helpers . . . guardian angels . . . teachers and guides . . . powerful ancestors . . . old and dear friends . . . some familiar, some not . . . but all smiling and nodding . . . gently approaching, one by one . . .

Come to show their admiration and respect . . . nod their acknowledgment . . . affirm your courage . . . offer a touch on the hand or shoulder . . . or bring a gift . . . set before you with gentle hands and smiling eyes . . . and you understand . . . that these are your witnesses . . . and they are welcoming you back to your own heart . . . and the richness of connection . . . laying at your feet the bounty of forgiveness . . .

And you can feel the velvety petals of your heart open like a flower . . . expanding from its center and filling your chest with its vast warmth and beauty . . . aware of all the peaceful power that resides there . . . and knowing that your heart is your home . . . the seat of your strength . . .

Understanding that the whole world pulses there . . . in the divine nexus of your heart . . . where all the delicate, luminous strands converge . . . glistening and glowing . . . in the unseen web that connects us all, one to the other . . .

And suddenly you are certain . . . you know with your whole being . . . that you are healing . . . that you will continue to heal . . . that your heart has always been whole . . . that whatever you thought was lost . . . still abides there . . . whatever seemed unforgiven . . . is redeemed there . . . that whatever appeared to be shattered by grief . . . is made whole there . . . that there is nothing in this world that can't be healed . . . in the vast space of your own open heart . . .

And so breathing in the power of this awareness . . . and breathing out the richness of your gratitude . . .

You can once again feel yourself breathing in and out of your belly . . . aware of your hands and feet . . . the support beneath you . . . and very gently . . . with soft eyes . . . allowing yourself to come back into the room . . . knowing in a deep place that you are better for this . . .

And so you are . . .

17 IMAGERY FOR A DEEPER LOOK AT THE SELF

This imagery is a good companion to both the Imagery for Confidence and the Imagery for Anger and Forgiveness. Or it makes a good substitute for the forgiveness imagery, if the idea of forgiveness holds no appeal.

It starts with the Peaceful Place Imagery that worked as a stand-alone exercise in stage one. Many people find that the opportunity to get some distance from themselves and see themselves with kinder eyes is a powerful experience.

Again, because the imagery requests a choice of a person or figure, it is a good idea to suggest to some people to pick just one for now, perhaps ahead of time (even though the unconscious might exercise its directorial discretion and change who it is that shows up). This will help those who otherwise might spend too much time trying to make the exactly right choice.

IMAGERY FOR A DEEPER LOOK AT THE SELF

Please take a moment or two to position yourself as comfortably as you can, allowing your body to be well supported . . . and gently letting your eyes close, if they want to . . . and arranging it so your head, neck, and spine are straight . . .

And letting your hands rest comfortably somewhere on your body . . . on your chest or midriff or abdomen . . . so you can feel the rise of your body when you breathe in . . . and the way it settles back down when you breathe out . . . and you're becoming more and more attuned to the feel of your breath moving in and out of your body . . .

And now, taking a nice, deep, full, cleansing breath . . . and breathing out, fully and completely . . . feeling the expansion of your belly with each breath in . . . and the way your body subsides with each out-breath . . .

And again, breathing in . . . and this time, imagining that you're sending the warm energy of your breath to places in your body that might be sore or tense or tight . . . and releasing the tension with the out-breath . . . so you can feel your breath going into those places . . . warming and softening and loosening them . . . and then, gathering it all up . . . and breathing it out . . .

So that more and more, you can feel safe and comfortable . . . relaxed and easy . . . watching the cleansing action of your breath . . .

And any unwelcome thoughts . . . those too can be sent out with the exhale . . . so that for just a moment, your mind is empty . . . free and clear space . . . and you are blessed with peaceful stillness . . .

And any emotions you might sense inside . . . those too can be noted and breathed out of your body . . . so you can be still and quiet . . . like a smooth and glassy lake with no ripples . . .

And now, if you would . . . see if you can imagine a place . . . where you feel safe and peaceful . . . relaxed and easy . . . and it might be a place you used to go to . . . or somewhere you go to now . . . or a place you've always wanted to be . . . it could be by the ocean . . . or in the woods . . . or in the mountains or desert . . . it doesn't matter . . . just so it's a place that feels good and peaceful to you . . .

And allowing the place to become real, in all its dimensions . . . looking around you . . . enjoying the colors . . . the play of light and shadow . . . the scenery, in all its appealing detail . . . looking over to your left . . . and over to your right . . .

And feeling whatever you're sitting against or lying upon . . . whether you're leaning against a friendly old oak tree . . . or lying on sweet meadow grass . . . or walking in the woods, on a fragrant carpet of spicy pine needles . . . or you might even be walking in the surf, with cool, wet sand oozing between your toes, and gentle waves lapping at your ankles . . . or maybe you're just sitting on a nice, warm rock in the sun . . .

And listening to the sounds of the place . . . birds singing . . . or the rustling sounds of a soft wind through the leaves . . . or the powerful, rhythmic crash of ocean waves . . . or the gentle soothing sound of a bubbling brook . . . just so you're letting your ears become attuned to all the beautiful sounds of this place . . . that is so safe and peaceful to you . . .

And smelling its rich fragrance . . . whether it's the sharp, bracing scent of salt sea air . . . the sweet, heavy fullness of flowers and grass . . . the pungent, dark green smell of peat moss in the forest . . . sometimes the air is so rich and redolent, you can practically taste it on your tongue . . .

And noticing the feel of the air on your skin as it caresses your face and neck . . . and it might be crisp and dry . . . or balmy and wet . . . so you're just letting your skin enjoy the nourishing presence of this place . . . that is so safe and peaceful to you . . . and letting its healing energy soak into your skin . . .

And as you become more and more attuned to the beauty and safety of this place . . . you begin to feel a kind of tingling . . . an energizing feeling in the air . . . and a sense that something wonderful is just about to happen . . .

And looking out in front of you . . . there's a shimmering in the air . . . a few feet away . . . looking like heat when it rises from a hot desert surface . . . and you can see . . . that this shimmering in the air is turning into a kind of a screen . . . a translucent screen . . .

And as you watch the screen . . . with a kind of peaceful curiosity . . . you gradually become aware of a form beginning to appear on it . . . becoming more and more defined . . . and you realize that this is the form of a very special someone . . . or being . . . radiating love and wisdom . . . and it might be someone you know . . . or perhaps not . . . it could be someone who loved you well from your past . . . maybe a special guide or teacher . . . a parent or grandparent . . . or even someone in your life now . . .

Or it could be a divine being . . . come to help you with this . . . or maybe a spirit guide . . . a guardian angel . . . a special animal . . . and you know . . . that it doesn't matter if you recognize this visitor . . . because you can feel the love and wisdom and goodness . . . the ability to see into the heart of things . . . deeply and clearly . . .

So you watch . . . peaceful and easy . . . as this figure becomes more and more defined . . . more and more three-dimensional . . . in whatever characteristic posture they have . . . wearing whatever it is that they wear . . . speaking in whatever way they speak . . . doing whatever it is that they do . . . crisp and clear in every dimension . . . *(pause)* . . .

And you can enter the screen, softly and easily . . . feeling yourself drawn to this visitor . . . wanting to have a closer look . . . undetected by them, you can slip into the screen . . . able to have a slow, curious walk around them . . . seeing them from every angle . . . the expression on the face . . . *(pause)* . . . the profile and the back . . . *(pause)* . . . coming around to the other side . . . as you sense the feel of the air around them . . . *(pause)* . . . the sounds of the breathing or the voice . . . *(pause)* . . . the scent of their skin or hair . . . *(pause)* . . . so you're just slowly moving around them . . . pleased to experience a full, rich awareness of them . . . with all of your senses . . .

And now . . . in the magical, safe space of the screen . . . somehow, for just a brief while . . . sliding past the boundaries and slipping into the body of this other being . . . and breathing their breath . . . for just a brief while . . . for the sake of understanding more . . .

And if there is any reluctance to doing this . . . just gently noticing it . . . and allowing yourself to soften all around it . . . for the sake of your own growth . . . and learning what you need to know . . . just an experiment . . . in breathing their breath . . . and looking out from the eyes of this other body . . . hearing, tasting, smelling, seeing from this other awareness . . .

Breathing deeply into this other being's body . . . and sensing the feelings . . . whatever they are . . . *(pause)* . . . and it might be a sense of warmth and peace and calm . . . or a soft expansion around the heart . . . maybe a solid, steady sense of clarity . . . or safety and comfort . . . whatever the feelings or sensations . . . just experiencing what it feels like here . . . in the muscles, skin, and bone . . . staying open and curious as to how it feels inside this other body . . .

And seeing out from their eyes . . . what the world looks like . . . sounds like . . . feels like . . . as you breathe with their breath . . . and feel with their feelings . . . gentle and easy . . . feeling their heart beating inside you . . . powerful and steady . . . *(pause)* . . .

And perhaps even seeing you over there . . . with these other eyes . . . looking over at you . . . and feeling who you are . . . taking in all that is under, around, and through the surface . . . to the essence of who you really are . . . seeing straight into your heart . . . taking in all the hidden splendor . . . all the vast beauty of your innermost being . . . *(pause)* . . .

Sensing what you are here to do . . . with all your unique gifts and special abilities . . . appreciating all the turns of the journey you've been on . . . seeing it all from this wider perspective . . . from this oasis of love and wisdom . . . comprehending the perfect timing of your path . . . and how you've walked it in your own unique way . . .

And so just taking a moment to experience this . . . gently and easily . . . with all the focus you can bring to bear . . . *(pause)* . . .

And now . . . very softly and easily . . . whenever you are ready . . . wishing this other awareness good-bye . . . in whatever way feels right . . . *(pause)* . . . and still infused with the richness and power of this experience . . . still feeling the expanded energy in your heart . . . very gently moving back into your own body . . . reinhabiting it fully and easily . . . feeling the familiar space . . . as you come back home to yourself . . .

Breathing into it with your own breath . . . through your own nose and mouth . . . back home . . . connected again to your body, your steadiest companion, and your oldest friend . . .

And sliding out of the magical, translucent screen . . . softly and easily . . . into your safe and peaceful place . . .

And very gently and with soft eyes . . . you can feel yourself coming back to your present surroundings . . . breathing very rhythmically and easily . . . into your own body . . . feeling your hands and your feet . . . your breath, deep in your belly . . .

Knowing in a deep place you are better for this . . .

And so you are . . .

18 IMAGERY FOR ACCESSING A SYMBOLIC ANSWER

This imagery takes advantage of the new levels of intuitive opening that often happen as a result of traumatic experience. The imagery is versatile and can be used for just about anything, because it offers help with an answer of any kind from the right side of the brain, in the form of a symbolic representation. It is particularly useful for dilemmas or issues that are hard to resolve. When the left brain keeps coming up with the same stale, circular conclusions, it's time to recruit the genius of the right hemisphere to help out. And of course, the trauma survivor has a built-in advantage, with an activated right brain and considerably enhanced intuitive capacity.

This imagery starts out with the heart-opening Imagery for Protection and Support that worked as stand-alone, de-stressing imagery in stage one. Opening the heart not only helps to regulate stress and balance mood but enhances intuitive capacity as well.

IMAGERY FOR ACCESSING A SYMBOLIC ANSWER

To begin with, please arrange it so that you're comfortable, either sitting or lying down, and your head, neck, and spine are aligned. See if you can take a moment to shift your weight, so that you're feeling well supported and comfortable . . .

And settling fully down into your body . . . taking a full, deep cleansing breath . . . *(pause)* . . . exhaling as fully as you comfortably can . . . *(pause)* . . . and another . . . breathing deeply, down into the belly if you can . . . filling your abdomen . . . and breathing out, fully and completely . . .

And once more, breathing in . . . and this time, imagining that you're sending the warm energy of your breath to any part of your body that might be tense or sore or tight . . . and releasing any discomfort with the exhale . . . so that you can feel your breath loosening and softening any tight places . . . and breathing them out . . . so that more and more, you can feel safe and easy . . . relaxed and comfortable . . . attuned to the cleansing action of your own breath . . .

And any unwelcome thoughts that come to mind . . . those too can be released with the out-breath . . . so that for just a moment, the mind is smooth and still . . . free and clear space . . . and you are blessed with stillness . . .

And any emotions that you are aware of . . . those too can be noted, and acknowledged, and released with the out-breath . . . so your emotional self can be still and quiet, like the mirrored glass of a lake . . .

And now . . . directing your attention inward . . . focusing on your heart . . . curious about how it feels all around and through your heart . . . with all the gentle focus you can bring to bear . . . detached and curious . . . and you might even want to put the flat palm of your hand over it . . . to help you focus your attention there . . .

As you connect to the powerful rhythms of your heart . . . sensing how it pulses life and strength . . . all through your body . . . and focusing your breath . . . so that you are imagining that you are actually breathing through your heart . . . as if the breath were actually coming in through your heart . . . and going out through your heart . . . to further focus your attention there . . .

So you can begin to feel a warmth and fullness . . . gathering in the center of your chest . . . as you continue to focus your attention there . . . and breathe your breath there . . . in and out of the very center of your heart . . . and just allowing natural feelings of love and care . . . to begin to collect there . . . all around and through your heart . . . (pause) . . .

And you might also become aware of the feel of the air immediately around you . . . a subtle energy, a bristle of aliveness . . . like a gently vibrating cushion of energy . . . softly surrounding and protecting you . . . gently vibrating and pulsing . . . and perhaps even sensing its sparkling dots of color . . . or hearing its gentle humming sound . . .

As you continue to breathe through the heart . . . sending the energy of the out-breath into this living, pulsing field of protective energy . . . adding to its density and size . . . making it more and more palpable . . . perhaps even sensing how it pulses in sync with the beat of your own heart . . . and inside the cushion . . . you can feel safe and protected . . . able to take in whatever is nourishing to you . . . but insulated from whatever you don't want or need . . .

And now, sensing this cushion of energy drawing to it all the love and sweetness that have ever been felt for you by anyone at any time . . . pulling in all the caring, all the loving-kindness that has ever been sent your way . . . every prayer and good wish . . . permeating and filling the field of energy around you . . . every smile, every nod of respect . . . every thank-you and gesture of gratitude . . . pulling it all in like a powerful magnet . . . calling every good wish home . . . and so increasing the powerful protective field all around you . . .

And perhaps even sensing around you . . . the presence of those who've loved and nurtured you . . . or those who love you now . . . or who will love you in the future . . . just the ones you want with you . . .

and sensing them around you now . . . maybe catching a fleeting glimpse of somebody . . . or noticing an old familiar scent . . . or hearing the familiar timbre of a dearly loved voice . . . possibly feeling a presence by your side . . . or the soft weight of a gentle hand on your shoulder . . .

People from your life . . . alive or long gone . . . there might even be a special animal . . . a powerful ancestor . . . a guardian angel . . . sweet spirits or magical beings . . . special helpers and healers . . . allies, teachers, and guides . . . dearest friends . . . all come to lend assistance . . . invoked by your intention to heal, fully and completely . . .

And some might be familiar and some not . . . it doesn't matter . . . just so you feel their protection and support . . . breathing it into your heart . . . letting it fill you . . .

As one of them . . . perhaps familiar, perhaps not . . . holds a gift for you . . . a gift that's specially covered and wrapped . . . something to help you with your puzzle . . . and you somehow know that this is assistance from the highest place, and for your greatest good . . .

A gift, lovingly offered to you . . . and as you unwrap it . . . what you find under the wrapping may or may not make sense to you . . . but you know . . . that this is something that can tell you what you need to know . . . offer a new way of looking . . . or a shift in feeling . . . a different perspective . . . *(pause)*. . . .

And it might be a complete surprise . . . what you discover under the wrapping . . . or maybe something very mysterious . . . or plain and simple . . . it could be something familiar . . . or amusing . . . or vague . . . it doesn't matter . . . because you can keep it . . . and hold it . . . and examine it again and again . . . from every angle . . . until you see what you need to see . . . feel what you need to feel . . . and know what you need to know . . .

Able to turn it in your hands . . . feel its texture . . . catch its scent . . . or hear its message . . . yours to keep . . . a powerful gift from a wise and loving ally . . .

And still smiling, the bearer of your gift bows . . . and, with a long and deep look, steps back . . . and you can feel peaceful and easy . . . knowing you can invite this visitor back whenever you wish . . .

And so . . . still breathing deeply and easily . . . still aware of the warmth in the center of your chest . . . and still sensing the cushion of protection all around you . . . you can once again feel yourself in the center of your body . . . peaceful and steady . . . feeling your hands and your feet on the ground . . . your breath in your belly . . .

And very gently, and with soft eyes . . . you can allow yourself to come back into the room whenever you wish . . . knowing in a deep place that you are better and wiser for this . . .

And so you are . . .

19 IMAGERY TO SUPPORT WEIGHT LOSS

It is not unusual for someone with post-traumatic stress to experience dramatic changes in weight. In the beginning stages of an acute stress reaction, with its surges of adrenergized hyperarousal, there is little appetite for food, and the body is likely to be speedily metabolizing whatever stores of fat there are.

With more chronic forms of PTSD, however, when the slowed-down numbing response sets in, a survivor can gain weight fairly easily. These shifts are all part of the general dysregulation that can occur.

This imagery is to help restore natural metabolism, using the body's basic process of converting stored fat into energy as the central metaphor for the whole person's releasing, focusing, and expressing inner energy and power. In addition, it grounds the body and generates appreciation for it. Other imagery, to increase feelings of safety and protection and to generate self-esteem, is included as well.

This imagery works well as an adjunct to standard healthy eating and strength training programs and can also be effective on its own.[1] It's a nice companion to the Imagery for Anger and Forgiveness—they are both about letting go of things that no longer serve us and just weigh us down.

Please begin by making yourself comfortable, shifting your weight so you're feeling well supported . . . *(pause)* . . . and gently allowing your eyes to close . . .

Letting your hands rest comfortably somewhere on your body . . . on your chest or midriff or abdomen . . . so you can feel the rise of your body when you breathe in . . . and the way it settles back down when you breathe out . . . and you're becoming more and more attuned to your breath, as it moves in and out of your body . . .

Inhaling deeply and slowly, all the way down into your belly if you can . . . *(pause)* . . . and breathing out, fully and completely . . . feeling the expansion of your abdomen with each in-breath . . . and the way it subsides with each out-breath . . .

And again, breathing in . . . and this time, imagining that you're sending the warm energy of your breath to any part of your body that's sore or tense or tight . . . *(pause)* . . . and releasing the tension with the exhale . . . so you can feel your breath going to all the tight, tense places . . . warming and loosening and softening them . . . and then gathering up all the tension . . . and breathing it out . . . so that more and more, you can feel safe and comfortable, relaxed and easy . . . noticing your breath . . . with friendly but detached awareness . . .

And any unwelcome thoughts that come to mind . . . those too can be sent out with the breath . . . released with the exhale . . . so that for just a moment, the mind is empty . . . for just a split second, it is free and clear space . . . and you are blessed with stillness . . .

And any emotions that are rocking around inside . . . those too can be noted and acknowledged and sent out with the breath . . . so that your emotional self can be still and quiet . . . like a lake with no ripples . . .

And now . . . see if you can turn your attention inward for a moment . . . to see how your body is feeling . . . noticing where it might feel tight or tense or achy or sore . . . and where it feels loose and easy . . . comfortable and open . . .

So you're moving your attention into your body . . . starting perhaps with your head . . . checking to see how it feels around your face and scalp . . . becoming aware of how it feels around your eyes . . . and in your jaw . . . and seeing how it feels deep inside your head . . . and you're just curious and neutral . . . friendly but detached . . . *(pause)* . . .

And moving your attention down into your neck . . . curious about any sensation there . . . *(pause)* . . .

And checking your shoulders to see how they feel . . . noticing any heaviness or tightness there . . . *(pause)* . . . as you continue to breathe deeply and easily . . .

Moving your awareness down into your chest . . . checking your lungs as they expand and contract to the powerful, steady rhythm of your breath . . . and it might feel a little heavy or tight in there . . . or maybe it's open and loose and easy . . . *(pause)* . . .

And seeing how it feels in your heart . . . *(pause)* . . . noticing any heaviness or tightness or sorrow there . . . or perhaps there are pleasant feelings of soft warmth and fullness . . . and you're just noticing, curious and relaxed . . . no praise, no blame . . . as you continue to breathe, deeply and easily . . .

And moving your awareness around into your back . . . noticing the feel of your back, all along the length of your spine . . . from your neck down to your tailbone . . . noticing places that might have absorbed extra stress . . . and noticing where it's feeling strong and comfortable and easy . . .

And coming back around . . . looking to see how it feels inside your belly . . . checking deep inside the abdomen . . . aware of any sensations there . . . as your body distributes nourishment and strength to every part of you . . .

And moving your awareness down into your bottom . . . checking to see how it feels along your whole pelvic floor . . . and noticing any comfort or discomfort there . . .

So you're just doing this inventory with the neutral eye of a camera . . . no praise, no blame . . . detached and curious . . . as you continue breathing in . . . and breathing out . . . fully and easily . . .

And moving your awareness down into your legs . . . sensing any feeling in your thighs . . . your knees . . . or in the calves . . . all the way down to your feet . . . all the way down to the very tips of your toes . . .

So you're just taking this space to reacquaint yourself with this body of yours . . . your oldest friend . . . your steadiest companion . . . noticing it . . . listening to it . . . and acknowledging it . . .

And letting your awareness sink down into it . . . settling your spirit all the way down into the welcoming spaces of your body . . . and just letting it drift down and settle into every corner . . . like a gentle, misty fog softly nestling into a lush, green valley . . . so you're fully inhabiting your body . . . feeling more and more the comfort, the rightness of being home . . .

And as you continue to breathe in and out . . . deeply and easily . . . and you might begin to notice a tingling in the air all around you . . . the pleasant, subtle feel of energy on your skin . . . tingling and vibrating . . . as if you were surrounded and protected by a magical cushion of air . . . alive with humming energy . . . tiny waves of it, sparkling and dancing with light and color . . . becoming fuller, denser, with every breath you take . . . more and more able to insulate you from whatever you don't want or need . . . *(pause)* . . .

And now, if you would, see if you can imagine that this cushion of energy is drawing to it all the love and sweetness that have ever been felt for you by anyone at any time . . . pulling in all the caring, all the lovingkindness that has ever been sent your way . . . every prayer and good wish permeating and filling the field of energy around you . . . every smile and thank-you . . . pulling it all in like a powerful magnet . . . calling every good wish home . . . and so increasing the powerful protective field all around you . . .

And sensing the presence of those who loved and nurtured you . . . just the ones you want with you . . . or those who love you now . . . or will love you in the future . . . feeling them around you now . . . maybe seeing a fleeting glimpse of somebody . . . or noticing an old, familiar scent . . . or hearing the well-loved timbre of a dearly loved voice . . . or the gentle weight of a loving hand on your shoulder . . . people from your life . . . alive or long gone . . . there might even be a special animal . . . a guardian angel . . . a powerful ancestor . . . sweet spirits or magical beings . . . perhaps familiar or perhaps not . . . it doesn't matter . . . just so you feel their protection and support . . .

And breathing in all that love and care, fully and deeply . . . all the way into your heart . . . filling up with it . . . feeling its warmth spread all through your body . . . gently pulsing out from the center of your heart . . . and diffusing all through your system . . . spreading widely and evenly, like ripples in a pond . . .

And you might even see this spreading as a beautiful color infusing your entire body . . . or as a humming vibration that tunes up the rest of you . . . like the low, powerful purr of a very finely tuned, powerful engine . . .

So more and more, you can feel a quickening inside of you, as energy spreads throughout your body . . . as centers deep inside the base of the brain broadcast signals to the glands that regulate the body's metabolism . . . causing a shift to occur . . . the way that moving the lever on a carburetor will make an engine start to idle faster . . . and use up more fuel . . . making it possible for it to spring into action more quickly and easily . . .

And so your body senses a shift . . . as a special deployment of eager hormones pours into your bloodstream . . . prodding the cells that hold extra stores of fat to release their contents . . . catalyzing the conversion of these tiny caches into looser, more flexible stuff . . . into fluid fatty acids that can easily slip into the bloodstream . . . and float downstream . . .

Where they are met and escorted by dashing young enzymes . . . clever fellows who know their way around the body . . . who can dance these tiny particles downstream . . . until they reach the entryway of an energy-hungry cell . . . where they charm their way through the membrane . . . gallantly holding open the door and dropping their partner off inside . . .

And once inside, these tiny particles can do what they were born for . . . gladly transforming themselves into heat and power . . . strength and growth . . . making you want to move and feel the pleasure of muscles working . . . the body doing what it was meant to do . . .

Tiny particles eagerly joining the exquisite dance of creation inside the body . . . helping to sculpt new muscle . . . to grow healthy new cells . . . delighted to fulfill their purpose and contribute to the whole . . . (pause) . . .

And knowing that it is not just the fat cells of the body that are releasing and converting their contents . . . but that you, too, are emptying out old pockets of stored pain . . . tossing out the crusty debris of long-held hurts and resentments . . . letting go of ancient fears . . . shaking off any leftover guilt or self-hatred . . .

Forgiving yourself and others for disappointments of the past . . . no longer willing to reinjure yourself with repeated visits to old wounds . . . but releasing it all . . . so your heart can be lighter . . . your body stronger . . . your life freer . . . with more choices, more energy, more aliveness available to you . . .

Better able to appreciate yourself just as you are, right now, in this very moment . . . better able to appreciate your body . . . your oldest friend, your steadiest companion . . . even with its alleged imperfections . . . and perhaps beginning to comprehend its true beauty, its awesome intelligence, and its faithful service to you . . .

And knowing that there will come a time when you'll be walking in one of your favorite places . . . aware of all the life and beauty around you . . . attuned to all the richness of the sights and smells and sounds of the place . . . of the delicious feel of the air on your skin . . . and maybe even taking pleasure in the way a soft fabric feels against your arms or legs . . .

Enjoying the easy, natural swing of your arms . . . the steady roll of your hips . . . and the way your feet touch and lift off from the ground . . . glad to make contact with the steady support of the ground beneath your feet . . . feeling the earth breathing its ample energy through the soles of your feet . . . grateful for so much strength and beauty, in so much abundant supply . . .

Knowing you are getting stronger . . . building muscle . . . gathering energy and power . . . clarity of purpose . . . feeling new stirrings of confidence . . . a clear sense of coming into your own as never before . . .

And suddenly you are certain . . . you know with your whole heart, with your whole being . . . that you can do this . . . that you can let go of needless baggage, piece by piece . . . that you are cleaning out the overstuffed closets of your heart, your mind, your house, your body, your life . . . and filling yourself up with the vast energy from your own open heart . . .

Knowing you have things to do, purposes to accomplish . . . that you require a strong, vital, healthy body for this . . . you require all your energy and power to fuel you . . . every part of you aligned with your sense of who you are and what you are about . . .

You again become aware of the protective cushion of energy and the allies around you . . . you might even see a nod, a smile, a gesture . . .

maybe hear an approving murmur, an encouraging phrase . . . perhaps even feel a loving squeeze on your shoulder . . .

And you know that they see it, too . . . that you can do this . . . that you can be stronger and surer and clearer than ever before . . . and they are your witnesses . . . your private cheering section . . . to see you through this and other things, too . . . always at your side . . . yours to call forth whenever you wish . . .

And so . . . feeling peaceful and easy . . . you once again become aware of your breath moving in and out of your body . . . fully and easily . . . perhaps feeling the need to stretch a little . . . and noticing how good it feels to move after being still for so long . . .

And so . . . very gently and with soft eyes . . . allowing yourself to come back into the room whenever you are ready. . . . knowing in a deep place that you are better for this . . .

And so you are . . .

20 IMAGERY TO SUPPORT RECOVERY FROM CHEMICAL DEPENDENCY

Chemical dependency is another frequent complication of post-traumatic stress, affecting a significant proportion of survivors with PTSD. Although alcohol and drugs can initially feel as if they are helping with symptoms, for many they eventually become a problem with a trajectory all its own, exacerbating and increasing the difficulties created by the traumatic stress. Once addiction is in place, the core of the trauma cannot be healed until it is dismantled. So most therapists and trauma treatment programs insist on sobriety before anything else.

This imagery is designed to help with recovery from chemical dependency and support motivation to stop using. It collaborates well with a twelve-step program and is also used in many residential treatment settings, for both adults and teens, as a valued component of treatment. Because of its self-soothing elements, it helps with the jangled nerves and hypersensitive skinlessness of early-stage withdrawal. At the same time, it supports skill-building in the art of self-regulation, as it offers a natural alternative to self-medicating anxiety with unhealthy substances to achieve calm. As a healthy replacement tool, it provides additional support for staying sober.

IMAGERY TO SUPPORT RECOVERY FROM CHEMICAL DEPENDENCY

To begin with, please arrange it so that you're comfortable, either sitting or lying down, so that your head, neck, and spine are straight, and taking a moment or two to shift your weight, so that you're feeling well supported and comfortable . . .

And settling your awareness down into your body . . . taking a full, deep cleansing breath . . . *(pause)* . . . exhaling as fully as you comfortably can . . . *(pause)* . . . and another . . . breathing deeply, down into the belly if you can . . . filling your abdomen . . . and breathing out, fully and completely . . .

And once more, breathing in . . . and this time, imagining that you are sending the warm energy of your breath to any part of your body that might be tense or sore or tight . . . and releasing any discomfort with the exhale . . . so that you can feel your breath loosening and softening any tight places . . . and breathing them out . . . and more and more, you can feel safe and easy . . . relaxed and comfortable . . . attuned to the cleansing action of your own breath . . .

And any unwelcome thoughts that come to mind . . . those too can be released with the out-breath . . . so that for just a moment, the mind is smooth and still . . . free and clear space . . . and you are blessed with stillness . . .

And any emotions that you might become aware of . . . those too can be noted, and acknowledged, and released with the out-breath . . . so your emotional self can be still and quiet, like the mirrored glass of a lake with no ripples . . .

And as you are breathing in and out . . . feeling the rise and fall of your breath in your body . . . you might begin to feel a kind of tingling . . . a pleasant energizing something in the air all around you . . . noticing more and more that the air is alive with soft, gentle, vibrant, humming energy . . .

And from somewhere above you, a cone of powerful silver-white light is gently and steadily moving down . . . forming a tent of soft, soothing energy all around you . . . surrounding and protecting you . . . muffling any harsh sounds or jarring noises . . . soothing your spirit . . . as it softly illuminates everything it touches . . . giving everything around you a fresh beauty . . .

You can feel the gentle energy of the light softly touching your scalp . . . caressing your brow . . . soothing and clearing, as it softly moves into your head and neck . . .

And soaks down into your shoulders with the softness of its energy . . . entering your chest . . . gently easing and massaging any tightness around the heart . . .

And continuing down your spine . . . soft healing filling your back and torso . . . moving into the layers of tissue, deeper and deeper . . . cleansing and clearing . . . opening and releasing . . .

Sending a warm, vibrating softness into any discomfort in the belly . . . feeling its healing magic soothe and calm any places that need it . . .

And flowing down into your legs . . . and filling your feet . . . all the way down to the tips of your toes . . .

So you're just letting the light work its soothing magic deep inside of your body . . . maybe noticing how it collects with deliberate intelligence into the deepest places where pain is stored . . . and feeling those places begin to open as you breathe into them . . . fully and deeply . . .

Breathing in, slowly and deeply . . . and breathing out, fully and easily, into the cone of light and energy surrounding you . . . that insulates you from whatever you don't want or need with its soft, tingling glow . . . breathing its healing magic in . . . fully and deeply . . .

So more and more, the healing energy of the light fills you and spreads throughout your body . . . catalyzing the birth of healthy, perfectly shaped cells to replace any weary, injured ones . . .

Strong, new cells that can accelerate the release of tired toxins that need to be discarded . . . sending old poisons on their way . . . out of the body . . . making room for rich, vital nutrients from the bloodstream . . . the arrival of new strength and vitality . . .

Elements in the blood stabilizing . . . muscle rebuilding . . . protective mucous linings forming . . . scar tissue shrinking . . . and blood vessels returning to normal size, shape, and resilience . . .

And feeling, too, the mind coming out of its fog . . . regaining clarity and focus . . . as energy increases . . . and mind and body become calm and stable . . . as your whole system cleanses and clears, rebalances and rebuilds . . .

And knowing that it is not just the tissues of the body that are letting go of whatever doesn't serve them . . . but that you too are emptying out old pockets of stored pain . . . letting go of ancient fears . . . tossing out the crusty debris of long-held hurts and resentments . . . shaking out leftover guilt and self-hatred . . .

Forgiving yourself for disappointments of the past . . . no longer willing to reinjure yourself by returning to visit old wounds . . . but releasing it all . . . so your heart can be lighter . . . your body stronger . . . your life freer . . . with more choices, more energy, more aliveness available to you . . .

Better able to appreciate yourself . . . better able to honor your body, your oldest friend, your steadiest companion . . . perhaps feeling glimmers of gratitude for its loyalty and patience . . . beginning to comprehend its true beauty . . . its awesome intelligence . . . and its faithful service to you . . .

Knowing you are getting stronger . . . building muscle and strength . . . gathering energy and power . . . clarity of purpose . . . feeling new stirrings of confidence . . . and a clear sense of coming into your own as never before . . .

And suddenly you are certain . . . you know with your whole heart . . . with your whole being . . . that you can do this . . . that every day, you are getting stronger . . . more and more able to look people in the eye . . . tell your truth . . . laugh from your heart . . . smell the morning . . . renew connections with those you hold dear . . .

Knowing you have things to do, purposes to accomplish, gifts to give . . . that you require a clear mind and a strong body for this . . . every part of you aligned with your sense of who you are and what you are about . . .

And so . . . feeling peaceful and easy . . . you once again become aware of your breath, moving in and out of your body . . . fully and easily . . . aware of your hands and your feet . . . perhaps feeling the need to stretch a little . . . and noticing how good it feels to move after being still for so long . . .

And so . . . allowing yourself to come back into the room . . . whenever you are ready. . . . very gently and with soft eyes . . . knowing in a deep place that you are better for this . . .

And so you are . . .

21 IMAGERY FOR CONNECTING, HEART TO HEART

This imagery exercise is done in pairs, combining imagery with light touch and imagining the flow of energy from the hands. It will relax and settle even the most agitated mind and works well in a support group setting. It is a potent exercise that opens the heart and drops awareness down into a place of deep healing and connection. It can be done with a friend, a relative, a fellow support group member, or even a stranger, as the connection goes beyond the social or interpersonal and straight into the heart. People are always surprised and moved by its power, and they usually don't want this exercise to end. Some joke that dicey committee meetings and tenuous diplomatic negotiations should start with this imagery.

This imagery requires an unusual seating arrangement. It asks that two people sit choo-choo style, one directly and closely behind the other, with both facing in the same direction. It is important to be comfortable and well supported during this ten-to-fifteen-minute exercise.

It should then be repeated with the positions switched, so that people can have the full experience of being on both the "receiving" and the "giving" end. So the person in the front moves to the back and the person in the back occupies the front seat.

For some trauma survivors, it's good to check with them first and explain the seating arrangement. A few will not want someone sitting directly behind them and may want to try a side-to-side arrangement instead. Still others may not be ready for the intimacy and feelings of lovingness this imagery generates. As always, timing is everything, and only the survivor knows whether an exercise is appropriate. There is only one expert on when, if, where, and how.

And one final caveat: teenagers who are propelled into roaring lust at the drop of a hat may find this exercise more trouble than it's worth. The goal of intimate connection through asexual touch—surprisingly easy for most people, including most trauma survivors—may just be beyond the reach of some of them, particularly the boys. On the other hand, many young people open like flowers to the feelings of unconditional love that this exercise prompts. So as with everything else, it must be decided on a case-by-case basis.

IMAGERY FOR CONNECTING, HEART TO HEART

Please arrange the chairs to sit choo-choo style, both of you facing the same direction, the person sitting in the back close behind the person in front. If the chair of the person sitting in the front has a back, it might be a good idea to turn the chair sideways, so your back is free and clear . . .

And making yourselves as comfortable as you can . . . sitting with your head, neck, and spine straight . . . and allowing yourself a full, cleansing breath . . . sending the warm energy of the in-breath to any part of your body that's tense or tight or sore . . . so it can soften and warm and loosen any discomfort . . . and you can release it with the out-breath . . .

So that more and more, you can be relaxed and easy, safe and comfortable, attuned to the cleansing action of your own breath . . .

And now, imagining a protective cushion of energy surrounding you, shielding the two of you from outside distraction . . . and keeping you safe and protected inside of it . . . sensing how the energy in this cushion has the magical ability to draw out of you anything that you might want to discard . . . so that anything you release is absorbed and neutralized by the energy of the cushion . . . making it an even stronger, more protective shielding . . . and inside, you can be safe and easy . . . relaxed and comfortable . . .

So you can just let yourself be . . . breathing in and out . . . deeply and easily . . . and perhaps becoming aware of the energy around the heart . . . aware of a warmth and softness that collects in the center of the chest . . . and just letting it expand, softly and easily, as you breathe fully, in and out . . .

And for the person sitting in the back . . . see if you can focus your attention on your partner . . . on the neck or shoulders or the back in front of you . . . settling your attention on what you might consider to be a particularly tender and vulnerable spot . . . a place that touches your heart . . . like the depression in the back of the neck . . . or the spot between the shoulder blades . . . and just allowing your own feelings of loving-kindness to collect in your heart for that appealing, tender spot that you're focusing on . . .

Maybe sensing some of what the back has carried . . . or the burden that the shoulders have known . . . or possibly feeling where tension or tightness is lodged . . . as your heart continues to warm and open and fill . . . with the vast energy of its own loving-kindness . . .

And gently placing the palm of your hand . . . down flat on the neck or shoulders or back in front of you . . . wherever it feels right . . . and just allowing the warm energy from your heart to move up to your shoulders, down your arms, and into your hands . . . and into your partner . . . to warm and nourish and replenish wherever it is needed . . . as you continue your focus on that vulnerable spot . . .

And the person sitting in the front . . . see if you can just allow yourself to receive . . . which is of course a great gift to give in and of itself . . . just letting your body soak up this rich, warm energy from this generous heart behind you . . . and letting the energy move through you . . . allowing it to go wherever it is needed . . . and remembering how good it feels to just allow yourself to receive . . . especially a gift offered so freely . . .

And for the person in back . . . just feeling the warm, rich energy flowing from your heart . . . down your arms . . . and through your hands . . . rich, powerful supplies from the vast riches of the open heart . . . just this gift . . . offered freely and without strings . . . and remembering how good it feels to be in touch once more with your own generosity . . .

Enjoying the richness of the connection . . . open heart to open heart . . . where the giver becomes the receiver and the receiver becomes the source . . . pulsing with the beat of one heart . . . *(long pause)* . . .

And whenever you are ready . . . gently allowing yourselves to disconnect . . . knowing in a deep place that you are better for this . . . more settled and steady . . . attuned to the powerful seat of the heart . . . connected with your own sources of love and wisdom . . .

And so you are . . .

(Now the exercise can be repeated, with the roles and seating reversed.)

This, then, is the complete guided imagery program for PTSD—twenty-one exercises, arranged in three stages of healing—yours to mix and match, as needed.

14 OTHER IMAGERY-BASED THERAPIES

Guided imagery is highly flexible and collegial, working well by itself but easily collaborating with other forms of therapy. It doesn't compete or interfere with other treatment methods but, like a good sport, supports them all, including talk therapy. Repeated use of imagery bolsters learning and integrates gains made from other modalities.

This is thanks to its capacity to work its gentle, subtle, but relentless magic deep under conscious radar, where technical distinctions matter little. It integrates growth, supports change, marshals courage, and boosts motivation by helping to cohere every part of the person—mind, body, and spirit—behind his or her intention to heal. In spite of how pretentious this might sound to some, I have to say that I believe imagery works at the deepest levels—the soul level, if you will—to bring every part of the person to bear, for the huge task of healing ahead. In that sense, it is truly a multisensory form of nondenominational prayer.

What I've been describing so far is the undiluted and unadorned variety of guided imagery. But there are other imagery-based tools, developed over the past two decades, highly targeted and carefully structured, that have been shown to be effective, practical, efficient, fast-acting, and accessible to many trauma survivors.

These new therapies, like pure guided imagery, lean heavily on right-brain functioning and also manage to successfully sidestep the roadblocks that traumatic experience imposes on cognition and language. They pierce symptomatology quickly and, for the most part, relatively painlessly.

Structured as a tightly sequenced, cognitive-behavioral method, with clear steps to follow, these therapies have more in common with one another than differences (although some of their practitioners might disagree), but their greatest similarity is the fact that imagery lies at the heart of each of them. Because they work at a cognitive and behavioral level, the changes are a godsend for speed but may lack depth. Often that is supplied by the survivor, who fills in the blanks with her own integrative work. But depth can also be supplied by the guided imagery program in this book, which can ensure that changes will be integrated at a deeper level.

The most promising and best-studied methods are described in this chapter. More information, for both survivors and practitioners—books, tapes, and training opportunities—are listed in the Resources section at the end of this book. For want of a better umbrella term, and for reasons that will become immediately apparent, I refer to these new methods as the *alphabet therapies.*

EYE MOVEMENT DESENSITIZATION AND REPROCESSING (EMDR)

EMDR is to date the most researched and well known of the new therapies and provides something of a procedural template for the other methods. In the ingenious way that innovation happens, you'll find many variations on this first theme.

The eye movement part is a bit of a misnomer, as EMDR's scope has expanded beyond its original tactic of having the survivor focus his imagination on traumatic images while moving his eyes back and forth, from side to side. It now also includes focusing on the distressing image while tapping back and forth on both sides of the body, or hearing tones in alternate ears from a headset, or experiencing the tingle of buzzers from tactile pulsars in alternate hands—indeed, any bilateral or two-sided stimulation.

This short-term process, discovered serendipitously by psychologist Francine Shapiro and then carefully developed into a method, appears to remove or significantly reduce the emotional distress associated with a traumatic image.[1] Additionally, it helps survivors integrate more positive ideas and thoughts around their trauma; and best of all, it is structured to accomplish this without unleashing a flood of disruptive symptoms.

There is some confusion over why EMDR works, but its practitioners swear by it. Research is somewhat equivocal but essentially positive, particularly for single-incident or single-image trauma.

Reading the description that follows is no substitute for getting trained in this technique. Shapiro has gone to considerable trouble to make sure that qualified practitioners are carefully trained and certified in the use of this method. That caveat in place, EMDR works something like this: after taking a history, the therapist and client together identify a distressing traumatic event or image to target for treatment. This comes to include any events or images from the past that seem to be related to the current source of distress. The therapist ensures that the survivor has some self-soothing, stress-reducing skills at the ready (a lot like the stage-one imagery in this book) to help handle any emotional distress that might come up during or between sessions.

Then the person identifies the most vivid image he has, as well as a negative belief about himself that the image has come to mean. He also identifies any emotions or body sensations that the image evokes. In other words, the process focuses not only on the image but on the cognition, emotion, and body sensation around that image. In addition, he is asked to give a numerical rating to the intensity of each of these things. He also identifies a preferred positive belief that is counter to the negative implication about himself.

The survivor is then instructed to focus on the image while simultaneously moving his eyes back and forth, usually following the therapist's fingers as they move across his field of vision for twenty to thirty seconds or more. Sometimes this is done with a light bar, hand- or knee-tapping, auditory tones, or other types of external bilateral stimulation. After this brief process, which Shapiro calls "dual attention"—on both the image and the external stimulus—the client is then instructed to let her mind go blank and just notice whatever thoughts, body sensations, and emotions come into her awareness. The degree of intensity is also noted and rated.

This process is repeated until she experiences no distress or significantly reduced distress from the image. If, at any time during the procedure, she becomes agitated, time out is taken to deploy the self-soothing techniques that were previously established.

Then the client is asked to think of the positive belief identified at the beginning of the session, or a better one if it has since emerged, and to again focus on the traumatic image while simultaneously engaging in the eye movements. After several go-rounds, the client usually reports increased adherence to this positive belief. Emotions and body sensations are noted, and positive shifts are accentuated in the same way.

The client is usually asked to keep a journal during the following week, to document anything else that might arise, and is encouraged to use the self-soothing methods if necessary. If indicated, follow-up entails working through, in the same way, any related images or any images emerging from the past or anticipated in the future that are connected with the original incident.

The goal is to eliminate emotional and somatic distress in a very short period of time, while producing cognitive insights and shifts in self-perception. Usually, because of the way the session is structured, and the distraction that occurs from the dual attention requirement, the survivor can do this without reactivating an ugly cascade of traumatic symptoms. As much as this might sound like hocus-pocus, it definitely works for some people, sometimes within the space of a single session. Many therapists mix EMDR with other methods during the course of their work. It seems to take to mixing well.

A very good example of EMDR occurred on the morning of 9/11, when a young woman, walking to work in Lower Manhattan, saw at close range the first plane hitting the first tower. She entered her workplace sobbing and in great distress, stating over and over again that she saw the plane hit the building, and that there was nothing but a big, black, burning hole. What, she wondered, had become of the people inside?

She was sent to a staff counselor, a traditional therapist who happened to also be trained in EMDR. When the distraught woman kept repeating, "I can't get this image out of my head," the counselor decided that if ever there was a case to use EMDR, this was it.

They quickly built rapport as they discussed her horror and disbelief at what she had seen. They went over her history. The method was explained to her, and very predictably, the woman targeted the image of the plane going into the building as the focus to work on. For her stress-reduction imagery, she identified a safe place to go to in her imagination—a spot by the seaside where she vacationed as a little girl with her family.

As an additional self-soother, she was coached to use the imagery of a TV remote device, which allowed her to immediately lower the volume, switch channels, or click the picture off altogether at the emergence of any overwhelming distress.

Once these coping mechanisms were in place, they began the procedure. She briefly focused on the horrifying image of the plane crashing into the building, while following her therapist's fingers, traveling back and forth, with her eyes. She identified her feelings (helplessness, disbelief, despair, horror, sorrow, revulsion) and rated the discomfort they produced. She noted her body sensations and where in her body they seemed to be located (queasiness in her gut, agitation, electricity buzzing through her body, numbness, pain in her heart) and rated those. And she also rated the intensity of the negative belief about herself that clearly emerged: *I am helpless.*

Each time they returned to the eye movement activity, they tracked the diminishing intensity of this cognitive belief, the associated discomfort in the body, and the painful emotions, on the rating scale.

Once the intensity was down, which took several sequences and possibly twenty minutes of clock-time, they discussed what might be a countervailing belief that was positive yet realistic. The young woman, a very religious, service-oriented person, heavily involved with like-minded people in her church, came up with: *I can do something to help.* She talked about ways that she, her family, and her church community could be useful to survivors and to affected families in her neighborhood. This positive belief was then intensified with the eye movements, just as the negative belief had earlier been diminished by them.

Her therapist, a rather measured woman who is not given to dramatizing her descriptions, reports that this woman left her office, still very upset, worried, and disturbed by the horror she had witnessed, but without the overwhelming emotions, scattered thinking, and inability to function she had come in with. She was focused and resolved—in spite of the fact that during that session, she and the therapist were interrupted by the news that a second plane had struck the other tower, establishing that this was a deliberate attack and not a random accident.

Suzanne Iasenza, Ph.D., a psychologist in private practice and associate professor of counseling at John Jay College of Criminal Justice, did a great deal of counseling in the aftermath of the attacks, both in her private office and with her students, who were all uniformed officers. She interspersed guided imagery, breathwork, hypnosis, and EMDR with her more traditional approaches. She reports:

> I was very grateful to have been exposed to these body-based techniques. My talk therapy training hadn't prepared me for 9/11. But my training in imagery, relaxation, EMDR, conscious breathing, and hypnosis was invaluable. They gave me something to do that actually helped, and a feeling I could be resourceful and of use, where many of my colleagues were at a loss in facing such extraordinary trauma.

She adds that because these techniques were simple, short term, non-verbal, and behaviorally oriented, they worked especially well for the police, firefighters, and National Guard, people whose mindset would never have allowed them to sign up for "therapy." They came in with complaints of insomnia, headaches, and agitation, asking for relief for those physical problems. Dr. Iasenza says:

> I felt that I could help them, that I had something to offer that was shorter in duration and that spoke directly to their complaints and body experiences. I was grateful to have something that could provide relief and didn't make them feel like "head cases."[2]

Manhattan marriage and family therapist Nancy Napier, L.M.F.T., was struck by how useful EMDR was for single-incident trauma:

> Sadly, we had a unique opportunity to observe EMDR's effectiveness when used immediately after a single-incident trauma, because of the large number of people who were simultaneously traumatized by 9/11. We were amazed at the response of people who received treatment within weeks of the attacks. With only a few sessions, they had significant and, it appears, lasting relief. They were of course deeply upset. But as far as I know, they did not go on to develop PTSD.
> I had never before been involved with helping people right

after something catastrophic had happened. I was used to dealing with people who had been traumatized in the past—sometimes the distant past.

I would have to say that when you can do something like EMDR soon after something happens, there's a good chance the traumatic effects will clear up. It's as though the trauma doesn't have time to burn its way into the brain. Habits aren't built yet. Responses haven't settled in. I've been in touch with some of these people, and two years later, they're still okay. I would have to say, I think it can save people a lot of grief later on.[3]

THOUGHT FIELD THERAPY (TFT)

TFT, a method developed by psychologist Roger Callahan, has elements in common with EMDR, but it introduces into the mix the client's tapping on specific acupressure points while focusing on the traumatic image—a kind of psychological acupressure, of sorts.

Borrowing concepts from Chinese energy medicine, the method is based on an idea, widely accepted in holistic health circles, that physical and emotional problems are a matter of blocked energy in the body. When clients are instructed to gently tap on critical acupressure points along the energy meridians of the body, the stuck energy is encouraged to flow and rebalance again.

According to Callahan, specific problems are connected to specific acupressure points, so he created targeted protocols, called algorithms, for the self-tapping sequence necessary to release each issue.

Callahan did not rely solely on the client's assessment of his own status with a numerical rating scale. He also incorporated a diagnostic process called Applied Kinesthesiology, or muscle testing, to get a physiological measure. With muscle testing, a procedure invented by a chiropractor named George Goodheart, to detect allergic and toxic responses to various foods and substances, the client holds her arm out at shoulder level and tunes in to a disturbing event or image, while the practitioner presses down on the arm. Under normal circumstances, she is able to resist the pressure and maintain the posture. But when she focuses on the traumatic event, the muscles are weaker, and the arm usually gives way.

The degree of muscle weakness reflects the extent of subjective distress that the issue is causing and usually matches the client's report of perceived distress.

Typically the therapist uses muscle testing, first to diagnose the severity of the distress and then, after a set of treatments is completed, to retest until the perceived distress is down to zero. An offshoot method, the highly regarded New Jersey training program developed by Sheila S. Bender, John H. Diepold, and Victoria Britt, called Evolving Thought Field Therapy, uses muscle testing to determine the most appropriate treatment points for each and every client.

According to Callahan, because most clients come to this treatment with considerable skepticism for what looks like some pretty peculiar hocus-pocus, the positive results they achieve cannot possibly be ascribed to placebo effect or positive expectation, since there is little of it. The technique seems to work on a substantial percentage of people whether they believe it will or not, and in one study, the improvement was sustained for at least six months.[4] Anecdotal evidence from practitioners shows that symptoms can remain in abeyance for years beyond that.

Interestingly, TFT and Callahan have been met with a great deal of skepticism and opposition from the clinical community—much more so than other methods that turn out to be quite similar. This is probably due to the aggressive way TFT was initially marketed, advertised, and priced; the claims Callahan made before any clinical trials could back them up; and the fact that subsequent methods established that his specific algorithms—marketed more or less as "secret formulas" available at exceedingly high cost—were not really necessary to effect a good result. As a result, the expensive trainings and technological accoutrements of TFT have been somewhat superseded by related but less expensive methods.

It is important to note, however, that Callahan's idea of connecting the two-fingered self-tapping of acupressure points to the unblocking of problematic thoughts and emotions was a valuable contribution that others were able to build upon. And in spite of the objections to his marketing, trademarking, and pricing decisions, there are hundreds of therapists, trained in his technique, who do excellent work with great integrity and at standard prices.

Nancy Napier is one such clinician, a traditionally trained Manhattan family therapist and trauma specialist, with an impeccable reputation, who uses EMDR, TFT, and other modalities with selected clients. She reports that Evolving TFT, with its strategic use of muscle testing and highly clinical focus, persuaded her to use the method:

> It probably could be used preventively as a form of care after a traumatic event such as 9/11, so people can minimize the effects of this kind of experience.
>
> Another thing I appreciate about these methods is the way they focus on the client's resilience, awareness, and strength—not the so-called "pathology."[5]

EMOTIONAL FREEDOM TECHNIQUE (EFT)

EFT is a less expensive outgrowth of TFT, and like TFT, it too is described as being "like acupuncture for the emotions, only without the needles." But along with its simpler, all-purpose tapping protocol, EFT also has people speaking affirmations and doing odd but apparently effective sequences of behaviors that include tapping, eye movements, humming, and counting. Developed by Gary Craig, a student of Roger Callahan, it combines some aspects of EMDR—the eye movements and the emphasis on shifting underlying cognitive belief systems—with a more generalized acupressure point tapping, based on TFT, plus some additional distraction techniques.

Because it dispenses with Callahan's secret formulas and provides a free downloadable manual on its website, EFT has managed to avoid much of the hostility from the professional community that TFT had heaped on itself, even though the EFT techniques and protocols are plenty strange-looking. Nonetheless, several respectable clinicians I know swear by it, particularly for single-incident trauma. And since one go-round takes only a few minutes and causes minimal distress, and a person doesn't have to believe it will work for it to be effective, common sense would dictate it is certainly worth a try before one attempts the more complex, time-consuming, expensive, and distressing methods of traditional treatment.

As with the other methods, the client in EFT is asked to identify a traumatic situation that continues to provoke extreme anxiety or other symptoms. He then does a preliminary patterned tapping on his own hand, accompanied by affirmative statements that address the distress, such as "I accept myself fully and completely, even though I am afraid of my nightmares."

The survivor then tunes in to the image of the traumatic event and reports on a scale of one to ten how distressing it is. He then engages in the prescribed series of activities, which used to include tapping on the hand with eyes open, eyes closed, looking left and right, rolling the eyes in one direction and then the other, then humming a few bars of a simple tune, then counting to five out loud, then humming again. These methods are continually being simplified, however, and the newer protocols are briefer.

The distress level is again assessed, and if necessary, the process is repeated, perhaps with some new tapping points. The sequence varies some from clinician to clinician, but this is the basic idea. Because the client is tapping himself, he can also take the technique home with him and initiate the process, if some residual anxiety or distress should surface later on.

Some people seem to clear their symptoms after one trial of this odd, autistic-looking sequence, and with minimal anxiety during the process. Others require several go-rounds and have an alleviation of symptoms but not a total improvement.

Many people report remaining symptom free for months and even years. Noted psychotherapist and author Bill O'Hanlon reports that he personally has observed the effects holding for as long as three years, which, at the time, was as long as he'd been using the method and tracking results. O'Hanlon alternates EFT with EMDR, depending on his intuitive assessment of the person and the situation. He too reports that some people seem to do well with one session, while for others it is more like peeling off layers, one at a time, before significant improvement occurs.

Here is a description of the effectiveness of EFT from someone who suffered severe depression and post-traumatic stress from sadistic, repetitive, childhood abuse, followed by subsequent molestation and rape:

> While tapping on specific easy-to-reach acupuncture points, I juxtaposed a negative statement with a positive to achieve results. I had been doing it this way and had gotten good results, but didn't like the idea of using negative phrases—I

was afraid I was just reaffirming the negative. So I tried it with just saying the positive. It didn't work as well.

I was intrigued, so I thought about it a lot, trying to understand what was going on. The conclusion I came to was that the negative aspect was already embedded in my body and mind, reflecting my perception of the original experience; it was there no matter how many affirmations I used. By acknowledging it openly, I avoided the "whipped cream on garbage" syndrome, and the negative eased out quickly.

Example: "Even though I feel awful, I deeply and completely accept myself without judgment." With surprising quickness, the negative disappeared, having received its due acknowledgment.

Or: "Even though I feel scared and alone, I choose to acknowledge the courage I have in doing this inner work." As I did the affirmation, I found that the strength of the negative statement diminished until it was no longer true, while the positive got stronger. I then adjusted the wording to reflect my progress as I went along. For instance, "Even though I still feel a little scared and alone, I choose. . . ."

It was amazing to me how quickly the shift took place. I liked that it allowed me the moment to acknowledge the feeling while not getting stuck in it, because it was paired with the positive. And because these affirmations are done while tapping on the acupuncture points, it had the effect of giving me some minimal movement to do (the lethargy of depression while trying to heal from abuse can be devastating), plus the clearing that happens as the meridians open up (as in acupuncture) provided a physiological release.

If I really couldn't bring myself to move, even imagining doing the tapping brought relief. For me it was an easy and powerful tool, and I continue to use it for all kinds of things and teach it to others who are similarly amazed by its effectiveness.

WHOLISTIC HYBRID EFT/EMDR (WHEE)

British psychiatrist Daniel Benor, in an effort to find a streamlined, sim-plified, but effective method to use with children, combined aspects of EMDR with EFT, calling his results by the rather exuberant acronym WHEE. For the inspiration for this idea Benor credits Asha Nahoma Clin-ton, a social worker he watched teach something called Seemorg Matrix Work, which combines alternate tapping of eyebrow acupressure points with the recitation of an affirmation, as a shortcut to using the entire se-ries of EFT points.

From EMDR he borrowed something called the "butterfly hug," where clients cross their arms so that their hands rest on the biceps of the opposing arm, and then they do alternate tapping on each arm with the hands. This bilateral tapping pose has the added benefit of being a rather comforting gesture in and of itself. Children and adults alike find it easy and pleasant. (This is one of the favorite exercises introduced to the children in Kosovo recovering from the trauma of war by a popular pro-gram implemented by the Center for Mind-Body Medicine in Washing-ton, D.C.)

To the butterfly hug, Benor added the EFT element of having people state an affirmation aloud—"Even though I have a fear of [fill in the blank], I completely and totally love and accept myself," or something broadly self-accepting along those lines.

Before and after using the technique, Benor has the survivor assess the intensity of the problem on a zero-to-ten scale, using a standard trauma assessment instrument called the SUDS (Subjective Units of Dis-tress Scale). Once the rating is down to zero, the person is guided to cre-ate a specific positive affirmation to replace the negative belief, reciting and tapping once more. Sometimes, in addition to the tapping, the client massages or thumps a critical spot on the upper chest, just below the col-larbone.

This gives the survivor a technique to use outside the office and out in the real world, whenever distress or panic gets triggered by external events. Because of this newfound ability to handle triggers, the person gets better and better at becoming conscious of the triggers and skillful at anticipating them and short-circuiting them.

Teenagers and kids who don't want to risk looking weird in front of their friends are taught to covertly tap with their tongue on their teeth on alternate sides of the mouth. Or a certain kind of breathing is suggested, with one hand over the center of the chest;[6] a light touch on the acupressure points of the eyebrows makes for another convenient stealth method that self-conscious kids and adults can deploy.

Dr. Martha Howard, a holistic physician trained in qigong, Chinese medicine, and acupressure, with a large medical practice on the north side of Chicago, reports enthusiastically on WHEE:

> After about six or so years of experimenting with tapping, EMDR, strobic phototherapy, EFT, and TFT, to see what would work for PTSD without retraumatizing the person, I determined that WHEE works better and is simpler than most of the other methods, since it combines the lateral "hemi sync" movements of EMDR with the tapping on the acupuncture meridians of TFT and EFT, plus the verbalized self-acceptance regarding the issues through the affirmations.
>
> People need something they can easily remember and do for themselves, and WHEE certainly fills that bill. It gives people something simple and immediate to hang on to, that's always available to them, no matter where they are. They become more aware, more mindful of their triggers, and more confident and self-reliant. It's very empowering.
>
> Eventually the practice breaks up any patterned response to the cues that trigger their panic or their other symptoms. It's a great example of something that promotes stress hardiness and breaks down habits of learned helplessness.
>
> I'm very encouraged and excited by what WHEE has done for my patients. The hardest thing about it is persuading people to try it, because it sounds almost too simple to be effective, and the results are almost too good to be true.

TAPAS ACUPRESSURE TECHNIQUE (TAT)

Originated by Tapas Fleming, a specialist in Chinese medicine, acupuncture, and yoga, the TAT method is similar to TFT, EFT, and WHEE, but instead of tapping while focusing on the distressing image, it offers a two-handed yogic pose, designed to get energy flowing again and release the trauma by applying acupressure to critical points on the front and back of the head, while the person recites or contemplates several key affirmations.

It works something like this: as with the other methods, survivors first identify a discrete trauma to work on—not a long-term or complex issue, but something particular and specific to begin with—and put their attention on it, rating it on a scale of zero to ten, with ten being the most distressing.

Then the person adopts the TAT pose, using three fingers of one hand to apply very gentle pressure to three acupressure points—at the bridge of the nose, one finger by each eye, and one at the center of the forehead—while placing the other hand at the base of the skull at the back of the head. The touch is light, not pressured. While in the pose, the survivor again places her attention on the trauma, remaining in the pose until she feels something happen—possibly a shift in energy, a release, an opening, a relaxation—or until one minute passes, whichever comes first, at which time she releases the pose.

The survivor again rates the trauma and puts her attention on whatever place in her body she wishes the healing to occur. This might be a weak back, sick stomach, tight jaw, or some other physical response. She then again adopts the TAT pose, while focusing her attention on what Fleming calls the "storage space," until she feels a change or a minute has passed, whichever comes first.

The trauma is rated again, and according to Fleming, if it is not at zero, other elements of the trauma are identified and processed in the same way, layer by layer, until the zero rating is achieved. The survivor is then encouraged to drink at least eight glasses of water in the next twenty-four hours, to help rinse and clear toxicity from the body.

Variations of this technique include adopting the pose while focusing on a positive image, stating affirmations that the issue is healing; that places where the issue is stored are healing; that secondary gains and motivations are healing; and that the self and others are forgiven for whatever part they may have played in the distress. Currently no research data are available on this method, but anecdotal reports are positive.

Marriage and family therapist Don Elium, a Bay Area clinician who is conversant with EMDR and EFT as well as TAT, finds TAT handy, easy for people to do, comforting, empowering, and highly compatible with psychotherapy.

> I've found TAT very effective at reducing the intensity of
> traumatic events, in anywhere from one to five fifty-minute
> sessions . . . I also use EMDR often, but sometimes issues are
> so intense that a person has to stop the eye movements. In
> these moments, I'll often turn to TAT, because it works well
> in conjunction with EMDR, and it is much gentler and more
> calming, while providing similar relief.

PROLONGED EXPOSURE THERAPY (PET)

PET was primarily developed and researched by cognitive-behavioral psychologist Edna Foa, Ph.D., to help reduce or eliminate the post-traumatic stress symptoms of survivors of rape, combat, and other traumatic situations.

Treatment typically consists of nine to twelve ninety-minute sessions, and after a certain amount of information is provided about the nature of traumatic stress, the survivor is guided to repeatedly reimagine the traumatic episode until, through sheer repetition, in the safe, supportive space of the therapeutic relationship, the emotional charge eventually dissipates. Usually the treatment protocol also includes the client listening to an audiotape of the session and reimagining the trauma once a day as well.

The imaginal exposure is coupled with "in vivo exposure," where the client is encouraged to gradually approach real-life reminders—situations and objects that had been feared and avoided because of their association with the original trauma. The least distressing is approached first, followed by the next, until a wide range of situations are "decontaminated."

PET is based on a cognitive-behavioral learning model. Practitioners believe that the technique works because, during the periods of imaginal and in vivo exposure, the feared negative consequences don't actually occur, giving the survivor a chance to learn a new set of expectations and associations and thus unlearn the old, fearful connections.

Another important part of PET is the discussion that takes place after the imaginal exposure. Through this discussion, dysfunctional ideas—for instance, "The world is a dangerous place" or "I am incompetent"—are identified and challenged, leading to a change in how the survivor views him- or herself and also the world.

Unlike EMDR, TFT, EFT, WHEE, and TAT, all of which use distraction devices such as eye movements, tapping, holding acupressure points, counting, phrase repetition, yoga stretches, and humming to automatically reduce or avoid emotional distress, PET uses no distraction. The survivor is tasked over and over again to hold the disturbing image in mind for at least twenty-five minutes or longer, sometimes at considerable emotional cost, while the anxiety floods, peaks, and then declines. The idea is that by repeating the process enough times, systematic desensitization occurs, and the person reestablishes her lost sense of safety.

Because of the emotional distress involved, and the length of time this therapy takes, some practitioners are reluctant to use prolonged exposure without first trying one of the more rapid and "less distressing" techniques. Nonetheless, the substantial research that has been done with PET has yielded a reliable success rate (generally about 60 percent) in reducing the symptoms of PTSD—at least for those who can tolerate the process long enough to benefit from it—making it one of the more respected PTSD interventions among traditional trauma therapists.

Some studies have PET performing equally well with EMDR (the most researched of the newer therapies); others show EMDR outperforming it by as much as 20 percent; and still others show PET to have the edge.[7] Clearly there is further testing and sorting to be done here, and many ongoing studies are currently in progress that will eventually tease out what works best with whom and when. In the meantime, a substantial number of clinicians are reluctant to use this method first, because of the head-on distress it imposes on their clients.

Linda Klein, M.D., a traditionally trained Cincinnati VA Hospital psychiatrist, has been using PET as part of a larger research study and has introduced it to several women vets with PTSD derived mainly from single-episode adult sexual trauma. She reports:

It takes some selling to get people to understand why they should approach something so painful rather than avoid it. Once we can get past that barrier, it gets much easier.

I usually ask them about all the things they'd like to be able to do again, like going to the mall, leaving the house, driving again, and so on, and that often tips the balance and helps them get started. Some strongly resist the in vivo exercises.

The actual imaginal exposure is very hard for people at first. Some have to stop and use their breathing and relaxation techniques before they can come back to it.

Usually by the fourth or fifth session [of ten] they start to notice some differences, both in the sessions themselves and out in real life. Once they have some success, it changes their ideas of themselves as incompetent. A very positive snowball starts rolling.

At the same time that they're realizing that it's getting easier, they are also able to organize the trauma more. It goes from coming in disconnected fragments to forming a sequence. They start making some sense out of the event, and you can see they are integrating it into their thinking process and memory.

Klein has her questions and caveats. She believes this method works best when people's lives are not in chaos, when they have some external stability and support, and when the trauma is more circumscribed.

I would use this technique very quickly in circumstances involving a single incident—adult rape, for instance. But I'm not convinced that it would work with combat veterans, who may have experienced hundreds of days of traumatic events.

This technique works best with fear-based trauma. It is not as helpful for patients who were perpetrators of violence in addition to being victims themselves, which can be the case with combat veterans. Edna Foa herself says that this method is not as effective when anger is predominant or when there is a reality basis for guilt.

Having been psychodynamically trained, I'm not used to being this directive or structured. But I'm learning there are real pluses. You are assured of covering what needs to be covered.

And I've seen some very impressive, exciting results. For instance, one phobic sexual assault survivor had moved back in with her mother, couldn't drive, and could stand to be alone in the house only if the TV was blaring. She has now moved out, gotten a roommate, registered herself back in school, and is employed. She still has her vulnerabilities, but she is coping really well and getting on with her life.

I've seen some vast improvements in symptoms like these. At the very least, I believe that all the women I work with in this study who are able to stick with the protocol will be improved. It's been a revelation and a real delight.

TRAUMA INCIDENT REDUCTION (TIR)

TIR is a very systematized, carefully structured method for guiding a survivor to review and describe his experience in order to reduce or eliminate any symptoms, distressing emotions, or unwanted attitudes from the trauma. The survivor first reviews the experience silently, in his imagination, from beginning to end, then reports what happened to a supportive, nonjudgmental, encouraging listener, repeating the process over and over again until the narrative stops changing and the emotional charge connected with the incident is gone. Sometimes, the survivor is then guided to address one or more earlier or similar incidents in the same way.

Created by Frank Gerbode and Gerald French, TIR is so carefully structured, so simple, and so dependent on its precise method rather than on its practitioner that facilitators needn't be therapists. Gerbode and French state that anyone properly trained in TIR can do it. It is nonhypnotic and entirely client-centered, and it has no fixed time for sessions—sessions are over whenever the process is completed.

The TIR protocol begins with the survivor identifying the issue or incident to be reviewed and, if it is a complex one, breaking it down to a very discrete, targeted segment to use as a starting point. Specific questions are asked about it to help the survivor locate and differentiate it, and then he is asked to go in his mind to the moment he feels the incident began. To use the analogy of a VCR, he rewinds the tape to the proper starting place but doesn't push "play" yet. (As with VKD, a method described later in this chapter, this process is extremely visual, and just by going through it, mastery and control over the images are gained. By virtue of being able to press "pause" on the starting point, the survivor is learning that he can control the images that torment him.)

Next the person—called the "viewer" in this system, not the "client"—is instructed to push the button and play the tape, usually watching and listening through without reporting on it. Then he is asked to tell what happened. The facilitator listens carefully and supportively, and provides the structure for the telling, but stays out of the viewer's way, never interjecting his or her own interpretations, personality, or ideas into the mix. The listener's job is to be interested but not interesting.

This process of starting with the single frame, playing the scene, reviewing it silently, and then telling what happened aloud is repeated at least five to ten times—sometimes well over twenty—until the incident stops changing. Most viewers are able to remember more details with each run-through. As long as the content or the affect of the narrative continues to evolve or shift in some way, the process is repeated.

Some survivors cannot relate in words what happened. These viewers are simply asked to say whatever they can, even if it is nothing more than the color of the sky at the time of the first frame and the fact that the doorbell rang. With each steady, patient, methodical pass through the incident, more and more words are usually able to come.

Eventually all the change that is to occur has happened. The viewer might become more and more relieved, or perhaps she discharges a lot of emotion until a peaceful stasis is achieved. Some viewers become better able to remember the incident, while others shift in their ability to think about it and analyze their reactions to it.

Sometimes viewers can shift only so far and then get stymied. When this happens, they are asked to see if perhaps the incident had an earlier starting point, or if a similar incident might also be at play, and then the process is repeated until the deeper shift occurs.

The most salient feature of this protocol is the way the listener-facilitator is trained to be a respectful, noninterfering, sensitive, observant, yet nonjudgmental sounding board, who nonetheless guides the process very actively.[8]

Although TIR has not been as thoroughly researched as EMDR, what studies have been done have found it to be extremely effective. TIR produced outcomes that were as impressive as those generated by other imagery-based methods, such as VKD and TFT. It outperformed PET in one study of traumatized crime victims, and delivered marked improvement to a population of female inmates with PTSD in another.[9]

Dr. Beverly Donovan, who uses TIR with many of her traumatized combat vets at the Louis B. Stokes VA Medical Center in Brecksville, Ohio, reports that she favors TIR for issues loaded with anxiety, fear, and grief but uses other techniques to help with processing guilt related to having perpetrated violence. Her experience is that TIR helps those who use it—sometimes dramatically and to a significant extent.

> The men like it. They feel progress has been made—progress that they can feel, emotionally . . . It's a very empowering thing, because it gives them and not the therapist the opportunity to be the active ones. They are the ones who come up with the revelations, the awarenesses. They figure it out for themselves . . . And they really feel different, emotionally, with it. The way it's structured is what makes it possible. It's amazing how they always come up with their own answers. In effect, they get to do their own cognitive therapy, but it's not just in their heads . . . they feel different . . . And that makes all the difference to them.

IMAGERY REHEARSAL THERAPY (IRT)

IRT reduces the severity of PTSD symptoms by helping survivors reinvent and reroute their nightmares. Based on a process called Lucid Dreaming, first introduced by sleep researcher Steven LaBerge, survivors use their imaginations to change the scenario of a recurrent nightmare into a more desirable and satisfying outcome, by writing down the new, improved version and then repeatedly imagining it or "rehearsing" it in a relaxed reverie state. Research shows that not only does this method help with the nightmares, it seems to improve general PTSD symptoms as well.

Typically, survivors meet for three-hour group sessions, where they talk about their nightmares and come up with alternate endings. The rewrite can involve one scene—one image—or the entire dream. Then, during daily, ten- to twenty-minute practice sessions, they imagine the new ending, until, after doing this for a month, there is a final group meeting where they discuss their results.

Implemented and studied by IRT's best known researcher, Barry Krakow, M.D., at the Center for Sleep Medicine and Nightmare Treatment in Albuquerque, New Mexico, results have been extremely promising. Pilot studies with victims of crime show that the technique yields substantial improvements in nightmare frequency, sleep quality, sleep impairment, and the more general symptoms of PTSD, anxiety, and depression.[10]

Krakow's reliance on the technique is based on the idea that nightmares may start out as a secondary symptom, but if they persist, they take on a life of their own, *retraumatizing* the person each time they occur. IRT interrupts the toxic feedback loop of this cycle.

Another research team that used this method with combat veterans and achieved excellent results concluded that IRT was effective precisely because PTSD is so much a condition of *images*—tormenting, out-of-control images—particularly for those who suffer primarily from nightmares and flashbacks.[11] With IRT, the survivor gains mastery over these images, curtails them, and even goes them one better, replacing them with empowering, nourishing, positive ones. Achieving control over their imaging process helps survivors conquer other anxieties and symptoms as well.

Dr. Donovan uses IRT with every vet in her Transcend program. Her approach builds on the Krakow method with a few additional elements.

In Donovan's protocol, the survivor identifies a recurrent nightmare— one that causes enough distress to qualify it as the one he most wants to modify. Using the journaling process in the group, the men write down what happens in the dream, all the way through, focusing on what they see, hear, feel, and smell in the dream. Other group members ask about it, to bring out even more details.

Then, borrowing from EMDR, Donovan has each man identify a limiting negative belief that he has about himself that devolves from the nightmare. For these vets, it's usually something like "It's my fault he died" or "I'm a coward" or "I'm a murderer." Then they are asked to come up with an alternate belief that is more positive. Here the group is usually recruited to help out, as the men tend to be judgmental and harsh toward themselves but more compassionate with one another. Alternate beliefs are usually something like "I made the best choice I could at the time" or "I learned from this and I know I'd never do it again." A volunteer scribe in the group writes it all down.

Then they create a new ending to the nightmare, with the help of the other men, when needed. They are asked how they would like to continue or extend the dream, so that when they wake up, they are in a peaceful state. Unlike Krakow, Donovan requires that the alternate ending *not* change the historical reality when someone is working with a repetitive nightmare about an actual event. If a buddy died, he still dies in the dream. But a redeeming third act can occur. Usually once the negative self-beliefs are identified, the men have an easy time coming up with their new endings.

Then, several times a day for three weeks, they work with the nightmare. The protocol: after a few minutes of listening to a tape of some relaxing imagery, they reimagine their dream with the new, extended ending, then repeat the changed belief to themselves, followed by a few more minutes of relaxing imagery. Those who have a religious or spiritual bent insert a prayer as well.

Donovan says that at the end of the three weeks, most veterans report a significant decrease in the frequency or intensity of their nightmares. Even though the Transcend program uses many powerful and effective techniques, she reports, the nightmare reprocessing method is a favorite.

> I love working with the nightmares, and the men are usually
> excited to do so as well. With these terrible dreams, they feel
> they have no control, that there is nothing they can do. But by
> working with them during waking hours, they can get at the
> key issues in ways that seem to satisfy the unconscious,
> especially once the negative self-beliefs are identified. So the
> nightmare frequency and the emotional distress greatly
> diminish.

I remember one guy—a tough, crusty curmudgeon of a guy who could describe his nightmare only in a minimalist way that never changed, never got elaborated. All he could say was, "Was in a foxhole, got hit, bled, thought I was gonna die." That was it. He didn't think much of the nightmare-reprocessing idea, but he found it so horrible to keep having this dream that he said he was willing to try anything.

His ending was something I never would have predicted for this tough guy. He extended the ending to seeing an angel coming down and picking him up out of the foxhole and taking him to the park and putting him down by his favorite big tree—the place he actually visited in real life to soothe himself. The angel then told him he was going to be okay, then flew off.

No one was more surprised than I when he reported, after several weeks, that he quit having the nightmare. Maybe it was the simple act of reminding himself, several times a day, in a relaxed, altered state, that he was safe. Maybe it was because the process reestablished his connection with his God in a feelingful, experiential way, several times a day. I don't know. But his nightmare was gone.

Sometimes some of the men might have an anniversary reaction. We encourage them to take out their notes and their relaxation tapes and go through the process again on their own. They now have the tools to use to calm themselves when they wake up, and it is empowering for them to know they can take credit for their success.

Donovan, like Krakow, says that she has no doubt that the process helps the men in other aspects of their lives as well.

It shows them they can be proactive; that they can take the initiative to deal with this, meet it head-on. And this generalizes to the rest of their lives . . . they see they can do something about their lives, that they have choices and can take steps, and it helps—sometimes very dramatically so.

VISUAL KINESTHETIC DISSOCIATION (VKD)

VKD is an imagery-based form of exposure therapy that softens the distress of reliving the trauma during the exposure phase of treatment by having survivors create at least two imaginary layers of distance between themselves and the trauma. People might be asked, for instance, to imagine that they are watching themselves *as* they observe themselves on a movie screen from the vantage point of the projection booth, with their hands at the controls. They are both in the projection booth, running the movie, and sitting in the theater, watching the movie, while at the same time, they are consciously processing the event with the therapist, aware that they are in fact sitting in the therapist's office, within the established safety of a structured, healing relationship. In other words, they are three times removed from the trauma as they remember it and process it.

Created by psychologist Erich Fromm and further refined by Neuro-Linguistic Programming innovators Richard Bandler and John Grinder, this process deliberately encourages survivors to detach from their bodies—a kind of conscious therapeutic dissociation—in what they call a three-point displacement, with the observing part of the mind *watching the experience* of *watching the experience* as the trauma is remembered, re-experienced, and noted. In this cushioned way, the person can reframe their traumatic incident, come to new conclusions about themselves and their lives, and get beyond it.

First, as in every technique, a sense of safety and comfort are established between the practitioner and the survivors. Then survivors are asked to form a picture of themselves (or imagine a sense of themselves) as they were before the traumatic event or events in question. Being very visually biased, Bandler and Grinder referred to this as a "stillshot." The survivors are then guided to the observer perspective and asked to watch themselves as they observe themselves reliving the trauma.

In this way, survivors might be asked to imagine themselves "floating out of themselves" up into the projection booth, where they watch themselves, also sitting in a theater seat, looking at the "younger" pretrauma self on the screen, as many times as it takes for them to become comfortable with the process, and becoming very skillful at willfully floating in and out of the body, to observe the observer. Just the very process of learning how to consciously dissociate is empowering, as most trauma survivors fade out without knowing it is happening. In learning to "leave" and "return," they become better at recognizing when they are "gone" and can consciously come back. As a result, they are more in charge of what is happening, and they are likely to be "home" much more of the time.

They are also told that they can modulate the degree of feelings they need to connect with, in order to get a clear, focused image of themselves at this earlier point in time. They are instructed to have feelings of strength and resourcefulness, as they watch the image. They modulate their feelings through the use of imaginary conceits such as "volume control" (increasing or decreasing the volume) and "color options" (making the picture go from color to black and white in order to decrease the emotional intensity, or saturating the picture with more color in order to increase it). In this way, they develop the ability to stay in control of their feelings by practicing on a nonthreatening focus—their pretrauma self—and keeping their hands on the imaginary controls.

They then play and replay the experience as many times as necessary, with their hands on the control buttons, until their symptoms drop in intensity and they are essentially desensitized. Then they are guided to "float" back into their present-day selves, where they are encouraged to make new meanings, draw different conclusions about themselves and the event. Frequently this aspect of the work—reframing the experience—will happen spontaneously, with very little guidance from the therapist. Survivors then offer their "younger" selves these new conclusions, and allow them to take the time to experience these new feelings of resourcefulness and strength. Then, in a final reintegration, the younger self is invited back into the body of the current self and joined with present-day reality.

This technique directly deploys imagery to take the edge off the exposure experience and make it gentler, kinder, and more tolerable. It is very similar to the guided imagery narratives offered on these pages, in which the survivor goes to a safe and comfortable favorite place (first level of distance), where he or she finds a magical screen (second level of distance) upon which certain healing things occur. But unlike guided imagery, this imagery leans very heavily on the visual sense and minimally on other sense perceptions.

In a well-known randomized, controlled University of Florida study by trauma expert Charles Figley, Ph.D., VKD was found to be as effective as TIR and TFT.[12]

SOMATIC EXPERIENCING (SE)

Somatic Experiencing, a method pioneered by biological physicist and psychologist Peter Levine, Ph.D., uses internal body awareness and kinesthetic sense as its touchstone. The central platform for SE stems from the idea that traumatic symptoms come from a frozen residue of energy trapped in the body from the traumatic event or events, which, because of the freeze response and its biochemical aftermath, still need to be resolved or discharged. By alternating body memories and sensations of safety and calm with carefully dosed body memories and sensations of the trauma; and by subsequently inserting alternative outcomes of successful "fight" or "flight" that are also imagined as felt sensation in the body (kinesthetic imagery), completion and healing can occur.

This process dovetails nicely with neurologist Robert Scaer's ideas about the physiology of trauma and has a great deal in common with a brilliant and subtle process created by psychologist Eugene Gendlin, Ph.D., called Focusing, that trains awareness on body sensation or "felt sense" rather than emotional or cognitive content, as the cleanest, quickest route to healing and resolution.[13] By having people gently and incrementally reimagine and reexperience the physical mobilization of whatever response they had at the time of the trauma, then slowly working in graduated "doses" to help them fully access and complete the locked-in or unexpressed reaction, Levine has created a powerful, direct, and effective therapy.

Along with the Focusing elements, SE uses the phrasing and the belief in spontaneous healing that are prominent in the hypnotic techniques of Milton Erickson, in a sequenced format that has similarities with EMDR, TFT, VKD, and EFT.

Although it is too new a technique to have controlled, randomized research behind it, it is gathering a great deal of support and intense enthusiasm from the growing community of therapists who work with it. SE's positive results, reported by scores of clinicians, fit nicely with a long-held guided imagery principle, that the most effective kind of imagery is *kinesthetic* imagery—imagery that elicits the feel and sensation of something happening in the body.

Neurologist Robert Scaer agrees:

In order to extinguish all of the traumatically-based procedural
memory that perpetuates the kindled cycle of trauma, it is of
critical importance to reconnect somatic awareness. The
guided somatic and kinesthetic imaging aspect is essential to
the efficacy of Somatic Experiencing . . . Ultimately imaging is
intimately involved in all somatically-based therapies.[14]

One variation of SE might look like this: survivors are initially dis-
couraged from simply telling their story as a complete narrative and instead are directed to identify the first moments they felt safe after the
trauma and focus on how that felt inside their body. If no such time exists,
they are guided to remember and reexperience other times of safety, relief, and calm. The most powerful occasion of peaceful relaxation becomes their oasis imagery—the place they reimagine and reexperience
when they become flooded with distress.

Then a deliberate process of "pendulation" or "looping" is begun,
where the therapist helps the survivor move back and forth between
small pieces of the highly charged, chaotic, traumatic material and the
calming oasis imagery. This looping back and forth helps discharge the activation in the nervous system that emerges as the person slowly works
through the traumatic event.

The key to SE is the way it brings attention to the sensations experienced in the body, rather than eliciting "mental" imagery that is strictly
visual. The specific oasis images are never suggested by the therapist but
rather are chosen by the survivor, from his or her own life experience.

The therapist then asks about the very first moment it was clear
something was wrong. Focusing on this image reactivates the threat
response—a massive jolt of body sensation. But rather than let that flood
the survivor, he or she is asked to "freeze frame" the moment and to
imagine moving away from it as far back as *the body* wishes to go in order
to feel safe. Thus the threat is located and isolated, while the survivor is
given something that wasn't available at the time of the original event—
some *time* and *space* in the imaginal world to deal with it.

In this way, he can imagine alternate responses to the event and play
with various imagined routes for getting himself out of harm's way. This

is a new chance to gain mastery over the moment and opens new avenues for discharging the energy that got frozen at the time.

When the practitioner asks what the body wants to do in response to what is now known as the threat, the survivor has the opportunity to investigate the sensations and impulses involved at the time, then tries out whatever additional responses the body feels impelled to make. It may be one or more flight responses, fight responses, or some combination of both. With each imagined response, energy is released, followed by a greater sense of calm and relief.

The survivor runs through the complete inventory of imagined responses to the event—always initiated from the same safe distance of the imaginal conceit of the freeze frame—until all the possibilities are exhausted. Completing these scenarios—sometimes in slow motion for added control and added effect—gives the person a chance to discharge the pent-up energy from the trauma, and a willingness to again trust himself and his body, as it becomes clear that he can indeed design realistic survival plans when given sufficient time to do so. If at any time during the process the person starts to flood with distress, he retreats to the oasis imagery established at the outset.

As Diane Poole Heller, Ph.D., explains, in describing a successful experience using SE with the traumatized survivor of a rear-end car collision,

> Simply having Marianne feel her body organize fight and flight responses and then feeling her body prepare to move or just move slightly and in slow motion, the body finds its greatest release. In most traumatic events, and typical of auto accidents, the body has little if any time to prepare, and these preparatory movements are overridden. By giving the body all the time it needs, it can then relax and shake off the excess energy left from the traumatic experience. Biological completion helps unlock the jamming in the nervous system and allows the client to integrate the experience so that they can indeed move on in life and become freer of the aftereffects of trauma . . .
>
> There is an experience of moving from fragmentation toward integration. Clients find that they can gradually slow down and maintain an integrated awareness from start to finish throughout the accident, including impact. Then

perceptually, the accident can move from seeming to be ever-present, or fixated in the future, back into the past where it belongs. Symptoms diminish. Triggers of fear, panic, and anger are extinguished as continuity of self is reestablished and the accident is experienced as truly over. With six months of Somatic Experiencing treatment, many of Marianne's phobias, as well as most of her physical and emotional symptoms, were resolved.[15]

Manhattan-based marriage and family therapist Nancy Napier, who is well trained and a trainer herself in traditional therapy, trauma therapy, clinical hypnosis, and meditation, says that after using SE with her traumatized clients, she realized what a superb grounding tool it was for anyone who walked into her office. She now uses aspects of it at some point in nearly every session, to help people connect with a fuller awareness of their bodies. She says it helps them access and process whatever it is they need to resolve in a more profound and integrated way.

TRAUMA PATTERN RELEASE (TPR)

Gestalt-trained therapists and energy healers Jim Kepner, Ph.D., and Carol DeSanto, M.A., have developed a specific technique called Trauma Pattern Release as part of their hands-on energy healing method called Nervous System Energy Work, which seems to be yielding promising anecdotal results, in spite of the fact that it is too early to point to research outcomes.

The TPR approach is a highly sophisticated synthesis of several methods: the energy healing protocols of the Reverend Rosalyn Bruyere; the tenets of Gestalt therapy; Robert Scaer's understanding of the nervous system's response to trauma; and the sequencing of behavioral techniques used by such methods as EMDR, EFT, and SE.

It is difficult to explain energy work to those who haven't had a direct experience of it as a practitioner or a client, but for our purposes here, suffice it say that it involves the transfer of subtle energy, or *chi,* from the healer to the client, usually by direct contact but sometimes through the air. This is done through the healer's intention, and her allowing a kind of universal healing energy to move through her and into the client's system, to unblock stuck energy.

The basic premise, derived from Chinese medicine, ayurvedic healing, and many Native American healing paradigms, is that a healthy body is a body that has energy moving freely throughout it, buzzing happily along the body's primary energy thoroughfares, or meridians, and spinning unimpeded in the central vortices, or chakras. Where there is physical or psychological dysfunction, energy is blocked or trapped. To use an electrical analogy, the healer acts almost like a transformer, accessing universal energy, transducing it, and focusing it toward the client, where it enters the general flow of the client's system and gently, subtly applies "pressure" on the stuck places, eventually releasing the trapped energy and helping it to either join the general flow or to discharge out of the body.

With experience, both healer and client invariably become more and more skillful at sensing the subtle movement of energy. Over time healers become quite adept at discerning differences in energy with increasing discrimination and certainty—not just from person to person but also between robust and weak areas of the same body. So too they can sense the differences as the client moves from one emotional state to another.

In the Kepner-DeSanto system, the issue that needs to be addressed is first identified. If the survivor completely dissociates or becomes fully triggered by the recall, it is too soon to use this method. However, if he can modulate his response to some extent, the work can move to the bodywork table.

The healer then stands behind the head of the client, who is lying face up, fully clothed, on a massage therapy table, and places his hands under the head, at the base of the skull, focusing on sensing the flow of energy through the nervous system. As she becomes more and more attuned to it, she matches it with her own energy, until a baseline of balance and calm is achieved, usually a matter of a few minutes or even seconds.

The healer then asks the client to evoke the trauma response just enough to feel it somewhat in his body, but without immersing himself in it. Most survivors find this an easy assignment and quickly manage to replicate a mild version of their body's response, just dipping their toes into the edges of the pool of sensation, so to speak. It of course helps that they are not asked to think about what happened, or to retell the content of the story. As the survivor dips lightly into the body sensations of the trauma, the shift from calm balance to mild agitation is immediately palpable between the practitioner's hands. She then matches this new pattern, until she is "holding" it, too, along with the client.

The survivor is then asked to intentionally distract himself from the trauma, thinking instead of something that is either neutral or pleasant. This leaves the practitioner "holding the distress," energetically speaking, and she then goes through a carefully structured, multidimensional guided imagery sequence for detaching and removing the energetic pattern and releasing it where it can do no further harm. (This, too, sounds like hocus-pocus, but again, clients report excellent results.)

The healer then reconnects with the client's nervous system and energetically fills the spaces cleared by the pattern with what Kepner and DeSanto call "high frequency energy."

The client is then asked to try to evoke the trauma pattern again and report whether the response is the same or different, and how. The healer pays close attention to what they are sensing in the spinal column and nervous system as a double-check on the client's feedback.

As with many of the other methods, sometimes the pattern is cleared. Sometimes it is diminished but still there, in which case another go-round is indicated. Sometimes the original response is gone, but a new and different layer surfaces, and that is then worked with in the same fashion. Once clearing is achieved, the client is asked to evoke an opposite, highly positive body sensation or memory, which the healer helps to anchor into the client's nervous system and energy field. The session closes with a general energy balancing and harmonizing, so that the client leaves the session in a calm and peaceful state.

Here is one severely traumatized woman's description of her experience on the receiving end of this protocol:

> This technique I learned from Jim Kepner, both as his client and as a student of energy healing. What I'm about to say will not do justice to it, but briefly, this was my experience of it: he would ask the person to access the thought-feeling of the trauma—just barely come up to the edge of it—no retraumatizing.
> Then he would feel the vibration in my nervous system,

join with it, and pull it out. It works! It gets to the very core of the disturbance that is still embedded in the body, even after the uncovering work of therapy is done.

I have tried to do it on myself, either imaging him doing it, or just doing it alone. Sometimes I pull it out through my head, sometimes the fingertips (where some of the meridians flow out).

I visualize the nervous system as you see it in anatomy drawings, branching out everywhere, seeing it as all lit up, which is not hard, because of trauma's electrical nature . . .

I think most trauma survivors identify with the feeling that the trauma is right in their nervous systems, which it is, so this also has logical appeal.

Although working on myself was helpful in a palliative way, and maybe I did achieve some of the change I was attempting, the result was not the same as when Jim did it. This is understandable in that I needed an energy stronger than the trauma I was carrying to move it out.

Of course, as our connection with the Divine gets stronger and we truly realize that that power is within us at all times, we can call upon it and use it. I continue to work toward that . . . but until that is more fully developed, I make use of both.

A NOTE ABOUT CRITICAL INCIDENT STRESS DEBRIEFING (CISD)

Since the early 1980's CISD has been the primary tool offered to people on or near the actual site of a disaster or in its immediate aftermath. Its very specific protocol has been used extensively to debrief early responders, such as police officers, emergency service workers, firefighters, rescue workers, and trauma survivors themselves. Created by two psychologists, George Everly, Ph.D., and Jeffrey Mitchell, Ph.D., it focuses on assessing and assisting people still reeling from overwhelming events with their immediate, practical needs.

One huge benefit CISD immediately conferred upon trauma survivors happened by virtue of its name. Because it is called *debriefing*—a happily masculine and military-sounding name, rather than *brief, supportive, reality-based, on-site therapy,* which is what it is, CISD is immediately palatable to its fairly macho recipients in the rescue industry, most of whom would have nothing to do with anything called by the sissified name of *therapy* or even *help,* for that matter. Policy makers should learn from this and call whatever interventions they decide are most effective by similar-sounding names, so that people can take advantage of them without embarrassment or worry.

The other thing CISD manages to do, to everyone's benefit, is steer well-meaning but misguided counselors away from insisting on imposing deeper levels of irrelevant and sometimes destructive psychotherapy on people at the site, immediately after a catastrophe. Instead, CISD helps people focus, in a very structured way, on what they need to do, right then and there, to assess their own safety, marshal available resources, ventilate some, receive emotional support, learn what to expect in terms of their future reactions, and in general anchor, ground themselves and get themselves home in one piece. This is truly a service.

Several recent reviews of the research literature have demonstrated, however, that CISD fails to deliver on its most ambitious promise of preventing the onset of PTSD symptoms later on. The ventilation encouraged by CISD does not defuse emotional responses to the traumatic event; nor does it provide "closure." In spite of dire warnings that failure to implement the CISD protocol will result in greater risk for responders and survivors for developing post-traumatic stress, the numbers have shown that this is simply not the case. Reviews of fifteen controlled, randomized studies measuring the efficacy of single session debriefing reveal absolutely no improvement in subsequent PTSD symptoms, and conclude that routine use of this intervention for prevention cannot be justified.[16]

Still, there is little doubt that CISD is helpful in the short term and is especially useful for helping people get organized and grounded enough to leave the scene of a terrible event and marshal the resources needed in the immediate aftermath of a disaster.

15 TEN INGREDIENTS FOR COMPREHENSIVE HEALING

In spite of the central importance of imagery as the critical, core component for healing post-traumatic stress, no book on recovering from PTSD would be complete without taking a good look at all the things survivors can do to help with their healing. Thanks to the resourcefulness of scores of trauma survivors and the inventiveness of equal numbers of their therapists, it is clear what those elements are.

People who have successfully transcended PTSD are usually those who have used several interventions—one or more of the imagery-based therapies, plus varying combinations of exercise, meditation, counseling, group support, medication, prayer, journaling, bodywork, expressive arts, and a cognitive understanding of the nature of the condition.

Perhaps in a few years we'll have a more streamlined way to heal traumatic stress, and the multifaceted approach I'm putting forth will look amusingly old-fashioned, quaint, and cumbersome. I hope so, and I expect so. But for now, it's the best we have. The ten-pronged approach outlined in this chapter has been distilled from interviews with more than sixty survivors and nearly as many therapists and counselors.

Survivors who fared best were the ones who researched their own options, found out about the new therapies, tried various combinations, and essentially took charge of their own healing. Others were lucky enough to stumble upon a savvy therapist who was willing to function as "general contractor," connecting them with one or more of these new techniques on an as-needed basis. Still others intuitively knew how to create for themselves the conditions and practices that healed them and didn't need the services of professional providers.

The pattern that emerges is clear: people who do well use one or more imagery-based therapies, while simultaneously working on themselves on many fronts and from many angles, sometimes in sequence but just as often in combination.

The ten-pronged approach includes these components:

1. Regular sessions or check-in times with a trustworthy therapist or counselor, who functions as the supportive anchor or "reality-check coach" at the center of the work
2. A support group or therapy group with fellow survivors who have faced similar traumatic circumstances
3. Some basic cognitive information on the nature of the PTSD and how it affects those who suffer from it
4. Phases of support, primarily from the class of antidepressant and antianxiety medication known as SSRIs—selective serotonin reuptake inhibitors, such as Zoloft, Paxil, Prozac, and Luvox—especially in the beginning, when symptoms are at their most severe and before self-soothing practices take hold
5. Some form of regular prayer for believers, and symbolic ritual for those with a more tenuous connection to matters of spirit
6. Developing skills at a regular relaxation, attunement, or self-soothing practice, such as guided imagery, self-hypnosis, progressive relaxation, breathwork, prayer, meditation, or all of the above
7. Some sort of physical exercise or moving meditation, such as yoga, tai chi, qigong, tai bo, aikido, karate, belly dancing, brisk walking, swimming, or aerobic movement
8. Some manner of bodywork, using modalities such as massotherapy, Therapeutic Touch, Zero Balancing, Myofascial Release, Polarity Therapy, Craniosacral Therapy, Reiki, and other forms of energy healing
9. Regular journaling in a personal diary or some other form of expressive practice, using dance, movement, poetry, or artwork
10. And, of course, guided imagery, both as a stand-alone healing modality, to help integrate deep change; and imagery as it appears

in one or more of the new, structured, short-term behavioral methods—the "alphabet therapies" such as EMDR, PET, and SE, described in Chapter 14.

In addition to these ten major components, many successfully recovered survivors were also involved in some sort of "therapeutic altruism"— voluntary service or meaningful work to help alleviate the suffering of others. Many also paid careful attention to diet, avoiding caffeine, alcohol, sugar, and other ingestible substances that exacerbated their symptoms. And, of course, those who were in recovery for chemical dependency also worked at maintaining their sobriety through their twelve-step program or in whatever way that worked for them.

At present, there are a few extraordinary trauma programs that are highly effective and that provide just this kind of multifaceted approach under one roof, but they are the exception. Here are two wonderful examples to emulate.

THE TRANSCEND PROGRAM FOR RECOVERING VIETNAM VETERANS

One such program is the extraordinary Transcend program, developed by psychologists Beverly Donovan and Edgardo Padin-Rivera (and further refined by Morgane Weekly, L.I.S.W.) at the Stokes VA Center. As I noted in the introduction, I had the privilege of sitting in on several sessions as an honorary staff person for the purposes of creating and testing out guided imagery for post-traumatic stress.

Qualified Vietnam vets participate in a thirteen-week, eight-person, inpatient treatment group, where they develop powerful cohesive bonds that interrupt the disabling isolation of PTSD, thanks to the intense commonality of their situations. These are all men who are in recovery from substance abuse and were severely traumatized in Vietnam.

The program also includes weekly individual sessions with one of the two Transcend group facilitators. Physical exercise a minimum of three times a week is required. In addition, the men must take on a project designed to help others, whether that be assisting a disabled patient, volunteering at a soup kitchen, working with Habitat for Humanity, or providing some other form of service.

The men also keep a daily journal, which they show to their individual therapist and share with the group, when moved to do so. Sometimes they are assigned a deliberately evocative writing task, designed to increase self-awareness and intimacy. One such ingenious assignment has each veteran write a letter to his father, telling him all the things he always wanted to say about their relationship. Not surprisingly, sharing this assignment dramatically increases the level of trust and closeness in the group.

In addition, the men are encouraged to paint, draw, write poetry, work with a form of Jungian art therapy called the sand tray, and express themselves in any medium that feels right and is available.

The men are taught about the nature of PTSD and get an explanation of their symptoms. The cognitive input is, in and of itself, a relief, putting to rest questions about their sanity, and it illuminates what they have been going through.

They are also taught a variety of relaxation and self-soothing skills, so they can have these methods under their belts before the work takes them to examining the more painful and frightening issues around their traumatic experiences.

In the beginning they are taught simple techniques, such as conscious breathing, progressive relaxation, and simple guided imagery. Later on they work with the more complex trauma-centered methods—guided imagery designed specifically to heal trauma, as well as several of the structured, imagery-based behavioral therapies mentioned in Chapter 14: EMDR, TIR, and/or IRT, depending on their individual needs. Always the regular support of the group and the individual sessions help to integrate new learning, bolster courage, and calibrate and celebrate progress.

Each group session closes with the ritual of the Serenity Prayer, spoken while everyone stands in a circle, arms around one another. The full program ends with a powerful ritual that sears the healing into the hearts of the changed men: they are driven by their therapists to Washington, D.C., where, at the National Vietnam Veterans Memorial, they recommit their lives back to themselves by writing promises to themselves to improve their lives and stop self-destructive behavior. Many also leave letters by the names of their fallen comrades.

Graduates of the multifaceted Transcend program have experienced a statistically significant reduction in their PTSD symptoms, as measured by the standard CAPS test (Clinician Administered PTSD Scale). Even more impressive, the reduction sustains itself at six months and again at twelve months. (Many programs show initial improvement, but by twelve months the symptoms are back, looking a lot like they did at the start.) And still more impressive is the dramatic reduction in measures of severity of addiction in Transcend graduates. These men, recovering from profound chemical addiction, not only reduced their using to near-sobriety levels at the close of treatment, but at twelve months, those numbers had gotten even better—a highly unusual uptrend in the world of chemical dependency.[1]

This outcome is in contrast to some important findings yielded by a randomized, wide-scale, multisite study within the VA system that compared the effectiveness of two kinds of group therapy: one type where the men discussed and processed their traumatic experiences, including learning some prolonged exposure (PET) methods; and the other where they discussed managing and coping in the present day but avoided trauma-focus. There were six members in each group, which met weekly for thirty weeks, followed by five monthly booster sessions. In spite of the superior number of therapeutic hours spent in these programs, the study found only modest improvements overall and, to the surprise of investigators, no significant differences between the two types of groups. However, there were more dropouts in the trauma-focused groups.[2]

HEALING THE WOUNDS OF WAR

Another highly effective, multifaceted trauma treatment program is Washington, D.C.'s, Center for Mind-Body Medicine's (CMBM) Healing the Wounds of War program, developed by Jim Gordon, M.D., and his team, for people living in Kosovo. A consistent group of volunteer mental health professionals travels from the United States to Kosovo, for intensive week-long work at regular intervals, with children whose parents were killed in the war and with bereft families who suffered multiple atrocities and losses. More important, they use the program as an opportunity to train local health care and teaching professionals in the various mind-body therapies offered, so that these teachers, doctors, and social workers can continue the work when the team goes back home.

Elements of this highly effective program are reminiscent of the Transcend program. It too uses ritual, at the outset and throughout. It began with the team going out to the villages, sitting with community leaders and villagers, and listening to a recounting of the horrors that had taken place. It was essential that the visiting volunteers simply listen in order to understand the depth of suffering. The villagers took the team out to the mass graves, many adorned with bouquets of plastic flowers, where they cried and grieved. They then took them back to their homes, to eat flia bread together. This ceremony began the subsequent collaboration and training, by Dr. Gordon and the CMBM team, of large numbers of mental health professionals and community leaders. The same quality of sensitivity and respect informed the work that followed.

As with Transcend, the work is built around small groups, where the bulk of the time together is spent. And even though the speaking is done through interpreters, it is surprisingly smooth and unencumbered. Each session begins with breathwork. Everyone learns how to soften their bellies and breathe deeply. The children are taught breathing with guided imagery—a favorite is imagining a balloon in their bellies that gets big as they breathe in and shrinks down as they breathe out.

After the brief meditative work with the breath come didactic segments about the nature of post-traumatic stress and the various ways to heal it. So again, as with Transcend, the program uses a teaching and training model, rather than a "fixing-curing" medical model, to avoid inadvertently pathologizing and demeaning people.

In the small groups participants are taught many tools: guided imagery to help them imagine a safe place, or to evoke their wiser self for dialogue and guidance; and other right-brain techniques such as conscious breathing, yoga, walking meditation, biofeedback using bio-dots (small plastic dots that can be stuck onto the skin, where they change color to reveal varying levels of stress), and all manner of journaling, such as dialogue with a symptom.[3]

There is also a great deal of dancing, shaking, and moving, a consistent favorite with adults and children alike, which no doubt helps to move the stuck energy of the physical trauma out of their bodies.

Art and drawing are also used extensively. On the first day, the children are encouraged to draw how they currently see themselves ; how they look with their biggest problems; and how they want to look in the future. The drawings are shared in the group. At the end of the week, they draw again: how they are now, where they want to be, and how they are going to get there. The differences in the pre- and post-artwork demonstrate the powerful recovery that takes place during the week.

And as with Transcend, there is always a return to ritual, particularly because the participants still feel a great deal of fear. During the team's first few visits after the war, Kosovo's cities and towns were still under heavy NATO guard. Indeed, some of the work took place in the very neighborhoods where family and friends were murdered. When the war ended, people went out into the towns and together took back their streets. In the plazas, people walked arm-in-arm in large circles, as if to see and experience that they were still alive.

Even the way people choose to take their turn at sharing in the small groups contains ritual elements. One of the volunteers, a gifted social worker and senior faculty member at the Mind-Body Center, Bob Buckley, L.C.S.W., wisely brought to the group a satin pillowy heart that quickly became the group's "talking stick," a wonderful symbolic device that empowered the speaker while at the same time underlining the need to speak from the heart. The ultimate goal of the program is to bring this healing mind-body-spirit approach to all the mental health centers and to incorporate it into Kosovo's medical and psychiatric training.

So as with the Transcend program, the Healing the Wounds of War program uses imagery, ritual, conscious breathing, meditation, movement, bodywork, expressive arts, journaling, cognitive input, and small group sharing to effect healing, in a context of mutually trusting and respectful relationship. Both programs use the multifaceted ten-pronged approach described here, deploying one or more methods from each of these ten areas.

Now to describe each ingredient in more detail.

FIND A SAVVY, SUPPORTIVE THERAPIST FOR AN ANCHOR

Not everyone needs one, but it is usually very helpful and sometimes essential to have a savvy therapist, counselor, or coach who knows about post-traumatic stress and is conversant with several of the right-brain methods that heal it, or who can refer to practitioners in the community who do. It helps enormously to have reliable referrals to trustworthy clinicians in a variety of practices. And this is the person the survivor can return to, to discuss the evolving reactions to the bodywork or the EMDR or the yoga practice—the consistent, stable, therapeutic "blankie" who holds a survivor steady as he learns and grows.

Some people, like Frannie, need to be seen two or even three times a week at first, for a year or more, before they can drop down to once a week and then move to occasional check-ins for "tune-ups." Flexibility is important for times when symptoms heat up again and there is a need for more intense and frequent support.

For others, weekly sessions aren't necessary, particularly after they've developed a good, strong working relationship with a counselor or therapist. Sometimes a friend or teacher will do the job, and sometimes people just use their own guidance. But maintaining a good therapeutic relationship, available to check in with, between alternative therapies, and to return to as necessary, is a good rule of thumb.

If your therapist insists on processing the traumatic events with you directly, before helping you find ways to regulate your anxiety or build up self-soothing skills, and if the discussion is causing you increasing distress, you're probably with the wrong person. To make things more complicated, it's possible that if you try to explain this and the therapist is unsophisticated about how to approach traumatic stress, they might tell you that you are being resistant to change, that direct processing is a natural part of the therapy process, and that things may have to get worse before they get better. Sometimes this is true. But make sure you are hearing it from someone who has earned some stripes in treating PTSD and knows what you are up against.

In addition, if you have post-traumatic stress, you might be more inclined to passively go along with the therapist's assessment, with little energy, will, or confidence to argue. That's one of the symptoms, after all.

But sooner or later you'll probably need to make a switch. The Resources section in the back of this book—especially the websites set up for specific techniques—can be one place to start finding a knowledgeable local practitioner. If you don't have the proactive energy for the networking involved, enlist some help from friends or family.

As for when it's appropriate to see a therapist: find a professional when your own attempts at managing symptoms aren't working, or when things have been getting worse instead of better for some time, or—always a good indicator—when you've worn out your friends, relatives, and colleagues. Or, as one astute client once told me, "I'm back because everyone in my life is sick of me. I'm giving them a break!"

LEAN ON A SUPPORT GROUP

A support group of fellow survivors who have experienced similar circumstances is an invaluable way to reduce the isolation, shame, and feelings of weirdness that trauma survivors usually live with. In addition, this kind of group provides a wealth of trustworthy wisdom, experience, and advice for suggesting effective methods and treatment tools, and processing reactions to them. Sometimes a support group makes a fine substitute for the anchoring function of a therapist, and often such groups arc less expensive, or even free.

Such groups can be found in local mental health centers, churches, Vet Centers, domestic violence organizations, rape treatment centers, family service organizations, and anxiety/phobia clinics at hospitals. Sometimes it's possible to do some horse trading, and in return for some effective treatment, a person might volunteer for a PTSD clinical trial at a local university or hospital—in the department of psychology, psychiatry, neurology, or behavioral medicine.

LEARN WHAT PTSD IS AND HOW IT ACTS

Anyone who has been reading this book and didn't skip over the first eight chapters has definitely brushed up on PTSD. Understanding the nature of this syndrome, and especially its physiological basis, will help make survivors feel a lot better about what's been going on with them and will provide a platform for self-understanding, compassion, and, most important, reassurance that they have not gone crazy. Hopefully it will enlighten friends and relatives, too. Attending seminars and community workshops can help as well. Other excellent books and websites are listed in the Resources section.

CONSIDER MEDICATION

Some people are emphatically antagonistic to the idea of medication, either philosophically or because they are afraid of becoming dependent on a crutch that will create more problems than it solves. I'm not an avid fan of pills myself. But certain kinds of medication, when properly handled, can be a very helpful short-term intervention that gets people over a difficult hump and serves their progress well. As a therapist, I'm happy to know they are out there, and having a good consulting psychiatrist on deck has served some of my clients very well. Nowadays even many traditional twelve-step programs have softened their hard line against meds, under the right conditions.

Consider medication when more and more of your energy is getting tied up in trying to keep yourself on an even keel, and attempts at self-regulation through relaxation, guided imagery, physical exercise, meditation, and other cognitive-behavioral controls just aren't doing it for you. Another indicator is when your normal eating and sleeping is compromised, or when you are enjoying nothing and every day is a struggle. It just doesn't have to be that hard.

The class of drugs known as SSRIs—selective serotonin reuptake inhibitors, like Zoloft and Paxil—are usually considered the first line of pharmaceutical defense for post-traumatic stress. When medication looks like a good idea, it is this class of drugs that research has shown to be the most effective at alleviating the broadest range of PTSD symptoms.

The SSRIs work by blocking a serotonin reuptake site on certain neurons, thus allowing more serotonin to be available in the body. This helps with PTSD's signature triad of symptoms—intrusive thoughts, hyperarousal, and numbing. SSRIs are also good at helping to counter depression, panic attacks, and obsessive-compulsive behavior. Especially in the beginning, when the new, self-soothing behavioral skills haven't kicked in yet, or at certain phases of treatment when symptoms are particularly intense, they can be a great help. They can produce side effects, such as insomnia, nausea, anxiety, restlessness, or lowered sexual responses.

When SSRIs aren't helpful or the side effects are too unpleasant, another type of drugs can be carefully considered—the MAOIs, (monoamine oxidase inhibitors, such as Nardil, known generically as phenelzine), which are antidepressants that work in a different way, by blocking the enzyme MAO, and thus preventing the destruction of serotonin and norepinephrine. MAOIs are good for intrusive symptoms, like nightmares, flashbacks, intrusive thoughts, and insomnia, but they don't help with numbing or hyperarousal. They can cause high blood pressure, and people are warned to avoid alcohol and eat carefully with this drug.

For most people, the TCAs —tricyclic antidepressants, such as Tofranil (imipramine) and Elavil (amitriptyline)—are a less attractive option for PTSD. They don't work as well as SSRIs or MAOIs, they take longer to kick in, and they have potential for more troublesome side effects.

The antiadrenergic agents, commonly used to treat hypertension, such as Inderal (propranolol) or Catapres (clonidine), work by blocking adrenergic responses. They have shown great promise in pilot studies for preventing the onset of PTSD, when administered right before or after a traumatic event, as well as the reemergence of symptoms, including nightmares, hypervigilence, insomnia, startle reactions, and angry outbursts, while improving mood and concentration. More study of this promising intervention is needed. Side effects include lowered blood pressure and pulse rate as well as depression.

Antianxiety drugs, such as Xanax (alprazolam) and Klonopin (clonazepam), have some ability to reduce insomnia, anxiety, and irritability, but they have not proven to be particularly useful for the primary PTSD symptoms. In addition, they can be addictive and they can exacerbate depression.

The important point here is to make sure that your evaluation for medication is done by a psychiatrist or neurologist or some other medical expert who is up on the latest drug trials for PTSD and who knows the difference between PTSD-induced symptoms and other conditions. This is not something to go to your family physician for, unless you are assertive enough to take along with you a book like Matthew Friedman's

Post-Traumatic Stress Disorder: The Latest Assessment and Treatment Strategies, turned to the medications chart on page 72, or some other knowledgeable resource.[4] The risk of being evaluated by a relatively naïve provider is that you may be overmedicated, not medicated enough, or prescribed something inappropriate or addictive.

USE PRAYER OR RITUAL

Because PTSD symptoms can be so overwhelming and feel so *big,* some form of prayer or ritual, regularly practiced, that invokes larger forces to come and assist with healing, can be a huge help. Whether it be a familiar set of rosary beads, sitting in quiet contemplation with centering prayer, or having a whole community pray together for the recovery of one of their own—it makes a huge difference to most people.

For those who have a more skeptical relationship with matters of spirit, any well-meaning ritual activity that symbolically invites archetypal assistance from the whole human race, or calls upon benign, fill-in-the-blank, invisible forces to lend their assistance, is all to the good. The writing of personal promises at the Vietnam Memorial serves the purpose for the Transcend men, as does taking back the streets and holding the talking stick for the recovering people of Kosovo. Ceremonial activity elevates the conversation, widens perspective, draws on strength, and gives heart to even the most cynical and weary survivor.

DEVELOP A SIMPLE SELF-SOOTHING PRACTICE

Essential to just about anyone suffering from PTSD is the acquisition of skills aimed at conscious relaxation and attunement. This ability to deliberately invoke a relaxed, peaceful state allows a survivor to not only get through the day but proceed with the more challenging aspects of the healing work that must be done, tasks that can exacerbate initial anxiety.

Any regular, simple practice that quickly soothes and settles—guided imagery, meditation, self-hypnosis, progressive relaxation, conscious breathing, or prayer—not only will create a generally calmer day but can be deployed throughout the day when anxiety mounts or ugly images intrude.

With regular use, these practices can become instantaneous tools for calming an agitated self. The more they are used, the more efficient they become. And knowing that they are internally available is the adult equivalent of having that threadbare but much-loved inner "blankie" at the ready.

ACQUIRE A REGULAR PHYSICAL PRACTICE

Even a body wracked by fibromyalgia or laid low by depression—indeed, particularly such a body—needs some sort of regular physical exercise or structured movement, even if the only thing that can be tolerated at the start is very gentle yoga stretching in a chair. Exercise is calming, energizing, oxygenating, and balancing, and it also helps move traumatic residue out of the muscle, tissue, and nervous system of the body.

Anything from simple aerobic exercise—running, biking, brisk walking, Dancercise, belly dancing, or swimming—to the moving meditations, such as yoga, tai chi, qigong, aikido, karate, tai bo, and the like, is bound to sooner or later reduce depression and anxiety and increase energy and emotional resilience.

It sometimes requires an act of will to engage in a moving practice when the heavy inertia of depression is waterlogging the limbs and sandbagging the spirit, but it's a fine antidote, and survivors shouldn't wait to *feel* like it to *do* it. Rather, they should do it so that they *will* feel like it—an act of faith and discipline, to be sure, but once started, these practices reinforce themselves with the positive, palpable changes they produce.

GET REGULAR BODYWORK

A broad range of body therapies provide a powerful therapeutic service, complementing the balancing and cleansing work of exercise and moving meditation, and most of them feel good, too, which is no small matter. There is quite a range of helpful modalities, some very gentle and some quite intense. Some of the better-known methods are licensed massage therapy (Swedish massage is the most common variation in the United States but by no means the only one), Myofascial Release, Polarity Therapy, Craniosacral Therapy, Zero Balancing, Alexander Technique, Ruben-feld Synergy, Shiatsu, Traeger Work, Rolfing, Core Energetics, Felden-krais, Somato-Emotional Release, Reiki, Therapeutic Touch, and other forms of energy work.

By dealing with the trauma as trapped energy in the body, and by hav-ing a practitioner work somatically to help move the energy blockages out of the neuromusculature, the survivor can ensure that emotional shifts and cognitive improvements are supported and sustained.

In addition, this kind of work can significantly alleviate many of the physical symptoms of post-traumatic stress. The gentler modalities dra-matically increase relaxation. Indeed, if you cannot self-soothe or settle down on your own, these methods will manually promote relaxation from the outside in, reminding the body of how it feels to be calm again.

And at a time when very little feels pleasurable, being physically touched in a nurturing, therapeutic, nonsexual way by a trustworthy pair of hands is a tremendous comfort. The majority of trauma survivors—even those who have suffered physical abuse, incest, rape, and other phys-ical violations—are amenable to this blessed antidote to violent touch.

Most licensed massage therapists are skilled in one or more of these techniques, and it is a good idea to discuss with more than one practi-tioner which methods they are certified to provide, and why they think one might be preferable to another for your particular set of circum-stances. Many of these modalities are equally effective, but some, such as Myofascial Release or Shiatsu, which work with acupressure points, may be too physically demanding or painful for someone with the tender spots of fibromyalgia but just right for someone else. Some survivors will refuse massage therapy but welcome Reiki or Zero Balancing because with the latter they can leave their clothing on. There is something here for everyone, and if time and resources are not in short supply, experi-menting with several can be a very good idea.

Again, this is another place where it helps to have a therapist, coach, or doctor who is familiar with the local resources and can make an in-formed referral for both a type of treatment and a specific practitioner. Various directories and professional organizations can be found in the Re-sources section of this book, but choosing a name from a list is taking a chance on quality. Nothing is better than word of mouth, from people with judgment who know you.

USE JOURNALING AND OTHER FORMS
OF SELF-EXPRESSION

Regular journaling in a personal diary is an important way to help process intense feelings, integrate disparate chunks of memory, let go of obsessive worry, and rediscover a coherent sense of yourself. It is a grounding, sanity-restoring activity that fits well at the end of the day. Many who have trouble talking or even thinking about themselves will still do bafflingly well at writing their thoughts and feelings down on paper. Journaling in the evening frequently becomes an anticipated part of the day, something that provides pleasure, refuge, and comfort as well as healing.

For others, especially children, expression through drawing, improvisational playacting, singing, or dancing serves the same critical therapeutic purpose. These right-brain activities provide access to feelings, memory, language, and thinking—often through the safety of symbol and metaphor—and help restore coherence and meaning to a trauma survivor's personal narrative. Here is a description of how author, composer, dancer, singer, and lawyer Rachel Bagby came to heal herself through music and dance:

> Most of the music on my CD arose as a healing response to trauma. *Full Woman* came in a dream, complete with hundreds of women and girls dancing a raucous dance of affirmation and power in concentric circles. Their movements included a kind of vigorous stomping that characterizes dances of protection that I've seen danced in several cultures since, by women indigenous to the Americas and Africa, in particular.
>
> *Full Woman* was born while I was healing from a period of multiple rapes in my twenties. I often felt particularly empty during that time, dangerously so. The dance dream of *Full Woman* and its accompanying music got me through a very rough night and kept me breathing.
>
> I have since led the dance with many, multigenerational groups of women throughout the Americas. Other women's choruses have also recorded the song. I still get letters and e-mails from women who use the music in celebrations of their daughters' menarche or their own menopause.

None of those other women know how *Full Woman* was born, but they feel the power of it.[5]

ENGAGE IN IMAGERY-BASED THERAPY

Imagery is at the core of healing trauma. Choose what is simple and doable and most compatible with your needs. The guided imagery in this book is organized in stages, to help you assess when to use which exercises. They can be recorded in your own voice, with your favorite music; or you can find these and other appropriate audio resources, offered by a host of practitioners, in the Resources section.

That section also offers web pages for the various new imagery-based therapies described in Chapter 14, many with listings of local practitioners or other ways to find specific help in that method.

And for those health care providers interested in getting more training in one or more of these therapeutic avenues, those programs are listed as well.

16 SURPRISE BLESSINGS: GIFTS IN THE RUBBLE

As hard and painful as the journey to healing is, once people come through it, they usually discover that it brings an unanticipated windfall of blessings. This bounty, bought, admittedly, at far too heavy a price, is almost always shared readily with others.

GENEROSITY

As Beverly Donovan, director of the Transcend program, says:

Those who are most successful in their own healing wind up with a tremendous amount of generosity toward others, because that's what continues to give their life meaning. First they must focus on themselves and their own healing, of course. And it takes time. That's what treatment is for. It's very hard, very intense work. And from there, their hearts begin to open. And that is something to see. Our guys keep on giving, in part because that's what they need to do to keep their recovery on track. It reminds them of where they've been and how far they've come.

Those who recover want to serve. The man who volunteers at the Hunger Center remembers when he was in the food line, and it feels right and good to be feeding others. There is a natural, unself-conscious charity that comes right from the heart.

Another aspect of this generosity is the openness that can be found among healed trauma survivors—an emotional honesty and a willingness to tell the truth, without artifice or guile, that creates an immediate, heart-to-heart connection with others.

JOY

Those who manage to emerge on the other side of healing have a lot to say about the excitement of being alive.

One woman who survived a terrible traumatizing year with cancer and several of its harshest treatments told me something I'd actually heard many times before: she was no longer worried about the everyday concerns and irritations that used to occupy her mind. She was instead flooded by the joy of being alive, with each magic minute of every miraculous bonus of a day. "I hope I can keep this feeling," she said, "because there's nothing like it!"

I didn't say what I was thinking, which was that if she lives as long as we all hope she does, she probably won't keep that feeling front and center 24/7, because it's just not in the nature of being human. And in a way, I hope she has the gift of so much time that she will again slip back into taking her life for granted. But certainly she'll be able to retrieve that feeling more easily than most of us, and the deep joy of being alive will always be part of her. I expect it will overtake her at delicious, random moments and take her breath away when she's least expecting it.

One woman equates her extraordinary capacity for joy with her ability to be fully focused, which she feels she learned from having to be hyperalert in order to survive growing up in her abusive family:

> To survive, I had learned to be exquisitely attuned to whatever
> was going on: overt actions as well as subtle nuances, veiled
> meanings, minor changes in facial and physical expressions. I
> am still very conscious, very aware, but it has transformed
> from a tense hypervigilance to an ability to be very focused on
> whatever I am doing. For example, when attending classes and

lectures, I know how to use my attention and focus so that I
learn the most; at concerts, I am fully aware of all the aspects
of the performance, and I come out of the performance feeling
nearly ecstatic with joy when others simply liked it. I think
these differences are because when our attention is not fully
focused, we are unable to fully take in the moment. Along the
same lines, people tell me that they feel fully heard when they
talk to me. I listen to others with my whole being, but now it is
not from fearfulness but just as a skill I developed.

A trauma survivor's joy is not to be confused with naïve pleasure, born of
ignorance and romanticism. It's fully seasoned by wisdom and knowing,
mature and unsentimental. It's as pure and unadorned, as shiny and
strong, as tempered steel.

COMPASSION

Similarly there is a deep empathy and nuanced compassion for others that
comes through, solid and true, in a healed trauma survivor. Facile judgments about right and wrong have gone by the wayside, because at the
profound depth they've been living, superficial black-and-white notions of
right and wrong make no sense.

One woman writes:

I saw so much suffering in the cult that I developed a keen
sensitivity to the suffering of others and a desire to alleviate it. An
awareness of others' pain became stronger than the awareness of
my own. Although that may have been a kind of defense
mechanism, the trait that developed from it stayed after the
trauma and prevented too much self-pity. Instead, a compassion
grew, which over the course of therapy could also start to include
a compassion for myself as well. This in turn flowered into what
others have called a warmth in me, in that there is no judgment
of myself or others, only compassion for the human dilemma we
are all in. Others say it makes me easy to talk with and to be with.

The capacity for intuitive understanding of what others feel, flourishing from all the experience with adrenergized fear and dissociated numbness, is often used to serve others. Many of the survivors I consulted turned out to be counselors and service workers themselves. As recovered trauma survivor and counselor Lynne Newman explains:

> When my mother would begin screaming and the physical and sexual abuse occurred, I left my body. From my "observation deck" on the ceiling, or the top of the refrigerator, my spirit was able to observe behavior . . .
> I came to know when the slightest sign of rage was beginning within my mother, and to flee to safer space so I didn't have to feel the pain . . .
> I learned to be a keen observer of people, and to feel the slightest stirring of emotional change. At that time it would have been called "hypervigilant."
> I understand now how it helped me become an empath, deeply sensitive to what people are feeling and thinking. . . . I am [now] able to deeply understand people and their responses to life, and their fear, and this helps me to help them understand themselves during my counseling and healing work.

What was once a symptom—poor sense of self and overly permeable personal boundaries—becomes a strength upon recovery, as this survivor notes:

> Traumatic situations had led me to sometimes merge with others, a lack of boundaries, but which allowed more information and insight to help myself. Now I can do it more consciously, using it when the other person has asked for help in understanding something in themselves.

HEIGHTENED CREATIVITY

My mailbox is stuffed with poems, stories, photographs, and artwork from scores of trauma survivors, many of whom came to discover their gifts for self-expression only as they were digging out from under their nightmares. Perhaps this is because their traumatic experiences were so big, they transcended everyday verbal expression; or maybe it's because all the creativity in the hyperactive right brain was so energized, this was where all that struggle and triumph had to be channelled. One survivor tells me it's the inevitable accompaniment of emotional healing and all the renewed excitement that comes with embracing life again. Another says it's just the release of all the natural self-expression that was for a while blocked by the trauma symptoms, finally liberated with recovery.

The artist Hollis Sigler's *Breast Cancer Journal* is an exquisite, powerful example of the way the communicative grace of art is used to release the traumatic wounds of cancer.[1]

One survivor with obvious intellectual gifts describes the creative, resilient thinking of a trauma survivor:

> As a young child, I was constantly trying to understand what was going on and to figure out how to survive. This taxed my brain to the fullest. I sense that this increased brain activity enhanced my native abilities, developing to the fullest my brain function and intelligence. The unusualness of my experiences further demanded ongoing inner adaptations to survive. I find now I am an excellent brainstormer in problem-solving situations. I am used to having to find multiple solutions and easily think "outside the box." Others say I am very creative; to me, it is just how I think. Also, when some solutions don't work, I just keep looking for more, an old habit that serves me well.

SURVIVOR POWER

There is a riveting teaching videotape about recovery from trauma that has the inspired title of *Strong at the Broken Places*.[2] On it, survivors are able to look back with awe at their own resilience and feel genuine appreciation and respect for what they've accomplished. Usually they can't grasp the enormity of what they've pulled off until they are out from under it for a while.

Numerous times people have told me about the experience of going back and reading their own journals, written when they were in the middle of terrible days and mind-numbing nights, filled with fear, shame, and rage, and for the first time comprehending the sheer courage it took them to just keep on going and get through it. Usually, until such a reminder, they've forgotten how bad it was.

One man who lost an arm, most of his shoulder, and part of his face in combat, who has since gone on to develop recovery programs for other vets, relates strongly to the mythic idea of the hero's journey. He says his path tested him and took him to the precipice, but ultimately it strengthened him and greatly enriched his life. It took time, it was a process, and it certainly wasn't easy, but he came out of it with the precious prize of knowing himself and understanding and respecting his own mettle. He takes great pleasure in improving the lives of others.

SPIRITUAL CONNECTION

Many survivors express gratitude for the renewed connection with the divine that their journey has brought them. They describe a more intimate relationship with their God. Often they talk about a newfound ability to source nourishment and renewal from every corner of the universe, every part of the natural world. There is a profound and palpable peacefulness that comes from deep inside of them. This inner light, capacity for joy, peaceful centeredness, acceptance of their own strength, and intuitive understanding of others acts subliminally to draw others to them. These are heroes who lead the way with equal measures of gentleness and personal power. And they remind the ones still struggling that they can reclaim their lives, too. As one survivor writes:

At this point in my life, I can see that I have not only healed in the minimal sense of no longer carrying a diagnosed emotional imbalance; I am thriving in a way that I would never have dreamed possible.

RESOURCES

Achterberg, Jeanne. *Imagery in Healing.* Boston: New Science Library, 1986.

Achterberg, Jeanne, Barbara Dossey, and Leslie Kolkmeier. *Rituals of Healing: Using Imagery for Health and Wellness.* New York: Bantam, 1994.

Allen, Jon. *Coping with Trauma.* Washington, D.C.: American Psychiatric Press, 1995.

Battino, Rubin. *Guided Imagery and Other Approaches to Healing.* Camarthen, UK: Crown House Publishing, 2000.

Biziou, Barbara. *Momentary Meditations.* New York: Four Worlds Entertainment (Audio), 2003.

Blanchard, Edward and Edward Hickling. *After the Crash.* Washington, D.C.: American Psychological Association, 2004.

Caldwell, Christine [Ed.]. *Getting in Touch: The Guide to New Body-Centered Therapies.* Wheaton, IL: Quest Books, 1997.

Cambridge Documentary Films. *Strong at the Broken Places: Turning Trauma into Recovery.* Cambridge, MA: 1998.

Cohen, Ken. *Qigong: Traditional Chinese Exercises for Healing Body, Mind, and Spirit.* Boulder: Sounds True (Video), 1996.

———. *Ken Cohen's Guide to Healthy Breathing.* Boulder: Sounds True (Audio), 1997.

Daleo, Roxanne. *MindWorks for Children.* Cambridge: MindWorks (Audio), 1996–2003.

Feinstein, David. *Energy Psychology Interactive.* Ashland, OR: Innersource, 2003.

Figley, Charles R [Ed.]. *Treating Compassion Fatigue.* East Sussex, UK: Brunner-Routledge, 2002.

Foa, E.B., T.M. Keane, and M.J. Friedman [Eds]. *Effective Treatments for PTSD.* New York: Guilford Press, 2000.

Frankl, Viktor E. *Man's Search for Meaning.* New York: Touchstone, Simon & Schuster, 1984.

French, G.D. and F.A. Gerbode. *Traumatic Incident Reduction Workshop Manual, Third Edition.* Menlo Park, CA: IRM Press, 1996.

French, G.D. and C.J. Harris. *Traumatic Incident Reduction.* Innovations in Psychology Series. Boca Raton, FL: CRC Press, 1999.

Friedman, Matthew J. *Post-Traumatic Stress Disorder.* Kansas City: Compact Clinicals, 2001.

Gallo, Fred. *Energy Psychology in Psychotherapy.* New York: W.W. Norton, 2002.

Gendlin, Eugene. *Focusing-Oriented Psychotherapy: A Manual of the Experiential Method.* New York: Guilford Press, 2001.

Herman, Judith. *Trauma and Recovery.* New York: Basic Books, 1997.

Illig, David. *Self Esteem.* Seattle: SuccessWorld (Audio), 2002.

———. *Reduce Stress & Anxiety.* Seattle: SuccessWorld (Audio), 2002.

James, John, and Russell Friedmann. *The Grief Recovery Handbook.* New York: Perennial, 1998.

Kabat-Zinn, Jon. *Full Catastrophe Living: Using the Wisdom of Your Body and Mind to Face Stress, Pain, and Illness.* Surrey, UK: Delta, 1990.

Kimerling R., P. Ouimette, and J. Wolfe (Eds.). *Gender and PTSD.* New York: Guilford Press, 2002.

Levine, Stephen. *Opening the Heart of the Womb* (Audio). Boulder: Sounds True, 1999.

Levine, Peter. *Waking the Tiger.* Berkeley, CA: North Atlantic Books, 1997.

———. *Healing Trauma: Restoring the Wisdom of the Body.* Boulder: Sounds True (Audio), 1999.

———. *Sexual Healing: Transforming the Sacred Wound.* Boulder: Sounds True (Audio), 2003.

Mehling, Betty. *Magic Island: Relaxation for Kids.* Northridge: California Publications (Audio), 1990.

Miller, Dusty and Laurie Guidry. *Addictions and Trauma Recovery: Healing the Body, Mind and Spirit.* New York: W.W. Norton, 2001.

Miller, Dusty. *Your Surviving Spirit: A Workbook of Spiritual Resources for Coping with Trauma.* Oakland, CA.: New Harbinger, 2003.

Miller, Emmett and Steven Halpern. *Letting Go of Stress.* Ashland, OR: Inner Peace Music (Audio), 2002.

Naparstek, Belleruth. *Staying Well with Guided Imagery.* New York: Warner Books, 1994.

———. *Your Sixth Sense.* San Francisco: HarperSanFrancisco, 1998.

————. Health Journeys Guided Imagery Audio Series. New York: Time Warner AudioBooks, 1992–2002.

Health Journeys titles relevant to Traumatic Stress:
o Relieve Stress
o General Wellness
o Relaxation & Wellness
o Healthful Sleep
o Ease Grief
o Combat Depression
o Healing Trauma (PTSD)
o Anger & Forgiveness
o Ease Pain
o Bienestar Global (General Wellness in Spanish)
o Affirmations
o Self-Confidence & Peak Performance
o Alcohol & Other Drugs
o Weight Loss
o Fibromyalgia & Chronic Fatigue
o Irritable Bowel Syndrome & IBD
o Your Sixth Sense

Phillips, Maggie. *Finding the Energy to Heal: How EMDR, Hypnosis, TFT, Imagery and Body-Focused Therapy Can Help Restore Mindbody Health*. New York: W. W. Norton, 2000.

Rossman, Martin. *Guided Imagery for Self-Healing*. Tiburon, CA: New World Library, 2000.

Rothschild, Babette. *The Body Remembers*. New York: W. W. Norton, 2000.

————. *The Body Remembers Casebook*. New York: W. W. Norton, 2002.

Scaer, Robert. *The Body Bears the Burden*. New York: Haworth Medical Press, 2001.

Scurlock-Durana, Suzanne. *Healing from the Core*. Reston, VA: Healing from the Core, 2003.

Shapiro, Francine. *Eye Movement Desensitization and Reprocessing (EMDR), Second Edition: Basic Principles, Protocols and Procedures*. New York: Guilford Press, 2001.

Schwartz, Jeffrey and Sharon Begley. *The Mind and the Brain*. New York: Regan-Books, 2002.

Sheikh, Anees [Ed.]. *Healing Images: The Role of Imagination in Health*. New York: Baywood Publishing, 2002.

Solomon, Marion F. and Daniel Siegel [Eds.]. *Healing Trauma: Attachment, Mind, Body and Brain*. New York: W.W. Norton, 2003.

Stamm, B. Hudnall. *Secondary Traumatic Stress: Self-Care Issues for Clinicians, Researchers & Educators*. Lutherville, MD: Sidran Press, 1999.

Terr, Lenore. *Unchained Memories: True Stories of Traumatic Memories, Lost and Found*. New York: Basic Books, 1994.

Van der Kolk, Bessel, Alexander McFarlane, and Lars Weisaeth, [Eds.]. *Traumatic Stress*. New York: Guilford Press, 1996.

Weil, Andrew. *Breathing: Master Key to Self-Healing*. Boulder: Sounds True (Audio), 1999.

Weinraub, Amy. *Breathe to Beat the Blues: Manage Your Mood with Your Breath*. Tucson: Yoga to Beat the Blues Productions (Audio), 2003.

Williams, Mary Beth and Soili Poijula. *The PTSD Workbook*. Oakland, CA: New Harbinger, 2002.

Winnecott, D.W. *Playing and Reality*. East Sussex, UK: Brunner-Routledge, 2001.

Yehuda, Rachel [Ed.]. *Risk Factors for Traumatic Stress Disorder*. Arlington, VA: American Psychiatric Press, 1999.

Web Pages
Relaxation Tools:
DesktopSpa Holistic Health Jukebox of Streamed Mini-Treatments:
      www.desktopspa.com
Health Journeys Guided Imagery Resource Center: www.healthjourneys.com
StressStop: www.stressstop.com

PTSD Resource Pages:
David Baldwin's Trauma Pages: www.trauma-pages.com
PILOTS Data Base: www.biblioline.nisc.com/scripts/login.dll
Jim Gordon's Center for Mind-Body Medicine: www.cmbm.org
Sidran Organization: www.sidran.org
National Center for PTSD: www.ncptsd.org
International Society for Trauma Stress Studies: www.istss.org

Guided Imagery Training:
The Academy for Guided Imagery (AGI): www.interactiveimagery.com
The Imagery Training Institute: www.imagery-training-institute.com
Nurses Certificate Program in Imagery (NCPI): www.imageryrn.com
The Bonny Foundation: www.bonnyfoundation.org/index.html

Imagery-Based "Alphabet" Therapies:
EMDR website: www.emdria.org
                www.emdr.com
Andrew Leeds' site: www.andrewleeds.net
Thought Field Therapy: www.tftrx.com
Thought Field Therapy Worldwide: www.tftworldwide.com/meetbdb.html
      (The BDB Group)
Gary Craig's EFT pages: www.emofree.com
Tapas Fleming's Acupressure Technique: www.tat-intl.com
Peter Levine's Somatic Experiencing: www.traumahealing.com

SE for car crashes: www.traumasolutions.com/about.shtml
Daniel Benor's WHEE pages: www.emofree.com/cousins/benor.htm
Kepner's & DeSanto's Trauma Pattern Release page:
      www.pathwaysforhealing.com
Gerbode & French's Trauma Incident Reduction Website: traumarelief.org
Barry Krakow's Nightmare Treatment page: www.nightmaretreatment.com

Trauma Therapist Directories:
www.emdrportal.com/practitioners.htm#top%20of%20page
www.3.bc.sympatico.ca/trauma/Directory.html
www.traumahealing.com/PractitionerRegistry.htm
www.energypsych.com

Energy Psychology:
www.energypsych.org
www.energypsych.com
www.innersource.net

Body Therapies:
www.reiki.org
Pat Ogden's: www.sensorimotorpsychotherapy.org/psychotherapists.html
www.hakomi.com
www.healingtouch.net
www.feldenkrais.com
www.therapeutic-touch.org/default.asp
Fritz Smith's Zero-Balancing: www.zerobalancing.com
Upledger Institute: www.upledger.com/home.htm

NOTES

CHAPTER 3: FIERCE UNDOING

1. Rachel Yehuda, Sarah L. Halligan, and Linda M. Bierer. "Relationship of Parental Trauma Exposure and PTSD to PTSD, Depressive and Anxiety Disorders in Offspring," *Journal of Psychiatric Research* 35, no. 5 (2001): 261–70.

2. Judith Herman, *Trauma and Recovery* (New York: Basic Books, 1997), 52.

3. Peter Levine, *Waking the Tiger* (Berkeley, Calif.: North Atlantic Books, 1997).

4. Viktor E. Frankl, *Man's Search for Meaning* (New York: Touchstone, 1984), 90–91.

5. Ibid., 48.

6. Ibid., 48–49.

CHAPTER 4: WHO SUFFERS: HOW, WHEN, WHERE, AND WHY?

1. William E. Schlenger et al., "Psychological Reactions to Terrorist Attacks: Findings from the National Study of Americans' Reactions to September 11," *Journal of the American Medical Association* 288, no. 5 (August 7, 2002): 581–88.

2. Sandro Galea et al., "Psychological Sequelae of the September 11 Terrorist Attacks in New York City," *New England Journal of Medicine* 346, no. 13 (March 28, 2002): 982–87.

3. On Southern France: Caroline Auger et al., "L'état de stress post-traumatique: l'après-déluge au Saguenay" [Post-traumatic Stress Disorder: After the Saguenay

Flood], *Canadian Family Physician* 46, no. 12 (December 2000): 2420–27. On Chinese earthquake: Chengzhi Zhao et al., "Prevalence and Correlated Factors of PTSD in Adolescents 17 Months after Earthquake," *Chinese Mental Health Journal* 15, no. 3 (May 2000): 145–47. On Italian landslide: Francesco Catapano et al., "Psychological Consequences of the 1998 Landslide in Sarno, Italy: A Community Study," *Acta Psychiatrica Scandinavica* 104, no. 6 (December 2001): 438–42. On Nicaraguan hurricane: T. Caldera et al., "Psychological Impact of Hurricane Mitch in Nicaragua in a One-Year Perspective," *Social Psychiatry and Psychiatric Epidemiology* 36, no. 3 (March 2001): 108–14. On Icelandic avalanche: Thorunn Finnsdottir and Ask Elklit, "Posttraumatic Sequelae in a Community Hit by an Avalanche," *Journal of Traumatic Stress* 15, no. 6 (December 2002): 479–85. On Gaza bombardment zone: Abdel Aziz Mousa Thabet, Yehia Abed, and Panos Vostanis, "Emotional Problems in Palestinian Children Living in a War Zone: A Cross-Sectional Study," *Lancet* 359, no. 9320 (May 25, 2002): 1801–04.

4. On German domestic violence survivors: Frauke Teegen and Johanna Schriefer, "Komplexe Posttraumatische Belastungsstörung: Eine Untersuchung des diagnostischen Konstruktes am Beispiel misshandelter Frauen" [Complex Posttraumatic Stress Disorders: An Investigation of the Diagnostic Construct in a Sample of Abused Women], *Zeitschrift für Klinische Psychologie, Psychiatrie und Psychotherapie* 50, no. 2 (2002): 219–33. On South African survivors: Jacqueline Bean and Andre T. Moller, "Posttraumatic Stress and Depressive Symptomatology in a Sample of Battered Women from South Africa," *Psychological Reports* 90, no. 3, pt. 1 (June 2002): 750–52. On U.S. Survivors: Laura C.M. Vogel and Linda L. Marshall, "PTSD Symptoms and Partner Abuse: Low-Income Women at Risk," *Journal of Traumatic Stress* 14, no. 3 (July 2001): 569–84, and Murray B. Stein and Colleen M. Kennedy, "Major Depressive and Post-Traumatic Stress Disorder Comorbidity in Female Victims of Intimate Partner Violence," *Journal of Affective Disorders* 66, no. 2–3 (October 2001): 133–38.

5. On Middle East: Thabet, Abed, and Vostanis, "Emotional Problems in Palestinian Children Living in a War Zone." On Kosovo: Amy L. Ai, Christopher Peterson, and David Ubelhor, "War-Related Trauma and Symptoms of Posttraumatic Stress Disorder Among Adult Kosovar Refugees," *Journal of Traumatic Stress* 15, no. 2 (April 2002): 157–60. On Sarajevo: Maureen A. Allwood, Debora Bell-Dolan, and Syed Arshad Husain, "Children's Trauma and Adjustment Reactions to Violent and Nonviolent War Experiences," *Journal of the American Academy of Child and Adolescent Psychiatry* 41, no. 4 (April 2002): 450–57.

6. On Zimbabwe: Anthony P. Reeler et al., "The Prevalence of Disorders Due to Organized Violence and Torture in Mashonaland Central Province, Zimbabwe," *Torture* 11, no. 1 (March 2001): 4–8. On North Korea: Yunhwan Lee et al., "Trauma Experience of North Korean Refugees in China," *American Journal of Preventive Medicine* 20, no. 3 (April 2001): 225–29. On Cuba: Eugenio M. Rothe et al., "Posttraumatic Stress Disorder Among Cuban Children and Adolescents After Release from a Refugee Camp," *Psychiatric Services* 53, no. 8 (August 2002): 970–76. On former Soviet

Union: Vladislav V. Ruchkin et al., "Violence Exposure, Posttraumatic Stress, and Personality in Juvenile Delinquents," *Journal of the Academy of Child and Adolescent Psychiatry* 41, no. 3 (March 2002): 322–29. On Tasmania: Rosie Bickel and Alistair Campbell, "Mental Health of Adolescents in Custody: The Use of the 'Adolescent Psychopathology Scale' in a Tasmanian Context," *Australian and New Zealand Journal of Psychiatry* 36, no. 5 (October 2002): 603–9. On Washington, D.C.: Roberto J. Valera, Robin G. Sawyer, and Glenn R. Schiraldi, "Perceived Health Needs of Inner-City Street Prostitutes: A Preliminary Study," *American Journal of Health Behavior* 25, no. 1 (January–February 2001): 50–59. On the United States: Anna Martinez et al., "Posttraumatic Stress Disorder in Women Attending Human Immunodeficiency Virus Outpatient Clinics," *AIDS Patient Care and STDs* 16, no. 6 (June 2002): 283–91.

7. Timothy H. Holtz et al., "Mental Health Status of Human Rights Workers, Kosovo, June 2000," *Journal of Traumatic Stress* 15, no. 5 (October 2002): 389–95.

8. J. E. Tedstone and Nicholas Tarrier, "Posttraumatic Stress Disorder Following Medical Illness and Treatment," *Clinical Psychology Review,* 23 (3): 409–448, May 2002.

9. R.C. Kessler et al., "Posttraumatic Stress Disorder in the National Comorbidity Survey," *Archives of General Psychiatry* 52 (1995): 1048–60.

10. Tarick Ali et al., "The Role of Negative Beliefs in Posttraumatic Stress Disorder: A Comparison of Assault Victims and Nonvictims," *Behavioural and Cognitive Psychotherapy* 30, no. 3 (July 2002): 249–57.

11. Stephanie J. Woods, "Prevalence and Patterns of Posttraumatic Stress Disorder in Abused and Postabused Women," *Issues in Mental Health Nursing* 21, no. 3 (May–June 2000): 309–24.

12. K. Ginzburg et al., "Trajectories of Posttraumatic Stress Disorder Following Myocardial Infarction: A Prospective Study," *Journal of Clinical Psychiatry* 64, no. 10 (October 2003): 1217–23.

13. Rachel Mary McNair, "Symptom Pattern Differences for Perpetration-Induced Traumatic Stress in Veterans: Probing the National Vietnam Veterans Readjustment Study," Ph.D. University of Missouri, 1999.

14. Matthew J. Friedman, *Post Traumatic Stress Disorder.* Compact Clinicals, Kansas City, MO, 2001.

15. A. Hautamaki and Peter G. Coleman, "Explanation for Low Prevalence of PTSD Among Older Finnish War Veterans: Social Solidarity and Continued Significance Given to Wartime Sufferings," *Aging and Mental Health* 5, no. 2 (May 2001): 165–74.

16. Edward W. McCranie and Leon A. Hyer, "Posttraumatic Stress Disorder Symptoms in Korean Conflict and World War II Combat Veterans Seeking Outpatient Treatment," *Journal of Traumatic Stress* 13, no. 3 (July 2000): 427–39.

17. Friedman, *Post Traumatic Stress Disorder,* p. 21.

18. B. Perry, "Incubated in Terror: Neurodevelopmental Factors in the Cycle of Violence." In: *Children, Youth and Violence: The Search for Solutions* (J. Osofsky, Ed.). Guilford Press, New York, 124–48.

19. Alastair M. Hull, David Alan Alexander, and Susan Klein, "Survivors of the Piper Alpha Oil Platform Disaster: Long-term Follow-up Study," *British Journal of Psychiatry* 181 (November 2002): 433–38. On English car collision: Richard A. Mayou, Anke Ehlers, and Bridget Bryant, "Posttraumatic Stress Disorder After Motor Vehicle Accidents: 3-year Follow-up of a Prospective Longitudinal Study," *Behaviour Research and Therapy* 40, no. 6 (June 2002): 665–75. On Chinese earthquake: Zhao et al., "Prevalence and Correlated Factors of PTSD."

20. Chia-Chuang Hsu et al., "Posttraumatic Stress Disorder Among Adolescent Earthquake Victims in Taiwan," *Journal of the American Academy of Child and Adolescent Psychiatry* 41, no. 7 (July 2002): 875–81. On loss of home: Caldera, "Psychological Impact of Hurricane Mitch." On loss of country or culture: H.B.P.E. Gernaat et al., "Veel psychiatrische stoornissen bij Afghaanse vluchtelingen met verblijfsstatus in Drenthe, met name depressieve stoornis en posttraumatische stresstoornis," [Many Psychiatric Disorders Among Afghan Refugees in Drenthe, the Netherlands, with a Residence Status, in Particular Depressive and Posttraumatic Stress Disorders: Community-Based Study], *Nederlands Tijdschrift voor Geneeskunde* 146, no. 24 (June 15, 2002): 1127–31.

21. Metin Basoglu, Ebru Salcioglu, and Maria Livanou, "Traumatic Stress Responses in Earthquake Survivors in Turkey," *Journal of Traumatic Stress* 15, no. 4 (August 2002): 269–76.

22. Janet E. Osterman, et al., "Awareness Under Anesthesia and the Development of Posttraumatic Stress Disorder," *General Hospital Psychiatry* 23, no. 4 (July–August 2001): 198–204.

23. Claes Lennmarken et al., "Victims of Awareness," *Acta Anaesthesiologica Scandinavica* 46, no. 3 (March 2002): 229–31.

24. Basoglu, Salcioglu, and Livanou, "Traumatic Stress Responses in Earthquake Survivors in Turkey."

25. On women's vulnerability: Carol S. Fullerton et al., "Gender Differences in Posttraumatic Stress Disorder After Motor Vehicle Accidents," *American Journal of Psychiatry* 158, no. 9 (September 2001): 1486–91. On gender percentages: Stein, Walker, and Forde, "Gender Differences in Susceptibility to Posttraumatic Stress Disorder," and Anne Jolly, "Évènements traumatiques et état de stress post-traumatique: une revue de la littérature épidémiologique" [Traumatic Events and Post-traumatic Stress Disorder: A Review from Epidemiologic Studies], *Annales Medico-Psychologiques* 158, no. 5 (May 2000): 370–78. On exposure to traumatic events: Ibid.

26. On British students: David G. Purves and Philip R. Erwin, "A Study of Posttraumatic Stress in a Student Population," *Journal of Genetic Psychology* 163, no. 1 (March 2002): 89–96. On French terror-bombing attack survivors: L. Jehel et al., "Étude prospective de l'état de stress post-traumatique parmi des victimes d'un attentat terroriste" [Evaluation of Post-traumatic Stress Disorders Among Victims, After a Terrorist Attack: A Prospective Study], *Encephale* 27, no. 5 (September–October 2001): 393–400. On Dutch adults: Michael Maes et al., "Risk and Preventive

Factors of Post-Traumatic Stress Disorder (PTSD): Alcohol Consumption and Intoxication Prior to a Traumatic Event Diminishes the Relative Risk to Develop PTSD in Response to That Trauma," *Journal of Affective Disorders* 63, no. 1–3 (March 2001): 113–21. On U.S. adults: Fullerton et al., "Gender Differences in Posttraumatic Stress Disorder After Motor Vehicle Accidents." On Spanish drivers: Borri R. Coronas et al., "Factores asociados al desarrollo del transtorno por esteres post-traumatico" [Factors Associated with the Development of Post-traumatic Stress Disorder," *Actas Españolas de Psiquiatria* 29, no. 1 (January–February 2001)] 10–12. On U.S. and Israeli inpatients: Yuval Neria et al., "Trauma Exposure and Posttraumatic Stress Disorder in Psychosis: Findings from a First-Admission Cohort," *Journal of Consulting and Clinical Psychology* 70, no. 1 (February 2002): 246–51. On Danish eighth graders: Ask Elklit, "Victimization and PTSD in a Danish National Youth Probability Sample," *Journal of the American Academy of Child and Adolescent Psychiatry* 41, no. 2 (February 2002): 174–81. On Chinese adolescents: Zhao et al., "Prevalence and Correlated Factors of PTSD." On Nicaraguan survivors: Caldera, "Psychological Impact of the Hurricane Mitch." On South Africans: Debra Kaminer et al., "Violent Trauma Among Child and Adolescent Girls: Current Knowledge and Implications for Clinicians," *International Clinical Psychopharmacology* 15, suppl. 3 (November 2000): S51–S59. On Vaucluse flood survivors: Pierre Verger et al., "Facteurs de variation des symptomes de stress post-traumatique cinq années après l'inondation de 1992 dans le Vaucluse" [Risk Factors for Post-traumatic Stress Symptoms Five Years After the 1992 Flood in the Vaucluse (France)], *Revue d'Epidemiologie et de Santé Publique,* v. 48, supp. 2 (August 2000): 2S44–2S53. On Winnipeg trauma exposure: Stein, Walker, and Forde, "Gender differences in susceptibility to posttraumatic stress disorder."

27. Robert Scaer, *The Body Bears the Burden: Trauma, Dissociation and Disease.* New York: Haworth Medical Press, 2001.

28. B.D. Perry et al., "Childhood Trauma, the Neurobiology of Adaptation and Use-Dependent Development of the Brain: How States Become Traits," *Infant Mental Health Journal,* 16(4): 271–291.

29. The poet Robert Bly likes to say that the corpus collosum (the interactive pathway between the hemispheres) in a man's brain is like a narrow country lane, while a woman's is more like an eight-lane superhighway.

30. Ronald Acierno et al., "Psychopathology Following Interpersonal Violence: A Comparison of Risk Factors in Older and Younger Adults," *Journal of Clinical Geropsychology* 8, no. 1 (January 2002): 13–23.

31. Mark Creamer, Phillip M. Burgess, and Alexander Cowell McFarlane, "Posttraumatic Stress Disorder: Findings from the Australian National Survey of Mental Health and Well-Being," *Psychological Medicine* 31, no. 7 (October 2001): 1237–47.

32. On Australia: ibid. On Israel: O. Taubman-Ben-Ari et al., "Post-traumatic Stress Disorder in Primary-care Settings: Prevalence and Physicians' Detection," *Psychological Medicine* 31, no. 3 (April 2001): 555–60.

33. On youth and PTSD: Gilbert Vila et al., "A Study of Posttraumatic Disorders in Children Who Experienced an Industrial Disaster in the Briey Region," *European*

Child and Adolescent Psychiatry 10, no. 1 (March 2001): 10–18. On Kobe survivors: Masaharu Uemoto et al., [The Mental Health of School Children After the Great Hanshin-Awaji Earthquake: I, Epidemiological Study and Risk Factors for Mental Distress], *Seishin Shinkeigaku Zasshi* [*Psychiatria et Neurologia Japonica*] 102, no. 5 (2002): 459–80. On Alabama children: Laura Stoppelbein and Leilani Greening, "Posttraumatic Stress Symptoms in Parentally Bereaved Children and Adolescents," *Journal of the American Academy of Child and Adolescent Psychiatry* 39, no. 9 (September 2000): 1112–19. On Briey survivors: Vila et al., "Study of Posttraumatic disorders in children."

34. Karestan Chase Koenen et al., "A Twin Registry Study of Familial and Individual Risk Factors for Trauma Exposure and Posttraumatic Stress Disorder," *Journal of Nervous and Mental Disease* 190, no. 4 (April 2002): 209–18.

35. Elklit, "Victimization and PTSD in a Danish National Youth Probability Sample," and Teegen and Schriefer, "Komplexe Posttraumatische Belastungsstörung."

36. On major depression: François Ducrocq et al., "État de stress post-traumatique, dépression post-traumatique et épisode dépressif majeur: la littérature" [Post-traumatic Stress Disorder, Post-traumatic Depression and Major Depressive Disorder: About Literature], *Encephale* 27, no. 2 (March–April 2001): 159–68. On mood disorders: Koenen et al., "Twin Registry Study of Familial and Individual Risk Factors."

37. Chris R. Brewin, Bernice Andrews, and John D. Valentine, "Meta-analysis of Risk Factors for Posttraumatic Stress Disorder in Trauma-Exposed Adults," *Journal of Consulting and Clinical Psychology* 68, no. 5 (October 2000): 748–66. On Danish eighth graders: Elklit, "Victimization and PTSD in a Danish National Youth Probability Sample." On Cuban refugees: Eugenio M. Rothe et al., "Posttraumatic Stress Disorder Among Cuban Children and Adolescents." On Kosovo survivors: Ai, Peterson, and Ubelhor, "War-related Trauma and Symptoms of Posttraumatic Stress Disorder Among Adult Kosovar Refugees." On life stress and child abuse: Brewin, Andrews, and Valentine, "Meta-analysis of Risk Factors."

38. On education and PTSD: ibid. On Turkish earthquake survivors: Basoglu, Salcioglu, and Livanou, "Traumatic Stress Responses in Earthquake Survivors in Turkey." On Afghan refugees in Netherlands: Gernaat et al., "Veel psychiatrische stoornissen bij Afghaanse vluchtelingen." On identical twin Vietnam veterans: Koenen et al., "Twin Registry Study of Familial and Individual Risk Factors."

39. B. Perry, Incubated in Terror: Neurodevelopmental Factors in the Cycle of Violence. In: *Children, Youth and Violence: The Search for Solutions* (J. Osofsky, Ed.). (1997) Guilford Press, New York, pp. 124–48.

40. Julia L. Perilla, Fran H. Norris, and Evelyn A. Lavizzo, "Ethnicity, Culture, and Disaster Response: Identifying and Explaining Ethnic Differences in PTSD Six Months after Hurricane Andrew," *Journal of Social and Clinical Psychology* 21, no. 1 (March 2002): 20–45.

41. Alyssa Lee, Mohan K. Isaac, and Aleksandar Janca, "Post-traumatic Stress Disorder and Terrorism," *Current Opinion in Psychiatry* 15, no. 6 (November 2002): 633–37.

42. On singles: Creamer, Burgess, and McFarlane, "Post-traumatic Stress Disorder: Findings from the Australian National Survey of Mental Health and Well-being," *Psychological Medicine* 31, no. 7 (October 2001): 1237–47. On teenage World Trade Center survivors: Daniel S. Pine and Judith A. Cohen, "Trauma in Children and Adolescents: Risk and Treatment of Psychiatric Sequelae," *Biological Psychiatry* 51, no. 7 (April 1, 2002): 519–31. On adults undergoing bone marrow transplant: Michelle R. Widows, Paul B. Jacobsen, and Karen K. Fields, "Relation of Psychological Vulnerability Factors to Posttraumatic Stress Disorder Symptomatology in Bone Marrow Transplant Recipients," *Psychosomatic Medicine* 62, no. 6 (November–December 2000): 873–82. On disturbance in social support: Brewin, Andrews, and Valentine, "Meta-analysis of Risk Factors," *Journal of Consulting and Clinical Psychology* 68, no. 5 (October 2000): 748–66.

43. A. Hautamaki and Peter G. Coleman, "Explanation for Low Prevalence of PTSD Among Older Finnish War Veterans: Social Solidarity and Continued Significance Given to Wartime Sufferings," *Aging and Mental Health* 5, no. 2 (May 2001): 165–74.

44. On panic attacks and 9/11: Galea, "Psychological Sequelae of the September 11 Terrorist Attacks." On Guam typhoon survivors: J.P. Staab et al., "Acute Stress Disorder as a Predictor of Posttraumatic Stress Symptoms and Depression After a Series of Typhoons," *Anxiety* 2, no. 5 (1996): 219–25.

45. Fullerton, "Gender Differences in Posttraumatic Stress Disorder," *American Journal of Psychiatry* 158, no. 9 (September 2001): 1486–91.

46. Charles P. Colosimo, "Use of Hypnosis in the Military," *Psychiatric Medicine* 10, no. 1 (1992): 149–67.

47. Daphne Simeon et al., "Hypothalamic-pituitary-adrenal Axis Dysregulation in Depersonalization Disorder," *Neuropsychopharmacology* 25, no. 5 (November 2001): 793–95.

48. Charles Andrew Morgan et al., "Relationship Among Plasma Cortisol, Catecholamines, Neuropeptide Y, and Human Performance During Exposure to Uncontrollable Stress," *Psychosomatic Medicine* 63, no. 3 (May–June 2001): 412–22.

49. Simeon et al., "Hypothalamic-pituitary-adrenal Axis Dysregulation."

50. On Ottawa ice storm survivors: Hymie Anisman et al., "Posttraumatic Stress Symptoms and Salivary Cortisol Levels," *American Journal of Psychiatry* 158, no. 9 (September 2001): 1509–11. On UN mine accident survivors: Elisabeth Aardal-Eriksson, Thomas Erik Eriksson, and Lars-Hakan Thorell, "Salivary Cortisol Posttraumatic Stress Symptoms, and General Health in the Acute Phase and During 9-month Follow-up," *Biological Psychiatry* 50, no. 12 (December 15, 2001): 986–93.

51. John W. Mason, "Marked Liability in Urinary Cortisol Levels in Subgroups of Combat Veterans with Posttraumatic Stress Disorder During an Intensive Exposure Treatment Program," *Psychosomatic Medicine* 64, no. 2 (March–April, 2002): 238–46.

52. Rachel Yehuda, "Low Urinary Cortisol Excretion in Holocaust Survivors with Posttraumatic Stress Disorder," *American Journal of Psychiatry* 152, no. 7 (July 1995): 982–86. On low cortisol levels persisting, see ibid.

53. Victor G. Carrion et al., "Diurnal Salivary Cortisol in Pediatric Posttraumatic Stress Disorder," *Biological Psychiatry* 51, no. 7 (April 1, 2002): 575–82.

54. Maes et al., "Risk and Preventive Factors."

55. Leslie K. Jacobsen, Steven M. Southwick, and Thomas R. Kosten, "Substance Use Disorders in Patients with Posttraumatic Stress Disorder: A Review of the Literature," *American Journal of Psychiatry* 158, no. 8 (August 2001): 1184–90.

56. Ibid.

57. Maes et al., "Risk and Preventive Factors."

58. Tamar Wohlfarth, Frans W. Winkel, and Wim Van den Brink, "Identifying Crime Victims Who Are at High Risk for Post Traumatic Stress Disorder: Developing a Practical Referral Instrument," *Acta Psychiatrica Scandinavica* 105, no. 6 (June 2002): 451–60.

59. Ali, "Role of Negative Beliefs in Posttraumatic Stress Disorder."

60. On fibromyalgia: Hagit Cohen et al., "Prevalence of Post-traumatic Stress Disorder in Fibromyalgia Patients: Overlapping Syndromes or Post-traumatic Fibromyalgia Syndrome?" *Seminars in Arthritis and Rheumatism* 32, no. 1 (August 2002): 38–50; Jeffrey J. Sherman, Dennis C. Turk, and Akiko Okifuji, "Prevalence and Impact of Posttraumatic Stress Disorder-like Symptoms on Patients with Fibromyalgia Syndrome," *Clinical Journal of Pain* 16, no. 2 (June 2000): 127–34; Ronald W. Alexander et al., "Sexual and Physical Abuse in Women with Fibromyalgia: Association with Outpatient Healthcare Utilization and Pain Medication Usage," *Arthritis Care and Research* 11, no. 2 (April 1998): 102–15.

61. Martin L. Pall, "Common Etiology of Posttraumatic Stress Disorder, Fibromyalgia, Chronic Fatigue Syndrome and Multiple Chemical Sensitivity via Elevated Nitric Oxide/Peroxynitrite," *Medical Hypotheses* 57, no. 2 (July 1, 2001): 139–45.

62. On Gulf War veterans: Dewleen G. Baker et al., "Diagnostic Status and Treatment Recommendations for Persian Gulf War Veterans with Multiple Nonspecific Symptoms," *Military Medicine* 166, no. 11 (November 2001): 972–81. On traumatized Lao and Mien refugees: Laurie Jo Moore et al., "Rheumatological Disorders and Somatization in U.S. Mien and Lao Refugees with Depression and Post-Traumatic Stress Disorder: A Cross-cultural Comparison," *Transcultural Psychiatry* 38, no. 4 (December 2001): 481–505.

63. Christine Heim, Ulrike Ehlert, and Dirk H. Hellhammer, "The Potential Role of Hypocortisolism in the Pathophysiology of Stress-related Bodily Disorders," *Psychoneuroendocrinology* 25, no. 1 (January 2000): 1–35.

64. Pall, "Common Etiology of Posttraumatic Stress Disorder, Fibromyalgia."

65. On combat veterans: Drue H. Barrett et al., "Posttraumatic Stress Disorder and Self-reported Physical Health Status Among U.S. Military Personnel Serving During the Gulf War Period: Population-based Study," *Psychosomatics* 43, no. 3 (May–June 2002): 195–205. On Israeli patients: Taubman-Ben-Ari et al., "Posttraumatic Stress Disorder in Primary-care Settings." On depression: Ducrocq et al., "État de stress post-traumatique."

CHAPTER 5: THE PHYSICAL EFFECTS OF TRAUMA

1. See Robert Scaer, *The Body Bears the Burden: Trauma, Dissociation and Disease* (Binghamton, N.Y.: Haworth Medical Press, 2001).

2. Ibid., 13.

3. Ibid.

4. Ibid.

CHAPTER 6: THE COGNITIVE EFFECTS OF TRAUMA

1. B.A. van der Kolk et al., "Nightmares and Trauma: Lifelong and Traumatic Nightmares in Veterans," *American Journal of Psychiatry* 141 (1984): 187–90.

2. J. Briere and J. Conte, "Self-reported Amnesia for Abuse in Adults Molested as Children," *Journal of Traumatic Stress* 6, no. 2 (1993): 21–31.

3. Retrieved traumatic memories have come under suspicion in recent years, and there is a lively debate in the field of psychotherapy about the reliablity and authenticity of such memories. Experienced therapists tend to know the difference. One major distinguishing feature of the real thing is the unique sensory detail in the content of the memory; another would be its fragmentary nature—a whole, intact, narrative memory suddenly emerging is extremely unlikely; another would be its emotional and sensory nature. On the other hand, a consideration that would make for second-guessing the memory would be the presence of a self-dramatizing component to the personality of the person reporting the memory; another would be an obvious interest of the therapist or counselor in this kind of material; a compliant, sensitive client might unknowingly try to supply what the therapist wants.

4. Bessel van der Kolk, *Traumatic Stress: The Effects of Overwhelming Experience on Mind, Body and Society.* (New York: Guilford Press, 1996), 233.

5. D. Bremner et al., "Deficits in Short-term Memory in Posttraumatic Stress Disorder," *American Journal of Psychiatry* 150, no. 7 (1993): 1015–19.

6. J. Krystal et al., "Toward a Cognitive Neuroscience of Dissociation and Altered Memory Functions in Post-traumatic Stress Disorder," in *Neurobiological and Clinical Consequences of Stress,* edited by M.J. Friedman, D.S. Charney, and A.Y. Deutch (Philadelphia: Lippincott-Raven, 1995).

7. B.D. Perry (1997) Incubated in Terror: Neurodevelopmental Factors in the Cycle of Violence. In Children, Youth and Violence: The Search for Solutions (J. Osofsky, Ed). Guilford Press, New York, 124–48.

8. J. Bremner et al., "MRI-based Measures of Hippocampal Volume in Patients with PTSD," *American Journal of Psychiatry* 152 (1995): 973–81.

9. M. Stein et al., "Neuroanatomical and Neuroendocrine Correlates in Adulthood of Severe Sexual Abuse in Childhood," paper presented at the annual meeting of the American College of Neuropsychopharmacology, San Juan, P.R., 1994.

10. R. Sapolsky, D. Packan, and W. Vale, "Glucocorticoid Toxicity in the Hippocampus: In Vitro Demonstration," *Brain Research* 453 (1988): 367–71.

11. S. Rausch et al., "A Symptom Provocation Study of Posttraumatic Stress Dis-

order Using Positron Emission Tomography and Script-driven Imagery," *Archives of General Psychiatry* 53 (1996): 380–87.

12. B. Naparstek, lecture at the Chautauqua Institute, Chautauqua, N.Y., 2001.

CHAPTER 7: THE EMOTIONAL EFFECTS OF TRAUMA

1. Judith Herman, *Trauma and Recovery* (New York: Basic Books, 1997), 42.

2. R.R. Grinker and J. Spiegel, *Men Under Stress* (Philadelphia: Blakeston, 1945).

3. Herman, *Trauma and Recovery*, 93–94.

CHAPTER 8: THE BEHAVIORAL EFFECTS OF TRAUMA

1. Michael Norman, *These Good Men: Friendships Forged from War* (New York: Crown, 1990).

2. J. Kaufman and E. Zigler, "Do Abused Chldren Become Abusive Parents?" *American Journal of Orthopsychiatry* 57 (1987): 186–92.

3. B. Perry, Incubated in Terror: Neurodevelopmental Factors in the Cycle of Violence. In *Children, Youth and Violence: The Search for Solutions* (J. Osofsky, Ed.) (1997). Guilford Press, New York, 124–48.

4. K.E. MacEwen, "Refining the intergenerational transmission hypothesis," *Journal of Interpersonal Violence* 9 no. 3 (1994): 350–65.

5. Judith Herman, *Trauma and Recovery* (New York: Basic Books, 1997), 114.

6. David Singh Narang and Josefina M. Contreras, "Dissocation as a Mediator Between Child Abuse History and Adult Abuse Potential," *Child Abuse and Neglect* 24, no. 5 (May 2000): 653–65.

7. According to Michael, cowboy poker is "a rodeo game where four players sit at a table in a rodeo arena and hold cards as if they were playing poker, and then they let a bull out and he usually destroys the table and whoever is sitting at it. The last person left sitting is the winner . . . anyway, I did that and won—one of the stupidest things I have ever done, if not the stupidest!"

8. Robert Scaer, *The Body Bears the Burden: Trauma, Dissociation and Disease* (Binghamton, N.Y.: Haworth Medical Press, 2001), 88.

9. B.A. van der Kolk, "The Compulsion to Repeat the Trauma: Re-enactment, Revictimization and Masochism," *Psychiatric Clinics of North America* 12, no. 2 (1989): 389–410.

10. R.A. Kulka et al. *Trauma and the Vietnam War Generation* (New York: Brunner/Mazel, 1990).

11. Jeffrey M. Lating, Megan A. O'Reilly, and Kimberly P. Anderson, "Eating Disordres and Posttraumatic Stress: Phenomenological and Treatment Considerations Using the Two-factor Model," *International Journal of Emergency Mental Health* 4, no. 2 (Spring 2002): 113–18.

12. Herman, *Trauma and Recovery*, 109.

CHAPTER 9: HOW AND WHY IMAGERY
HEALS TRAUMA

1. Anxiety and depression: C.H. McKinney et al., "Effects of Guided Imagery and Music (GIM) Therapy on Mood and Cortisol in Healthy Adults," *Health Psychology* 16, no. 4 (1997): 390–400. Blood pressure: J.M. Hermann, "Essential Hypertension and Stress. When do Yoga, Psychotherapy and Autogenic Training Help?" *MMW Fortschritte der Medizin* 144, no. 19 (2000): 38–41. Cholesterol: P. Bennett and D. Carroll. "Stress Management Approaches to the Prevention of Coronary Heart Disease," *British Journal of Clinical Psychology* 29, pt. 2 (1990): 1–12. Lipid peroxides: R.H. Schneider, "Lower Lipid Peroxide Levels in Practitioners of the Transcendental Meditation Program," *Psychosomatic Medicine* 60, no. 1 (1998): 38–41. Cuts: C. Ginandes et al., "Can Medical Hypnosis Accelerate Post-surgical Wound Healing? Results of a Clinical Trial," *American Journal of Clinical Hypnosis* 45, no. 4 (2003): 333–51. Fractures: C.S. Ginandes and D.I. Rosenthal, "Using Hypnosis to Accelerate the Healing of Bone Fractures: A Randomized Controlled Pilot Study," *Alternative and Complementary Therapies in Health and Medicine* 5, no. 2 (1999): 67–75. Burns: R.B. Fratianne et al., "The Effect of Music-based Imagery and Musical Alternate Engagement on the Burn Debridement Process," *Journal of Burn Care Rehabilitation* 22, no. 1 (2001): 47–53. Blood loss in surgery patients: H. Dreher, "Mind-body Interventions for Surgery: Evidence and Exigency," *Advances in Mind-Body Medicine* 14 (1998): 207–22. Hospital Stays: L.S. Halpin et al., "Guided Imagery in Cardiac Surgery," *Outcomes Management* 6, no. 3 (2002): 132–37. Immune function: J.H. Gruzelier, "A Review of the Impact of Hypnosis, Relaxation, Guided Imagery and Individual Differences on Aspects of Immunity and Health," *Stress* 5, no. 2 (2002): 147–63. Arthritis pain: L. Sharpe et al., "A Blind, Randomized, Controlled Trial of Cognitive-behavioural Intervention for Patients with Recent Onset Rheumatoid Arthritis: Preventing Psychological and Physical Morbidity," *Pain* 89, no. 2–3 (2001): 275–83. Fibromyalgia: P. Whiting et al., "Interventions for the Treatment and Management of Chronic Fatigue Syndrome: A Systematic Review," *Journal of the American Medical Association* 286, no. 11 (2001:): 1378–79. Medical procedures: G.H. Montgomery et al., "Brief Presurgery Hypnosis Reduces Distress and Pain in Excisional Breast Biopsy Patients," *International Journal of Clinical and Experimental Hypnosis* 50, no. 1 (2002): 17–32. Hemoglobin A1c: Richard S. Surwit et al., "Stress Management Improves Long-Term Glycemic Control in Type 2 Diabetes," *Diabetes Care* 25 (2002): 30–34. Motor deficits in stroke patients: S.J. Page, "A Randomized Efficacy and Feasibility Study of Imagery in Acute Stroke," *Clinical Rehabilitation* 15, no. 3 (2001): 233–40. Children's fear of MRI: G. Smart, "Helping Children Relax During Magnetic Resonance Imaging," *American Journal of Maternal Child Nursing* 22, no. 5 (1997): 237–41. Children's fear of needle sticks: Rachel E. Albert, M.S.N., R.N., preliminary doctoral dissertation results presented at the annual scientific meeting of the American Pain Society, Atlanta, 2000. Bulimia: M.J. Esplen et al., "A Randomized Controlled Trial of Guided Imagery in Bulimia Nervosa," *Psychology and Medicine* 28,

no. 6 (1998): 1347–57. Infertility: A.D. Domar et al., "Impact of Group Psychological Interventions on Pregnancy Rates in Infertile Women," *Fertility and Sterility* 73, no. 4 (2000): 805–11. Weight loss: D.L. Johnson and R.T. Karkut, "Participation in Multicomponent Hypnosis Treatment Programs for Women's Weight Loss with and without Overt Aversion," *Psychological Reports* 79, no. 2 (1996): 659–68. Concentration: D.L. Porretta and P.R. Surburg, "Imagery and Physical Practice in the Acquisition of Gross Motor Timing of Coincidence by Adolescents with Mild Mental Retardation," *Journal of Perception and Motor Skills* 80, no. 3, pt. 2 (1995): 1171–83.

2. Indeed, D.W. Winnicott, the pediatrician-psychoanalyst who coined the term "transitional object," considered all play, creativity, and religion to be derivatives of this earliest of phenomena. D.W. Winnicott, *Playing and Reality* (Sussex, UK.: Brunner-Routledge, 1999).

3. Viktor E. Frankl, *Man's Search for Meaning* (New York: Touchstone, 1984), 48–49.

4. Ibid., 49–50.

5. Perry B.D. (1997) "Incubated in Terror: Neurodevelopmental Factors in the Cycle of Violence." In *Children, Youth and Violence: The Search for Solutions* (J. Osofsky, Ed). Guilford Press, New York, 124–48.

6. Heightened sensitivity can be found in the paralimbic belt, parts of the limbic system, the insular cortex, the posterior orbitofrontal cortex, the anterior cingulate cortex, and the anterior temporal cortex.

7. B.A. Kolk, "The Psychobiology of PTSD," in *Traumatic Stress,* edited by Bessel van der Kolk, Alexander McFarlane, and Lars Weisaeth (New York: Guilford Press, 1996).

8. On restoring biochemical balance: C.H. McKinney et al., "Effects of Guided Imagery and Music (GIM) Therapy on Mood and Cortisol in Healthy Adults," *Health Psychology* 16, no. 4 (1997): 390–400. Mindfulness meditation: R. Sudsuang, V. Chentanez, and K. Veluvan, "Effect of Buddhist Meditation on Serum Cortisol and Total Protein Levels, Blood Pressure, Pulse Rate, Lung Volume and Reaction Time," *Physiology and Behavior* 50, no. 3 (1991): 543–48. Yoga: T. Kamei et al., "Decrease in Serum Cortisol During Yoga Exercise is Correlated with Alpha Wave Activation," *Perceptual and Motor Skills* 90, no. 3, pt. 1 (2000): 1027–32. Qigong: B.M. Jones, "Changes in Cytokine Production in Healthy Subjects Practicing Guolin Qigong: A Pilot Study," *BMC Complentary and Alternative Medicine* 1, no. 1 (2001): 8. Massage: T. Field et al., "Alleviating Posttraumatic Stress in Children Following Hurricane Andrew," *Journal of Applied Developmental Psychology* 17, no. 1, 37–50.

9. The work of psychologists Joen Fagan, Ph.D., and Irma Shepard, Ph.D., at Georgia State University in the 1980s amply demonstrated the power of hypnosis for helping people who dissociate, even people with the most extreme diagnoses such as multiple personality disorder.

10. Pir Valayat Inayat Khan, *Introducing Spirituality into Counseling and Therapy* (New York: Omega, 1999).

11. Jon Kabat-Zinn, as described on his website, www.mindfulnesstapes.com, and in his two books, *Full-Catastrophe Living* (New York: Delta, 1990) and *Wherever You Go, There You Are* (New York: Hyperion, 1995).

12. Jeanne Achterberg, Barbara Dossey, and Leslie Kolkemeir, *Rituals of Healing: Using Imagery for Health and Wellness* (New York: Bantam Doubleday Dell, 1994).

13. Sandra Smeeding, Susan Osguthorpe, and David Bradshaw, "The Application of Guided Imagery and Music for Control of Pain and Anxiety Before and After Surgery," in draft proposal, April 24, 2003.

14. Ronald C. Albucher and Israel Liberzon, "Psychopharmacological Treatment in PTSD: A Critical Review," *Journal of Psychiatric Research* 36, no. 6 (2002): 355–67.

15. Michael Persinger, "The Tectonic Strain as an Explanation for UFO Phenomena: A Non-Technical Review of the Research, 1970–1990," *Journal of UFO Studies*, 2 (1990): 105–137.

16. These are all Gestalt-trained mental health professionals who practice in Cleveland Heights, Ohio.

17. There is one mention of the word *God* on the Affirmations side of this audio program, which says, "I know I am held in the hands of God, and I am perfectly, utterly safe." Luckily, it comes as one of the very last lines in the entire audio program. Had it been spoken any earlier, she probably could not have responded positively to it. Although we get occasional complaints about this unexpected reference to God, we get hundreds more comments pointing to that one line as being particularly helpful.

CHAPTER 10: GENERAL GUIDED IMAGERY WISDOM AND TACTICS

1. Phaedra Caruso, "A Comparison of Guided Imagery Techniques with Chemotherapy Patients," Ph.D. diss., California School of Professional Psychology, Alameda, Calif., 1999; and Trudy D. Helge, "A Comparison of Three Audio Guided Imagery Tapes on the Self Efficacy of Cancer Chemotherapy Patients," Ph.D. diss., California School of Professional Psychology, Alameda, CA, 1999.

2. Personal conversation with Phaedra Caruso, December 22, 2003.

3. Training Programs for this sort of practice are offered by the Academy for Guided Imagery and by NCPI, both of which are listed in the Resources section.

4. See the Resources section.

5. The intense amplification of a superior microphone, however, will result in the need for good digital editing as well, because every pop and click, slurp and smack, will be amplified as well. It's quite a symphony!

6. Steven Mark Kohn, *Music from Health Journeys*, Health Journeys, Akron, Ohio, 1999; *Inward Journey: More Music from Health Journeys*, Health Journeys, Akron, Ohio, 2003.

7. Eller, L.S. Guided imagery: A nursing intervention for symptoms related to infection with HIV, Ph.D. dissertation, Case Western Reserve University, Patricia

Flatley Brennan, Ph.D., R.N., F.A.A.N., Director. Dissertation Abstracts International, DAI-B 55/04, 1376. (AAC 9423416), 1994.

8. Trial and error experience has taught me to be partial to Steven Mark Kohn's *Music from Health Journeys*, track 1, for the closest fulfillment of these requirements without losing universal appeal to a broad audience. I would recommend it under any circumstances, but full disclosure requires I mention that my company produces this CD.

9. Colonoscopy: D. Smolen, R. Topp, and L. Singer, "The Effect of Self-selected Music During Colonoscopy on Anxiety, Heart Rate, and Blood Pressure," *Applied Nursing Research* 15, no. 3 (2002): 126–36. Breast biopsy: M. Haun, R.O. Mainous, and S.W. Looney, "Effect of Music on Anxiety of Women Awaiting Breast Biopsy," *Behavioral Medicine* 3 (Fall 2001): 127–32. Radiation therapy: M. Smith et al., "Music as a Therapeutic Intervention for Anxiety in Patients Receiving Radiation Therapy," *Oncology Nursing Forum* 28, no. 5 (2001): 855–62. Ventilator therapy: L. Chlan et al., "Feasibility of a Music Intervention Protocol for Patients Receiving Mechanical Ventilatory Support," *Alternative Therapies in Health and Medicine* 7, no. 6 (2001): 80–83. Coronary bypass surgery: S. Barnason, L. Zimmerman, and J. Nieveen, "The Effects of Music Interventions on Anxiety in the Patient After Coronary Artery Bypass Grafting," *Heart Lung* 24, no. 2 (1995): 124–32. COPD: S. McBride et al., "The Therapeutic Use of Music for Dyspnea and Anxiety in Patients with COPD Who Live at Home," *Journal of Holisitic Nursing* 17, no. 3 (1999): 229–50.

10. For a thorough discussion of pros and cons, see Rubin Battino, *Guided Imagery and Other Approaches to Healing*, (Carmarthen, U.K.: Crown House, 2000), 117–33.

11. L. Root et al., *Trauma-Specific Guided Imagery: A Systematic Evaluation of an Adjunct Intervention to Group Psychotherapy*. Poster session, annual meeting of the International Society for Traumatic Stress Studies, New Orleans, 2001.

CHAPTER 12: GUIDED IMAGERY FOR THE SECOND STAGE OF TRAUMA

1. Variations of this imagery appear both in Belleruth Naparstek, *Staying Well with Guided Imagery* (New York: Warner Books, 1994), and Belleruth Naparstek, *Your Sixth Sense* (San Francisco: HarperSanFrancisco, 1997).

2. From Belleruth Naparstek, *Healing Trauma (PTSD)* (New York: Image Paths, 1999).

CHAPTER 13: GUIDED IMAGERY FOR THE THIRD STAGE OF TRAUMA

1. A controlled pilot study by Dr. Jeff Rossman, director of behavioral health at Canyon Ranch in the Berkshires, found that a variation of this imagery doubled weight loss in a behavioral program; and Green Mountain at Fox Run reports excel-

lent results as well. In both centers, the imagery is one element in a larger behavioral program.

2. Excerpted and adapted from *A Meditation to Help You with Weight Loss* from the Health Journeys Guided Imagery Audio Series, New York: Time Warner Audio-Books, 1997.

CHAPTER 14: OTHER IMAGERY-BASED THERAPIES

1. F. Shapiro, *Eye Movement Desensitization and Reprocessing: Basic Principles, Protocols and Procedures,* 2nd ed. (New York: Guilford Press, 2001).

2. Telephone interview with Suzanne Iasenza, Ph.D., July 2, 2003.

3. Telephone interview and e-mail correspondence with Nancy Napier, L.M.F.T., July 2003.

4. C.R. Figley et al., "A Clinical Demonstration Model for Assessing the Effectiveness of Therapeutic Interventions: An Expanded Clinical Trials Methodology," *International Journal of Emergency Mental Health* 1, no. 3 (1999): 155–64.

5. Telephone interview and e-mail correspondence with Nancy Napier, L.M.F.T., July 2003.

6. This comes from yet another meridian-based energy therapy, derived from TFT, called Touch and Breathe (TAB), created by psychologist John Diepold, Ph.D.

7. PET and EMDR: Christopher William Lee et al., "Treatment of PTSD: Stress Inoculation Training with Prolonged Exposure Compared to EMDR," *Journal of Clincial Psychology* 58, no. 9 (September 2002): 1071–89; Gail Ironson et al., "Comparison of Two Treatments for Traumatic Stress: A Community-based Study of EMDR and Prolonged Exposure," *Journal of Clinical Psychology* 58, no. 1 (January 2002): 113–28. Steven Taylor et al., "Comparative Efficacy, Speed, and Adverse Effects of Three PTSD Treatments: Exposure Therapy, EMDR, and Relaxation Training," *Journal of Consulting and Clinical Psychology* 71, no. 2 (April 2003): 330–38.

8. Gerald D. French, M.A., C.T.S., and Frank A. Gerbode, M.D., C.T.S., *Traumatic Incident Reduction Workshop Manual,* 3rd ed. (Menlo Park, CA.: IRM Press, 1996); and Gerald D. French and Chrys J. Harris, *Traumatic Incident Reduction,* Innovations in Psychology Series (Boca Raton, FL.: CRC Press, 1999).

9. Charles R. Figley et al., "A Clinical Demonstration Model for Assessing the Effectiveness of Therapeutic Interventions: An Expanded Clinical Trials Methodology," *International Journal of Emergency Mental Health* 1, no. 3 (1999): 155–64; Lori Beth Bisbey, "No Longer a Victim: A Treatment Outcome Study for Crime Victims with Post-traumatic Stress Disorder," Ph.D. diss., California School of Professional Psychology, San Diego, 1995; Pamela Vest Valentine and Thomas Edward Smith, "Evaluating Traumatic Incident Reduction Therapy with Female Inmates: A Randomized Controlled Clinical Trial," *Research on Social Work Practice* 11, no. 1 (January 2001): 40–52.

10. B. Krakow et al., "An Open-label Trial of Evidence-based Cognitive Behavior Therapy for Nightmares and Insomnia in Crime Victims with PTSD," *American Journal of Psychiatry* 158, no. 12 (2001): 2043–47; and B. Krakow et al., "Imagery Re-

hearsal Therapy for Chronic Nightmares in Sexual Assault Survivors with Posttraumatic Stress Disorder: A Randomized Controlled Trial," *Journal of the American Medical Association* 286, no. 5 (2001): 537–45.

11. D. Forbes, A. Phelps, and T. McHugh, "Treatment of Combat-related Nightmares Using Imagery Rehearsal: A Pilot Study," *Journal of Traumatic Stress* 14, no. 2 (2001): 433–42.

12. Charles R. Figley et al., "A Clinical Demonstration Model for Assessing the Effectiveness of Therapeutic Interventions: An Expanded Clinical Trials Methodology," *International Journal of Emergency Mental Health* 1, no. 3 (1999): 155–64.

13. Eugene Gendlin, *Focusing* (New York: Bantam Books, 1982).

14. Robert Scaer, e-mail communication, January 22, 2004.

15. Counselor and co-author with Laurence Heller, Ph.D., of *Crash Course: A Self-Healing Guide to Auto Accident Trauma and Recovery* (Berkeley, Calif.: North Atlantic Books, 2002).

16. Steve J. Lewis. "Do One-shot Preventive Interventions for PTSD Work?: A Systematic Research Synthesis of Psychological Debriefings." *Aggression and Violent Behavior*, 8(3): 329–43, May–June 2003; Jonathan I. Bisson, "Single-session Early Psychological Interventions Following Traumatic Events," *Clinical Psychology Review* 23, no. 3 (May 2003): 481–99; and Arnold A.P. Van Emmerik et al., "Single Session Debriefing After Psychological Trauma: A Meta-analysis," *Lancet* 360, no. 9355 (2002): 766–71.

CHAPTER 15: TEN INGREDIENTS FOR COMPREHENSIVE HEALING

1. Beverly Sue Donovan, Edgardo Padin-Rivera, and Sean Kowaliw, "Transcend: Initial Outcomes from a Posttraumatic Stress Disorder/Substance Abuse Treatment Program," *Journal of Traumatic Stress* 14, no. 4 (2001): 757–72.

2. Paula P. Schnurr et al., "Randomized Trial of Trauma-focused Group Therapy for Posttraumatic Stress Disorder," *Archives of General Psychiatry* 60, no. 5 (2003): 481–89.

3. This sort of journaling protocol, along with many others, can be found in Ira Progoff's *At a Journal Workshop* (New York: J.P. Tarcher, 1992).

4. Matthew J. Friedman, M.D., Ph.D., *Post Traumatic Stress Disorder: The Latest Assessment and Treatment Strategies* (New York: Compact Clinicals, 2000).

5. Rachel Bagby is author of *Divine Daughters: Liberating the Power and Passion of Women's Voices* (HarperSanFrancisco, 1999) and creator of the track, "Full Woman," on the audio CD *Full* (1994), available from www.cdbaby.com/cd/bagby.

CHAPTER 16: SURPRISE BLESSINGS

1. Hollis Sigler, Susan M. Love, and James Yood, *Hollis Sigler's Breast Cancer Journal* (New York: Hudson Hills Press, 1999).

2. *Strong at the Broken Places: Turning Trauma into Recovery*, Cambridge Documentary Films, 1998.

ACKNOWLEDGMENTS

I am indebted to the innovative work and questioning minds of the pioneer clinicians, theorists, and researchers who changed forever the way we look at traumatic stress, making it possible to alleviate a tremendous amount of suffering as never before. My special gratitude is for the work of Viktor Frankl, Marion Woodman, Bessel van der Kolk, Francine Shapiro, Robert Scaer, Judith Herman, Jim Gordon, Edna Foa, Stephen Levine, Bruce Perry, Peter Levine, and Eugene Gendlin.

Scores of gifted practitioners have shed light and illuminated my thinking. My deep thanks first and foremost to Beverly Donovan and Edgardo Padin-Rivera for teaching me so much. Their compassion, patience, and humanity, along with their ingenious work, inspires me daily. I am in awe of the elegant work and deep commitment of Suzanne Iasenza, Nancy Napier, Frances Baker, Bob Buckley, Arlene Geller, Leslie Root, Anne Chapman Kane, and James Stone. I thank Martha Howard, Tapas Fleming, Gary Craig, Linda Klein, Allan Schore, Charles Figley, James Kepner, Carol DeSanto, Monette Park, Kathy Sievering, Laura Chapman, Cary Sanchez, Linda Gould, Warren Fry, Ellie Lottinville, Bill O'Hanlon, Daniel Benor, Don Elium, Diane Poole Heller, Kathie

McFarlane, Mimi Butterfield, Terry Sparks, Rosalyn Bruyere, Babette Rothschild, Michael Oruch, Barry Krakow, Fritz Smith, Mary Beth Williams, Donna Eden, David Feinstein, Gerald French, Frank Gerbode, David Baldwin, Rachel Yehuda, Daniel Goleman, Matthew Friedman, Daniel Siegel, Edward Blanchard, and Frank Ochberg.

Without the voices of many, many invisible heroes, this book would have no heart. My deepest gratitude goes to the trauma survivors who were so generous, forthcoming, and honest in their conversations with me, even when those conversations cost them comfort, sleep, and peace of mind for a few hours or days. I have permission to name: Reverend Doug Taylor, Dianne Schwartz, Jan, Lynne Newman, Randy, Julius, Bill, Walter, Greg, Cathy L., Dooley, Susan P., Elisabeth Pozzi-Thanner, Elsie Rose, Gary, Julie White, Kathy, Laurie, Michael "Mikey" Risenhoover, Suzanne, Walt, Chris, Rosemary, Dawn, Simone, Karen, Carole, Fred, Leslie, Andy, Debi, Annette, Jim A., Jim P., John R., John L., Julie, Emma, Betsy, Rebecca, Robin, Sarah, Sylvie Anne, Vicky, William, Keith, Therese, Lewis, Mark, Linda, Candace, Heather, Raymond, Judy, Teresa, Maureen, Sharon, Christine, Robert, Gary, Barb, Julie, Suzee, Lorna, and Emily—thank you all, named, nicknamed, pseudo-named and unnamed.

I thank my friend and business partner, George Klein, who supported and endorsed all these years of PTSD obsession with his ever-present generosity of spirit, kindness, wisdom, and view of the bigger picture. I thank everyone at my company, Health Journeys Inc. (Where would I be without them?), starting with our gifted CEO, Dan Kohler, and including, in order of appearance over these past fifteen years, Steve Kohn, Bruce Gigax, Cheryl Pomeraning, Karen Wilkerson, Cindy Stalnaker, Rich Coleman, and Mary Hamilton.

I am blessed to have Loretta Barrett as my literary agent and Toni Burbank as my editor. It doesn't get any better than this.

My heart smiles at my smart, funny, and unique adult children, who work to make the world a better place, and who also look out for me, make me laugh, enrich my life, show me what I don't know, and keep the various strange, technological devices in my home and office in working order. Thank you, Aaron and Joanne, Keila and Tom, and Abe.

And for my one and only Art with the Heart—dear husband, best friend, cheerleader, ally, coach, honey, and early morning jokester—I thank you for everything, always.

INDEX

ABOUT THE AUTHOR

Belleruth Naparstek, LISW, BCD, is a psychotherapist, author, and guided imagery innovator. She is the creator of the *Health Journeys* guided imagery audio series. Her recordings are used by major pharmaceutical and insurance institutions, as well as by more than 1,500 hospitals, mental health, and recovery centers nationwide. They have been distributed by the Veterans Administration, Oklahoma City, Columbine High School, Kaiser Permanente, and the Red Cross, as well as numerous rape crisis and domestic violence centers. In addition, her audio programs have been used in 24 clinical trials that have established the efficacy of guided imagery use for several psychological and medical challenges. A regular speaker at conferences nationwide, she is also the author of *Staying Well With Guided Imagery: How to Harness the Power of Your Imagination for Health and Healing* and *Your Sixth Sense: Unlocking the Power of Your Intuition.* Belleruth has been featured in *Fitness Magazine, Glamour, Cosmopolitan,* the *Wall Street Journal,* and *Prevention Magazine,* as well as on *The Today Show, 20/20,* and *CBS Health Watch.* She obtained her master's degree in clinical social work from the University of Chicago, and now lives in Cleveland, Ohio.

For more information, and for a resource guide to trauma therapies and practitioners, please visit www.healthjourneys.com. The website also maintains Belleruth's updated speaking schedule. Continuing education credits are offered for selected events.